"*Citizen of Nature* is the first full biography o. ____ the most complete. . . . Drummond delves deeply into Mills' complex personality and the triumphs and controversies of his intensely full life."
—*Peak and Prairie* [Rocky Mountain Chapter of the Sierra Club]

"The first full-length examination of Mills and his work. . . . [A]n incisive account of a complex, controversial, and often difficult man who touched millions of lives in his time and whose legacy has a vivid relevance today."
—*Estes Park Trail Gazette*

"Drummond . . . offers here an impressive biography of a man who from age nineteen aspired to be nothing short of John Muir, the nation's most renowned naturalist. Readers of *Kansas History* will be interested to learn of [Mills'] Kansas upbringing."
—*Kansas History*

"This book is the enjoyable, acutely analytical story of an intriguing and influential mountain man, a story that also offers a good bit of lore about the mountain environment and catches the atmosphere of the early-day conservation movement. . . . Drummond's assessment of Mills' achievements is always reasoned and supported."
—*Wichita Eagle*

"Alex Drummond . . . has produced what is very likely to become the definitive biography of Mills. It is exhaustively researched and very readable."
—*Rocky Mountain Nature Association Quarterly*

"By portraying Mills as the product of the mountains he loved and in the context of contemporaries such as John Burroughs, John Muir, Stephen Mather, and Pinchot, Drummond successfully explains how much poorer the American landscape would be today if not for Mills' efforts back then. Read *Enos Mills: Citizen of Nature* and you never will feel the same again on public land."
—*Fort Collins Coloradoan*

"At last, the first in-depth biography of the Rocky Mountains' greatest conservationist—warts and all."
—Peter Wild, author of *Pioneer Conservationists of Western America*

"An extremely valuable contribution to American conservation literature. Alexander Drummond's comprehensive work on Mills brings to light the many sides of a very gifted innovator and fascinating character."
—Michael Frome, Ph.D., author of *Regreening the National Parks*

Enos Mills. *Courtesy, Enos Mills Cabin Collection.*

Enos Mills
Citizen of Nature

by Alexander Drummond

UNIVERSITY PRESS OF COLORADO

Published by the University Press of Colorado
5589 Arapahoe Avenue, Suite 206C
Boulder, Colorado 80303

The University Press of Colorado is a cooperative publishing enterprise supported, in part, by Adams State College, Colorado State University, Fort Lewis College, Mesa State College, Metropolitan State College of Denver, University of Colorado, University of Northern Colorado, University of Southern Colorado, and Western State College of Colorado.

The paper used in this publication meets the minimum requirements of the American National Standard for Information Sciences—Permanence of Paper for Printed Library Materials. ANSI Z39.48-1992

Library of Congress Cataloging-in-Publication Data

Drummond, Alexander, 1938–
        Enos Mills: citizen of nature / by Alexander Drummond.
            p.   cm.
        Includes bibliographical references and index.
        ISBN 0-87081-407-9 (cloth: alk. paper) — ISBN 0-87081-669-1 (pbk: alk. paper)
            1. Mills, Enos Abijah, 1870–1922. 2. Naturalists—United States—Biography. I. Title.
QH31.M47D78   1995
333.78'2'092 — dc20
[B]   95-38668

11 10 09 08 07 06 05 04 03 02   10 9 8 7 6 5 4 3 2 1

For
Jennifer and Roger

Contents

Illustrations

Preface

Enos Mills (1870–1922) was a citizen of nature by birthright and persuasion. Nature commanded his allegiance not through its immutable laws but through what he saw as its innate aesthetic and moral appeal. It was for him a creative pageant that gave inspiration for his own growth and self-definition. In wild nature he saw birds and animals in charge of their own destinies, able to achieve individuality, free choice, and enriched lives despite the dominant influence of their genetic heritage. They, and nature generally, supplied a moral standard by which Mills measured human progress; and they suggested to him a universal democracy of cooperative citizenship among all living things.

None of these ideas, however, characterized the Enos Mills I first heard about as a fifteen-year-old summer ranch hand working half a mile down the road from the site of his famous Longs Peak Inn. That grand old log structure on the eastern edge of Rocky Mountain National Park had burned just four years earlier, and Mills had been gone for one generation — thirty-three years. I was too young to ponder Mills the conservationist and park advocate, or Mills the naturalist, or public speaker, or writer, or advocate of alternative education. As a young climber testing my nerve and balance on the vertical granite of Longs Peak, I was roused instead by tales of Mills the intrepid mountaineer. He could roam the windswept winter tundra for days at a time with not so much as a bedroll, a climbing friend of mine said, with an intriguing mixture of admiration and skepticism.

Now, nearly four decades later, I have been able to return to the subject and to condense my personal vision of Enos Mills into this volume. I am a specialist in none of his fields of endeavor yet have come to fully appreciate the range of accomplishments in which he gained recognition. Journeying into his age without the credentials of a professional historian, I have been encouraged at every step by friends and readers of my drafts to tell Mills's story with fresh awareness, free of both the burden and the privilege of credentials. Mills was a man to whom we must respond with common sense or not at all, for he fashioned his life and his message for universal comprehension.

I have sought to discover who Mills really was and how much of his revered John Muir was in him, how he acquired his beliefs and acted on them, and what his beliefs and actions mean to us today. His story cannot be told through dispassionate scholarship alone. His life begs interpretation, and to that task I have inevitably brought some of my own biases. I have come to agree with Howard Zinn that all history — in which I would include the history of an individual life — expresses points of view. My story of the life and work of Enos Mills, following no formulas for biographical narrative, is but one of many that could be told. Mills was a colorful and a controversial man, one easily subject to a biographer's own ambivalence. If readers themselves arrive at a feeling of ambivalence about Mills, it would not, in my opinion, be an inappropriate result. To understand him as a man of striking originality and creative force, undercut by confusing and sometimes disruptive character traits, is to understand him fairly and realistically. Such a view, acknowledging complexity and contradiction within the same man, would be a distinct advance over the good guy–bad guy polarization that now splits — almost painfully — the collective memory of Mills, especially in the region where he lived. Discouraged by that polarization from relying on local opinions to evaluate Mills, I have attempted to find the most objective evidence and to discuss it as frankly as possible.

I am indebted to Elizabeth Mills, granddaughter of Enos Mills, for making the files of the Enos Mills Cabin Collection (at the original homestead site) freely available to me, late, but not too late, in my research process. These materials, only now being given sufficient order for scholarly use, are a valuable supplement to the Mills Papers donated by the family to the Denver Public Library in the 1960s. My relations with the Mills family have been for the most part shaky, worsened by my probing into sensitive areas. Among family members given a chance to read the manuscript, two declined, one read it with approval, and one registered strong dissent. *Enos Mills* should not, on balance, be considered a family-authorized biography. I am nevertheless indebted to all family members for withstanding the intrusiveness of the biographical process and its sometimes painful clashes with inherited family history.

We are lucky at this point to have nearly half of Mills's own books back in print, allowing modern readers to compare their own perceptions of him with those presented here. It has been my pleasure in the late stages of preparing this biography to know James H. Pickering, the resourceful editor of four of Mills's books, reissued in the late 1980s. His lucid commentaries and text annotations will be as useful to Mills's readers as they have been to me. He, along with many others, has been a steady source of encouragement, for which I acknowledge heartfelt thanks.

Abundant gratitude is also extended to the following people for their advice, discussion, text review, production assistance, or creative prodding: Stanley Boucher, Liz Caile, Franklin Folsom, Joyce Gellhorn, Forrest Ketchin, Stuart Krebs, Rachel Paul, Walter Richards, Janet Robertson, Charles Trench and A. Gayle Waldrop; and to the following for assistance in locating research materials and photographs: Lennie Bemiss (Estes Park Public Library); Peter Blodgett (Huntington Library, San Marino, California); Helen Burgener (Library of Rocky Mountain National Park); R. L. Carter (Cunningham Memorial Library, Indiana State University); Ola May Earnest (Linn County, Kansas, Historical and Genealogical Society); Eleanor Gehres (Denver Public Library, Western History Department); Rebecca Lintz (Colorado Historical Society); Carol McBryant (Rocky Mountain National Park, Interpretation Division); Jack Melton (YMCA of the Rockies); John Shelly (Pennsylvania State Archives); Cynthia Stevenson (The Holt-Atherton Center for Western Studies, University of the Pacific, Stockton, California); Lynn Swain (Estes Park Area Historical Museum); David Wake (Museum of Vertebrate Zoology, University of California, Berkeley); and to staff members of numerous libraries and archives around the country, who searched their records without finding traces of Enos Mills.

The lengthy task, now completed, has taught me why authors unfailingly reserve their greatest thanks for their own family members. I happily join that tradition, thanking all loved ones in my life, who have been of uncommonly good cheer throughout the process.

Alexander Drummond
WARD, COLORADO

Speak of me as I am; nothing extenuate,
Nor set down aught in malice.

—Othello, V, ii

Prologue:
Enos Mills in His Time and Ours

Nineteen-year-old Enos Mills attributed the course of his future to an accident: Had he not met the famous naturalist John Muir (1838–1914) one December day in 1889, he would have found no focus for his life. "I owe everything to Muir," he wrote. "If it hadn't been for him I would have been a mere gypsy."[1]

The boy had traveled to San Francisco that fall when the Anaconda Mine in Butte, Montana, was closed and most of its workers idled by an underground fire. Mills, a toolboy in the huge industrial mine, hung around to watch the excitement created by the fire, later writing about it for the *Anaconda Standard*. Then already a seasoned traveler, he struck off for the West Coast. The meeting of the vast Pacific with the continent's plunging headlands may have thrilled the youngster from Kansas, just as the meeting of the rolling prairies with the eastern wall of the Rockies had when he first went west at age fourteen.

In an undated one-page autobiographical essay, Mills wrote that one day on the beach, he saw a small group gathered around a man "intensely explaining" a handful of plants. When the group dispersed, Mills ventured forward, inquisitively presenting a plant someone had pulled by its long root from a sand dune. He received what Muir could deliver as no one else could: a "stirring biography" of the plant, the full story of its "manners, customs, and adventures." Mills probably learned then and there that every living thing has a place, a purpose, a unique story, and a connection to all else in creation.

Mills walked with the fifty-one-year-old Muir several miles to the trolley line, captivated, as all were, by Muir's famously vivid and voluble conversation. When they parted, Mills had an invitation to visit Muir at his home in Martinez. During the walk, Mills said, Muir "incited me to do many things, some of which I fear will not be done by the time I reach three score and ten." He tried mightily to do them, aspiring to be nothing short of John Muir of the Rockies.

"The two Johnnies": John Burroughs *(left)* and John Muir, famous writer-natural-ists whom Mills idolized and emulated, were photographed together in Yosemite National Park by noted Estes Park photographer F. P. Clatworthy. *Archives, University of Colorado at Boulder Libraries, general 2059.*

How well he succeeded in his relatively brief life of barely more than two score and ten is an important part of the story of Enos A. Mills.

But though Mills would have probably been something different without Muir's influence, he would surely not have been a gypsy. Mills, by the time the two met, was decidedly ambitious and consciously in the process of making himself. Already on his own for five years, he had begun to learn a love of mountains, mountaineering, and nature watching. He had a sense of his place in the growing West — not yet guessing how he might try to influence that growth — and a dawning sense that society could stand some improvement. He had a natural proclivity for confrontation and thought for a time of becoming a lawyer. He had put down the kind of roots that gypsies lack, anchoring them to his small homestead near Estes Park in the Colorado Rockies. He had an urge to guide people into the transcendental world of lofty peaks and through the infinitely rich galleries of nature's wild treasures. He was anything but a drifter, and his life would have coalesced, with or without Muir. Yet Muir, once in his life, became the polestar on which he set his distant, if not his daily, course.

Muir was, in fact, more of an abstract inspiration than a readily available role model. There was far less substance to the personal connection than Mills liked people to suppose. Their correspondence was scanty, probably not beginning until 1902; it was always brief and never discussed ideas. Muir never managed to visit Mills in Colorado, even after Mills's famous Longs Peak Inn attracted notable leaders in many fields, including naturalists of stature. Mills visited Muir sporadically in California — usually while on the road during his public campaigns — and without doubt drew renewed strength and inspiration; but at no obvious point, even when circumstances might have suggested it, did Muir's influence change the course of Mills's actions. Though Mills actively sought the identification and even itemized his similarity with Muir in some of his writings, he may have diminished his own importance by appearing to be a mere imitator of the more famous Californian. Mills's fixation on Muir makes the theme an indispensable part of his biography, but a story of greater interest is his separate development as a regionally distinct and nationally prominent naturalist, speaker, writer, and advocate for conservation.

It is certain, nevertheless, that from the first meeting with Muir, the boy readily absorbed what was available from any encounter with Muir: a jubilant sense of wonder for natural creation in all its variety and richness. Muir could talk endlessly and fascinatingly about mountains and glaciers, rocks and ice, flowers, animals, and birds; about the glory of roaming the mountains, heedless of destination or physical discomfort, without equipment or firearms, and with only meager food; about swaying in windstorms at the tops of trees, of slipping behind waterfalls to see moonlight through the ribbons of water; about running out into the night to hear Yosemite's walls reverberate in an earthquake and shake down tons of loosened granite. Even a boy of Mills's age could see that Muir's rhapsodic outpourings expressed serious purpose and were illuminated by an original and powerful mind. Muir indeed fascinated and attracted the company of eminent scientists, President Theodore Roosevelt, and the great philosopher Ralph Waldo Emerson.

Mills had the excitability and depth of appreciation to embrace nature on Muir's highly charged and romantic level. Already used to roaming wild places, he acquired more and more of Muir's habits of indifference to comfort, food, and the constraints of scheduled time. His disregard for safety went beyond Muir's — up to, and often over, the brink of calamity. He absorbed Muir's sense of poetic inspiration in the lives of every plant, creature, and physical feature of the earth; and, like Muir, he was able to inspire others with a sense of wonder, both in person and in his more than a dozen books. And he absorbed and translated into action Muir's conviction that nature loved so deeply must be protected from those who love money more.

Muir was in simplest terms for Mills what he remains today for millions in the new conservation era: the quintessential example of boundless and passionate love of the outdoors — its beauty, its immense plenitude, its right to exist apart from human concerns, but also its infinite blessing to the human spirit. Muir remains a central fiber of today's conservation ethos, and the power his legacy gives it is the crusading power of love of nature and love of life — forces no amount of greed can crush. Interest in Muir continues to grow, with new books about him appearing regularly and much of his own writing back in print. Stephen Fox, setting out to write a general history of American conservation, concluded that Muir should be the organizational focus for his book. The title, appropriately, became *John Muir and His Legacy: The American Conservation Movement*. Its biographical portion — the first Muir biography to profit from personal papers and manuscripts released for scholarly use in 1977 — shows Muir as a man who spent his whole life going between "sets of polar opposites" in a "rhythm of bondage and release": between "people and nature, civilized constraints and wild freedom, love and loneliness." Fox concludes that Muir's tension expressed in acute form the need of modern man for both civilization and release from civilization; and that "through working out his private quarrels, Muir was to become the central figure in the history of American conservation."[2] The recognition that wilderness is a necessary part of civilization — rather than its antagonist — has been one of the major cultural contributions of twentieth-century conservation.

Mills, too, moved from long solitary periods in the wilds to an application of his acquired knowledge to public causes. He never renounced civilization to the extent the young Muir had. He valued the bonds of domesticity more than Muir, and he suffered the frustration of not acquiring them until late in his life. Mills perceived nature's gifts to humanity more broadly but less profoundly than Muir. Both knew that by preserving nature we preserve part of our own spirit and secure one recess of our existence against the onslaught of our own materialism. Both men contributed to the ideas, rhetoric, and practical politics that helped implant that notion into twentieth-century consciousness. But the pressures and opportunities of Mills's life brought out differences from Muir that emulation could not bridge and that led him ultimately to understand man's relation to nature differently.

Those differences — despite no discussion of Mills himself — are brought into greater relief by Michael Cohen's 1984 study of Muir's "spiritual journey" in *The Pathless Way: John Muir and American Wilderness*. Cohen's analysis of how Muir's understanding of nature evolved and how he acquired his sense of the "right relation between Man and Nature" focuses most closely on Muir's deeper and more radical vision — a vision lost to most of his followers and to conservation history generally.[3] Insights into Muir such as Cohen's help illuminate today's newer currents in conservation thinking, and — partly by contrast — help to define what Enos Mills achieved and stood for in the formative stages of the American conservation movement.

What Mills drew from the inspiration of Muir — and other historical figures he admired — made him, if nothing else, indomitable. And what his own temperament added to that made him at times impossibly pugnacious. He was, in the words of one commentator, "as combative a character as the West had seen in all its combative history."[4] Once in the public arena, Mills fought for his causes until he dropped, almost literally in his tracks, at age fifty-two.

Many have pronounced harshly on Mills's public crusades as being "marred by conflicting aims and an aggressive self importance." In a 1979 article on Mills, Carl Abbott continues that, as a public advocate, Mills was a "tragic figure." Historians, one should hope, would prick up their ears at mention of a "tragic figure" and go at once to investigate. They would find tantalizing scents along the way, such as Robert Shankland's notion — in his biography of the first National Park Service director, Stephen Mather — that Mills's temperament was "one of the most famously choleric ones of his time." But, argues Abbott, Mills's refusal to submit his ideas to critical analysis and his habitual condemnation of all who opposed him resulted in a "self-imposed and self-righteous isolation" that left him "with no followers except his wife and few friends to defend his accomplishments."[5]

Esther Burnell Mills (1889–1964), Mills's wife for the last four years of his life, did just that. She gathered and published Mills's remaining writings, adding three posthumous volumes to the dozen already in print. She continued to operate his famous Longs Peak Inn until 1945, maintaining its unique character. Though heavily burdened in continuing the business, she was said to have concealed her stress from the view of guests and to have "unfolded to them her own charming spirit and the spirit . . . of the mountains she loved." She raised the daughter that she called "the greatest possible joy to her father," and died at age seventy-five in 1964.[6]

Thirteen years after Mills's death, Esther Burnell Mills coauthored *Enos Mills of the Rockies* with Hildegarde Hawthorne, a granddaughter of Nathaniel Hawthorne and herself a Mills admirer. Though published by Houghton Mifflin as a biography for juvenile readers, the work is laced with material meant for adults and often pointed at Mills's adversaries — of which, by the time of his death, there were many. The political batterings that Mills took and dealt in his last years left his reputation in need of repair, and to that task Esther set herself with a widow's devotion and perspective. Lacking the time and training to accomplish her task in depth, she built her case for Mills on sentiment and avoided questions of rigor by directing her narrative to young readers. But there is no mistaking the book's intention of scoring points for Mills with a wider audience. Its tone of hagiography is apparent to any modern reader; its biases and errors — especially errors of omission — are not. In it, Mills is scrubbed clean to reveal only his most endearing qualities — and there were many of those, too. The book is readable, and, though factually flawed, it is reliable in its devout loyalty to preserving the image of the famous man whom Esther won and lost in so brief a span. Its chief merit now is to reveal both how Esther saw her husband and how Mills may have seen himself.[7]

Well before, and long after, the appearance of *Enos Mills of the Rockies,* idealized accounts of Mills made their way into newspaper stories, popular nature writing, and the growing literature about America's national parks. Romanticized and wholly agreeable versions of Mills passed almost by formula into pre–World War II national park books, invariably attaching to Mills his coveted epithet, "Father of Rocky Mountain National Park." Conspicuously held up for admiration in many narratives about him was the tale of the triumph of a sickly youth made strong and hopeful by outdoor

living — a theme that had already become the backbone of Mills's
own conservation message to the nation.

As the story of American conservation began to be written in
more detail during the postwar growth of American environmental
consciousness, Mills's reputation was forced to compete with those
of a growing number of significant figures from the past. Now simple idealizing worked against him, for it was necessarily based on a
lack of specifics. Hans Huth's 1957 *Nature and the American: Three
Centuries of Changing Attitudes,* for example, calls Mills "one of
the greatest pioneers of the conservation movement . . . who was
self-taught, a pure idealist, independent, and endowed with extraordinary will power." Yet Huth's treatment of Mills is exceedingly
brief and does not explain why Mills was a great pioneer. Roderick
Nash's classic *Wilderness and the American Mind* cites Mills only a
single time — as a national park advocate. And no works on Muir,
past or present, give Mills more than brief mention. Post–World War
II Forest and Park Service histories, and histories of the State of Colorado, have likewise dealt with Mills only sketchily, though sometimes provocatively. Several bestow on him the title "John Muir of
the Rockies." One calls him "the first professional environmentalist
in the Rockies," and another, citing some of his conflicts with governmental agencies, tags him as "an unpredictable friend and a formidable enemy."[8]

Peter Wild's inclusion of a chapter on Mills in his 1979 *Pioneer
Conservationists of Western America* gave renewed visibility to
Mills in the same year that Carl Abbott published his first of two
Mills essays. And C. W. Buchholtz's 1983 history of Rocky Mountain National Park highlighted Mills's importance to the development of the Estes Park area and various aspects of the national park
movement.

Wild cites several reasons for restoring Mills to a place in history. Like Muir, Mills both helped to catalyze and gained popularity
through the back-to-nature sentiment in the decades following the
proclaimed end of the frontier era in 1890. Mills "celebrated the last
wild remnants of the Rockies even as he realized that industrial society was taming the wilderness he loved," says Wild. Particularly
interesting are Mills's "perceptions of one world passing while the
other emerges." The fervent tone of Mills's nature writing, traceable
to his profound solitary experience in the wilds, places him in the
tradition of Muir and Thoreau. That tradition, Wild believes, gave

birth to the modern impulse to preserve nature in America rather
than in Europe. Mills furthermore often had charm and substance as
a distinctly Rocky Mountain writer, and his books, Wild notes, are
amply sprinkled with heady passages, wry humor, suspense, good
story telling, and a wealth of sharp detail. "For many Americans,"
adds James Pickering in a 1988 essay, "Enos Mills remained to the
end of his life the most accessible and attractive writer-naturalist of
his generation." Mills's importance endures, writes Paul Brooks in
his 1980 *Speaking for Nature,* as part of the distinguished tradition
of literary naturalists who have "enlarged our understanding of the
natural world and strengthened our sense of kinship with it."[9]

Much also recommends retelling the story of Mills's life within
the historical period it spanned. "For historians interested in examples of self-made men on the late nineteenth-century frontier," Carl
Abbott notes, "the life of Enos Mills is almost too good to be
true."[10] The child of pioneer parents, Mills began his life in the era
of Reconstruction following the Civil War, the time of America's
development toward a modern industrial society. As a young man
Mills worked on the range with cowboys, in mining camps with
miners, and in uncharted territory with surveyors. He dropped in on
isolated settlers in the high Rockies and interviewed them to find out
why they were there. A seasonal laborer until 1902 and a later friend
of the socialist labor leader Eugene Debs, he witnessed the growth
and radicalization of the labor movement but escaped its violent and
tragic clashes with militia-backed corporations. He witnessed the
growth of capitalism from its uncontrolled excesses in the robber-
baron era, to the introduction of government regulation and the
growing partnership between government and business to modern
political capitalism. A born reformer, Mills lived his most active
public years in the Progressive Era — the "Age of Reform" that in
many ways left society's deeper problems unchallenged. Mills's place
in the mentality and practical achievements of that era is an important part of his story.

Mills witnessed and was part of the growth of American conservation from the first designations of federal forest reserves in 1891
to the powerful era of Progressive conservation under Gifford Pinchot and Theodore Roosevelt, which brought institutionalized
resource management and technocratic efficiency. The parallel
growth of amateur preservationism inspired by Muir sought to save
America's wildlands not only from the havoc wrought by settlers

and large-scale corporate abusers, but increasingly as well from the very technocrats who had taken over their management. Mills's alignments in these conflicting ideologies beg closer examination. Much can also be learned from exploring Mills's attitudes toward the end of the pioneer age, planned settlement through governmental reclamation programs, national nostalgia for outdoor and country living, and the rise of the western vacation industry. The subject of whether the West's prosperity should ultimately rest on extractable resources or on its scenic beauty remains of central importance today.

Though he shunned pure science as an oppressively dry discipline, Mills was part of the new scientific age. He dabbled in scientific exactitude, often invoked scientific rationality, yet believed in "poetic interpretation" of the facts. He followed Thoreau, Muir, and John Burroughs into a brand of natural history quite different from that of formal science, yet, like Muir and Burroughs, was at times ranked among the top naturalists of his day. Mills replaced his own religious heritage with a scientific outlook that precluded metaphysical or spiritual searching and led him occasionally into derisive anti-clerical jabs.

Mills believed profoundly and literally in the principles of democracy and reacted with anguished belligerence to its flaws and to the needed give and take of practical politics. He believed ardently in personal freedom, in creating the opportunities and conditions for everyone to grow, and in the right of everyone to start life anew, at whatever age and for whatever reasons. The West, and the great outdoors, were the places where he believed that renewal could occur best. He championed equal rights and opportunities for women and was instrumental in getting women's groups active in conservation causes. He was wildly enamored of play, and saw everywhere in the wilds evidence of individual and evolutionary growth nurtured by that most remarkable instinct. He preached learning through direct experience, fun, and unfettered curiosity; he both loved and was loved by the children he taught. He had bizarre eating habits and usually ate little, but drank corrosively powerful coffee. He spent a week among road-crew convicts and concluded that their self-governed community was healthier than society on the outside. "During the last fifteen years of his life," said his inn manager, Emerson Lynn, Mills was "the most colorful man in the Estes Park community."

That distinction can easily extend to the whole Rocky Mountain region and beyond.[11]

The reissue of eight of Mills's books in recent years signals reviving interest in the man and his work. Surviving family members have reissued his 1905 *Story of Early Estes Park,* his 1914 *Story of a Thousand Year Pine,* and (through New Past Press), his 1920 *Adventures of a Nature Guide.* Comstock Editions have twice reprinted Mills's important 1919 work *The Grizzly, Our Greatest Wild Animal,* without, regrettably, any modern scientific critique of its continued validity as a work of natural history. Park Service naturalist Tom Danton's foreword to the reissued *Adventures,* on the other hand, usefully reasserts Mills's importance as a naturalist and founder of outdoor interpretation, while Michael Kiley's introduction to the same work explores Mills's deeply experiential approach to nature and to the art of "nature guiding." James H. Pickering's introductions to reprintings by the University of Nebraska Press of Mills's first four major published works and of Joe Mills's idealized autobiography, *A Mountain Boyhood,* (1926) provide compact and informative reviews of the lives of Mills and his younger brother and the regional context of their lives. New information presented about Joe — the lesser known of the two brothers — helps elucidate both Joe's own achievements and the similarities and differences from Enos that played out so dramatically in the brothers' relationship. Individual Mills stories also continue to be popular. His famous first-person narrative "Snow-Blinded on the Summit," for example, has been reprinted half a dozen times since 1980. It is one of sixteen stories gathered into a new Mills anthology, *Radiant Days,* edited and insightfully interpreted by John Dotson.

Mills's writings reveal little private biographical information but leave many traces of the man behind the narrative voice and the created image. From the time he left home at age fourteen, Mills was self-made; creating an image for public consumption became the inevitable result of personal experience translated to a first-person literary format. As didactic purpose entered his work, he was frequently an outright propagandist who used his subject matter to create sentiment and win support. Because his own persona was partly literary device, part of the challenge in recounting his life is to disentangle the strands of what he wanted to be, thought he was, and said he was.

Had Mills lived longer he would have doubtlessly penned his own life story, for one of the concepts that interested him most was that all living things have their biographies. The nature writer is both the reporter and the biographer of animals, birds, trees, and mountains. Mills wanted to know how every creature got to be what it is, what "adventures" it had experienced, and how its life and character could be read from its surroundings and behavior, its shape, deformities, and scars. To be marked by life was the sign of having lived.

Of all the images by which Mills invoked biography, the gnarled trees at timberline were the most vivid and the most emblematic of his own life. Their struggle to survive and advance at the last frontier of growth was, for Mills, heroic evidence of the persistence of life in the face of overwhelming odds. Shorn of their branches upwind but proudly streaming them downwind, they were for Mills flags of a victorious will to live and a defiant struggle against the injunction "This far and no farther." Mills struggled to the frontier of his own limitations where forces beyond his power stopped his advance but could not send him in retreat for shelter. He stood his ground in defiant self-assertion, tenacious in purpose and faithful to his causes to the very end. In the records of nature, where the persistence of life counts for more than regal stature, Mills lives on as illustriously as his taller contemporaries.

PART I

Boy Meets World: A Fast Start

CHAPTER 1

Farm Boy on the Kansas Frontier

His mother was small and plucky, feisty if necessary, dark haired and dark eyed, quick with her hands and feet, able to outrun her chickens and cows, and given to singing "all day, every day, all her life." Ann Lamb Mills (1837–1923) was a nature lover who gave her son his deep sentiment for the outdoors and probably also his lifelong admiration for women. Remembering his debt to her in an autobiographical sketch written for the Saturday Evening Post in 1917, the forty-six-year-old Mills wrote that it was she who had first interested him in natural history, "firing his imagination" with stories from her own experiences "among peaks and streams." Her stories, he told one journalist, were the first things he remembered in his life. It was usual for Mills to proclaim the equality of women in public, as he did no fewer than four times from the podium of a national parks conference in 1917. Twice at that conference Mills said that women are physically and mentally the equals of men in outdoor pursuits. And as nature guides for the national parks — requiring the gifts of "a philosopher and a friend and an instructor" — women, he insisted, would be "in many cases even better than men."[1]

Stories, based on personal experiences and able to "fire the imaginations" of others, would be the ingredients of Mills's own creative achievement, just as it had been the gift of Ann Lamb Mills to her children. Mills would learn to see all of nature as a storybook to be absorbed and retold, to be made vivid and palpable in the telling, to enrich the world of the listener, and to show that birds and beasts are sane, healthy, vibrantly alive, and morally correct. Not morally clever, like the talking animals of fables and concocted children's stories — he abjured those as falsifications. But yet animals who could feel and think, who had time and inclination to loaf, to play, and to visit their relatives — animals who inhabit the world as our companions, who "in their desire for human society" will sometimes even leave the forest to live near human habitation and "confidingly raise their families in the scenes where children romp and play."[2]

The world of nature that Enos Mills received from his mother was a world of intuition and remembered experience, a world compatible with a child's world, valuable more for the feelings it evoked than its precise meanings. The genius of that world for Mills would later be John Muir, who also listened to nature's stories and told them back, who also made nature vivid and palpable and fired the imaginations of all who read or listened to him. As the teller of nature's stories, Muir would become Mills's Shakespeare, "the greatest genius that ever with words interpreted the outdoors."[3] Mills would see the essence of Muir in his fusion of thought and feeling, of scientific fact with poetic interpretation. As a youngster with an eye for detail and later with Muir as his model, Mills would also learn to add fact to sentiment — fact observed, deduced, or drawn from the inner eye of imagination. The search for facts would bring him to the outskirts of science, to a precinct where knowledge was a blessing, but erudition was unwanted baggage. Facts by themselves were dry and weary; illuminated by imagination, they shone with the light of poetry.

The experiences "among peaks and streams" that Ann Lamb Mills inspired her children with occurred during the summer of 1860, when she ventured to the Colorado gold fields with her husband and three other men, all related. News of the Pikes Peak rush of '59 had reached eastern Kansas, where the interrelated Mills and Lamb families had settled two years earlier. Ann Mills had lost her first three children, all at ages under three, and perhaps sought personal renewal on the frontier of the high Rockies. Elkanah Lamb (1832–1915), a cousin of both Ann's father and her own husband, chronicled that trip in his 1906 autobiography. Lamb wrote that for the small party finding gold was secondary to the adventure and the romance of the West. They went, he said, from "a desire to see the Western plains, the buffaloes, wild Indians, and the Rocky Mountains."[4]

Those fabled Rockies, the feverish gold camps, the characters of the raw West, and the adventurous journey out and back — all was stuff to nourish the attitudes and ambitions of the Mills children. Perhaps more than her experiences of nature in that summer of 1860, Ann Mills gave to her children a vision of the West as a place of robust virtues, a frontier that both demanded vigor and gave vigor to life, that bred a quality in men and women already recognized as the pioneer spirit. Those were among the qualities of the West that Enos Mills would later want preserved in national parks and that Joe Mills (1880–1935), Enos's younger brother by ten years, would depict as an aficionado of western Americana.

Joe Mills gave his mother heroic stature in relating his parents' goldrush adventure in a 1926 autobiographical narrative, *A Mountain Boyhood*. Joe trimmed the size of the party from four men and a woman to only his father, prostrate on the wagon planks from mountain fever, and his mother, singlehanded driver of the pony team for several weeks. One evening as she cooked, twelve Indian braves filed into her camp, watched silently while she prepared a buffalo stew, then snatched and hid the kettle when she turned her back for a moment. "With sudden ferocity," Joe wrote, the ninety-two-pound pioneer wife "swept around the circle slapping the surprised braves, pulling their hair and demanding the kettle." The group's chief was revealed as the culprit, and when the hot brew spilled over his legs at Ann's tug on his blanket, "the fellow leaped high into the air, and vanished into the night, leaving the brass kettle behind him."[5]

Elkanah Lamb's version of the episode was notably different. The other Mills in the group, rather than Ann's husband, was ill with fever, and two, not twelve, Indian braves rode into camp. After eating some cold biscuits and looking the party over, they "unceremoniously departed," Lamb reported, mentioning neither Ann nor the buffalo stew. Perhaps Joe knew of no better way to express his "lasting admiration for [his] plucky mother" than with a tale of pioneer heroism which, if stretched, conveyed at least that she *could* have sent the twelve braves packing. It was, withal, a tale told at the expense of the Indians, who were reduced to cowardly buffoons, and it was a tale that kept Joe from attempting a deeper rendition of who and what his mother really was. Nothing in the writings of Enos Mills, who was singularly reticent about personal and family matters, sheds any further light on the character of the mother both boys admired.

With established farms in Linn County, Kansas, awaiting their return, the party's failure to find gold was of little consequence. But had they not already put down roots in Kansas, they might have stayed in Colorado to do their plowing along the bottomlands of the streams issuing onto the plains from the Rockies' east slope. Many had done just that, and Colorado agriculture was in a prodigal infancy, selling crops and hay for hungry miners and their livestock.

The party arrived home to the Kansas famine of 1860–61, caused by drought and searing southwest winds. They had in fact cut short the gold-digging adventure because of that famine and their concern for family members left behind. Kansas territory was not only hungry and thirsty but also torn by escalating warfare among its own settlers. The issue was slavery, and the tensions that would soon ignite the Civil War had already stirred up bloody skirmishes along the Kansas-Missouri border. A law of 1854 allowed Kansas to choose its future as a slave or a free state, with the result that pro- and antislavery groups had promoted settlement into the territory, each seeking to dominate the opposition in numbers and influence. Bitter feuding among the settlers gave the territory the name "bleeding Kansas."

About thirty-five members of the Lamb and Mills families, linked since the 1820s, had settled in the troubled border country, some less than five miles from Missouri, a staunch slave state. Quaker ties made them devout abolitionists, and Elkanah Lamb's father had harbored fugitive slaves on the underground railroad in northern Indiana before the families moved to Iowa in 1852 and to Kansas in 1837. Lamb's autobiography describes raids by pro-slavery ruffians who rode into Kansas from Missouri, called settlers to their doors on pretext of business, then murdered them in cold blood. Three miles from Lamb's farm, a rabid pro-slavery propagandist rounded up six citizens at a trading post and executed them. Both sides committed revenge murders, and the gangs of terrorists often rode through the countryside singing, jesting, and dangling stolen goods and live chickens from their saddles. These were the "crimson crimes and dark deeds," Lamb wrote, "that put to shame and condemnation" man's innately "sympathetic, kind and affectionate" nature. Joe Mills's autobiography said more simply, "The eastern Kansas border during the trying times of the early sixties was perhaps the worst place in all the world to live."[6]

Not far from the Mills home, five miles south of Pleasanton in Linn County, Union and Confederate forces fought one of their battles on Kansas soil. Joe Mills credited his father with having fought in the battle of Mine Creek, while Elkanah Lamb wrote of his capture by ruffians posing as Union soldiers. Threatened with execution by a pistol held to his head, Lamb miraculously escaped. Overwhelmed by his experience of "God's special providence," he underwent an intense religious conversion and was born again "to do the will of God." Soon ordained as the Reverend Lamb, he would play a prominent role in the life of the younger Enos Mills.

Though Lamb rejected slavery with apparent sincerity, he retained ingrained attitudes that gave his writing an unthinking and often insolent hypocrisy. Late in life when the experience of years might have given him wisdom or at least discretion, he tritely propounded the white man's right to inherit the earth. "Seemingly the red man and the black man have not the capacity or the necessary willpower for the improvement or possible development of nature's grand and prolific resources that are comprised in soils, forests, and mineral fields," he wrote; "and therefore, it appears to be destined for the white man."[7] The assumption that nature's riches belonged without qualification to humans and to the exclusively deserving white race was a bedrock Western attitude that the conservation movement, starting in Mills's youth, would need laboriously to revise. If Lamb influenced Mills's early assumptions about the use of natural resources, he could not prevent his later shift to the preservationist wing of the conservation movement led and symbolized by John Muir.

As a religious influence on Mills, Lamb would accomplish little. Young Mills was not cowed by Lamb's thundering sermons and his intimidating presence — six feet, five inches tall and clad in a long, coatlike, black Sunday frock. Mills may at most have taken on some of Lamb's habit of moralizing, but he became, and remained, largely a religious skeptic, quick to criticize Christian hypocrisy. Though Ann Mills's father was a Quaker preacher, Enos Mills, Sr., (1834–1910) was a professed agnostic with no tolerance for organized religion until he approached its fringes as a Freemason later in life. As a twenty-five year old, Mills learned explicitly from his father in a letter what he must have absorbed while still a youngster at home. Perhaps responding to an inquiry from his son, Enos, Sr., wrote that he did not know whether or not there was a god, that his belief would not change the facts anyway, that he tolerated charitable Christianity but despised "sensational" Christianity, and that he "would not give a farthing to have the orthodox religion spread over the earth a foot thick."[8]

On matters of religion, the two dominant male figures in Mills's life prior to his meeting Muir thus stood at opposite poles. Lamb, though often bigoted and an incessant moralizer, was personally generous and a profound nature lover. Enos Mills, Sr., also far larger physically than his son, appears to have been pragmatic in both thought and deed, a man with perhaps less personal warmth and passion than Lamb.[9] There is no evidence that these contrasting influences ever caused Mills to struggle with metaphysical questions or spiritual doubts. It was in his nature to look around and to draw on the currents of the times that he liked. Although nature came as close as anything to being his religion, he never followed Muir into a view of nature suffused with spirit or a "soul life," or modeled, as it was for Emerson and the naturalist Louis Agassiz, on an idea of God in every plant and animal.

When Enos Abijah Mills saw the light of day on April 22, 1870, the world, in broadest terms, was no better or worse than it had ever been. The Civil War was five years over, and the land, both North and South, now agonized over how the rebel states should rejoin American democracy. The East was thickening with industrial growth, while the West — including the newly purchased Alaska — still offered a frontier for those needing or wanting new lives. Enos Mills belonged to the generation, born in the last third of the nineteenth century, that set the twentieth century on a course we still recognize today. Churchill, Gandhi, FDR, Lenin, Henry Ford, Albert Schweitzer, Frank Lloyd Wright, Freud, Jung, Caruso, Stravinsky, Eliot, Yeats, Madame Curie, and Einstein, are but random samples of twentieth-century genius born and formed before our century began. Mills entered the 1900s old enough to know something of life, but young enough to want to change it. It was with the new century that he would identify and in which he would place his hopes for an improved humanity.

In Mills's birth year of 1870, the United States had 39 million inhabitants, fewer than half a million of them in Kansas. But the new state, admitted in 1861, was growing fast: from 107,000 in 1860 to 996,000 in 1880. Those sunbaked wheatlands would bring forth the poet Edgar Lee Masters, fiction writers Damon Runyan

Enos Mills, age eight. *Courtesy, Enos Mills Cabin Collection.*

and Dorothy Fisher, and newspaper greats Frank Irving Cobb and William Allen White — the last of these a later acquaintance of Mills's in Colorado. In an age when geographical theories of culture abounded, it was easy to suppose that the boundless sweep of the Kansas sky gave inspiration to aviator Amelia Earhart or to Walter Beecher, Clyde Cessna, and Glenn Martin — all Kansans and all famous aircraft entrepreneurs. Or that the tiresome prairie distances turned the mind of Walter Chrysler to automobiles. Or that its unrelieved flatness prepared Kansan William Starrett to build New York's Empire State Building. Such notions were doubtlessly plausible to Mills, who liked to repeat the adage that "history is geography set in motion." And whatever the inspiration of the land itself, the people, said William Allen White, are "hard-working, highly literate, and easily excited." All of those qualities stamped Enos Mills as a true native Kansan.[10]

Young Mills did not know who his famous contemporaries would be, nor yet guess his own destiny as a Rocky Mountain hero and national celebrity espousing the power of nature to cure what ails the world. Kansas life still dealt with fundamentals, and the births of a few men and women destined for greatness was not conspicuous. The persistent problem of growing food was aggravated by severe drought again in 1873, but the determined settlers were learning about drought-resistant wheat strains, and the Jayhawk state progressed toward prosperity.

The construction of railroads in the late sixties opened the colorful era of longhorn cattle drives from Texas along the famous Chisholm Trail to Kansas railheads. During Mills's youth heroes such as Wyatt Earp, Wild Bill Hickock, and Bat Masterson made their mark, and the Kansas towns of Abilene, Dodge City, and Ellsworth thronged with cowboys who spent their wages on women and hard drinking after months in the saddle.

When Mills was born, the Atlantic cable was five years old and the Suez Canal had just begun service. Clipper ships still graced the high seas but would soon be replaced by throbbing steamers. By the time Mills was ten, telephones, phonographs and electricity were common in some parts of the country, and in another ten years the pride and optimism of the new technology would be reflected in the great Chicago World's Fair of 1893. An admiring Enos Mills would be on hand to share in the fair's utopian visions.

Other frontiers besides the American West were still plentiful. Schliemann had started to excavate Troy, and Livingstone to explore the Congo. The Matterhorn had yielded to human daring, and the English Channel would soon yield to human endurance. Greenland's interior had been penetrated, and a generation of daring polar explorers — Scott, Amundsen, Shackleton, Cook — were boys of Mills's age who would later set new standards for courage and fortitude against the hardest of hardships.

Barnum's circus, opened in 1871, proclaimed American hyperbole, and "Barnumizing" — vulgar sensationalizing of every exploitable object — would become a later source of Millsian condemnation. If the bigness of Barnum verged on vulgarity, the bigness of Walt Whitman created a vibrant new vision of the American spirit for those who dared to understand. Ralph Waldo Emerson, at the peak of his fame, had pronounced favorably on that vision as the "most extraordinary piece of wit and wisdom America has yet contributed."[11]

The two summers before Mills's birth were John Muir's first summers in the Sierra mountains of California, his most precious years of wild freedom. The valley of Yosemite and the High Sierras to the east were more beautiful than anything he had ever seen, and with a gift for thinking backward and forward in geological time, he could see each moment as part of a continuously unfolding perfection. Muir began a period of phenomenal creativity during the years of Mills's earliest infancy, progressing within five years, according to his biographer Frederick Turner, from "an unknown itinerant laborer looking for work" to a "naturalist with standing in American scientific circles, the acknowledged expert on the life of the Sierras, and a writer of reputation."[12] His rustic but shrewdly perceptive glaciology brought him instant notice when he published an article in the December 5, 1871, issue of Horace Greeley's *New York Tribune* declaring that Yosemite Valley must have been carved by glaciers, not created by a 3,500-foot collapse of the earth's crust, as California's state geologist, Josiah Whitney, had concluded. More articles followed on sundry topics, and well-known magazines competed for them. By the late seventies, Muir was a minor celebrity, widely read and praised even by literati.

Muir had survived a boyhood of harsh physical and emotional punishment by a religiously obsessed father — first in Scotland, then on a Wisconsin farm, where the toil was unremitting. Even where abnormalities at home did not inflict their abuses, Muir's life exemplified the severe toll that pioneer life took on frontier children, and he retained a lasting aversion for both its drudgery and its wasteful disregard for the land. One of the outspoken critics of pioneer life's toll on children was Isabella Bird, a solitary Victorian traveler who settled briefly in the mountain valley Mills would later inhabit and whose writings Mills later knew and admired. "One of the most painful things in the western United States and territories," she said, "is the extinction of childhood. I have never seen any children, only debased imitations of men and women, cankered by greed and selfishness, and asserting and gaining complete independence of their parents at ten years old."[13]

Enos Mills's departure from home at age fourteen does not imply circumstances in the Mills family approaching those of Isabella Bird's doleful scenario. Pioneer hardships apparently yielded to the industry of Mills's capable parents and mutual support among the related families. The boy emerged from childhood with a hopeful outlook on life and a distinctly positive assessment of pioneerdom. There is nevertheless a perceptible if subtle sense in *Enos Mills of the Rockies* — virtually the only account of Mills's youth — that something was not quite right in the Mills family, that young Enos stood somewhere in the confusing terrain between uncommunicating parents. The lad suffered some kind of digestive disorder that was perhaps caused by wheat allergy but was intensified by emotional stress and was interpreted by his father as stubbornness. The Hawthorne-Mills biography, perhaps reconstructing things Mills himself had said, draws a portrait of dichotomy between the parents where there should have been teamwork to mitigate the boy's distress. Ann Mills's role seems to have been one of rescuing her frail son from an insensitive and overdemanding father. Mother and son collude to avoid father's stern table discipline; they share companionship while father "is busy with the newspapers." And Ann Mills suggests her son's departure from home to escape his father's unrealistic expectations for his participation in farm work. If most of what Esther Burnell Mills and Hildegarde Hawthorne knew of Mills's childhood came from Mills himself, the salient fact about the boy's father was how he himself perceived him. But against that conclusion must be placed the possibility that the authors of *Enos Mills of the Rockies* themselves recoiled from paternal domination and put their sympathies in the more familiar domain of Mills's mother. Detached from

The Mills family shortly before Enos *(top left)* departed for Colorado at age four-teen. Sisters with Mills in rear are Sarah, Belle, and Ella; in front from left are Enoch (Joe), Naomi, parents Ann Lamb Mills and Enos Mills, Sr., and Horace. *Linn County, Kansas, Historical Society.*

the emotion of his departure in later years, Mills gave the offhand explanation that his health required a mountain climate, while his parents were unable to leave the plains.

If the boy's early separation from a mother he loved and a father who expected much but responded little left a permanent mark, it can perhaps be seen in Mills's later glorification of play as a lifelong urge and privilege, his eagerness to adopt John Muir as an alternative father figure and to proclaim him as "the factor of my life," his intense desire to advance the social standing of women, and in some personal insecurities that limited his tolerance to criticism and brought him in frequent conflict with former allies. Enos Mills grew into a colorful, principled, highly idealistic but short-fused and often pungently disputatious man. He was a man by turns kind, generous, suspicious and spiteful; a man at times expansively and at times pet-tily eccentric; a man who won loyal friends and bitter enemies; and a man admired by millions across the country. He was able, like all men of ability, to focus his strongest energies to meaningful activity, yet he also expended much of his energy on mistrust and personal vendettas.

The stirring drama of a boy leaving home at age fourteen is firmly enshrined in the Mills legend. But what is missing in *Enos Mills of the Rockies* and virtually all early and most modern accounts is the fact that family members were waiting to help and guide the boy at his destination in Colorado. Living near Estes Park village, preaching the Gospel, and guiding vacationers up Longs Peak was none other than Reverend Lamb. Transferred by the United Brethren church to Colorado in 1871, Lamb had spent much of his time on the itinerant preaching circuit in northeastern Colorado's thinly settled districts. He moved to the Longs Peak area in 1875, cutting the first road in from Estes Park, eight miles below, and began offering guided climbs up Longs Peak in 1878. Nearing fifty years old, he turned the property, the guiding, and the small cattle operation over to his son Carlyle and moved with his wife, Jane, to another cabin nearby. Jane, a solicitous and warm-hearted woman, gave young Mills some of the motherly attention he had left behind; one of his sisters was also living nearby, in Fort Collins. Lamb, his grown son Carlyle, and another son, Lawrence, also in Fort Collins, could all provide the boy with some degree of adult male guidance. The boy's move to Colorado appears, in short, to have been a practical transfer to the care of relatives and was probably decided with the help of the family doctor. The epic flavor of a sickly youth who faced the world alone at age fourteen needs revision without belittlement: Leaving home was in any case a major event in his life and the catalyst for his phenomenal self-development. One of its immediate benefits, Mills said in his 1917 self-portrait, was that it allowed him to "escape most of public school." That meant, in Mills's terms, that he was spared the stifling drudgery of rote education and left free to discover the world for himself.

In one of the few glimpses Mills gave of himself as a youngster still at home, the ingredients of an ardent, self-taught nature investigator are already evident. No exception to any boyhood norm in preferring the open fields and woods to farm chores, Mills found himself one day testing the local maxim that a skunk can throw its scent no more than eight times straight:

We came upon a skunk crossing an open field. There was no cover, and in a short time each of our three cur dogs had experienced twice and ceased barking. Each of the [two other] boys had been routed. All this time I had dodged and danced about enjoying these exhibitions and skunk demonstrations. . . . After eight performances I felt assured that of course he must be out of eradicator. But he wasn't. For years I avoided the skunk, the black and white plume-tailed aristocrat.[14]

We see a boy capable of the intense delight of curiosity. In his dancing about on the periphery of the action, there is a hint of both delicacy and good sense. The future naturalist was well positioned to keep score on the skunk's emissions, and only when assumption overruled detached observation did Mills mix his presence into the investigation and suffer the consequence.

Such events as this made the proverbially monotonous Kansas farmland anything but monotonous for the young boy. Enos Mills, despite frailty, was eager to learn and keen of eye, and where there is a will to look closely, no place on earth is barren. Where the land was unplowed, "big bluestem" and other prairie grasses grew higher than a man's head, for eastern Kansas lay in that matchless belt of fertile savannah called the tallgrass prairie. Hidden in the majestic grasses were creeks and hollows, skunk and badger dens, raccoons, coyotes, muskrats, deer, and, in their seasons, birds and flowers galore. Knowing the land intimately was the alternative to taking in all of Kansas in one undifferentiated glance, and it was to detail that Enos Mills turned. As a young naturalist two decades later, he would proclaim that minute and repeated inspection of the same territory was the way of true observation, and he would find that point articulately set down for him by John Burroughs (1837–1921), the Hudson River naturalist — an idol second in rank only to John Muir.[15]

CHAPTER 2

Adolescent among the Mountains

"I believe that any person with a fair constitution, who settles in any portion of Colorado, stands a better chance of enjoying a healthful life, and of finally attaining the full period allotted to man — three score years and ten — than in any other part of the Union." So declared pioneer Colorado physician F. J. Bancroft in a letter to the Territorial Board of Immigration in 1873, three years before Colorado became a state. In wooing new settlers to Colorado, the Immigration Board stressed good health along with economic opportunities, and by the mid seventies there was widespread promotion of Colorado's health-restoring climate, targeted to both tourists and new settlers. Enos Mills was one of the roughly one-third of all new settlers between 1880 and 1890 that could be classified as health-seekers.[1]

Tuberculosis and asthma were said to respond the best to the miracle climate, but epidemic diseases were reduced to "very mild forms" if they reached Colorado at all, Bancroft insisted. For statistics, one needed only to compare Denver's ten-per-thousand death rate (the lowest in the country) with New York City's thirty-two-per-thousand and New Orleans's fifty-four-per-thousand. The life-giving ingredients of Colorado's climate were said to be its pure, dry air, its high altitude, bright sunny days, "uniform and highly electrified atmosphere," and the "brilliant and grand scenery, which produces cheerfulness and a contented frame of mind." Mills would later popularize the curative power of the mountain climate that restored his own health, stressing especially the beneficial effects of high altitude. As for scenery, he would later agree: Why should it not promote good health if it pacifies the mind and body, performing what in modern terms would be called stress reduction? The populace Mills would later address as a spokesman for outdoor living was fast succumbing to the pace and pressures of urban life. One Colorado guide of the time ascribed Colorado's healthfulness to the opportunity it afforded people to "escape for a time from the fierce struggles and intense mental strain of modern civilization."[2] The cure, for many, consisted simply in getting away from it all.

Health resorts had developed rapidly in the seventies, led by Manitou Springs at the foot of Pikes Peak with a summer population of 2,000 who took the waters of six separate springs, each with its own name and chemical analysis. At Idaho Springs, discovery of the miracle mineral radium in the waters in 1881 brought a booming business under the slogan that "the stretcher is carried in only one direction." Travelers' guides to Colorado such as Frank Fossett's 1879 *Colorado* and George Crofutt's 1881 *Grip-Sack Guide to Colorado* helped to spread the word. If they were at times unrealistically rhapsodic, they did not contrive to deceive. Coloradans boasted of their climate because they believed in it. And Isabella Bird, lavish with her praise only when it was deserved, wrote, "The climate of Colorado is considered the finest in North America, and consumptives, asthmatics, dyspeptics, and sufferers from nervous diseases, are here in hundreds and thousands, either trying the camp cure for three or four months, or settling here permanently." "In traveling extensively through the territory . . . I found that nine out of every ten settlers were cured invalids. Statistics and medical workers . . . represent Colorado as the most remarkable sanitorium in the world."[3]

If Kansas was the cause of Enos Mills's indigestion, then such a barrage of encouraging testimony for the curative power of the neighboring state must have seemed ample grounds for sending the boy off to get well. In the spring of '84 the fourteen-year-old bid his family farewell, walked and hitched rides to Kansas City, and — according to family lore — earned his train fare by working a short stint in a bakery. In a few weeks, Enos Mills boarded a train for Denver with a choice of three lines, the first completed in the year of his birth. The reddish-haired adolescent's feet may not have touched the floor as he sat on the coach seat, and the world outside must have seemed immense as the train entered the treeless expanses of the western Kansas and eastern Colorado prairie. The prairie was limitlessly flat in the larger perspective, but in the near view it rose and fell in rhythmic swells, like long ocean rollers stopped in their heaving by the desiccating sun. Somewhere to the west was that ocean's rocky shore.

Even if the boy had had no one to care for him, he could have been confident that the young state — admitted to the United States in 1876 — had its share of enterprising new settlers and an abundance of work. The newly reissued *Grip-Sack Guide* (1884) had advertised, "There is always work of some kind for those who honestly seek it. Make a name for honesty, sobriety and reliability, and you can soon attain any position and salary that your abilities will warrant. If you are not such a person, *stay away* from Colorado and let your friends, if you have any, support you in idleness." Wages ran from two to three dollars a day for the majority of jobs — jobs in railroad construction, quarrying, wagon-making, blacksmithing, the flourishing building industry, and mining and farming. Board and room consumed about half those wages, leaving a margin for the thrifty to advance their condition.[4]

Colorado had just finished a boom decade from 1870 to '80 in which the population had increased from 40,000 to 194,000. Five colleges and eight railroads had opened, statehood had been won, and the discovery of silver at Leadville had produced a stampede second only to the California goldrush of '49 and '50. Mining stimulated business, and the railroads helped businesses capture trade from the mining areas. Keeping pace with demand, agriculture doubled its production and livestock increased eightfold. The population density in 1880 was just under the two per square mile needed to designate Colorado — in Census Bureau terminology — as "settled" rather than "frontier." And indeed many mountain areas were fairly swarming with every form of life that precious metals could attract. After a lengthy tour of one mining area, the *Grip-Sack* authors reported, "We made . . . over 3,400 miles, and was [sic] never out of sight of civilization *one hour at a time*. People are scattered all over the country, prospecting, mining, stock raising, cutting grass, building bridges and wagon roads, publishing newspapers, building smelting works and mills, erecting large business blocks, and prosecuting all kinds of business enterprises with a *vim, vigor,* and *push* that says: 'This country is good enough for us. We have come to stay.' "[5]

Estes Park, young Enos Mills's destination, was neither a fashionable spa nor a feverish mining camp. It was a benign summer resort with a population of 150, depicted by an etching in the *Grip-Sack*

Guide that showed a tranquil scene of men and a sleeping dog around a campfire, fishing poles and rifles propped nearby, and a canoe lolling on the water behind. Though there was some modest dairying, lumbering, and halfhearted mining, taking care of the summer visitors was fast becoming the base of the village's economy.

Twenty-two miles into the state, the train came to First View, 4,593 feet high on the high rolling prairie, and Mills got his first distant glimpse of the mountains that would change his life. Closer in, the mountains dominated the whole western horizon, and their late spring snow cover set them off resplendently against the temporary green of the prairie. That view, after hundreds of miles of unrelieved prairie, is thrilling to anyone who has witnessed it. Not anywhere to the east — clear to the Atlantic seaboard — is there a comparable view. Only the Alps, the "storied monuments of poetical legendary fame," provided a reference point, and against them all comparisons were made. Coloradans had already decided that the Alps were no match in grandeur for the Rockies, and the state had proclaimed itself the Switzerland of America. One of the country's most famous and authoritative travel writers, Bayard Taylor, made liberal use of that epithet in his 1867 book *Colorado: A Summer Trip,* and Samuel Bowles, the famous editor of the Springfield *Republican,* had published a book entitled *The Switzerland of America* in 1869. Isabella Bird had picked up the theme too, exclaiming, "The Alps, from the Lombard Plains, are the finest mountain panorama I ever saw, but not equal to this."[6] Colorado's preoccupation with outclassing and outboasting the Alps would later serve Enos Mills well in his campaigns for scenic preservation and the creation of Rocky Mountain National Park.

The fourteen-year old stepped off the train in Denver into a city which had grown by a phenomenal 45,000 inhabitants to a total of 70,000 in the last four years. No city in the world had increased comparably in population, wealth, or substantial improvements, claimed the *Grip-Sack Guide.* Where Isabella Bird had found only ugly makeshift structures in 1873, Denver now had 10,000 buildings, many in brick and stone. Flagstone sidewalks and 400,000 young trees bordered the streets. Eight railroads entered the city from all points of the compass, and a complete municipal railway system served the inner city with forty-six cars and 230 horses. There were sixteen public schools, a posh opera house built by silver king Horace Tabor, an academy of music, theaters, over three dozen hotels, as many drugstores, and hundreds of luxuriously furnished private residences.

The burgeoning Rocky Mountain metropolis was a locus for some of Enos Mills's later activities. Now, mountain-bound, the boy had only a quick look, but enough of a look to see that Denver was going full tilt toward a position of western leadership. Traveling north on the Greeley, Salt Lake, and Pacific branch of the Union Pacific, Mills had options for stage connections to Estes Park from Longmont and Loveland — unadorned towns that had pleased Isabella Bird no more than Denver but that had added size and refinements in the intervening decade. Most impressive to the practiced eye were the irrigation works, with numerous canals over thirty miles long to channel the mountain waters as they flowed onto the plains and spread over thirsty crops of wheat, corn, and sugar beets. Preaching forest preservation, to hold irrigation waters in snowy "reservoirs," would be one of Enos Mills's opening sallies into matters of western conservation and one of his lasting concerns.

An eight-hour stage ride finally brought the lad to the valley that contained "health in every breath of air," the valley of which Isabella Bird had rhapsodized: "I have just dropped into the very place I have been seeking." For her, for Enos Mills, and for millions since them, the intermountain vale of Estes Park was — and is — "perfection," a place "that satisfies [the] soul."[7] Approached from most directions, it is a valley looked into from its rim, as into a hidden Shangri-La. The floor is at 7,500 feet, the rim rippled with granite outcrops 1,000 to 2,000 feet higher on three sides. On the fourth side, the 12,000 foot peaks of the Continental Divide bear the chisel marks and some of the ice of the ancient glaciers that fashioned spires, sheer walls, and bowl-shaped cirques out of the high peneplain. The lower hills rise to meet the divide in tiers that force the eye to climb. The grassy valley and surrounding ponderosa forests are sunny and open but change to denser spruce higher up. The streams, flat and meandering in the valley, enter it and leave it again through rushing canyons.

Crowning the view of the high peaks and rearing 7,000 feet over the valley is the bare granite head of Longs Peak, gone from view during the climb from Longmont or Loveland but now magnetically close at hand. Longs Peak is a mountain of blunt strength, boldly individual and forbidding yet inviting. Its vertical sweep both elevates the spirit and evokes the horrors of falling. Blocklike and heavy with girth and mass, it occupies the sky but does not pierce it. It does not soar, being stationary; and it does not brood, lacking cause or means for brooding. Longs Peak is a presence, a presence over the valley of Estes Park, and Enos Mills was now drawing close to it — close to the mountain whose character he would mingle with his own. Between the youth's eye and its 14,255-foot summit lay seven miles of clear, thin air.

However perfect and soul-satisfying this valley was, and however bracing the view of Longs Peak and its court of lesser royalty, it was a boy of only fourteen who stood at the stage stop and had to ponder the next moment of his life. Everywhere he looked was up, and he was smaller than anything around him. Barely past childhood, facing the complexities of adolescence, and troubled by physical disorders as yet undiagnosed, Enos Mills stood on the threshold of his new life. But for the time being — in 1884 and well beyond — there is nothing to indicate that Lamb and his warmhearted wife, Jane, would have refused young Mills any attention he required. We do not know whether he declined a probable invitation to stay with the Lambs and earn his keep (as he did the next two summers), whether Lamb had lined up other arrangements through his local acquaintances, or whether Mills resolutely asserted his grownupness and sought at once to make his own way. In any event, he found work and lodging at the Elkhorn, one of the early Estes Park lodges, founded in 1877 by the family of William E. James.[8]

James had come to Colorado in 1873 or '74, seen the Estes valley on a hunting trip, and stayed to settle. He started out in the cattle business, but every summer people came to the ranch and begged to be allowed to stay. Each winter James built another cabin to house them, and soon found that there was more money in caring for summer tourists than in raising cattle. That fact, characteristic of Estes Park so early in its history, stuck fast in Enos Mills's memory and became a germinal idea in his conservation ethic.

While Enos Mills washed dishes, chopped wood, carried the mail, helped out in the commissary, and occasionally served guests their afternoon tea, the rascally four-year-old daughter of the house, Eleanor James, combed the fur of Tommy the cat, dressed him in doll's clothes, and took him riding in her doll buggy. Once Tommy sat in a high chair at the table and was served a boned trout but abused the privilege by snatching a guest's trout as well. Not many years later Eleanor enticed the children of guests to a swimming

Arriving in the Rocky Mountains as a fourteen year old, Mills was one of many who came West seeking improved health. Outdoor living was the chief ingredient of his cure. *Denver Public Library, Western History Department.*

hole, where they innocently paddled around in their birthday suits until they were discovered. Eleanor's favorite prank was to escape her 8:30 bedtime and spy on the adults, seeing "a great many things I was not supposed to see."[9]

Though remembered from a distance of fifty years, Eleanor James Hondius's memoirs provide one of the early accounts of resort life in Estes Park and a choice description of Elkanah Lamb preaching his sermons of hellfire and damnation. Through the decades the Elkhorn remained one of the centers of Estes Park life, popular for its lighthearted gaiety, and host to many distinguished visitors. Its fare included fish and steak fries, Sunday lectures or musicals, treasure hunts and bridge tournaments, baseball games, mock cowboy and Indian battles, dinner dances that required rounding up blind dates for the unattached ladies, an annual cabaret performance, and a harvest moon party to end the season. How much of the style of the lodge portrayed by Eleanor James Hondius had evolved during Enos Mills's summer there in 1884 is not certain, but its rudiments were surely apparent. In setting the tone of his own Longs Peak Inn twenty years later, he had the Elkhorn and others like it for comparison, and sought to create for his guests a strikingly different experience.

Though always diligent when he was working, Mills decided early that work for work's sake alone is a perversion that neither man nor beast should obey. Play, work's liberated opposite, quickens the mind, gladdens the heart, and rescues civilization from despair and decay. Animals, Mills came to believe, have known and practiced such a doctrine all along. Muir as a young man had said, "Idle sentimental transcendental dreaming is the only sensible and substantial business that one can engage in." That translated later to the maxim that work should resemble play to the greatest possible extent. "Longest is the life," Mills would later repeat from Muir, "that contains the largest amount of work that is a steady delight."[10] While he sought the work that would be his form of delight, the youth was content to earn wages, to save through abstemious living, and thus to buy installments of freedom prolonged by the absence of currency in the backwoods, where he began spending much of his leisure time. For the next three winters a farm or ranch on the Colorado plains took him on as errand boy, and the Lambs provided similar employment at Longs Peak House beginning in his second summer at Estes Park. Both arrangements left Mills time to roam the wilds, to learn his woodcraft, and to observe all he could about Colorado's flora and fauna, from the treeless plains to the highest peaks.

Even when performing menial tasks, Mills did not uncouple his mind or earn his wages by rote. He felt himself part of exciting tides in the growth of the West. The work he did and the personalities he met had vivid substance that shaped him as a westerner and gave him needed depth as a later spokesman for western interests. Working at the Elkhorn introduced him to a clientele with standing, and prepared him for his earliest stabs at journalism — writing summer vacation gossip in the late nineties. The cattle ranch gave him a romantic sense of the cowboy's contribution to the history of the West and an understanding of the cowboy era's demise. An even deeper immersion into the world of metal mining — after 1887 — showed him social and ethnic diversity among workingmen, boom-town vitality and vulgarity, and the beginnings of labor organization in an industry soon dominated by large-scale capital.

During his winters on the Colorado plains, Mills kept a sketchy diary that shows that he earned his keep by performing a wide variety of chores. The boy's exposure to the world of the cowboy during this period left a deep impression, for the cowboy's days of glory were coming to an end with the fencing of the prairie by homesteading ranchers and farmers. Seeing the cowboy's transient place in history, Mills later characterized him as a breed who "tarried for a brief moment on the frontier, . . . [yet] made great changes throughout the West, and hastened its final development."[11] Of all the frontier virtues that Mills probably discovered first among the cowboys, he prized most the ethic of asking no questions about a man's past. He would come to view the West as a place where people could "start over" and he ardently defended a man's — and a woman's — right to carry no burden from the life left behind.

CHAPTER 3

Self-Discovery Begins

It was time for Enos Mills to plant his feet on the summit of Longs Peak and to sink roots that would attach him permanently to the soul of the mountain. Perhaps just looking at it, he had already begun to think of Longs as his peak, where he could make clear to people what a wondrous thing nature is, and through nature, life. And perhaps he already saw the peak as an axis of stability to which he could unfailingly turn for strength, definition, and certainty.

He got his chance in summer 1885, assisting Carlyle Lamb lug up some of the camera equipment for a guided party. The twenty-three-year-old son of Elkanah Lamb had reason to plan his trips well and to measure the capabilities of his parties, for in late September of the previous season he had allowed a client to perish from exhaustion and exposure by continuing up the peak when her growing fatigue should have warned him to turn back. He had in fact tried to, but Carrie Welton's determination to make the peak had overridden his better judgment. Whether Carlyle was reticent about the loss or willing to discuss it openly with Mills as they passed a marker placed in Carrie's memory, the boy had to look upon the spot where a hopeful and vital young person had died. And he had to form some opinion about why. "The guide should have refused to go farther," Mills wrote of the tragedy in 1905. And though it was a reproach, Mills knew the difficulty of overriding a client's enthusiasm. Carlyle was too young at his trade to have known what Mills learned later: "Guides on mountain peaks must sometimes be imperators." As a guide for 257 Longs Peak ascents, Mills would learn many times that people are potentially more lethal than the laws of gravity or the sudden shifts of weather. And he would often

In the first two decades of the century, Longs Peak became synonymous with the name of Enos Mills. He descended the great east face, shown here, in June 1903. Ice field at base of face is Mills Glacier, lake is Chasm Lake. *Courtesy, Enos Mills Cabin Collection.*

say during his guiding years that he could never learn enough about human nature.[1]

The youngster knew the moment he set foot on the summit of Longs Peak that summer day in 1885 that he wanted to be a guide on the great peak. Had he been alone on the summit he might have burst out in the same wild ecstasy that had stirred Muir when he first stood above Yosemite's great walls. Perched like Muir on high granite, Mills could see as much thrilling space at his feet and as many tall peaks at his back. Longs Peak is a worthy counterpart of the great shouldering masses of Yosemite granite and a rude twin of the spectacular Halfdome. Both are plated with sloping granite on three sides and sheared vertically on the fourth. Halfdome looks to have stayed longer in the sculpture studio for a final glacial polishing. It looks finished and on exhibit, while Longs Peak tells of work still in progress by an artist hacking at his object with uncontrolled forces. Today, Longs Peak as quickly evokes the name of Enos Mills as Halfdome does of John Muir, and each is a centerpiece of a national park that each man helped to found.

Neither Longs's great eastface Diamond wall nor Halfdome's sheer north face was scaled until the era of modern rock climbing — both in the 1960s. But below and around Longs's Diamond are eastface routes — dozens, and of every degree of difficulty — that challenged serious climbers as early as the 1920s. And between all those routes is a passage where goats might go and a nervy man could follow without a climber's paraphernalia: first up a steep snow arm, then along the wide, mid-peak Broadway ledge, and then through dripping, rubble-filled chimneys to stable blocks below the summit. Reversing that route to descend the peak is a possibility not the least bit obvious from the summit, and one only gulps at the amount of air at one's feet in peering down the abyss. How remarkable, then, and consummately foolish, yet brilliantly executed was Reverend Lamb's descent of that east-face passage alone in 1871, before anyone had ever touched that face, upward or downward. That he lived through it was a grand stroke of beginner's luck, for it was his first climb of Longs, backed by virtually no previous experience.

Already an Estes Park legend before Lamb wrote of it in his 1906 autobiography, the adventure reinforced the certainty of Lamb's great physical prowess, and revealed a source of primal energy behind his thundering sermons. He was a man not meek in peril and relied on God to see him through; yet he had a perfect

Young Mills *(at right)* first climbed Longs Peak in 1885 and went on to climb it 304 times more, 257 of them as a guide. *Denver Public Library, Western History Department.*

sense that God could at any moment hand him over to gravity. Escaping from the chimneys (where more than one climber would later fall to his death), Lamb traversed Broadway ledge to the ice-glazed snow arm, now called Lamb's slide. He slipped and slid, miraculously caught himself on a projecting rock, righted his over-coat, hacked a toehold in the ice with his pocketknife blade, and was at last flushed out to safety at the peak's base. If mountains could blink with astonishment at the temerity of humans, Longs would have blinked as Parson Lamb brushed himself and walked away, still six feet five inches tall, and ready to continue the Lord's work. As Enos Mills peered into the awful abyss where Lamb had disap-peared, he could not have guessed he would be next to try. But not yet. Lamb's feat remained unrepeated past the end of the century.

As for the easier side of Long Peak, it was — Mills would later quip whenever asked — "no more than a hard day's work." And he must have been right, for by the centennial anniversary of the peak's first ascent in 1868, over 100,000 had trodden the summit boulders. That, some would point out, is an implausibly large number of peo-ple willing to put in a hard day's work without wages. But work for recreation's sake was fast gaining credence. Mark Twain, in sum-ming up Tom Sawyer's fence-painting trickery, had put it this way: "Work consists of whatever a body is *obliged* to do, and . . . play consists of whatever a body is not obliged to do. . . . Constructing artificial flowers or performing on a treadmill is work, while rolling tenpins or climbing Mont Blanc is only amusement." The era was becoming conscious of the worth of leisure activity, and climbing mountains provided a simple illustration of values: The work and discomfort are worth it. Today, as then, some understand, and some don't. For those who understand, the summit of Longs Peak is "half-way to heaven," according to one climber's entry in the peak regis-ter. "But," the epigram cautions, "only a misstep from hell." The toll that Longs Peak would take — starting with Carrie Welton in 1884 — numbered twenty-two by the centennial year and forty-one by 1991.[2]

By the time Enos Mills climbed Longs in 1885, the peak was an adventure known and sought by outdoor enthusiasts, featured in some of the alpine journals, and climbed by about 100 people a year for the last several years, according to Frederick Chapin's 1889 book *Mountaineering in Colorado: The Peaks About Estes Park*. The climb and the exalted moods it evoked were things worth writing

The Rev. Elkanah Lamb, a fire and brimstone preacher, nature lover, and relative of both of Mills's parents, helped the fourteen year old start his new life in Colorado. The two later clashed. *Courtesy, Enos Mills Cabin Collection.*

about, and first-person narratives abounded to such an extent that by 1874 one editor wanted no more. "The Longs Peak communication is decidedly well written but the subject is threadbare," said the editor of the *Boulder News* in declining to print another account. And no wonder, for literary justice had already been done to the ascent at least twice over, both by literary women widely read in their day. The first was Anna E. Dickinson, a celebrated lecturer and essayist, a forceful voice in the abolitionist movement, and a sturdy mountaineer who had climbed New Hampshire's Mt. Washington twenty-seven times. Miss Dickinson climbed Longs in September 1873 as a guest of the famous Hayden survey, and Mills included her account in his 1905 booklet *Early Estes Park*. At virtually the same spot where Anna Dickinson sat around the fire with Professor Hayden and his party, Isabella Bird sat a few weeks later with the redoubtable "Rocky Mountain Jim" Nugent, a poetic and sensitive "desperado" who was said to be cultivated and intelligent when sober, violent and dangerous when drunk. The sublimated infatuation between Isabella and her rugged guide provides the first tale of romance on Longs Peak, a tale that lives on today, even in a recent opera. As a Longs Peak guide with couples of every description in his charge — married, engaged, or strangers until the day of the ascent — Mills would have abundant opportunity to observe how romance blossomed or wilted on the slopes of his mountain.

Chasm Lake, sunk into the floor of Longs Peak's east-face amphitheater, was still spotted with icebergs that July day when Mills first peered into it from 2,000 feet above. Cupped by so much perpendicular granite, the lake was a thing of wonder to the boy and he might at once have called it what he called it the rest of his life: utterly wild. The lake's outflow stream washes over sloping rocks, meanders briefly over a meadow and plunges into a pool of peacock blue, then courses the base of a moraine deposited by the glacier responsible for Longs Peak's present look. Both the remnant glacier and its moraine now bear Mills's name. Peering from the top of Longs, the boy could see the stream finally lose itself among boulders and trees as it dropped away east of the peak. Yet he probably knew already where it entered the Tahosa Valley and veered to join the northern branch of the St. Vrain River. The Tahosa Valley had not yet acquired its name and would do so only thirty years later, under heated controversy.

Mills's homestead cabin is now a registered historical landmark, a family-run museum, and a starting point for nature tours in Mills's own tradition. *Denver Public Library, Western History Department.*

The lodge and utility buildings of Longs Peak House, toylike in the view from Longs's summit, occupied meadowland near the valley's upper end at an elevation of precisely 9,000 feet. The place, now ten years old, was prospering under Carlyle's management. Mentioning no family link, or even any acquaintance between Mills and the Lamb family during the boy's previous summer in Estes Park, *Enos Mills of the Rockies* announces a first and casual meeting in 1885 when Mills happens by to inquire about vacant acreage next to Longs Peak House: unclaimed, Lamb informs him. And though Enos Mills could file on it only when he reached twenty-one, nothing apparently prevented him from putting a structure on it. That August, the fifteen-year-old started felling and notching trees for his own cabin, and in the fall, when the Lambs left for the lowlands, he stayed on, relishing the perfect peace of the high-country Indian summer and the measured labor that brought his cabin slowly into being. "Measured," for he later explained that he learned to pace his work and to intersperse it with rest and leisure by following the example of the beaver, which earns its epithet "busy" only sporadically.

October snows finally forced the boy back to the prairie for another winter on the ranch, and he rotated seasonally between working there and in Longs Peak House until his first mining venture in fall 1887. Alone in the valley after the others had left, he discovered "solitude, boiled down, refined, and twenty-two-carat."[3] But that solitude gave the boy generous amounts of time to finish and occupy his cabin, to develop a passion for watching wild animals, and no less a passion for tramping through the mountains in pursuit of everything that inspired him or aroused his curiosity.

Nature in the wild surroundings of Longs Peak was a virtual paradise for roaming and for gaining high places, for dallying by brooksides and for hiding to watch wild creatures. The accommodating forests let the boy make his way even without trails. They were forests without the entanglements of the denser eastern forests and without the lurking hazards of the dark forests of myth. Nature was her plain self, made of rocks and trees, soil, streams, lakes, snowbanks, flowers, and vestigial glaciers. It was an Eden, but not an Eden of biblical prescription, shadowed by an impending expulsion. It was, as John Muir believed of his beloved Sierras, unsurpassable by heaven. Ranging into the higher valleys, the boy eagerly discovered that the same stone surfaces etched and wedged toward gradual soil by the roots of alpine flowers had once been polished by Pleistocene ice; in the place of hanging glaciers were now "hanging gardens."

In these high and wild spaces, Mills found regenerative powers that reddened his blood and pumped life into his frail constitution. He felt that all was right with the world — his world and probably the rest of the world, too. The mountain streams, he would later insist, made a music that improves a man's character, and the solitary water ouzel bobbed up and down to be in harmony with the water's flow. In the bright reality of so hospitable a surrounding, palpable dangers seemed as absent as superstitious ones. These Rocky Mountains — indeed all of wild nature — seemed safer than any place on earth, able to protect humans as well as heal them. Muir would later reinforce that conviction in his young admirer, but the roots of it lay in Mills's experience at the foot of Longs Peak. Nature's essential safety would become a cornerstone of Mills's outdoor philosophy.

Nor did safety in the wilds require the ministrations of a benign and all-encompassing "mother nature." Just as life-giving as nature's stiller moods were its expressive outbursts. The youngster loved to be stirred, battered by fierce winds, and stung by winter cold. Several times in his youth he hauled an elkskin sleeping bag up to timberline during violent Rocky Mountain chinooks, which often gust over 100 mph. Staring wide-eyed in the dark, he imagined he was lying in a diver's suit on a beach during an ocean storm. "At times I was struck almost breathless by an airy breaker, or tumbled and kicked indifferently about by the unbelievable violence of the wind," he wrote. And as he lay there through "hours of Niagara," he experienced "weird and strange feelings," and felt the "good old world grow better."[4]

Probably no outdoorsman in the West surpassed Mills's familiarity with winter and his willingness to live in it with virtually no protection for weeks at a time. He would deservedly earn the reputation "snowman" before he was thirty years old and before his three-year stint as the state's first snow surveyor. In what must have been one of his first Colorado winter adventures, the adolescent sat on one of his upturned snowshoes and rode it like a sled down an immense snow-chute off the western side of the Continental Divide. Careening at high speed over a patch of glare ice near the bottom, Mills landed headfirst in a clump of trees — battered but so exhilarated that he labored back up the 1,000-foot gully to repeat the daredevil ride just at dusk. Then he camped in a snowbank to have a third go at it in the morning.

If his later experiences cast any light on this one, Mills risked much to gain thrilling sensations. His name in fact became associated in popular legend with euphoric experiences afforded only by great daring. And though his later account of the snowshoe ride included a rhetorical wish for "a dozen other boys to try it with me," Mills — like Muir — averred that his most meaningful experiences were solitary. The hundreds, probably thousands, of nights that Mills gloried in his campfire high in the mountains, or left deliberately in the middle of the night to climb snowy peaks by moonlight, were habits in the repertory of many nineteenth-century romantics, yet they were highly specific and emotionally charged experiences that left their permanent imprint on him and his attitudes about the vital powers of nature over man.

Plunged into his immense private world of mountains, Mills was perhaps still young enough to have felt some of that intuitive oneness with nature that children inherit, then lose to their maturity — a oneness that makes a child "a part of things, unaware of endings and beginnings, still in unison with the primordial nature of creation." When Mills wrote later about his most intense moments outdoors, he said he found himself "on the edge of things" and found nature so richly suggestive that it was "eerie." It was not the eeriness of Wordsworth's mysticism, though he knew and quoted the quintessential English nature poet. It was not the eeriness of states of existence beyond the present and palpable, nor the "spiritual glow" of an Emersonian nature that illuminated Muir's thinking and written imagery. Nor was it the quivering mystery of nature that caused Mills's later acquaintance Ernest Thompson Seton to "bite the twigs in a craze of longing and inexpression."[5]

The eeriness that Mills experienced drove him remorselessly into danger. Always unintentionally, but with astonishing frequency, Mills began to step over the "edge of things" into mid air. The mature mountaineer as often as the neophyte plunged from trees, mountains, and boats; slipped, tripped, and capsized; was plucked from his perches by avalanches; and was held in the iron grip of electric currents high on stormy peaks. Mills would experience more than a score of near-fatal mishaps and would apply his skill more to extricating himself from danger than to avoiding it. His compulsion to fall — whether or not the Jungians could build a case on it — discloses a puzzling dimension to his character, particularly since the same trait showed up in his brother Joe.

Soon enamored of "poetic living," Mills was greatly pleased when things looked or felt "artistic," when nature's ways were themselves "poetic," when he, through his adventures, could arrive at and at times tumble over the "edge of things." Living poetically, that ardent habit of nineteenth-century romanticism, had been equally the motto of the flamboyant Byron and the reclusive Thoreau. As the notion lost depth with the waning of romanticism, many clung to it self-consciously; some, like the adventurer Richard Halliburton, carried it well into the twentieth century as both a consuming life style and a profitable vocation. In choosing the ways of a backwoods romantic, Mills, like Muir, experienced poetic highs in the raw wild elements far from the European landscapes where romanticism was born and far from the salons where its poetry was cultivated. The terms "poetic" and "artistic" lodged permanently and to a degree self-consciously in Mills's outdoor vocabulary, yet his belief in them was uncontrived, for as a youth alone in the wilds he made them discoveries of his own.

For Mills the human drama was poetic too, and his early involvement with the developing West and its means of livelihood shaped his sensibility at the same time the stronger impulses of nature were forging it. The story of Mills's life became one of combining the two. Unlike Muir, who in most of his moods appeared to prefer nature to humanity, Mills would come to prescribe nature as a social medicine out of a profound commitment to mankind itself. During fifteen years of tramping through the West and making its wild creatures virtually his next of kin, Mills was also looking at humanity and thinking about its destiny. His starting place was the hurly-burly of boomtown mining.

CHAPTER 4

From Mines to Muir

Scant seventeen, part cowboy, part homesteader, and nascent mountaineer, Enos Mills went north to Butte, Montana, in fall 1887 to
earn wages in the mining camp that was called the biggest, busiest,
and richest in the world. Mills's work-for-freedom formula would
prosper through the relatively high wages offered to laborers in the
boom years following Butte's rise to second place among the silver
producers of America and its spectacular shift to copper.

Marcus Daly's Anaconda complex took Mills on as a toolboy —
a "nipper" — who brought sharp drills to the men in the drifts and
returned the used ones topside. No longer a live-in errand boy of relatives or friends, Mills was now one of 2,500 employees in a city of
heavy industry. Butte's monthly payroll was over half a million dollars and growing fast. By 1890 the Anaconda alone employed 3,000
men, produced 3,000 tons of ore a day, and led Butte to an annual
production of $30 million in metal. The boy from Kansas was a
wage earner in a highly integrated corporate structure and would
make it his primary — but always seasonal — source of livelihood
until 1902.

If Mills's virtue had been perishable, Butte, a center of hellraising
nonpareil, was the town to spoil it. The copper camp had sixteen
gambling halls and 212 registered saloons — one of them was nearly
a block long, and many of them had not closed for a single minute
since opening day. Venus Alley and Galena and Mercury streets supplied erotic temptations in every price range. And everywhere could
be seen chronic drunkards, drug users, professional hoboes, and
pimps. In the notorious "Cabbage Patch," makeshift dwellings,
saloons, and brothels were set amid waste dumps and rubbish. But
the boy soon had a seasoned view of boomtown revelry and saw
beneath the surface uproar to a wholesome vitality. "Butte has no

Butte, Montana, where Mills worked seasonally in the copper mines from 1887 to 1902, was a huge industrial complex whose pollution effects are still felt today. *Denver Public Library, Western History Department.*

bad men," he reflected later. "The police have only common experiences and the sheriff might easily be mistaken for a visiting drummer. Like all mining towns it is saturated with saloons and charged with chance. . . . Butte is world-known for spirited receptions to prominent visitors and the crowd that greeted one lecturer was so large he thought he saw everyone in Butte. The city is ever ready to honor genius, reward talent or welcome merit."[1]

So the lad had a tolerance for the seamy side of life and an admiration for high spirits whatever their object. Values weren't too far wrong if miners tipped their hats to genius; less, after all, can usually be said of respectable society. The carousing, gambling, and whoring were in the end harmless, and the real spirit of Butte was a positive and fun-loving individualism. As one recent writer on the copper camp muses, "Butte was tough, yet Butte was tender. Stark and ugly, warm and unpretentious, fatalistic yet fun-loving and convivial, the city left visitors aghast, but it struck an enduring affection and loyalty in the hearts of its people. Once known, Butte was never forgotten."[2]

Young Enos Mills *(far left, first row on bench)* among the hardened miners at Butte, Montana, late 1880s. *Denver Public Library, Western History Department.*

Butte's residents and visitors also saw healthy democracy under the throbbing day-and-night revelry. Rich, poor, worker, groomed lady, and prostitute — all could mingle on the street on common terms. Marcus Daly, the Anaconda's powerful and brilliant boss, went drinking with the workingmen. The dominant Irish, idolizing Daly, clinging to their ancestral ways, many speaking Gaelic, brawled often enough with their rivals, the Cornish "Cousin Jacks." But they had a solidarity as workingmen. Next to these master hardrock miners worked Finns — masters of timbering — other Scandinavians, Welshmen, Scots, Germans, French Canadians, Jews, and blacks. There was something big enough and rich enough in Butte to equal the visionary hyperbole of Walt Whitman. These were the workers of America, swinging their picks in unison. "That camp was the most democratic place I've ever lived in," raved one journalist. And Mills's own friend of the nineties, Robert W. Johnson, recalled that "the rush of the little democracy was in [Mills's] veins too."[3]

Butte's no-questions-asked tolerance of every sort of individualism boldly underscored what Mills had experienced among the

"Butte is world-known for spirited receptions to prominent visitors," Mills wrote. Here, the visitor is Theodore Roosevelt, c. 1900. *Montana Historical Society.*

cowboys. The wide-open city offered the freedom for any kind of eccentricity and relished the outlandish characters it bred — characters like Blasphemous Brown, famed for his swearing; Liz the Lady, a renowned hermaphrodite; Chicken Lee, who raided chicken houses and fought with a straight razor; Fay, the Lady Barber, murderess of at least three boyfriends; Fat Jack Jones, gaunt hack-driver in top hat who careened through the streets with celebrities; and Dublin Dan, whose "Hobo retreat" dispensed free stew for the bums and whose cronies once waited outside a revival meeting with signs saying, "For a good cold scoop of lager after the service . . . go to Dublin Dan's just around the corner."

Mills probably never told his wife and future biographer all he experienced during his Butte years, and she in turn probably did not expect him to. Esther Burnell Mills accepted a liberal view of Butte as a place that was "busy in a hundred ways, . . . working and playing hard, and reaching out for whatever the world could give it." But at the same time she stressed that Butte had its genteel side, with wealthy residential areas, good schools, churches, several newspapers, a university club where intellectuals read verses and discussed issues, elegant clubs for cultural entertainment, and a first-rate library. The library, she asserted, is where Enos Mills spent his spare time. Having gladly escaped further schooling when he left Kansas, Mills had diligently poked at his books in Estes Park and on the ranch, working to become a self-educated man. Now he had for the first time a well-stocked library and was staggered by its wealth of human knowledge. Robert W. Johnson tells us that Mills read the words of men who had revolutionized thought, including Huxley, Tyndall, Wallace, Darwin, and Spencer, as well as the freethinkers Tom Paine and Robert Ingersoll, "general history," Shakespeare, and John Fiske's "cosmic philosophy."

But Mills perhaps knew by instinct, and later preached, that books are a bloodless substitute for life. It was in the contrast between the worlds inside and outside the library, in the comparison of raw life with literature, that the boy probably found his intellectual awakening. "God bless every man who swung a mallet on that staunch and tiny craft," he blurted out to Johnson as he recounted the adventuring spirit of a Robert Louis Stevenson South Sea tale. Deep currents in Mills spoke for immersion before reflection, for life before literature. And had he drifted too far into books, a warning would have brought him back: "If a lad does not learn in the streets, it is because he has no faculty of learning," wrote Stevenson, at once and forever a favorite in Mills's literary pantheon.[4]

How much Mills learned in the streets of Butte is something about which he was characteristically reticent. It would have been an unusual boy who failed to try the bars a few times, to try a few games of pharaoh or stud poker, and to satisfy an adolescent's curiosity about the opposite sex. His later preoccupation with more serious pursuits and his testy expectation that others should do the same, marked him as slightly prudish, though bits of evidence here and there suggest he was not, and his belief in the cultural importance of play had enough latitude to encompass naughty merrymaking. Sometime during his Butte years, wrote his friend Johnson, Mills drifted into a bar, probably in Spokane, was set upon by two roughnecks, and escaped by convincing them he was the notorious gun-slinging outlaw "Bobby Burns of Butte."

If Mills was drawn to the "edge of things," he had it in Butte, in the very midst of human company. How, he must have puzzled, did the camp's bizarre characters come to be what they were? Butte must have helped force upon him the conviction that every living thing has a life story and that the instinct of the writer must be to find and tell that story. But had writing alone been his goal, the great broth of life in Butte would have surely provoked his first serious literary efforts. Instead, he left its literary possibilities virtually untouched. Butte was significant to him for its vision of life, its raw experience, its vitality, and its counterpoint to his outdoor solitude. It probably contributed to his own headlong approach to living and no doubt helped prepare him to write, though he wrote almost nothing about Butte itself. Though visibly interested in becoming a writer, he had a fortunate modesty, a slow beginning, and an avidity for living that made him want to fill his lungs with life before giving it voice. While he acquired his experience of the world, he dabbled and ruminated with his pen just as he should have, and without literary pretension: a poem about the mountains of Montana, practice essays on Lewis and Clark, past civilizations, right and wrong, the ideal of liberty, a polemic against vaccination, an account of the great fire in the Anaconda Mine — in short, principles, morals, and manageable slices of life. In summers at Longs Peak he reported vacation tidbits for the *Denver Times* and *Republican* and practiced the scenic descriptions he would later need for his serious writing. However much he labored to master the rudiments of writing, he never stopped living in order to write. His gift in the '90s was to sample the world alone, among men, and among the works of men.

If Butte's soul was big enough to embrace a heroic view of America, it was a soul nevertheless laced with contradictions. There were disturbing flaws in the democracy that tolerated every sort of eccentricity, the worst of which was ethnic abuse against immigrants from Italy and southeast Europe, and especially the Chinese. In a stunt of ghastly cruelty, a Chinaman was strung up in Butte's first hanging, for no other reason than "for the hell of it." The earth itself, battered open to extract its riches, was shocking testimony that civilization brought a destroying power along with its creating power. During Mills's first year in Butte, the Anaconda alone used 15 million board feet of timber and 75,000 tons of coal. Daly and his partners could not be bothered by federal restrictions against commercial timber cutting of public lands. And in the nineties, when the creation of federal forest reserves and revised homestead laws tightened federal regulations, they purchased large tracts of timberland for as little as $2.50 an acre, usually by fraudulent means. Though Mills never made any explicit connection, his distrust of monopolies and the congestion of wealth may have entered his developing view of the world early in his time at Butte, as he saw the Anaconda buy up huge reserves of ore, coal, and lumber and then expand to urban real estate, farmland, hotels, rails, water and electrical works, and more mines from Chile to Alaska. The Anaconda would eventually hold Butte and Montana itself in a powerful, strangulating grip.

And what's the goal of it all, anyway? Mills might have asked. "Many may make a large fortune, who remain underbred and pathetically stupid to the last," said a Stevenson essay that became a lifelong favorite. But the idler, the man who really cares for life, "has had time to take care of his health and his spirits; he has been a great deal in the open air, which is the most salutary of all things for both body and mind."[5] In Stevenson's "Apology for Idlers," Mills found the ethic he needed to combine his intense capacity for hard work with his equally intense love of creative freedom. Idleness, leisure, curiosity — all shibboleths in Mills's cosmology by the time he began writing — were habits, said Stevenson, of regeneration rather than degeneration.

Regeneration was, indeed, one of Mills's most spectacular achievements during the 1890s, a decade in which he left his sickly youth behind and blossomed into such robust health that he could later claim, "I'm never ill, never." In Butte he lifted Indian clubs to put muscle on his slight frame and did a colon therapy for his digestive ailment. The problem all along, a visiting eastern physician told him, was his inability to digest starchy foods. The cure: fast for ten days, drinking only water. Then watch what you eat. The prescription stuck. Already a mincing eater by default, Mills now made necessity a virtue. For the rest of his life he would preach the power of abstinence from food to strengthen the organism. Fasting sometimes to the point of emaciation — "to give his system a rest" — would become one of the most visible and most talked about characteristics of the famous outdoorsman, and put him in league with John Muir, whose indifference to food was legendary.

Whatever digestive frailties Mills had to overcome, the rest of his constitution weathered an environmental assault that withered even the trees. Modern pollution pales next to that of the copper city in the 1880s, when smoke emissions were unchecked by any regulations or any common concern. The ore treated in Butte every twenty-four hours gave off 300 tons of sulfur and was spiked with enough arsenic — claimed local wits — to kill the cats who licked it from their whiskers. Worse than the smelters were the open pits, up to a block long, filled with ore and logs and allowed to burn for days to roast out the sulfur. Travelers said they had only the hacking coughs of their invisible forerunners to guide on when they crossed the flats of South Butte, where all landmarks were extinguished. Public opinion and the press at last waged a smoke war in the early nineties, forcing passage of antiroasting ordinances and the installation of abatement devices on smelters. By that time, by official count, only four trees remained alive in all of Butte.

A measure of Mills's progress toward full health was his putative refusal to be vaccinated against smallpox on the grounds that a person in good health won't get the disease, and that "if vaccination prevents smallpox, those who are vaccinated have nothing to fear from those who are not." Specifying the date of the incident only as "several years later," *Enos Mills of the Rockies* tells us that Mills backed up his conviction by going to the pest-house and rubbing his hands on diseased inmates. The story cannot be verified, but it is consistent with the strident logic and self-assurance that Mills later applied to his public causes.[6]

If Mills bristled with native distrust at the idea of a municipally mandated vaccination, he gave no sign of refusing the liberal benefits showered by the Anaconda on its employees. With the welfare and loyalty of its workers in its own interest, the Anaconda management took progressive steps in sponsoring health plans, hospitals, kindergartens, and public libraries. It gave out free turkeys at Christmas, rewarded loyal workers with leases on choice ore veins, funded college educations for promising children of the poor, and provided small brick houses for families of workers killed on the job. It was a kind of industrial feudalism, but it also reflected management's respect for a workforce that was fully unionized and wielded social, economic, and political power. Labor analysts say that even Butte's capitalists paid homage to the unions, and that part of the unions' strength lay in friendly relations with management — particularly at the Anaconda. Marcus Daly and one of the owners, "Uncle George" Hearst (father of William Randolph), were both rags-to-riches folk heroes who maintained a strong empathy with the men and were their companions in the streets and bars.

Unionism in Butte began after a peaceful and successful strike by mine workers in 1878 to protest an arbitrary wage cut — the first strike in Montana's history. Workers formed the Butte Working-men's Union (BWU) in June 1878, and quickly added to their ranks experienced miners migrating to Butte who had won fights in Nevada's silver mines. Some of Butte's mine owners took advantage of ethnic rivalries by mixing their workforces to break up class solidarity. But when the chips were down, union strength united even ethnic factions. Occupying a large union hall in 1885, the BWU reorganized to the Butte Miners' Union (BMU), created split-offs for smaller craft organizations, and joined the all-inclusive Knights of Labor. The next year, the BMU formed the Silver Bow Trades and Labor Assembly and became the greatest stronghold of unionism in the intermountain West. Mills's first view of organized labor was that it had the power to achieve its aims and that it was capable of harmonious relations — or at least a fruitful tension — with management. Though confirming records were apparently destroyed by later fires in Butte, there is every reason to suppose that Mills was a union member, too. By the time labor-management relations deteriorated at Butte and grim warfare erupted all over the mining West, Mills was out of the workforce but attracted to socialism and doubtlessly sympathetic to the workers and the men who led them.

Mills apparently experienced no difficulty in breaking off his employment to return to Longs Peak each summer and in resuming work each fall. That pattern continued for at least half the years until 1902, some of his other winters being spent in mines in Ward and Cripple Creek, Colorado. Mills last appeared in the Butte city directory living at 23 West Quartz Street, employed at the Parrot Mine, another large operation under Anaconda ownership. He had risen from toolboy to miner to engineer, probably operating a topside hoist. Such positions offered better pay and job safety and were often obtained through personal connections.

It was shortly after Mills's arrival for his third season of mining in fall 1889 that underground fires stopped the Anaconda's operations and set the stage for his journey to California and his fortuitous meeting with John Muir. Muir, now in his fifties, still longed for the primitivism of his early years in Yosemite and still valued wilderness and wild places above any works of man. He had married in 1880, taken over the fruit farm of his wife's family, and fathered daughters in 1881 and 1886. Eight years as an industrious and successful gentleman farmer had sapped his strength and spirit, leaving him feeling cut off from his "real work," learning "nothing . . . that will do me any good," and "degenerating into a machine for making money." Encouraged by his wife after seven years with no wilderness trip, Muir at last went off to Mt. Shasta and the Cascades and saw the need to get out of farming and to return to studying and writing about nature. It was a partially restored John Muir that Mills met that December day in 1889.[7]

Having newly discovered what he needed and taken steps to pursue it, Muir perhaps imparted to Mills an impassioned message that work must impart meaning and joy. If he formulated for Mills his maxim that life is longest when it "contains the largest amount of work that is a steady delight," it was a fitting utterance for a man now past fifty who felt his life ebbing when work was merely work and returning when work meant more than money-earning. But how sober even that maxim was, compared with Muir's feathery insouciance as a young recluse in Yosemite when he had insisted that "idle sentimental transcendental dreaming is the only sensible and substantial business that one can engage in."[8] Conditioned then or later by his reading of Stevenson, Mills may have seen the profound and paradoxical quality in Muir by which "idle sentimental transcendental dreaming" had prepared him to make a deep and practical impression on the world. That dreamers may, in the end, be the greatest doers was an underlying theme in the life and work of Mills as well, and certainly part of his legacy from both Muir and Stevenson.

Muir, at the time of the meeting, had just resumed writing after a dormancy of ten years. Sponsoring and prodding his literary renewal were both his wife and Robert Underwood Johnson, editor of the influential *Century Magazine,* which had published some of Muir's essays in the seventies. Johnson chided Muir for having dried up, and now sought his help in promoting legislation to establish a Yosemite National Park. Muir was to write two inspirational essays and to apply his unmatched knowledge of the region in helping to draft the bill. When Mills met him, or soon afterwards, Muir was working on the articles, and passage of the Yosemite Park bill in September 1890 rewarded his labors with a magnificent victory.

If young Mills had more than just a passing acquaintance with Muir, he could have witnessed the influence that a nature writer can exert on public and political consciousness. Political influence was new to Muir too, and his career as a conservation activist was just at its beginning, backed by Johnson and other influential people whom Johnson steered his way. With that weight, therefore, Muir's message must have impressed Mills: "Take your stories of the Rockies to the people choked up in cities, urge them to see the wild places of the West, arouse their interest in preserving this primal beauty."[9] That mission, in many intertwined variations, set the course of the rest of Mills's life.

But the nineteen year old was not yet a naturalist, and lacked both the knowledge and the fame that would soon propel John Muir to the front guard of the young conservation movement. Mills had to have his *Wanderjahre,* to become a recognized symbol of the outdoors, and to acquire a public voice. It is uncertain how much time the two actually spent together in that winter of 1889–1890 and in fall 1890, when Mills took courses at Heald's Business College in San Francisco. But the boy must have had enough access to his formative father to get what he needed. Inspired by Muir's suggestions, he set off on explorations through Yosemite and Kings Canyon and the big trees, worked down the eastern side of the Sierras to Death Valley, then north to Mono Lake, Virginia City, and Reno. He went up the coast to the redwoods and down the coast to San Diego and the offshore islands.

As he saw the places Muir told him about, Mills perhaps saw them with Muir's own eyes, and Muir, hearing of the boy's travels, perhaps relived a measure of his own years of freedom. In both was an unquenchable fire to live poetically and a rare taste for observing nature by living in it on its own terms. For the next decade and a half, Mills would spend as much time outdoors in the wilds as indoors or at work. He would roam through much of the West and eventually in all the states and Alaska, but most extensively in the hills of his own adopted Colorado. He would follow and watch every kind of animal and bird, delve into the lives of every tree and flower, and contemplate the evolution of mountains, glaciers, rivers, and lakes. He would defy gravity and the elements to scale peaks, to snowshoe through the winter wilderness, to careen down rivers on makeshift rafts. By the time he acquired and became the host of Longs Peak House (later Inn) in 1902, he was known as one of America's most daring woodsmen, was emerging as a naturalist of stature, and had begun writing. For him, as for Muir, experience in the raw wilds was the teacher for later accomplishments among men. It was as a woodsman that Mills simultaneously discovered his true self and began to create an image of himself for the public — a public eager for new heroes in an age that feared it had gone soft with the passing of the pioneers.

Part II
Self-Made Man

CHAPTER 5

The Adventure Seeker

Enos Mills headed into the rugged Uncompahgre mountains of southwestern Colorado late one fall, taking almost no food, no bedding, and — despite the imminence of winter — no snowshoes. As he climbed, a prospector shuffled by, leaving the high country to avoid being trapped by the first and proverbially heavy snow. For two days Mills climbed and photographed the 14,000-foot summits of the Uncompahgre group, and as he settled down by his fire on the third night, he "saw a cloud-form in the dim, low distance . . . creeping up into my moonlit world of mountains."[1]

Just after midnight, rain and snow awakened him. In the inky darkness he packed up to make a dash for the lowlands, knowing that without his snowshoes his predicament would be "as serious as to be adrift in a lifeboat without food or oars in the ocean's wide waste." Instead of retreating to Lake City down his ascent route, he headed for the railroad village of Ridgway, diagonally across broken and unfamiliar mountains and canyons.

Quickly soaked and chilled, he groped down a rugged mountainside for 1,000 feet, prodding with a stick like a blind man for dropoffs before each step. The roar of a torrent told him he had reached the bottom, but the swollen stream was boxed by rock walls and he had to retreat upstream half a mile to find a crossing. Groping in the darkness, he found a log and balanced his way across. Then he mounted the valley's opposite side, dropped over a ridge to the Little Cimmaron River, and found another log ("a long, vibrating bridge") in the dripping blackness. He climbed out of that valley, hoping to cross one more ridge and drop to the Uncompahgre River, which he could follow out to Ridgway.

But that last ridge was a fearsome peak, Mt. Coxcomb by name, and "not one of the 'eternal hills' but a crumbling, dissolving, tumbling, transient mountain . . . eagerly moving from its place in the sky to a bed in the sea." In the soaking rain and snow it was as unstable "as if it were composed of sugar, paste, and stones." Mills saw changes "that on most mountains would require ten thousand years or more." Monoliths of water-soaked rock and soil "indulge[d] in a contest of leaning the farthest from the perpendicular without falling, . . . then gravity drag[ged] them head foremost . . . down the slope." Below, "the gulches feast[ed] on earthy materials."

Mills tried to follow up one of the slender ridges but the poor footing and the darkness forced him into a gully. As he gained elevation, snow replaced rain, and when the clouds momentarily parted, the drenched traveler was awed by a pinnacled ridge of "snow-covered statuary — leaning monoliths and shattered minarets, all weird and enchanting in the moonlight." Then came darkness again, and redoubled rain and snow.

Slipping mud and stones warned Mills to get out of the gully. Then a huge crash and roar, followed by bombardments of flying rock debris came at him as a landslide bore down from above. He tried to scramble out of the gully, slipped and tumbled back in, then, groping blindly, he connected with a tree root and just managed to pull himself out of the way of the rushing flood of mud and rock. As he paused to listen to the "monster groan and grind his way downward," more rocks from the cliff above pelted his stance. One broke a bone in his left foot, and he lost consciousness.

Mills awoke near daybreak, lying drenched and half frozen in the mud and snow. He bandaged his foot, then climbed up toward the shoulder of Mt. Coxcomb, still hoping to descend its back side. But the steepness and the crumbling cliff forced him to retreat back to the Little Cimmaron. The descent of less than two miles took him twenty hours, and during that day and night — until he lost track — he counted the echoing roar of forty-three "fallen cliffs." Everywhere the earth had "fleshy areas [that] crawled, slipped and crept." Trees lost their foundations, drooped forward, and fell. The slide that had narrowly missed him had plowed down a stand of towering spruces more than half a mile below. Elsewhere, Mills saw a clump of trees move intact with its sliding foundation to a new position down the slope.

By afternoon the air turned colder, and snow began to pile up. At twilight the limping mountaineer met a sow bear with cubs; he stood still, they passed. Then came night again, and no letup to the snow. At two A.M. he finally reached the river and searched for a log to get him over the torrent and beyond the slide debris. Finding no log, he tried to wade, but at midstream struck his broken foot, flinched, and lost his balance. Swept away in the current, unable to see, he battled his way across by sheer determination, and at last pulled himself out. He lurched a few steps and then collapsed in the snow. Only a fire could save him, but with soaked wood, snow still falling and now fifteen inches deep, and the trees dripping water, what were the odds? But some Promethean force made him prevail, and an orange glow of light and warmth came to life in all that awful darkness and wetness. He warmed himself beside the blaze for two hours and was then fit enough to continue down to the valley. Shortly before daybreak he came to a trail he knew and by nightfall reached Ridgway and a doctor's office.

That is a Millsian adventure of the sort that filled his years from the early nineties until about 1905 and established his reputation as one of the West's most skilled and daring woodsmen. The episode contains all that was quintessentially Mills: extraordinary risk taking; a radical neglect of equipment and comfort; a near-starvation diet; consummate wilderness skills, including firemaking under nearly impossible conditions; navigating through unknown and treacherous territory in storm and darkness; not one but several near brushes with death; extraordinary will power; unshakable confidence in his ability to survive; and about the whole thing a miraculous and storylike quality.

Though he began writing about his adventure tales while he was still living them before 1905, his principal output and his real fame as an outdoor writer came after he had achieved national recognition as a lecturer. It was from the podium, in thousands of lectures in which he wove his tales of adventure into his messages about saving the forests, that he learned to gauge the desires and tastes of his audience. He learned that adventure, bravery, and risk taking, combined with a romantic appreciation of the outdoors and faith in nature's life-restoring qualities, were an eminently salable commodity. He discovered, in short, that he had something America wanted. And once his principal literary output began in 1909, his books flowed — with parts appearing first in magazines — at an average of nearly one a year for the rest of his life. The Uncompahgre adventure is representative of Enos Mills the adventure seeker, recollected or created by Mills the writer.

We cannot be sure exactly what Mills was like in the reckless abandon of his young manhood. Putting himself on record primarily in magazine stories, he was subject to the relatively simplistic standards that prevailed during the "golden age of the magazine" after 1900 when — unlike the more elevated tone of earlier magazines — entertainment was the definitive ingredient. "Good easy reading for the people — no frills, no fine finishes, no hair splitting niceties, but action, action, always action," prescribed editor Frank Munsey for the new mass-consumption magazines.[2] Mills furthermore wrote many of his stories for youth magazines such as *Youth's Companion* and *The American Boy*, where he exemplified not only daring and courage but also will, determination, and victory over a sickly youth. That message appealed to adults as well, and some of Mills's almost larger-than-life heroism may have been his own declaration that frailty of constitution had been irrevocably conquered. He was a man not merely regenerated by nature but regenerated from the most frail of beginnings. He was one of those thousands who came west seeking health, and he made himself the embodiment of the maximum possible attainment from the least promising beginnings. That process could not have happened on the farm, nor in any city, nor perhaps within the confines of regular employment. Health and strength came from the free and open life in nature, and Mills was an example for all to see. Writing most of his adventure narratives when he had a strong ideology to promote, he could show the vitalizing power of outdoor experience by making himself a symbol of death-defying, and hence life-affirming, vitality.

It was characteristic of Mills never to suggest that his real self was any different from the man he portrayed in his writing. If Rousseau is right that no writer ever achieves full honesty about himself, we can suppose that Mills — especially in times of intense public involvement — romanticized his younger years of freedom; that he to some degree fit his image to magazine standards and perhaps even enjoyed the simplified, courageous hero that resulted; and that he found it useful and natural to promote his public causes through his own example.

We should at the same time note that Mills was something of a legend before he recorded most of his exploits in magazines and books, and that he personally impressed many people who themselves spoke of his extraordinary qualities. Throughout his life, Mills had ardent admirers — many of them journalists — who did as much as or more than Mills himself to give him legendary status. They included his friend and frequent camping companion of the 1890s, Robert W. Johnson, who wrote admiringly of him in the 1924 memorial edition of *Rocky Mountain National Park;* J. A. Maguire, editor of the Denver-based *Outdoor Life*; John Sherman and Frank Harrison, editors of major newspapers in Chicago and Peoria, Illinois; Colorado journalist and historian Arthur Chapman, who published articles about Mills in *Country Life* magazine and in a separate booklet; journalist Earl Harding, who wrote a grandly heroic — and the only — account of Mills's 1903 descent of the east face of Longs Peak; Philip Ashton Rollins, Western writer, historian, and fellow grizzly bear aficionado, who also wrote of Mills in the 1924 issue of *Rocky Mountain National Park;* and John T. Jacobs, author of the introduction to Mills's posthumous *Bird Memories of the Rockies,* who found Mills "intensely original" and beyond question, "a genius." All of these, and others besides, regarded Mills with admiration amounting in some cases to awe; and part of what they admired in him was his phenomenal intensity and success in outdoor pursuits.[3]

Given, however, only Mills's own after-the-fact record of most of his actual adventures, what can we say about him as a woodsman? We find first of all that he worked hard to gain his competence. While still a teenager he apparently tried to learn by reading about other adventurers. An explorer, he decided, must combine and surpass the qualities of "a captain, pilot, scout, surveyor, [and] timber cruiser." More important, even a boy, "though he does not wear buckskin and have a beard," can be an explorer by going somewhere new even if it is close to home.[4] Mills read about the Lewis and Clark and Pike expeditions, and about the miraculous escape of John Coulter from the Blackfeet and his 100-mile return to safety without even his clothing for protection. Later Mills said he followed portions of the routes of all three.

While still a youngster, probably during his stay at the eastern Colorado ranch, he fashioned his own initiation rite that weaned him permanently from excess camping gear. Carrying a neophyte's turgid baggage out onto the prairie, he camped one night in needless comfort. Next day he wandered off from his gear to watch some antelope, lost his way in the rolling, treeless expanse of prairie, and could not find his way back. After spending the night without supper or bedding, he retraced his roundabout route and discovered he had slept within 500 feet of his gear. As he approached it — our eyebrows go up a bit at this — a sudden prairie whirlwind spiraled it into the air and scattered it over the prairie. Impressed by the lesson, Mills left the gear where it landed. "I did not need it and never went back for it," he said. "From that time I planned to 'go light.'" From then on, Mills improvised his shelters. He camped under rocks and logs, or in crudely hollowed snowdrifts. Like Muir, with whom he said he camped, he eschewed tents, even when he accompanied scientific parties that made them available. At times he carried a heavy elkskin sleeping bag — the one in which he was so thrillingly battered by "wind surf" and "hours of Niagara." In his most active and mobile periods he left even bedding behind and slept in snatches beside a fire. When wood was scarce, that meant more wood gathering than rest. "Until daylight released me" describes the marginal comfort of many of his nights.[5]

Stung by the humiliation of getting lost on the prairie, Mills never forgot that woodcraft begins with the ability to find your way. "I hit upon this plan," he wrote, "which I have since used hundreds of times. I imagined myself attached to camp with a line and reel which promptly pulled in slack and also kept a steady pull on myself. At all times I knew where camp was and where I was. This plan kept before me a map picture of the locality and mentally showed me camp. I could estimate the distance." That method finally became pure instinct, and Mills could speak confidently of "ever having my reckoning without stopping to take it."[6]

Mills also trained himself to be able to raise a blaze under any conditions. He carried three sets of matches, packed watertight; he scraped pitch from tree trunks and carried it for quick-starting tinder; and he always had a stub of candle to nurse wet wood into flame, even in windy conditions. He had heard of men becoming so chilled and helpless that they perished even after reaching shelter. "With wit and muscle dull," they could not manage even to strike a match, he said. "Wit and muscle dull" is today's hypothermia, and Mills — small, wiry, often meagerly nourished — must have needed his firemaking skills to function automatically when he became deeply chilled. Once, in zero-degree weather, he descended an ice slope, prevented by his precarious stance in axe-hewn steps from "hurrying, arm-swinging, and dancing." He arrived at an abandoned cabin "benumbed almost beyond movement," and clumsily dropped his matches to the floor. He was unable to pick them up with his wooden fingers, but his unimpaired skills took charge: He "mashed sensation" back into his stiffened lips, then lay on the floor, picked up a match with his mouth, struck it on a stone, and plunged it into his pitch splinters. Later he trained himself to hold a match with numb hands by splinting it crudely to a finger with a twist of handkerchief or even bark.[7]

"Years of training," Mills wrote, "had given me great physical endurance, and this, along with a peculiar mental attitude that Nature had developed in me from being alone in wild places in all seasons, gave me a rare trust in her and an enthusiastic though unconscious confidence in the ultimate success of whatever I attempted to accomplish outdoors."[8] Part of that trust stemmed from having developed the mental conditioning not to fight adversity, and Mills went so far as to refer once to his theory of nonresistance. Though never elaborated, that principle is evident in some of his survival tales. Immobilized by an early snow, for example, he splashed down an unfrozen stream rather than exhaust himself in waist-deep drifts. A herd of deer doing the same thing showed him the wisdom of his choice. He slept when and where he could, rather than on a regular schedule. When nights were too cold he napped during the day, often sharing sunny slopes with animals there for the same reason. He believed that animals use their acquaintance with every opportunity afforded by their territories to endure storms, to find the earliest grass in spring, the places with the fewest flies, and the best escape routes from enemies. Nature thus provides its own clues to survival, and Mills came to view it as richly supplied with resources for whatever he undertook. To his stern training as a woodsman it was natural for him to add his growing abilities as a naturalist. He learned to visualize all the resources of any territory he entered, and even in a high, dry desert in Nevada, he had only to head for a mountainside island of aspens to find a flowing spring that the trees had "signalled with a flag of gold."

Lacking size and brawn, Mills developed courage, skill, sinewy endurance, and an extraordinary indifference to creature comforts — a hardness for which Muir was a renowned model. It was Muir who merely crawled under matted trees and hungered beside a small fire. It was Muir who was said to be "as innocent as a child . . . of the art and convenience of camping as ordinarily understood." And it was Muir who carried so little in the mountains that he was known to say that all he needed in preparation for going was to jump over the back fence. Muir had seen mountain men "heartily content to 'rough it' and sheepherders who lay down to sleep with less care [for comfort] than their dogs."[9] How much Mills actually knew of Muir's camping habits until Muir's books appeared — well after Mills's own outdoor learning years — is uncertain. But in his writing he compared himself to Muir, who he said "neither fished nor carried a gun . . . frequently went hungry; many times was without bedding; [and] often . . . was entirely alone for weeks."[10] Not fishing was for both a matter of disposition, while going without firearms was for both a private conviction and a public declaration that nature has no hazards requiring a response with bullets. Going hungry, if partly inspired by Muir, became Mills's own outdoor specialty and part of his own legend. He ate but once a day in the woods, and even at home never ate breakfast and generally had no more than ten meals a week. His declaration to a reporter, "I'm never ill, never," was said with a vehemence that clearly locates his notion of health in low food intake. Though it would be hard to say who ate less — Mills or Muir — Mills made food a frequent subject of discussion, while Muir largely ignored it.[11] Mills undoubtedly had more of an axe to grind; fasting, discovered in Butte, had been the key to leaving his sickly youth behind. And in generalizing personal victory to universal principle, he invoked his greatest idol in the animal world, the grizzly bear — unweakened and "ready for action" even after several foodless months in hibernation.

Muir's staple in the wilds was a sack of breadcrumbs. Mills's was a starchless equivalent: a pocketful of raisins. A few handfuls lasted him for several days and a few pounds for treks of two weeks or more. Though raisins kept him alive, they replaced none of the flesh that fasting removed. The Mills of Colorado lore was an emaciated mountaineer descending unexpectedly from the snowy heights, face often blackened against snowglare. "Here's the Snow Man again — worse starved than ever," exclaimed the conductor of a mountain narrow-gauge when Mills boarded the train one night.[12] Even Mills's own friends feared he would starve to death on his nearly foodless winter treks and coaxed him to eat by sending food packages to mountain towns where they expected him to call for mail.

Mills paid no heed and said he sometimes fed the donated food to mining-camp horses.

Raisins became inseparably linked with the name of Enos Mills in Rocky Mountain lore, and as he gained fame as an outdoorsman, the raisin legend grew. Reporters began to write that he "lives entirely on raisins," "eats . . . nothing else," "walks thirty miles a day on them," and "requires no other diet." And Mills may himself — tongue in cheek perhaps — have helped that myth along. Declining the Southern delicacies served to him by his New Orleans hosts on a later lecture tour, Mills explained, "I eat nothing else but raisins . . . half a pound a day, the year round."[13]

At home, Mills in fact ate a reasonable diet in small amounts, avoided rich foods and desserts, and preached for both humans and animals that diet conditions disposition. In the wilds he sometimes supplemented raisins with chocolate and with roots, berries, mushrooms, and tree bark. "Even at times," he said when he was "most active in exploring or mountain-climbing, I repeatedly lived for two weeks or longer with nothing but these." In Alaska he said he walked 200 miles living only on wild plants after his guides deserted him and absconded with the supplies. Among natural survival foods Mills seems to have preferred the inner bark of aspens, available even in winter. Raw, roasted, or boiled, he found it "tender and juicy."[14]

Whether consisting of raisins, bark, or nothing at all, Mills's fare was meatless for weeks at a time. Yet he never appears to have taken up vegetarianism, though precedents abounded from Ben Franklin in the eighteenth century to flourishing vegetarian societies throughout the nineteenth century. Once, while exploring the smoldering ruins of a forest fire, his fast only two days old, his appetite was suddenly aroused by the discovery of a fire-roasted deer. He knelt and began to eat. As he ate, a grizzly bear came along and stopped to watch. Mills feasted on, and when he at last had had his fill, he stood and addressed the bear: "Come, you may have the remainder; there is plenty of it."[15] That fascinating and slightly macabre scene in the blackened forest can be taken as an index of Mills's willingness and perhaps desire to be regarded as a man of bizarre pursuits and eccentric habits. It had the flavor of a ritualistic immersion in the organic processes of nature but was, Mills could say with composure, perfectly fundamental woodcraft.

No doubt a significant part of Mills's cult of hungering was his notion that forgetting to eat is the habit of those who truly live. John Muir — with allowances for *his* legends — was so intense in his conversation that once on a camping trip he failed to notice a succession of six trout served to him and then removed from his plate and eaten by others. Mills made that intensity his own, too. Whether looking for fossils, inspecting trees, watching animals, or climbing winter peaks, he typically forgot to eat. Later he announced that children in his nature school usually forgot to eat their lunches, too. And even animals, he believed, were capable of responding to values higher than food. The black bear would rather play than eat, he said, and a grizzly that once came into his camp was so curious about his yellow slicker hanging on a tree that he ignored Mills's exposed food.

Striking in many of Mills's adventures as a young man was his wanton disregard for precautions. Going into the high Uncompahgre without snowshoes or waterproof clothing was a willing self-deception. "I allowed myself to believe that the golden days would continue," he said. That lesson was never learned, and a conspicuous number of Mills's survival episodes began with the same scenario: trapped by early, heavy snow. His greatest act of negligence was to continue traveling over high-altitude snowfields after losing his snow goggles ("The wild attractions of the heights caused me to forget the care of my eyes.")[16] Soon snowblind (*too* soon, according to modern medical knowledge) Mills faced the ordeal, or rather the supremely exciting adventure, as he regarded it, of traveling three days through the wilderness without eyesight. Both incidents are clues to a dominant theme of Mills's adventures and to a significant difference from Muir: Mills habitually, and perhaps compulsively, got himself into serious trouble, and was what we would call today distinctly accident prone. He tumbled from trees and rocks and mountainsides; broke through the ice of lakes and rivers; was swept away by avalanches at least three times, and had boat or raft accidents on the Missouri and Colorado rivers, an Idaho lake (three miles from shore), and the Alaska coast. Adventure, as Mills portrayed it in his writing, more often than not consisted of rescuing himself from his own predicaments. The Uncompahgre escape was one of his lengthiest survival feats, surpassed perhaps only by his three-day snowblind trek. On another winter trip he became lost in a blizzard, fell through a snow cornice, landed on a mid-cliff ledge, was nearly knocked off by another piece of the fractured cornice, lost but recovered one of his snowshoes, clawed his way back to the ridge, descended the other side as avalanches raced down nearby, fell through the ice of a stream, made a fire to dry his clothes, and next day was swept off in an avalanche but was miraculously spit off to the side before it plunged over a cliff. John Muir, by contrast, fell once — when he said his visit to the city had degraded his mountain faculties — and was greatly disturbed by it. He was daring and took chances, but remained in control and never blundered wantonly into accidents. Not in the whole of his career did Muir have the quantity of narrow escapes that Mills had on any one of many excursions. Muir furthermore disliked heroics and no doubt saw accident proneness as a sign of being out of tune with nature. Mills was almost comically blind to how badly his repeated mishaps reflected — or at least reflect by today's standards — on his mountaineering skills. "Adventure," noted the famous polar explorer Vilhjalmur Stefansson, no doubt *too* restrictively, "is a sign of incompetence."[17]

The sheer number of Mills's mishaps, their often fantastical character, and the frequent role of luck in saving him, casts doubt on their authenticity. Several more examples are illustrative: Mills, suddenly an expert skier, outruns a pursuing avalanche; another avalanche comes after him into a prospector's cabin where both he and the prospector escape without a scratch even when the avalanche flings a spruce tree like a javelin through the roof. When an obdurate mule named Satan resists Mills's efforts to lead him under a tree out of the rain, Satan's stubbornness proves providential: Lightning strikes and demolishes the tree. In Colorado's San Juan Mountains, a quick instinctive U-turn by a horse Mills is riding saves him from certain death by an avalanche. In a burning forest where Mills and his dog, Scotch, are trapped and Mills is immobilized, Scotch carries his jacket — on Mills's command — to a nearby stream, soaks it, and brings it back for the two to crouch beneath as the flames roar by. And when on a winter trip the two slip and begin to fall down an ice slope, the rope connecting them catches on a nubbin of rock and brings them to a stop.

Mills never confessed to fabrication or even exaggeration, and disapproved strongly of misleading people about anything to do with the outdoors. The readers of his own time had a thirst for real and vicarious experience and drank deep, uncritical drafts of the elixir he proffered. His stories established him as a genuine Rocky Mountain hero and his reputation has worn surprisingly well. Bill

McKibben's appreciative 1989 "Hero of the Wilderness"[18] — the title is significant — accepts on good faith Mills's death-defying escapades, including the one most troublesome to many mountaineers today, his snowblind trek (a subject to which we return in Chapter 20). The truth, no doubt, is that Mills experienced many adventures which did not result in calamity — climbing Longs Peak in winter winds was one — and there is no question that he became a hardened, daring, and capable mountaineer who spent phenomenal amounts of time alone in the wilderness for over fifteen years. Writing primarily about his narrow escapes — and many no doubt were authentic — he introduced a misleading bias that we must mentally edit in considering his great years of mountain adventuring.

We must likewise make allowances for the attitudes and emotions he portrayed or failed to portray. Though he occasionally explained his near-disasters as youthful recklessness and wondered himself how he had managed to survive some of them, the more prominent themes of his adventure tales are unflappable courage, fearlessness, and nonchalant self-possession. His twenty-hour decent from Mt. Coxcomb to the Little Cimmaron, drenched, with a broken foot, and on a slope continuously discharging rock and mud slides, was "painful though intensely interesting travel." When he crawled from the river and fell into the snow, his failure to get a fire going would have surely meant his end, but he recalled with studied sureness, "I was not discouraged even for a moment, and it did not occur to me to complain." And of the adventure as a whole: "It gave me no concern that I recall." Similarly, finding himself snowblind alone in the wilderness, he was "only moderately excited, feeling no terror," and the trip that began with his falling through a snow cornice was "the most thrilling and adventurous that has ever entertained me on the trail."[19] Almost nowhere in Mills's writing does he confess panic or pain, or fear that he could lose his nerve. Coming through his scrapes alive and claiming it never occurred to him to be frightened can be easily mistaken for boastfulness and — worse — denies us access to the inner man and to the inner resources Mills must have had in addition to his physical skill and training. Mills risked simplifying himself to a stock character of "true life" adventures and never sought to explore their psychological dimensions.

Instead, the message and the mood he sought to convey was poetic gratification. Mills clearly sought existential highs through the elevated awareness that danger and deprivation gave him. How much of the poetry he lived and how much he added as a writer is unclear. But if he added some or much of it later, he nevertheless seems to have had the raw material to work with, and material of the sort that showed he was sensitive to deep suggestions and meanings in outdoor adventure. When he called his descent from the crumbling walls of Mt. Coxcomb "painful but intensely interesting travel," he meant perhaps not so much to discount the pain as to signal the heightened awareness pain gave him while descending with a broken foot. The theme of heightened awareness is more explicit in his tale of climbing 14,350-foot Blanca Peak in winter. The whole recollected fabric of the adventure — staggering to a homestead ill from drinking contaminated water, a delirious night spent being nursed on sage tea by an aged couple, challenging the peak the next day, escaping its treacheries, his supreme moment of triumph on the summit, physical exhaustion and mental clarity on the descent, almost clairvoyant guidance in reaching his goal in the dark, the soft tones of Spanish coming from an adobe house and their evocation of a brief job he had had in the California orange groves among Mexican workers — that whole sequence had, as Mills thought and wrote about it later, a dreamlike quality and was in his deepest sense "poetic." When he was "swept irresistibly" toward the summit of the peak, he had felt that "there are times when Nature completely commands her citizens." And when he was forced by exhaustion during the descent to lie down every few minutes, he discovered that his mind was "clear and strangely active." Likewise, whatever the actual truth of the ski chase, with an avalanche in hot pursuit, Mills discovered clarity of vision during a leap over a gully: "It was like leaping into the dark, and with the leap turning on the all-revealing light. . . . My senses were keenly alert, and I remember noticing the shadows of the fir trees on the white snow and hearing while still in the air the brave, cheery notes of a chickadee."[20]

Circumstances and context enriched the imagery of many of Mills's narratives and often added a specificity that offset the fiction-like quality of the story line. When he hunched, for example, in a deserted cabin after a day filled with narrow escapes, he discovered a musty pamphlet on palmistry wedged between the logs. We can imagine him leaning toward the warmth of the stove, affirming life in the aftermath of mortal danger, and absorbed by the strange occult message of fate inscribed on a human palm. Mills also regains both some of our confidence and our affection through his spontaneous joy. Riding in a treetop in violent wind — as Muir sometimes did too — he was spontaneous and childlike ("such wild, exhilarating joy I have not elsewhere experienced"). And he projected that joy even onto the tree: "I could feel in the trunk a subdued quiver or vibration, and I half believe that a tree's greatest joys are the dances it takes with the wind." Mills also felt the deep currents of life's poetry when his solitude conjured visions of himself as the only human in a prehuman nature or as a quester in some "legend-weaving age." When strange "storm-made . . . tree forms" appeared and vanished in the shifting projections of light from his fire, coyotes howled and foxes replied with "mocking laughter," Mills became a "primitive, crouching fire-worshipper in a new and unexplored world." When he climbed Longs Peak in 100 mph winter gales, sometimes holding on with his hands and letting himself be pushed up feet first, the wind became his playmate. "It was seriously splendid to play with those wild winds," he wrote, and we understand with him that people who care seriously about life play, and find in play some of life's deepest and richest meaning.[21]

Mills said, "I know what it is to be alone on high peaks with the moon." He said, meaning something genuinely deep, "I went beyond the trail." And he expressed the bounty of life with simple but often offhand declarations such as "I have had my share." While Mills's glib disclaimers of fear diminished the sense of what he really experienced, he redeemed some of that fault through the at least brief glimpses his writing gives into the poetry he must have lived in the solitary outdoors. Reckless, inspired, marveling at everything, Mills's ultimate outdoor being — and one that we at last accept — was that of a manchild using danger and hardship to arrive at poetic rapture. We do not question his belief in life's imperative to explore, grow, and develop; or his abhorrence of "stagnation;" or his personal identification with the grizzly bear, who "is innately an adventurer . . . [whose] curiosity does not allow him to live in a rut [and who] is always learning . . . keeps alive and growing."[22]

Mills had no dull and conventional past to repudiate, for his life was his own early enough that all his development was self-motivated. His own life, formed primarily in the outdoors, was the source of his belief that nature both demands and develops one's highest creative faculties. Mills was a rough-hewn artist, driven by curiosity and creative energy and invoking the "poetic" and the "artistic" as the essence of vital living. He combined the inspiration

Both a dreamer and a doer, Mills pursued a poetic ideal of enriching life. *Courtesy, Enos Mills Cabin Collection.*

he drew from the solitary world of nature with his developing social consciousness to form his basic attitudes about life and the power of outdoor living to create full and whole human beings. Mills the public man was already being formed in the wilderness, and as a public man he would draw inexhaustibly from the cup of life that he first filled in the remote wilds of the Rocky Mountains.

CHAPTER 6

The Budding Naturalist

Throughout his career of reckless and exhilarating adventure, Mills was equally the naturalist, pursuing the story of every plant, animal, and rock and always ready to stop what he was doing in order to investigate new events that caught his attention. For Mills as for Muir, fusing adventure with nature observations was living at its best, and in those wonderful years of freedom, Mills was bound, he said, by "neither the calendar nor the compass."[1]

Mills became, as befits any naturalist, a sentient presence in nature, knowing it even when his attention was required elsewhere. When, in storm and darkness, he straddled a dead tree over the flooding Cimmaron River and read from the arrangement of branches what kind of tree it was, the fact stuck in his memory, although it wasn't needed at the moment. And when he climbed Longs Peak in 100-mph winds he made scientifically meaningful observations of clear-air turbulence over the Continental Divide in the midst of exalted and death-defying play.

In the mold of Muir — and somewhat unlike the sedentary Burroughs — Mills developed observational and mountaineering skills with a mutual resonance. His blind descent from the Continental Divide was his most drastic fusing of those skills, and, though his later narrative gloried perhaps excessively in the virtues of imagination, it dramatized how vitally complementary mountain and nature craft are.

Mills's abilities as a mountaineer and naturalist developed more or less simultaneously, but the inoculating experience that put nature resolutely into his blood came while he was still a neophyte in the world of high mountains. The rafters of the fifteen year old's rude and not yet finished cabin near Longs Peak were chosen as a nesting site by a pair of bluebirds. The boy was struck by a sense of destiny: beautiful, sensitive creatures had arrived from unknown parts to add their nest to his, and it seemed as though nature itself had descended on him and intended to stay. Lest he disturb the birds, the boy left the roof unfinished until they had hatched and reared their young. They returned for three more seasons, rearing prodigious families, lovingly watched by the youngster, himself scarcely out of the parental nest.

To the boy's sense of destiny was added the weight of responsibility when misfortune struck in the fourth season. A trigger-happy boy from a group of tourists camping nearby approached Mills's cabin while he was away and shot the nearly tame adult birds. Mills was crushed by the loss. "I can never know how much or how deeply this tragedy influenced and colored my life," he wrote. It "asked me to be far more than I had ever been and different than I had ever dreamed of being." What he felt was asked of him was to be a parent to the orphaned nestlings, and the depth of his experience centered on his assuming that responsibility as thoroughly as if the young birds had been his own offspring. With profound parental devotion he nourished them on crumbs, grubs, and insects. He made them toys — a striped ball, wood shavings in a box, an envelope hung from a string — to ensure them the crucial gift of play. He talked to them as to children: about their "late parents," about the "ways of other birds," about the birds they would meet in the south in winter. When the bluebirds could walk but not yet fly, they followed their young foster father around his cabin and scurried behind him when he went to his brook for water. They rejoiced at his return from longer absences, "forgetting even hunger for a time in their gladness." That was perhaps Mills's first evidence of food's subordination to higher passions, even in the animal world.

Mills felt his love requited in full measure, especially by his favorite of the birds, Little Blue. He described the experience that was perhaps the single greatest influence in bonding him with nature:

> He sometimes lighted on my table, I think, for the purpose of having me talk to him. . . . After the first few words he looked up into my face and stopped all activities, listening to the end with perfect attention. . . . One morning . . . with half-opened and fluttering wings, he began a

low, sweet, whispered warble — the lovesong of the bluebird — all the while looking intensely at me, with almost passionate interest. . . . This was a dear experience to have with a dumb friend, and it was deep enough for tears.[2]

In gaining the trust of a wild creature, Mills must have felt accepted into something larger and universal, where the separation between man and nature dissolves. The bird — and with it all of nature — came forward to be touched by his humanity. In the tiny creature were latent faculties that awakened to kindness, to caresses, to human sympathy and joy. Mills's deepest view of life would never depart from a belief that between humans and animals there can exist a universal bond of understanding and mutual justice. His parenting experience instilled in him a gentleness — a sweetness even — that remained throughout his life and was for some his most memorable quality. But a poignant and perhaps tragic part of his story is how, under the growing pressure of public life, his nature-bred purity of heart could not always sustain him or express the rightness of his causes; feeling attacked and betrayed, he sometimes reacted with an aggressiveness that ended once-valuable alliances.

Conversing with his young bluebird flock started Mills on his lifelong practice of talking to wild creatures to win their trust. He always spoke, he said, in a natural conversational way, sympathetically, and about something definite. Animals "soon came to know that they were in a safety zone around my home," and "once they lost fear they became curiously, watchfully interested in every move I made." Rabbits, squirrels, and chipmunks hopped about his cabin unafraid, and often rushed to him for safety when frightened. Once a flock of chickadees landed on him and took over his head, arms, and shoulders. Yet Mills claimed no special powers, stressing only his patient efforts to condition wild creatures to trust his presence — a process he called getting acquainted "on the installment plan." And though Mills's ability with animals was extraordinary, the message he preached was universal and egalitarian: all men and all animals can be friends.

While Muir missed the wildness in domestic animals, Mills held them in nearly the same esteem as their wild forebears. Muir found barnyard sheep to be degenerate, man-made caricatures of the robust, wild variety. Horses could not follow him where he wanted to go, and dogs were rarely his companions. The more poignant, for that reason, was Muir's famous adventure with the dog Stickeen, whose bravery in following him into and back out of danger on an Alaskan glacier caused Muir to look "with deeper sympathy into all my fellow mortals."[3] Mills was not perplexed by any boundary between wild and tame. As a boy and throughout his life he had a knack with horses that won him praise even from his father. Some of the hired horses at mining camps and his faithful dog, Scotch, were his closest companions in life-or-death situations. Scotch, indeed, seemed to take on Mills's persona and was remembered by many as the colorful co-host of the famous Longs Peak Inn. The crossover from wild to tame that distinguished Mills from Muir would later express symbolic and practical differences in their conservation codes. Muir clung to the wholly wild, while Mills accepted the graftings of civilization onto the wild to "make it ready" for use by the masses. Muir would be, in greater measure, a prophet of today's wilderness ethic.

Mills's natural curiosity tutored him to scrutinous observation, and almost as soon as he arrived in the Tahosa Valley he began spending large amounts of time looking at everything around him. His favorite haunt close to his cabin was Lily Lake, several acres large and with sand and grassy shores, pinewoods behind, and cliffs to the north. He could dash there in half an hour from his cabin, and he went in every season and at every hour of day and night. Bears, beavers, wildcats, lions, bighorns, coyotes, weasels, gophers, snowshoe rabbits, and birds from pipits to eagles came to the pond. "It was a never-ending surprise to me that so many live things came to one place and that so many different ways of birds and animals could be learned in one little spot," the boy marveled.[4] Simple landmarks were his reference points to events and changes between visits. On one log, at different times, he saw a lion napping, magpies romping, a squirrel hiding cones, a coyote crouching to snatch its prey, and a weasel dealing savage death to a mouse. Bluebells arched over the log in summer and a snowdrift buried it in winter. Over the drift ran the tracks of squirrels, rabbits, porcupines, mice, weasels, and mountain sheep. He developed to a fine art his ability to "read the news" from tracks wherever he saw them.

Mills lacked a schooled conscience about what ought to interest him or ought to be important, and thus he developed the art of truly looking — a faculty that many naturalists labor long to acquire. It was as notable to him that beavers brush away flies from their noses as that they engineer consummate water works. He watched them comb their fur as avidly as he watched them chew down trees, and he noted how they carry mud on both land and water. He watched them scratch what itched and romp in carefree play. In rare moments, the tireless young observer was galvanized by sudden drama in the lives of those methodical beavers. Once a wolf attacked, and they fled in the nick of time; and once a bobcat attacked and was defeated by the brave water engineers, turned to awesome warriors. Mills's many years of beaver observations became the basis for one of his best works of natural history, his 1913 *In Beaver World*.

In spring, Mills learned the blooming time of every wildflower. In fall he pondered why some aspens turn yellow before others. He determined that most animals live and die close to where they are born. He concluded from his own observations that bears eat mostly mice, and that catching anything takes perseverance. As Lily Lake's natural history and its annual continuity became encyclopedic in young Mills's mind, he caught the rhythm of the place and a sense of nature's drama over a longer term than most of us ever experience. It was a dramatic lesson for him to watch a coyote try for six years to catch the same marmot off base and finally succeed. That is nature's way, and to have come on the scene only when the coyote got its meal would have been to miss an important lesson.

Mills said he sometimes sat nearly motionless for as long as three days. He watched beavers in a small area for a solid week. In winter he camped near the yarding areas of deer and elk to watch how they coped with snow and cold. He watched individual birds and mammals from dawn to dusk to see the full range of their day's activities. He said he was oblivious to rain, cold, and insects, and that if nothing was stirring, the scene itself gave him "primal and poetic" inspiration. "Watch and wait" was his slogan and his tested field technique, though it was far from being his alone. The famous nineteenth-century American naturalist Gilbert White preached it, and both John Burroughs and John Muir popularized it. "All things are on the move, and are sure sooner or later to come your way," said the congenial Burroughs. "The great globe swings around . . . like a revolving showcase." Mills often cited Burroughs on that point, but coined it in his own way as well: "In a bit of wild space across which a primitive man could have hurled his spear," he said, he had witnessed "comedies, courtships, feasts, fights, and frolics." For Muir any area, no matter how small, was so teeming with life that he said he would be "gladly willing to be fenced in upon it for all eternity."[5]

But it was with the fire of John Muir in his veins that Mills could as quickly abandon his stationary observations to become a nimble rover in search of "encounters." Athletic and mobile like Muir, Mills camped in all of the states and Alaska, Canada and Mexico, avidly studying each new environment. Lily Lake was his version of John Burroughs's Slabsides, a microcosm revealing endless secrets to his patient eye. But whole mountain ranges, the whole West, the whole continent, was the vast domain he shared in spirit with John Muir. He said that going into new environments to see how the animals lived was his greatest passion. And what he was bent on finding, he sought with tenacious energy. He searched for days to find a coyote den with pups. He followed woodpeckers all day to see how many trees they bored into for insects. By following the tracks, scat, and food caches of two lions for several days, he learned that one ate well while the other nearly starved. He followed a bighorn flock for five days through what now covers a large part of Rocky Mountain National Park and monitored a grizzly for its first seven days after hibernation to see what it ate. Such arduous feats, and his habitual tramping through forests and valleys or along the fringes of timberline for days and weeks, and in all seasons, became Mills's trademark as a naturalist.

It was his vitality and confidence in the outdoors that enabled Mills fearlessly to share close quarters with grizzly bears and become one of the most celebrated grizzly fanciers in the American West. He and a few others of his time were the first to insist categorically that grizzlies properly treated and understood are not to be feared, and that they are noble friends whose extraordinary character, intelligence, and prowess demand our highest admiration. Frightened by his first grizzly encounter as a youngster, Mills learned through his own experience not to fear the great bear. He later recorded a wealth of observational and historical data in his 1919 book *The Grizzly, Our Greatest Wild Animal*.

Mills was not above feeding birds and small mammals so that he could watch them better, and he even dragged large carcasses to spots where he could watch carrion eaters work them over. He planted a china egg in a hen's nest to see what a marauding skunk would do with it. He threw peanuts into the grass in rapid succession to test a jay's memory, and once when he threw a teddy bear at a jay the testy bird retaliated by snatching away three pencils from his open pencil box. When a mother bear sent her cubs up a tree to wait while she went off somewhere, Mills tried to catch and kidnap them, finally sawing off a branch to dislodge the uncatchable rascals. With boyish prankishness he lobbed a stone into a lake near a grizzly sow swimming for shore with a cub perched on her back. What fun to see her spin around and paddle off in the opposite direction, her cub capsized and now clutching frantically to her tail.

Animals, like atoms, can be disturbed by the act of observing them, but in such times, the sacrifice of science was of no concern. Nor is it irrevocably upsetting that Mills cut a tree branch to catch bear cubs, even though it ill suited him as a future conservationist. As a nature-enchanted youth and later as a mature naturalist, Mills made nature's wild creatures his playmates and learned something about them in the process, scientific or not. For all his intense seriousness, nature was first of all his playmate and science was first of all adventure.

With the artistic impulse so compelling an ingredient in Mills's sensibility, he had to decide early how he would align with formal science, art's perceived opposite. He knew that science was a force upon the world not to be denied. But a poetic approach to comprehending the natural world quickly germinated in him to accompany the poetic stimulation of raw adventure that gave his life aesthetic and physical intensity. It was a quest for poetic sentiment, more often than science, that gave him his needed observational tenacity and drove him, for example, to follow timberline for hundreds of miles along connecting mountain slopes to absorb its dramatic moods.

A hand lens and an altitude barometer in his pocket and a low-powered microscope at his cabin for counting finely spaced tree rings gave Mills a sense of precision and allowed him to stand with one foot in science while his still vague faculties of poetic perception were forming. Counting whatever could be counted was a residual habit of Victorian science but was a healthy stimulus to Mills's curiosity, even when as a child he wanted to know how many times a skunk can "fire." Now alone in the wilds, there was much to count: How many trips must parents of young birds make each day to stuff their gaping beaks? How many trips does a squirrel make to its granary? How many seeds are held there in storage? How many nuts fit into a chipmunk's cheek pouches? How many cones per tree? Trees per acre? How much silt is washed from forested slopes and from burned-over slopes?

Though he increasingly called himself a "poetic" observer of nature and shunned the aridity of pure science, Mills was, nevertheless, also a man of facts. Acquired at first to satisfy his curiosity, facts later punctuated his colloquial natural history with scientific authority. And the fusion he sought as a developing writer about nature would be the "poetic interpretation" of solid factual information. Crediting Muir with teaching him greater observational rigor, Mills developed an eye for detail, intense powers of observation, and a nervous awareness that kept his attention focused persistently on its subject. His nerves, said his friend Philip Ashton Rollins, "were keyed always to racing speed," and he "threw into his love [of nature] the entire measure of his brain."[6]

Mills's overriding interest in animals was to learn how they live and behave. He called each observation a "story," and each story had to make a valid factual contribution to his growing comprehension of the animal's life history. He approached his task like a reporter "with a nose for news." He dug hard for his stories, but without rigid investigative tools. His tools, said Rollins, "were a camera, his eyes, his brain, and a pair of bounding feet." He had little interest in morphology, classification, or controlled experimentation. Like Burroughs, he may have failed to record many of his observations in his journals. And he probably wrote his nature essays as much from memory as from carefully documented observations. He had abundant precedent in both Muir and Burroughs for a casual approach to science. In Burroughs, for example, he found a spokesman for the validity of learning through direct personal experience:

> I myself have never made a dead set at studying Nature with note-book and field-glass in hand. I have rather visited with her. We have walked together or sat down together, and our intimacy grows with the seasons. What I have learned about her ways I have learned easily, almost unconsciously, while fishing or camping or idling about. My desultory habits have their disadvantages, no doubt, but they have their advantages also. A too strenuous pursuit defeats itself. . . . To absorb a thing is better than to learn it, and we absorb what we enjoy. We learn things in school, we absorb them in the field and woods and on the farm.[7]

With kindred sentiment, Muir shocked a group of scientists when he told them of his habit of sitting down beside a new plant "to make its acquaintance and hear what it had to tell" or beside boulders to ask "whence they came and whither they were going."[8] Muir impressed scientists with his knowledge, powers of observation, and native insight, but he was not one of them. He wanted more from science than it could give, and his answer — even more ardently than Burroughs's — was absorption by total immersion. Muir's and Burroughs's examples were dispositionally agreeable to Mills as a self-taught naturalist, for they liberated his conscience from a commitment to formal study. He saw through them both that he could become a lyric spokesman for nature without painstaking years of formal training; that he could teach himself what he needed to know, and that that was in fact preferable to academic knowledge.

As Mills's range of outdoor experience broadened, he developed a correspondingly comprehensive vision of all life in the forest. He later told his readers not always to look for the sensational but to savor even the routine details in the daily lives of creatures and plants. Get to know them as personal friends, and marvel at the uniqueness of each one's personal destiny: trees bent or straight, healthy or diseased, split by lightning, scarred by fires, lived in by creatures, deformed by earth slides, avalanches, or altitude; animals hungry or well fed, sure-footed but occasionally maimed by a fall; a bear with missing claws; a skunk and a young grizzly, each troubled by a thorn in its foot; the orphaned young of both mammals and birds raised by foster parents; and so on, in myriad profusion.

Mills looked assiduously for the interactions between individuals of the same and different species — events the untrained or unpersistent observer rarely witnesses. His writings are filled with fascinating encounters that enlarge our appreciation of the tightly woven fabric of the biological community. We learn that forest animals intermingle as prolifically as those of the barnyard, if we will only take the time to watch them. He saw wolves pestering both mountain lions and bears, robins and jays harassing a sleeping owl, and skunks driving other animals away from their food. He watched a horned owl land on a tree branch next to a wild turkey, gradually crowd the turkey to the branch's end, and then attack when the turkey took flight. He saw chickadees, brown creepers, and woodpeckers cooperatively gathering food, and saw birds join forces to drive off invading hawks and owls.

He discovered a male redwing blackbird practicing bigamy, with two nests and separate mates in each. Several times he saw male robins feeding young bluebirds, and on the mountainside behind his cabin two robins fed a blind and helpless jay until the old bird died. He saw coyotes watching the flights of buzzards and hastening to the feast when the buzzards landed. Coyotes, he noted, sometimes traveled with mountain lions or followed the trails of bears and human hunters to live from their discarded scraps. He observed relay hunting by both wolves and coyotes, and on the prairie he watched coyotes holding the attention of prairie dogs while other coyotes attacked them from behind. He saw animals feign injury to decoy intruders away from their young, carry food to their young by circuitous routes, and move them to alternate dens when there was a danger of discovery. He watched antelope mothers leave their young in the care of other mothers while they went for water and then return the favor. He saw coyotes lure hunters away from wounded companions, and he witnessed otters and squirrels wail and wander for days in search of their dead mates.

Mills watched so much and became attentive to so many details that unseen events became as vivid for him as those he observed. Tracks, matted grass, feathers, fur, or blood, conjured for him dramatic scenarios of what had happened. He learned to see plants in their seasonal metamorphoses and their evolutionary changes; to see mountains rising and crumbling again to soil; to imagine the individual crystals of glaciers cutting rock like so many billions of miners' drills; to mentally span ten thousand years from the time alpine lakes were born from retreating glaciers until they were filled by encroaching meadows. For Muir the ability to expand the range of the senses was the essence of imagination and a faculty "infinitely superior to our physical senses." Muir "saw" rock crystals "in rapid sympathetic motion," and "heard" sounds from the "sweet music of tiniest insect wings" to the "sound of the stars in circulation."[9] Mills practiced and later preached rigorous training of the senses to gain all from them that was possible, and then, like Muir, went beyond them to extract further data from the realm of "true imagination."

Working hard at his craft as an observer, Mills came to see that animals, like humans, have good days, bad days, successes, failures, accidents, and injuries. In hardest times, survival might depend on the most meager thread. Other times afforded leisure, time for sunning, wandering with no particular goal, "visits to friends and relatives," and play. Mills was intrigued by the role of chance in animals' lives and of their constant need to respond to the unexpected. "Responsiveness" became a cardinal virtue that he looked for in animals and humans alike.

The governing principle was of course survival, and "safety first" became Mills's insightful explanation for much animal behavior. He believed explicitly in evolution, and as much as he came to glorify the leisurely sauntering and playfulness of animals, he never overlooked their imperative to stay alive and reproduce. Safety first and not cowardice caused the coyote to flee the frontiersman, he preached. Who wouldn't flee the superior killing power of a rifle? And safety first applied diverse means to the same end: a mother bear with the power to fight guards its cubs closely, while a mother antelope whose defense is speed of escape, must ignore her young when predators are near to avoid betraying their location.

To illustrate how the sudden intrusion of an unfamiliar object will trigger an alarm response in virtually every animal, Mills told how a landscape painter had sent the local fauna — including a grizzly — into panicked flight by popping open an umbrella over his canvas. He said he unconsciously used that same principle to advantage when he once surprised two wolves in an enclosed wooded area. He knew — popular myth notwithstanding — that under normal circumstances he had nothing to fear from wolves. But these wolves, sensing they were trapped, snarled and crouched as if to leap. Needing something to keep up his courage, Mills decided to snap a picture of them. "This," he said, "effectively broke the spell, for when the Kodak door flew open they wheeled and fled."[10]

As his awareness of the imperatives of survival deepened, Mills admired evolutionary success whenever he saw it. He marveled that birds have populated deserts, jungles, and polar latitudes. He was impressed that antelope have resisted extinction for over two million years, while numerous other animals in North America have come and gone. The antelope taught him a willingness to revise his conclusions when new data challenged old: observing antelope on the plains convinced him that they will detour widely and tackle significant horizontal obstacles to avoid jumping vertical obstacles. The pronghorn "has not learned high jumping," he concluded. But later in a wooded region of Yellowstone, he saw them hurdling timber as easily as deer. "I suppose," he confessed, "it will never do to reach final conclusions concerning what an animal will do under new conditions."[11]

Mills's intense passion for gathering experiences and observations marked him with the distinctive and colorful persona of a naturalist par excellence. Talking to and climbing trees, tapping hollow trees with the butt of his hatchet to see what would fly out, stooping to examine everything in his path, sprawling on frozen beaver ponds to watch the beavers swimming below the ice, spending days and weeks in the wilds living mostly on raisins, kneeling to feast on a fire-roasted deer — in all these ardent and strange ways, Mills became a Rocky Mountain legend. As stories about him circulated, he became for some of the single-minded stockmen and prospectors an apparition of unfathomable peculiarity.

Once, three prospectors who were sure that Mills had a secret mine, stealthily followed him over a high pass, then watched as he examined and talked to the trees. They saw him mark off an acre and count all the trees in it, then lie on the ground to study a piece of wood with a hand lens. They came out of hiding and rushed over to view his gold nugget, cursing loudly when they saw it was only a piece of wood. Off Mills went again, and the sleuthing sourdoughs next found him sitting in a large tree preparing to measure its girth. Mills cheerfully began to explain the tree's chronology, its diseases, the forces that had shaped its growth. But it only made him seem more peculiar. "Though I had . . . done them no harm, they seemed to consider my incomprehensible performance a personal affront," he wrote of the experience. He leaped from the tree, dodged three heavily booted kicks, then gladly complied with an order to vanish into the woods. "This is just what I wanted to do," he said, and went his way, "unhampered by further misunderstandings of the scientific spirit."[12]

That tone — jaunty, almost impish — reveals how Mills had grown into his role as eccentric seeker of knowledge in a world of material values: earnest beyond the grasp of the mountain argonauts, friendly, harmless, glad to impart his knowledge, and with a somewhat studied innocence — amply peculiar, in short, to satisfy any era's popular conception of a field naturalist. Aligning himself with the scientific spirit while eschewing its formal rigor, viewing nature with the inner eye of imagination one moment but scanning it with a hand lens the next, Mills was becoming the model of an inspired amateur, soon to take his place among those curious turn-of-the-century hybrids of science and sentiment that we remember today as popular naturalists who taught others largely through the medium of inspiration.

CHAPTER 7

A Woodsman Ponders Politics

The vale of Estes was resplendent as usual on the Fouth of July 1897, as a crowd gathered to hear twenty-seven-year-old Enos Mills orate on the meaning of Independence Day. The valley's grassy floor still wore early-summer green and the peaks of the Continental Divide were flinging torrents of meltwater off toward the lowlands. The streams bore trout, some destined to land on holiday platters. Those who fished for them or hiked in the cool forests felt nature's resuscitating power and swore to the gift of renewed life bestowed by this valley. Vacationers wrote home to their sweltering relatives — a debilitating heat wave hung over the Midwest — and canny businessmen saw that the cool altitudes of the Rockies were a commodity potentially more lucrative than timber, mining, or beef. Estes Park had arrived as a vacation center and had largely escaped the economic slump afflicting much of Colorado in the nineties.

Mills's oration was the first Independence Day address given in the park, and though no record is available of what he said, a Fourth of July text written a year later has survived. Whether a practice essay or the text of an intended speech, Mills's "American Liberty" gives a glimpse of his developing political attitudes and may have incorporated ideas spoken publicly in 1897. Mills said that the Declaration of Independence was a turning point not just in American history but in all human history. "It placed all in Paradise again," he exclaimed. Before that bold declaration, "life was hardly worth living," and the world "was not adapted to raising good people." History was an endless succession of useless wars, broken homes, saddened hearts, and the horrors of feudalism and slavery. "The worst stain over all the desolate past," he stated gravely, "is the accursed treatment of women."

As women were at that time merchandise, a cargo of them was shipped from England and sold to the men of Jamestown as wives. They sold for about 120 pounds of tobacco apiece. . . . No wonder women hate tobacco! Think of all the moonlight walks that tobacco prevented! Imagine a young man walking up to a pair of bright eyes and exclaiming, "You're worth your weight in tobacco!" How different now! Today as lovers stroll happily along the flowery, shady, or moonlit pathway of courtship, the young man gallantly and repeatedly assures her that she is worth her weight in gold. And what young man is there who has not reached that point of delicious uneasiness where he said, at least to himself, "I'd give the world for her."[1]

The passage ingenuously mixed Mills's politics and youthful idealism. Though his sentiment was stirring, it missed the opportunity to denounce all merchandising standards as measures of human worth. Did he in fact mean that women were still commodities, though raised in value from tobacco to gold to "the world"? How much could the hyperbole of impassioned courtship improve their condition? Mills's ingenuous if slightly flawed reasoning hints of his longing to pledge the world to a mate of his own. Little did he know he would have fully twenty years still to wait and to view marriage with an outsider's idealized longing. During that time he would acquire the occasional epithet "Hermit of the Rockies" and would alternately boast of needing no woman and confess his longing for love and family.

He ended his text by challenging complacency and preaching greater vigilance over America's precious freedoms. He made skirmishing references to the "country's great dangers and great wrongs," and to its greater peril "from forces within than from the entire Spanish [soon to be defeated in the Spanish-American War], or any other unjust nation without." He wondered whether "the grand government of the United States will ever fall," whether poets would someday write, "here the fair cause of freedom rose and fell." And throughout his text Mills could not refrain from picking at that unforgivable flaw in American democracy: "Is the condition of woman in the United States what it should be in the land of liberty?"

In lamenting America's ills, Mills was close to the spirit of his age, for the late nineties saw the beginning of the great age of reform that lasted through World War I. The Progressive Movement touched virtually every aspect of American life in promoting a return to the economic individualism, political democracy, and moral and

civic purity people believed had existed before the great corporate
takeovers and institutionalized political corruption. Some were satisfied by changes little more than cosmetic, others wanted a fundamental restructuring of society. The most optimistic were confident
that creative solutions could be found for whatever problems needed
to be solved.

The Progressive cast in Mills's mindset was reflected in photographs that, by his late twenties, began to show the expression of a
reformer. A photo taken after his 1897 oration shows the solicitude
of the bluebird father generalized to paternal concern for all humanity. With it is a hint of Victorian rectitude that some might have
found churchly. But those who knew him found religion absent from
his world view. Rationalists like Tom Paine and Robert Ingersoll
spoke to Mills as Elkanah Lamb's fire and brimstone could not. Still,
there was in Mills's character and expression a consuming need to
proselytize. He was precocious, proud, public-spirited, bursting with
opinion, and always ready for debate. His manner projected moral
purpose and a degree of forwardness. He was self-assured from having spent over half his life on his own and was deepened by knowledge of life at the bottom of mines. Travel and self-study had
broadened his observations but not eradicated his innocence. And
his expression was perhaps even etched with a streak of paradox
from having peered into the abyss of death in the name of exalted
play. Mills in his young life had been places.

Yet he was not, at twenty-eight, an active politico and perhaps
sensed that he still had more to learn. "It is wrong to entertain any
belief without thorough investigation," he wrote. And believing
that, he lingered in the role of critical observer. His Fourth of July
text, though notable for its indictment of injustice and its defense of
women, was just as notable for its lack of references to specific
issues of the day. Had suffrage granted to Colorado women in 1893
improved their condition significantly or not? What stirred him
about the Spanish-American War, which made the United States a
major imperial power as well as a self-proclaimed guardian of freedom? Had he considered joining the flood of volunteers from Colorado to fight in the war, or had he already formulated the doctrine of
pacifism that he left among his undated papers? "It is better to live
for your country than to die for it. If we really live *for* it, there will
be no need to fight."[2]

How did Mills view the defeat of the People's Party in the election of 1896, which so crushingly neutralized the attempt of the farming and mining states to carry their economic concerns onto a national political ticket? How did he judge the massive consolidations of wealth into scandalous Wall Street fortunes? What, as a mine worker, did he think about the radicalization of labor in reaction to the growing power of capitalism? Mills was gripped by the troubles of the not-so-gay nineties and deeply disturbed by that greater danger from within than from without. But he was not yet publicly articulate about what was wrong or how it should be repaired.

Mills's demanding dictum that it is wrong to entertain any belief without thorough investigation expressed a preoccupation with right and wrong that went deep in his character and was a constant preoccupation of the age in which he lived. He tried an essay on the subject and began with the sweeping declaration that "the Right and the Wrong cover every thought, desire, and act of life." In a passage resembling one by Elkanah Lamb, Mills asserted that Right "is an everlasting principle [that] never changes . . . no matter what we think about it." It produces "good actions," while Wrong "brings forth evil." He recognized that something short of absolute standards probably governs the real world ("Man is mortal and few of his decisions . . . are absolutely good or wholly bad") but rejected a relativist stance: "However, Right and Wrong must not be qualified." So conditioned, Mills tended to view politics always in adversarial terms and suffered correspondingly from a deficit of political finesse when he later committed himself to what he believed was undebatably right.[3]

Mills's developing political makeup had remnants of his Kansas heritage as well. Learning what he could of the Kansas-Missouri border warfare of the late fifties, he concluded that it was "an event unparalled in history"; he was struck by how savagely both sides fought for values they were convinced were right. Though never wavering from his revulsion to the idea of slavery, his heritage from the troubled region of southeastern Kansas left him with a tolerance and even a compassion for the South. He credited the South for being the first to champion the cause of Cuba's independence from Spain, forgetting, or never knowing, that the motive of the antebellum South was to annex Cuba as a proslavery state. Kansas politics were for Mills a dizzying seesaw of change, and he once quipped,

"Kansas should be a healthy state, for in its youth it had several constitutions." He admired the transformation of the arid land to a thriving farm state and joked about its ability to surpass its crop of grasshoppers with "more wheat, and . . . more populists than any state in the union." He lamented that noisy real estate developers had replaced the quiet Indians and that politicians had "howled down" the coyotes. Changeable and paradoxical, Kansas was "not the first who with best intentions have incurred the worst." Kansas was for Mills a kind of metaphor for the "most loved and despised" and for alternating "woes and glory." Just those antipodes would later characterize Mills's own life.[4]

While questions about his Kansas heritage still occupied him, Mills had for consideration a simpler political digest in the short thirty years of Estes Park history — a history that gave him almost an allegory of democratic evolution and American self-determination. When Joel Estes first settled in the valley in 1860, he and his family "were monarchs of all we surveyed. . . . There was absolutely nothing to dispute our sway."[5] Soon there was, however, for the valley fell under the shadow of foreign aristocracy. An Irish baron, the Earl of Dunraven, sought to make the valley his own. Dunraven had the acquisitive instinct of an immensely wealthy nobleman, but he used American-style corruption to buy American soil. Hiring bogus settlers to claim tracts under the homestead laws and then to sign them over to him, Dunraven soon owned 8,000 acres and controlled another 15,000. The practice was common throughout the West as wealthy individuals and corporations — the Anaconda among them — sought to gobble up mineral, timber, or grazing lands.

Not about to take the insult lying down, the park's settlers quickly maneuvered to block Dunraven's scheme, and eventually the Earl left the valley. Later, the park's settlers showed no more tolerance for get-rich capitalists than they had for Dunraven. When a toll road into the valley continued to charge a toll — and even raised the rates — after its charter expired in the nineties, one Estes Park resident tore down the toll gate. He was arrested and fined but promptly tore the gate down again. Joined by Abner Sprague, a later Estes Park notable, he took the battle to court and won. "The toll company was defeated and these two men deserve the honor of giving Estes Park a free road," wrote Mills admiringly.[6]

With that as perhaps his earliest inspiration, Mills came to view roads as inviolable fixtures of democracy. Roads were for the people, regardless of rank or status. Controversy over the ownership and use of roads sparked one of his first overt political statements and provoked his last and most painful political battle twenty years later. Here is Mills in 1903 taking issue with a newspaper that had cited mismanagement of roads in Denmark as evidence of the failure of government ownership:

You state that much consternation has followed the government ownership and mismanagement of these roads. The fact that consternation followed government mismanagement is a point in favor of government ownership. Private-owned roads in this country are frequently mismanaged, and often afflict people with shameful abuses — yet the people generally calmly acquiesce. There is always a chance of ending a wrong when the people are aroused against it. Government ownership gives the people direct and sensitive interest in a road's affairs, and abuses at once arouse them, and being stockholders the abuse can be quickly stopped. The gigantic railroads privately owned in this country often inconvenience or plunder the public, yet their enormous power makes them almost impregnable against public attempts to stop their wrong doing. As people long ago found concerning government — the only way to control a great power is to own it.

Mills then raised a paean to socialism:

Denmark's temporary failure in public ownership is hardly a case against socialism. Probably Denmark's trouble was caused by the evil influence of some private monopoly. Socialism is the public ownership of all monopolies. Monopolies, for dividends, are great corrupters, because of their irresponsible power while in private hands. Both logic and example show that the evils arising from monopolies decrease as the number of them under government ownership increases.[7]

In another letter to the newspaper, Mills criticized the high cost of the postal service as the result of exorbitant freight rates charged by the railroads. The answer, he repeated, is public ownership of the sort that has made New Zealand "without doubt the most prosperous and contented country on earth." Bringing the argument down to the scale of local experience, he noted that "for years a toll road literally collected a tithe of the earnings in Estes Park. Abner Sprague broke up this toll road, and now the Park is just beginning to prosper." Again Mills raised the banner for socialism:

Socialism, like liberty, comes slowly — on the installment plan. As socialism insists that each shall have what he produces, it follows that those who have must produce. What is there in their plan to excuse your repeating the thoughtless remark that it would "deaden ambition and encourage laziness"? Had you said that the present system of society deadens ambition and encourages laziness, considers dishonesty the best policy, makes Standard Oil divine and rewards food adulterers, your statement would not have been so disputable. The charge that socialism would encourage laziness, like the charge of monkey descent against Darwin, is a current expression which strictly truthful people cannot make use of without showing vague information on the subject.[8]

Mills's defense of socialism was as explicit a statement on the subject as he ever made. Having begun his own entrepreneurship as an innkeeper, he was not opposed to privately owned business. His distinguishing point about business was that those things affecting all people should be owned by all people. His notion of socialism did not include class struggle or revolution; it closely resembled the moderate socialism of Edward Bellamy, whose famous utopian novel *Looking Backward* profoundly influenced Mills's generation. Accident or not, *Looking Backward* provided a blueprint for most of Mills's social ideas.

Published in 1887 and called by some historians the single most influential book in the whole fifty years from 1885 to 1935, *Looking Backward* contrasted an ideal society of the future with a scathing indictment of the late nineteenth century. That indictment inspired the zealous generation of journalists that included Ida Tarbell, Lincoln Steffens, and the "muckrakers." Mills's later friend Eugene Debs poured over it in prison in 1895 and said that it helped cement his own conversion to socialism. Mills took easily to Bellamy's belief that human nature is basically good and will not tolerate corruption once it is brought into view. Bellamy's ideal state came about nonviolently because society's ills had finally been perceived by all. "Public opinion had become fully ripe for it, and the whole mass of the people was behind it," wrote Bellamy.

The people of the United States concluded to assume the conduct of their own business, just as 100 odd years before they had assumed the conduct of their own government, organizing now for industrial purposes on precisely the same grounds that they had then organized for political purposes. At last, strangely late in the world's history, the obvious fact was perceived that no business is so essentially the public business as the industry and commerce on which the people's livelihood depends, and that to entrust it to private persons to be managed for private profit is a folly similar in kind, though vastly greater in magnitude, to that of surrendering the functions of political government to kings and nobles to be conducted for their personal gratification.[9]

Social justice, equal opportunity for women, the redemptive power of parks, the value of recreation and leisure, the right to redirect one's life at any point, a hatred of public corruption and amassed wealth, an insistence on honesty in journalism, a faith in technology, and a belief that prisons are counterproductive were Millsian notions closely akin to those of Bellamy. Later, in one of his most famous forestry addresses, Mills even adopted Bellamy's technique of looking back from a more nearly perfect future to promote a reform agenda.

In 1903, when Mills ventured his opinion on socialism, hundreds of thousands of Americans, appalled especially by the brutal suppression of strikes, were beginning to think of socialism as the necessary and inevitable wave of the future. While Progressives wanted to correct the system's worst faults, socialists wanted to overhaul the whole system. Conservative socialists like Victor Berger stressed change through education and the democratic process, while revolutionaries like Eugene Debs stressed replacing the whole capitalistic system. Part of the appeal of socialism for Mills was doubtless its scientific and logical framework ("Great inventions and grand thoughts will preserve liberty," he said) alongside its optimistic faith in a coming utopia. And its main appeal, furthermore, could stir his sentiments without nudging him very far away from his basically Progressive outlook. Both, after all, proclaimed a saner, higher, and nobler social order. As a young entrepreneur, Mills was also spared conflict over the ownership of private property, for socialism both allowed it and said with fervor that workers would own their homes for the first time. And far from reducing personal initiative, the socialism of Mills's day claimed passionately that it would elevate the outlook and performance of workers by rescuing them from the pitiless exploitation of capitalists — a notion Mills clearly implied in his missives to the *Loveland Reporter*.

Mills probably gained some exposure to socialism during the nineties in Butte, where *Looking Backward* and many of the utopian novels it spawned were no doubt available. And though the Anaconda treated him well as a wage earner, there was plenty for him to see that stood in ugly contrast to what seemed right and reasonable in the socialist perspective. The very year that Mills signed onto the Anaconda payroll, Marcus Daly, the mine's operational genius, and William A. Clark, arch frontier capitalist on the way to becoming one of the world's richest men, began a feud that lasted twelve years and debauched Montana politics. In 1890, according to *Enos Mills of the Rockies*, Clark singled young Mills out to be his personal secretary following necessary business training, which the youth secured at Heald's Business College in San Francisco. Mills returned to Butte and took the job, but within a few weeks galloped off to explore Yellowstone Park. Had he remained employed under Clark, his ideals would soon have clashed with those of Montana's most infamous money baron.[10] Surpassing even the sordidness of his feud with Daly were Clark's outrageous acts of bribery to win himself a seat in the U.S. Senate — a feat soon undone by a Senate investigation that declared his election void.

In continuing his sporadic association with the Anaconda, Mills saw it swallowed up by a huge trust that put it and virtually all of Montana into the hands of Wall Street. Stock manipulation schemes — with the infamous Standard Oil pulling the strings — outrageously gypped the small investors. Ever-worsening pollution downwind from the Anaconda killed large numbers of livestock, but the company claimed with haughty impunity that any abatement of pollution would be injurious to the nation's security. Fraudulent acquisitions of land and timber resources brought only a timid rebuke from the U.S. courts several years later. The consolidations of the majority of all Montana mining, along with huge holdings of urban real estate, farmlands, hotels, rail and water works, and over half the state's newspapers, made the state little more than a colony. The people were powerless and prayed for the day of "Montana's redemption from the rottenness of corporate domination."[11]

Though Mills witnessed generally good labor-management relations in his early Butte years, things changed with the huge consolidations at the turn of the century. The new and largely insensitive corporate managers quickly alienated the workers and their unions. Tensions steadily mounted, confrontations resulted, and in a pattern common all over the mining West, federal and state troopers helped the business establishment crush unionism. In Colorado, the Western Federation of Miners adopted the platform of the Socialist Party of America in 1902. The next year, violence began to erupt in the gold town of Cripple Creek, where Mills had worked in the winter of 1896–1897. In retaliation against union demands for decent wages and an eight-hour working day, Colorado governor James Peabody led corporate interests in open warfare against organized labor, which brought about the crushing defeat of union power throughout the Colorado mining industry.

In that political climate, Mills's reliance on the socialist democracies of Denmark and New Zealand to state his case for socialism seems far removed from the issues he might have confronted given his long involvement in the mining industry. Nor did he take socialism with him into his active public life as a conservation crusader. Locally he remained simply a "man of unusual social ideas" and an all-purpose "mugwump" in the midst of an overwhelmingly conservative and Republican population.[12] As Mills entered the arena of public causes, he sought support for them wherever he could get it without making partisan commitments of his own. If he remained always a socialist at heart, he paradoxically succeeded best with Republican administrations and with influential Republican backers such as J. Horace McFarland of the American Civic Association and George Horace Lorimer of the *Saturday Evening Post*. It was in fact the breadth of the Progressive Era's reform impulse that allowed Mills to follow his own conscience and to pursue his own concerns without closely allying himself with any party interests.

Mills's friendship with Debs began in 1913, and they no doubt exchanged ideas on many subjects as they hiked in the forests around Longs Peak. Debs's deeply committed and humane character is certain to have appealed to Mills, for Debs — like Bellamy, who had influenced him — was one of those great, unselfish personalities who worked unremittingly for human freedom and justice. Debs drew worshipers by the thousands to his speeches and rallies. His oratory, falling to a whisper and rising to a booming appeal for justice to all humanity, was a model Mills might have drawn upon in his own persuasive speech-making. But whatever influence Debs might have had — before or after they met — Mills cannot be called a socialist in any truly functional sense. Debs — who said that merely believing in socialism does not make you a socialist — probably gave

Mills humanitarian inspiration more than political substance.[13] Debs ranked with Mills's other crusader heroes, such as William Lloyd Garrison, the abolitionist, the feminist Elizabeth Cady Stanton, and the freethinker Robert Ingersoll. All exerted a powerful personal force over their followers. Mills's agenda soon after 1903 would shape itself around nature as civilization's panacea, and it was Muir, consequently, who remained his most important model. Interestingly, we hear nothing from Mills about Muir's own political hero, Henry George — another foe of the abuses of private ownership and an inspiration for the later wilderness movement.

Though Mills's defense of socialism came halfway through Theodore Roosevelt's first term, his actual development to a practicing socialist may have been deflected by his admiration for the president. Roosevelt's personal charisma and pragmatic vigor captured allegiances from across the political spectrum and — it was often said — "made the nation one man." Muir lamented the "mad, God-forgetting progressive days" and refused to join Roosevelt's conservation program, yet even he was captivated by Roosevelt as a man.[14] For Mills's acquaintance William Allen White, the famous Kansas editor and frequent summer resident of Estes Park, it took only one exposure to Roosevelt's personality and to his *American Ideals and Other Essays* to become a loyal and lifelong Rooseveltian, and to abandon his virulent racism, social Darwinism, and glorified vision of laissez-faire capitalism ("Let selfishness go unchecked, it's nature").[15] Roosevelt professed a "distributive justice" in which the professional classes, small businessmen, and independent farmers would give a fair share to the working man. Likened to a "respectable revolution," such a scheme may have seemed to Mills able to accomplish what Bellamy had called "change through universal consensus." And Roosevelt's conservation program had a social dimension in proclaiming public interest against private exploitation that made sense to Mills, too.

Roosevelt, furthermore, commanded both Muir's and Mills's highest respect as an outdoorsman and naturalist. All three believed that deviating from the laws of nature is invariably fatal to civilizations. Mills, even toward the end of his life, still held Roosevelt in esteem as one whose deep acquaintance with nature was "ever . . . helpful in making the right decisions and in getting results."[16] Brought into Roosevelt's active ranks as a conservation spokesman from 1907 to 1909, Mills gave no public evidence of whether his socialism still existed or had melted into the broader Progressive mold. As his perspective turned increasingly to nature as the arbiter of human affairs, he retreated from partisan demonstrations of his views and the controversies he became embroiled in had no overtly partisan slant. Under Roosevelt, Mills's public life began a complex course that would take him from dedicated government service to a deep distrust of one agency two years later and essentially all government a decade later.

CHAPTER 8

Enos Mills, Longs Peak Guide

The mountaineer who played so carelessly with his own life took meticulous care of the 257 parties he guided up Longs Peak. If flirting with death was a compulsion of his solitude, placing himself in charge of others was perhaps a form of self-correction. And he had some slogans to validate: "Nature is safe," he insisted, and climbing Longs Peak is "simply a day's work crowded with enjoyment." Mark Twain, we recall, had proved that some kinds of work are worth it, and had chosen mountain climbing as the best example next to painting fences. John Muir, meanwhile, was making it known that "one must labor for beauty as for bread."[1]

Longs Peak is, furthermore, "almost free from danger," Mills said — safe enough, in fact, for everyone except invalids, the morbidly height-shy, and those who rake out their whole catalog of existential worries while standing on narrow ledges. One illustratively narrow ledge highlighted Mills's route up the peak, the standard route still used today. That ledge, called "the Narrows," overlooks — said Mills with relish — "unbannistered space." Indeed, though nowhere difficult, Longs Peak's tourist route shares close company with frightening precipices and has a certain intricacy that can quickly bring trouble when climbers stray off course or weather conditions change. Like any high peak, Longs can summon villainous weather out of an empty sky in a matter of minutes.

Most mountain visitors in Mills's day concluded that a guide was mandatory. One article said flatly that without a guide's protection, "Climbing is destructive to human life." In an age when people were reawakening to outdoor adventure but no longer commanded native outdoor skills, they could be led by a guide where they could not otherwise go. They could experience the mountains as both safe and thrilling, civilized and savage. By 1915, three-fourths of all Longs Peak climbers used guides.

Mills cut a fascinating figure to his clients because he had acquired a legendary aura: He appeared to have come from realms of profound adventure that had bestowed on him bounteous health, optimism, and unequivocal self-direction. As they clung to the peak's rocky slabs — even when clinging was unnecessary — Mills could be coaxed to describe his adventures there in winter, such as his weight-less February dance in the roaring gale that floated him to the top and spiraled his hat off toward the heavens. When Longs Peak rum-bled and grew slick in summer storms, Mills could turn his clients' fear to worshipful John Muirish awe for nature's irrepressible wild-ness.

The image of Mills as a weightless and free spirit was expressed by this message to him from an admiring guest of Longs Peak Inn: "Having seen you walk as one who floated with the wind I had a vivid picture as I read of your going to and fro upon the mountain-tops. I envy you that power to get about, the power to see all you can see and the life out of doors."[2]

That is exactly the effect Mills wanted to have, for he believed that the guide's own person should embody the lessons of his profes-sion and that his force of personality should leave a lasting inspira-tion. There is clearly intended metaphor in his belief that the guide can "encourage people to go into new fields . . . to advance, and get somewhere."[3]

One of those who felt that extended inspiration was inn guest Earl Harding, who found that, as Mills guided him up the peak, he was able to "forget all dreads, fears and limitations of life . . . to feel all that comes of triumph and of high resolve — and more." Mills the inspirational guide and Mills the reckless and solitary mountain-eer were subjects of equal fascination to Harding during his stay at Longs Peak Inn in June 1903. Mills had just returned from descend-ing Longs's great east face, the first to repeat Elkanah Lamb's nearly suicidal feat of 1871. Mills feigned stoic reticence. He said that he was just out after pictures and had slipped into some water. But Har-ding coaxed the story out of him and recorded it. His hyperbole might have embarrassed Mills, yet it displayed exactly those hectic and heroic values that characterized Mills's own first-person narra-tives. Harding wrote:

Lost in the wonderland of the skies, the very ozone intoxicating, reason lost and some wild impulse bidding him play with death, a mountaineer, bronzed, muscular, rugged, started down the East Precipice of Longs Peak — the most hazardous descent in America — heedless of all there was of danger in the three thousand feet of almost perpendicular cliff. . . . Peril was lost sight of in the etherial [sic] excitement that comes from facing death.[4]

At an impasse and forced to find a way down or stay there "and starve," Mills slithered his way down a water-filled rock groove and made it to a ledge, "thrilled with exhilaration such as few mortals live to experience." Falling snow, ice, and rocks pelted the dauntless mountaineer, and once he was knocked out but fell with his head in a snowbank whose "cooling compress soon brought him to his senses." Finally an avalanche shot down an adjacent gully and Mills hopped aboard to ride it like a runaway train for 800 feet until it stopped next to Chasm Lake. Out from under the snow he popped, indestructible as he had been on all his solitary adventures. The puff and adulation are Harding's, but the incidents must have been supplied by Mills and all are familiar in the Millsian repertory of mishaps.

"Hereafter," he told Harding, "I shall confine my climbing to places where the wealth of scene is sufficient reward; conquering crags and descending precipes just for the doing of it is folly; my adventure was foolhardy — but it was worth the cost." Mills delivered that declaration a few days later on the summit of Longs Peak as the two looked over the dizzying chasm of the east face. If Harding reported the conversation correctly, we can take Mills's east face descent as his last major feat of risk taking — or rather his intention that it be his last. For that next winter, 1903–1904, and the following year, 1904–1905, he had some of his narrowest escapes from snowslides and probably made his blind three-day descent from the Continental Divide as well.

If controlled mastery of danger rather than reckless folly had characterized Mills's solo feats, he might have claimed with some validity that self-testing honed the faculties he needed as a guide. It was true, in any event, that Mills took guiding as a profound mission and made his clients' safety a cardinal principle. He climbed Longs in every kind of weather and at every hour of day and night to know all possible dangers. Once, at least, he returned from an

Climbers ascend the "Trough" on Longs Peak. As a professional guide, Mills reduced party sizes and added nature lore to his excursions to awaken permanent interest in the outdoors. *Denver Public Library, Western History Department.*

ascent, rested only a few minutes, then climbed to the top again with thirty to forty pounds of rescue equipment on his back.

With quick, catlike attentiveness to everything around him, Mills epitomized the "peculiar alertness" he said a guide must have. That alertness saved at least one client from certain death. A garrulous and constantly chattering man, failing to notice Mills's sign of caution, stepped onto a patch of early-season ice and shot off down the slope. Mills instantly leaped to a point of rocks piercing the ice patch and grabbed the man by the coat, slowing his speed and deflecting him sideways — with Mills still attached — off the ice. Mills said casually that he had been ready to execute the maneuver for years.

The lucky man should have heeded some of Mills's alpine advice: "Do most of your talking while at rest." "Thoughtfulness and deliberation are essentials of mountain climbing." "Climb slowly." "Look before stepping."[5] Such is the wisdom of guides everywhere, but it sounds curiously incongruous from the man who in solitude slipped, slid, and fell more times than all his clients put together.

Mills's safety record as a guide was unblemished, but he had plenty of trials and once almost had four Carrie Weltons on his hands. Unlike Carlyle Lamb, who allowed his tiring client to coax him to continue, Mills as a young guide once prodded his unfit party beyond their endurance, thinking it was the guide's responsibility to get them to the top. The four were unaccustomed to walking, and, worse, were of that species so foreign to Mills, people who "apparently lived to eat." When they reached the top, all four collapsed. By the time Mills got them started down, a storm struck and daylight faded. Rain fell off and on all night, and the temperature dropped below freezing. Mills prodded, coaxed, and helped, step by step. The foursome stopped incessantly to huddle, shiver, and whimper. It was long after midnight when he at last got them to timberline and revived them by a fire. A misjudgment had nearly brought tragedy, but superior training has prevented it: Mills stayed with his party, found the way in a wet, black night, kept his nerve, and disciplined his exhausted and frightened group.

Managing people, Mills learned, is the guide's ultimate and toughest task; his lament that he could not prepare himself enough for a knowledge of human nature summed up what he saw as the greatest of all mountain hazards. Mills learned that large parties inevitably developed frictions, and that parties bent on speed learned the hard way that speed and altitude don't mix. Seven healthy football players provided Mills with his most triumphant example of the latter. The young men hired him for an ascent, then set off at a blistering pace, with "the evident intention of killing me off." Mills stuck to the fastest pace he knew he could hold, and finally began to overtake the athletes as they dropped by the wayside, green around the mouth. "Another long-haired brave tumbled down," Mills noted as he passed the second of them. "Only two of those husky, well-trained athletes reached the summit," he chuckled. The young men were further chastened as they sat in the inn that evening and watched Mills leave to guide another party up the mountain by moonlight.

Moonlight ascents were a guiding specialty of Enos Mills's, the romantic aficionado who made moonlight so much a part of his solitary adventures. Oddly, he did not think of climbing Longs by moonlight until another — H. C. Rogers, in 1896 — had done it, but then he added it to his repertory and made a substantial number of his guided ascents at night. He could give his clients an other-worldly experience that many had never before approached in their lives. The moonlit peak from the Boulderfield floated huge and ethereal, silent except for the slapping of water on rocks as it ran down from the snowfields. The Keyhole was a forbidding allegorical passageway, the Narrows a place of breathless silence where silhouettes crept one by one, the Homestretch a staircase of bright granite lit up like marble, the summit a place of rejoicing as the climbers shivered and counted the lakes to the west while they waited for the warming touch of the sun. Habits have changed, writes Longs Peak chronicler Paul W. Nesbit, and fewer today go to discover and contemplate the peak's nighttime mysteries.

Mills learned, as all guides learn, that at times he had to take absolute command. Some people, not responsive to suggestions, had to be ordered not to roll rocks. Some, plucky but too sick to go on, had to be forced to stay and wait. And some, suddenly hysterical, had to be calmed, sometimes physically restrained. One of Mills's favorite guiding tales was that two daughters of a minister arrived at the Narrows and simultaneously became hysterical. It was no place for ceremony, Mills decided. In some kind of maneuver strangely suited to the location, he pushed the feet from beneath one of the young women, tripped the other on top of her and sat down on both. When the father arrived, his face, Mills said, "vividly and swiftly expressed three or four kinds of anger before he grasped the situation." It should be added to Mills's credit that he did not capitalize on hysterical-lady-climber tales and never portrayed women as more giddy or prone to losing their heads than men.

"The trail . . . is probably without a rival as a place for making 'matches,'" said Mills, always wholesomely interested in the interplay between the sexes. His anecdotes of romance on Longs Peak show his enjoyment of love's triumphs and foibles, his amused tolerance of lovers' quarrels. High mountain ascents create a "natural sociability," altitude "makes the reserved talkative," and climbing brings out everyone's true character, Mills believed. No wonder, then, that he saw lifetime friendships both begin and end, and acquaintances inflame to love as he led his guests up out of the ordinary world.[6]

One couple met at the base of the peak and was engaged before reaching the top. One young couple in Mills's charge continued with him up the mountain over the protest of their chaperone, who was too exhausted to continue. On another climb, three young couples confronted their true natures for the first time. The first, soon to be married, quarreled and split up for good. The second quarreled but made up, at least for the rest of the climb. The third reversed roles: The young woman, cool for years to her suitor's attentions, began to grow amorous as he expressed impatience with her clumsy performance as a climber. When he began avoiding her altogether, she pretended to sprain her ankle. That relationship was broken forever too, and doubtlessly for the better. The three malcontent couples finally worked themselves into a mighty row, then turned their wrath on Mills, and "united to roast" him.

Did Mills have romances of his own up there in his most vivid element? Were there flirtations, seasonal romances, letters afterward, and perhaps deeper entanglements? Or was there an awkward failure of the trail to make any matches, however temporary, for the solitary mountaineer, despite his distinction as a guide and as the keeper of a thriving mountain inn? The record is missing, and that is itself perhaps revealing. We know only that any real romantic fulfillment continued to escape Enos Mills throughout his years of guiding.

After 1906 public life took Mills out of active guiding, but his last summer ended that career with éclat. In August 1906 alone, he climbed Longs thirty-two times in thirty-one days, six of those times by moonlight. And on each of those days he made a sixteen-mile round trip to Estes Park by horseback or wagon. On one day he made two wagon trips and one horseback trip to Estes Park, then climbed the peak by moonlight. And in one sixty-hour stretch he neither ate nor slept.

It was neither quarreling lovers, nor hysterical ministers' daughters, nor humbled football players who gave Mills his most memorable experiences as a Longs Peak guide. Instead, it was an eight-year-old child named Harriet Peters. She was his youngest client, and with disarming charm and childish innocence epitomized the kind of instinctive curiosity Mills wanted everyone to have. Harriet marveled at the "brave little trees" that live where they have "to stand all the time in the snow." She wanted to know how the beaver sharpen their teeth, and who had bitten off the cony's ears. She left Mills without an answer when she asked why the cony doesn't go down the mountain and live by the brook where there is more hay. On the summit of Longs Peak she asked, "Where did all the rocks come from?"[7]

Mills and Harriet Peters, Longs Peak summit. Mills wears hobnail boots, the standard footgear until rubber lug soles were developed in the 1950s. *Denver Public Library, Western History Department.*

Harriet was Mills's model client, but even most adults, he discovered, had a latent curiosity about nature that the guide could arouse by supplying interesting facts about plants, animals, and the geology along the route. All of Mills's self-taught knowledge of nature came to a focus in what he came to call nature guiding. Just as peak guiding gave him the opportunity to inspire people to "advance and get somewhere," nature guiding was his way of awakening people to the miracles and mysteries of the whole outdoors. And that, he believed, was tonic to the human disposition. It improved people's interactions, deepened their acquaintances, and gave them a happier outlook. Mills later rounded out the concept of the nature guide, making it the direct antecedent of the ranger-naturalist in today's national parks, and giving his name a secure place in the history of outdoor interpretation.

CHAPTER 9

Nature Instructs: Self-Improvement Through Play

Floating effortlessly on a current of rising air, a column of butterflies mounted Longs Peak in single file as Enos Mills peered over the edge from the peak's 14,000-foot summit. Cresting the top, the fragile-winged creatures dropped 400 feet off the peak's south wall, circled west to re-enter the updraft, and repeated their ride. Mills had seen these mysterious processions before and wondered what they meant. At last he was convinced: "Butterflies, as well as other life, play."[1]

This was exquisite play, a soft, summer version of Mills's wild, buoyant dance up the peak on February gales. "The irresistible call to play," he had called it then. What eloquence he now saw in the response of these delicate insects to some primitive visceral thrill! And what excitement in the belief that an irresistible urge to play runs through all of nature.

A grizzly bear egged on by that urge flung himself onto the overhanging lip of a snow cornice as Mills watched from below. The bear fell with the collapsing snow to a snowfield below, playfully rode to its bottom, then climbed up for a second ride. This time he flung himself in cartwheels from the top of the slope to gather speed.

A discarded sardine can rattled with strewn gravel when an otter bounded past it. The animal jumped with fright, then stopped, circled the can, sniffed and inspected it, and at last began to cuff and chase it like a kitten with a ball. As Mills watched from his hiding place, another otter joined the play, and together they batted the can about and raced to pounce on it.

Watching animals indulging in the sensations of motion, frolicking with objects, chasing, scuffling, and engaging in other forms of play stirred Mills's deepest admiration for nature's wild creatures.

Play was the profoundest connecting link between animals and humans and an index for his appreciation of each species. He read about play in both Darwin and Wallace, owned works by the psychologist William James, who pondered its significance, and could have read numerous other writings on play available before 1900. By the time he wrote most of his own animal essays, he perhaps knew the 1898 or 1911 English editions of Karl Groos's *The Play of Animals,* a German philosopher's "first systematic treatment" of the whole subject, first published in 1895.

Mills saw play as a potent force enhancing both individual lives and each species' evolutionary progress. "Playing animals are most likely to survive and leave offspring," he wrote. "Those alert and quick to re-adjust themselves to the ever-changing conditions — those surviving, succeeding and evolving — are those ever loyal to life's best ally . . . play." For Mills and for many others, that idea seemed to apply equally well to humans. Play for both children and adults was a rediscovered ideal of the Progressive Movement, and finding it vigorously practiced in the animal world gave the nature-conscious era assurance that it was a healthful and natural function. Mills's vast store of experience in watching play in the wilds later gave him shamanistic fervor in preaching its benefits to an age eager to accept his gospel that "life . . . is not all struggle" and that play is "Nature's great way."[2]

Theories of animal play in Mills's time were well on the track of those accepted today. Play was seen as something far more significant than a mere rehearsal of skills needed for adult living. Virtually the full range of play behaviors had been observed, together with their broadening influence on animals' adaptability in meeting new situations. Clear distinctions were recognized between play and "serious" behaviors, and animals were observed — correctly — sometimes to go back and forth between the two. Mills occasionally saw animal play "end in a row" when the protagonists lost their tempers.

It was supposed that animals sought "fun" for its own sake and that the pleasure of play was both physical and mental. Animals were believed capable of pretending and make-believe in some of their games, and even a kitten, said Karl Groos, requires a "conscious act of self-deception" to bat a ball back into motion once it has stopped rolling and ceased being a "prey." That conscious self-deception, he said, "involves some of the most subtle psychological elements of the pleasure that play gives." Play was observed to be practiced by adult animals as well as by young, and Mills, like others, correctly supposed that it promotes sustained fitness and resiliency for efficient living.[3]

Mills went so far as to insist that the play instinct asserts itself even during times of stress. A wounded grizzly sow that he tracked for several days seemed to him to take time out to play, though she was pursued by hunters and was weak from loss of blood. He saw her stand on her hind legs and strike "playfully" at grasshoppers with her single front paw — the other had been severed by a bear trap — and finally pirouette in a full circle. In the stream of animals fleeing a forest fire, Mills saw two bear cubs stop for a "merry romp," and noted that "even the threatening flames could not make them solemn." Other fleeing animals stopped to watch and "momentarily forgot their fears."[4]

Modern biologists might quarrel with those interpretations and with Mills's frequent claim that a bear would rather play than eat. Animals apparently play only when they are free from concerns about cold, heat, food, sex, and sleep. Play indeed represents freedom "from the driving demands of instinct." Mills came closer to that notion in his observation that beavers diligently finish their necessary work and then play. Squirrels, too, seem to have a period of play when their winter food stores are in, and birds have long been known to do their most original singing outside the reproductive season. Mills generalized those lessons and offered them for imitation by an overstressed society: Animals work less than we and play regularly all year.

To the extent that play signifies a release from the immediate demands of survival — to the extent that playful actions are "unhooked" from the motivations that drive serious behavior — modern ethologists see in it one of the roots of human freedom of action. Play furthermore fosters the development of cooperative skills among animals and improves their flexibility in social situations. Mills linked team play to cooperation and mutual aid among animals and said that in mutual aid "appears to be the beginning of a conscious consideration for the rights of others."[5] Belief in play's social benefits transferred easily to the human domain and became a cornerstone in theories of youthful character development at home, in schools, and in the children's summer camps that proliferated at the turn of the century.

Mills said that watching animals play claimed a large share of his field time, and his writings abound in freshly original observations of play behavior in the wilds. Here, for example, is a stunning scene of wolves at play with a blowing tumbleweed:

A tumbleweed in a Wyoming windstorm furnished the plaything in an exciting game for a pack of wolves. I watched the play from the shelter of a ravine. Flying before the wind, the tumbleweed bounded a ridge with a huge wolf after it. Closely pressing him came a pursuing pack of twenty. A lull in the wind and the tumbleweed, colliding with the leading wolf's head, bounded off to one side. Other wolves sprang in the air after it, but the wind carried the tumbleweed along and the entire pack rushed in pursuit.

This big, much-branched, ball-shaped weed was two feet in diameter. When it touched the earth the gale swept it, bounding forward and rolling over and over, across the brown, wide plains. After it came the closely massed wolves. Just as those in the lead were nearing this animated plaything it was caught by a whirlwind and pulled high into the air. Two wolves leaped and tried to seize it. Several sat down and stared after it as though it were gone forever. The tumbleweed commenced to descend, but buoyed up by the air it came down slowly. The pack surged this way and that, as the weed surged in descending, to be beneath it; and while it was still several feet above them a high-leaping fellow struck it head-on and sent it flying to one side. It disappeared in a hollow and the wolves vanished after it.[6]

The passage continues as the wolves burst into view again ("as intense and . . . serious as football players") still pursuing the tumbleweed with the concentrated energy of the swerving and lunging pack. Then, like much animal play, the game ended as abruptly as it had begun.

Another lengthy passage, describing a grizzly sporting with a floating log in a river, has the same kind of closely observed detail. The playful bear stands the log on end in the water, tries to climb it, capsizes, lies upon it, capsizes again, pushes it under water, loses it in its buoyant rebound, recaptures it, and so on. "I found afterwards," Mills wrote, "that the grizzly had rolled the log into the water a short distance upstream from where I came upon him. . . . He may have rolled it over to see if there were insects beneath, but, accidentally or intentionally, he had rolled it into the water." The possibility that the bear chose its toy and set it in motion is consistent with the finding of modern ethologists that brown bears — which include grizzlies — sometimes play by repeatedly carrying objects up a slope, dropping them, and chasing after them.[7]

Otters, Mills discovered, appeared to prepare their slides in advance of using them, evidence (articulated earlier by John James Audubon) of a highly developed play instinct. Once, in the wintry recesses of the Medicine Bow Mountains, he saw fourteen otters sliding silently in the moonlight. Where had so many otters come from in this otter-sparse region, he wondered? The scene was poetic in all Mills's favorite ways, and the sleek "forest gypsies" were still sliding on the moonlit snow when Mills finally slipped off to his campfire late at night. The next day, he followed the tracks converging on the slide. Four otters had come from a stream five miles away over a high ridge, and he surmised — otters being good travelers — that some had come from over twenty miles.

In that intricate community of interacting species scarcely noticed by most humans, animals sometimes play with each other or watch each other play with absorbed curiosity. Twice Mills saw a bear and a coyote playing together, with sparring, dodging, and elaborate make-believe in which one pretended to sleep while the other tried to surprise him. He watched a bear try without success to engage a stodgy porcupine in play. Groos cited cases of a tame deer inviting her playmate dogs to chase her by tapping them with her front hooves, and of a raccoon in the wilds repeatedly heckling a badger who was trying to sleep. Mills saw numerous instances of heckling and teasing among animals, as well as games of tag, hide and seek, and follow the leader — all forms of play still recognized today.

Birds stopped to watch the grizzly sporting with his log in the river, and Mills saw both birds and squirrels watch otters on their slides. He said he found otter slides several times by following grizzly tracks leading to them, for the mighty bear, he discovered, was an enthusiastic spectator of otters at play. That habit of animals to watch each other was for the famous philosopher Arthur Schopenhauer, half a century earlier, the most human of all animal qualities.

At times animals played or watched others play with such intensity that they forgot their own safety. Groos reported the case of a rabbit easily snatched by a fox as it watched sporting bucks. Harpooners said they could sometimes approach sporting seals unnoticed. And in an observation nicely befitting the Rocky Mountain setting, Mills saw a grizzly, raised with forefeet braced on a rock, watching a fly fisherman. With each cast of the line the bear's head moved back and forth, and for several minutes he seemed lost in concentration. Then suddenly he seemed to come to his senses and ran off in fright.

Groos reported that the seductive power of curiosity caused apes repeatedly to steal glances at a snake they morbidly feared, by opening the lid of the box in which it lay coiled. The biologist George J. Romanes attributed to curiosity even the moth's flight into flames. Not so, say modern biologists, but the long-standing observation that gazelles and chamois could be captured by attracting them with unfamiliar objects remains a valid testimony to curiosity's great pull on animals. In the West, before Mills's time, it was a common though unsportsmanlike practice to lure curious antelope into close firing range by displaying a red flag.

Mills found, on the whole, though, that curiosity enables an animal to anticipate and avoid danger. With rustic circularity he said, "Curiosity prevents oncoming events from being thrust on the curious." He considered curiosity as indispensable for effective living as the closely related gifts of play, imagination, and creativity. Without the modern terminology to describe it, he correctly perceived curiosity as the faculty that enlarges an animal's combination of experiences and prompts it to try new behaviors that lead to new skills and knowledge not otherwise accessible.

Grizzlies were again at the head of the class, and, in an utterance Mills would surely want to be remembered for, he said, "Behind the word curiosity the grizzly bear has put a world of meaning." And he urged others to watch them to see what he meant. He saw in the grizzly a curiosity-driven restlessness that led him off in search of new experiences and new sensations, and caused him to abandon the familiar to explore the unknown. A modern naturalist describes the grizzly's curiosity behavior as a sort of "groping" quality that looks for and tries to generate new experiences.[8]

Like the indelible portrait of a grizzly moving its head in rhythm to the casts of a fly fisherman, many of Mills's observations of animal curiosity involve grizzlies and have a distinctly Rocky Mountain flavor. When Mills signaled to a miner with a mirror from a mountaintop — doubtless his own form of play that day — a grizzly stopped to watch. When a wheel broke loose from a miner's cart and rolled down the mountainside, a grizzly went to see what it was.

And when an umbrella blew away from a mountain-top landscape painter and scudded over the tundra, a grizzly watched in fascination. That overweeningly curious grizzly who came into Mills's camp to inspect his yellow slicker — ignoring his nearby food — helped urge Mills to his conclusion that bears would rather play than eat. The bear had in fact followed Mills all afternoon to view his slicker — Mills must have deduced that later — and in the process sacrificed several hours of food-gathering time. He had perhaps also waited two or three hours near his camp — probably without food as well — for Mills finally to retire.

Mills himself was sometimes the object of grizzly curiosity. One bear followed him all day, then sniffed him in his bedding at night. Unafraid, Mills lay still and watched, then saw the bear, his curiosity satisfied, walk quietly away beneath the stars. Another time Mills sat motionless for a long time by a streamside rock watching water ouzels, then suddenly smelled bear, heard a twig snap, and looked up to see a grizzly leaning over his rock. "He looked at me with intense interest," Mills said. "His curiosity absolutely dominated."[9] In much the same way, a curious mountain lion came to inspect Mills while he sat dozing against a tree stump. Before he had slept, the surrounding snow was trackless; when he awoke he saw lion tracks leading to and away from the stump. Lions have that curious habit, modern experts agree. Morbidly shy on the one hand, they sometimes follow humans from sheer curiosity. In one recent instance in Colorado — noticed only when the snapshots were developed — a lion watched a group of picnickers from an overhead tree.

A favorite Millsian theme was that animals are far more aware of our presence than we of theirs, and that we see them so seldom because they have seen us first and fled. Mills was fond of saying that bears know more about people than people know about bears. And contrary to John Burroughs, who believed that all animals instinctively fear men, Mills believed that all animals desire man's acquaintance. He saw the fun-loving black bear as a boy in disguise and said that nothing would give him greater delight than to romp with rollicking, irrepressible children whose parents have blackened his character. In Yellowstone, Mills wrote, a grizzly did just that — leaping into a stream where some boys were bathing and causing "great excitement and merriment."[10]

Irrepressible himself, Enos Mills ran and played tag with black bears in Yellowstone, played elaborate hide-and-seek with a prospector's tame yearling cub, and succeeded once in engaging a wilderness bear in full-fledged play. The bear had climbed a low tree and could not escape the pole that Mills gently prodded him with to get him to come down. The frightened bear batted at the pole defensively, but Mills persisted until the bear at last comprehended that play was meant rather than aggression. Soon he was playing with the pole "as merrily as ever kitten played with a moving, tickling twig or string."[11] Scenes such as that helped to set Enos Mills apart from other men as a Rocky Mountain original: In his floppy hat, face grimy from his fire, standing beneath a tree with a pole, certain or heedless of his own safety, and convinced of the bear's innate desire to play, he sought, as he had with the Longs Peak winds, to make nature his playmate in the wilderness of the American West.

Did he know what this shadow-thing was? Mills wondered as he watched a grizzly chase and box his own shadow. And was all this just jolly make-believe? Make-believe was for Mills another wondrous aspect of the animal world. Lions fought elaborate imaginary battles in pantomime — W. H. Hudson had watched them do it for hours at a time in South America. Owls made faces and hammed it up, the jay was a master of vaudeville and impersonation, and games of hide and seek surely required the capacity to pretend. In that last category, none excelled Mills's own dog, Scotch, who could seem to be watching something far away while all the time watching Mills, and could hug the earth, pretending to be hidden, as Mills called, Where is Scotch?

The prairie dog, an animal with elaborate social habits, gave Mills an example of what he cautiously put forward as an instance of an animal skit:

> One of their plays consisted in a single dog mimicking a stranger or an enemy. A bunch of dogs acted as spectators while an old dog highly entertained them by impersonating a coyote, at least his exhibition reminded me very much of a coyote. The old dog imitated the coyote's progress through dog town with the usual turning, looking, smelling, and stopping. He looked into holes, rolled over, bayed at the heavens, and even tried the three-legged gallop. During most of his stunts the spectators were silent but toward the last he was applauded with violent cursings and denunciations — at least so it sounded.[12]

More bizarre, and suggesting ritualistic behavior, was an apparent mob execution by prairie dogs in which an old member of the colony, having apparently committed some offense, was pushed into an exitless hole and buried alive. The mob then danced a "barbaric triumphal war dance upon the buried one," Mills wrote.[13] Darwin himself had described animal executions, and other nineteenth-century naturalists had speculated on the meaning of executions among rats, cows, crows, and other species.

The grizzly became for Mills the model of an animal who "takes time out to relax and to build and restore himself in play," and who "refuses to live in a rut," "seeks self-improvement," and strives always to be "alive and growing." Clearly living his own life by the same principles, Mills strikes us as having identified personally with his king of beasts. It is at times as Mills's alter ego that the grizzly masters its habitat with all faculties and senses engaged, that he explores life with boundless curiosity and the élan of play, that in his solitary existence, where he is required to "learn everything for himself," he is "a mind seeking facts." Through the grizzly, Mills could tell his readers to approach life with a sense of wonder and adventure. "Had he been a child, with the power of speech," Mills wrote of the grizzly, "he certainly would have asked questions. Often his expression, his attitude, indicated that he was saying to himself: 'What was that? What caused it? Where did that noise come from? What are those strange shadows running from, and how can they move without a sound?' "[14]

There seemed in this great bear even to be a sense of aesthetic appreciation, causing him to watch sunsets, thunderstorms, shooting stars, and rainbows with rapt attention. There is known to be a degree of aesthetic perception in highly evolved species, and, as apes show artistic discernment in their own paintings, the grizzly, Mills seemed to suppose, saw that nature — the nature that Mills found everywhere "artistic" — was beautiful.

The remarkable endowments and what we can rightfully call the nobility of this great bear are being newly appreciated in our own age as civilization chooses whether to force him farther into exile or to give him the domain he needs. We are learning to measure the grizzly's worth both by the worth of any living creature and by his inspirational value to humanity as a great masterpiece of evolution. Mills cared as ardently about the survival of the grizzly as about anything he fought for.

One day he climbed up a mountain to view a forest fire and found a grizzly already there, already watching the fire. Too absorbed to notice Mills, the bear watched the bursts of flame and smoke and listened to the fire's explosive roar. For several minutes Mills stood near the bear, looking with him on the furnace of destruction. Perhaps the bear's own domain was engulfed and this fire about which he was merely curious would force him to seek new territory. He at last saw Mills, bared his teeth, and fled. That grizzly, and all grizzlies, continued to flee — from loss of habitat, from traps, from bounties and uncontrolled hunting, and finally from Colorado altogether. The bear who shared that mountaintop with Mills did not know that he stood next to a friend within the race of the enemy. Nor did he know how vital the survival of his own species would be to man's own salvation from himself.

CHAPTER 10

Longs Peak Inn: "Higher than any Hotel in the Alps"

Two lively grizzly cubs romped on the grounds of Longs Peak House, tussled and tested wits with Enos Mills's dog, Scotch, and sometimes ran foot races with Mills, now the inn's owner and host. Occasionally a lucky guest got to frolic with the cubs, which Mills said he had found orphaned on the lower slopes of Longs Peak and brought home in a gunny sack. That verve was matched the same month of June 1903 by Mills's careening descent of Longs Peak's east face. His spirits and energies were in high gear. Five months earlier he had made the first winter ascent of Longs Peak and throughout the winter had snowshoed over the state's mountain ranges on official assignment to measure the snowpack. In spring he prepared for his second summer as fledgling entrepreneur in the resort business, and in June he put the operation solidly into motion.

Though zoobound a year later, the grizzly cubs, Johnny and Jenny, were the very thing Mills and his new inn stood for: furry and irrepressible versions of Mills's own wilderness persona, and the symbol of his resort as a nature retreat par excellence. Here was deep-woods intelligence brought in for close view. When Mills pushed a penny around the floor with one finger, Johnny and Jenny imitated him perfectly, pushing it with a single claw. When they were chained and romped their separate chains into a tangled mess, they could systematically maneuver in reverse to untangle themselves. When Scotch shrewdly placed a bone just beyond Johnny's reach, bear intelligence prevailed: Johnny turned around at the end of his chain and reached out with his hind paw to gather in the prize. The precocious bears swung in a hammock, rocked in a rocker, rolled a

Johnny and Jenny. *NPS photo.*

blown-out eggshell without breaking it, and learned to lift milk sau-
cers from a table and gulp the milk like thirsty kids.

Mills had purchased Longs Peak House in 1902, acquiring the
main house and guest facilities, several surrounding buildings, and
160 acres adjoining his own cabin. Guiding for Carlyle Lamb
through much of the nineties, Mills had had ample time to size up
the business, which had grown from a largely dairying operation in
the early eighties to a busy climbers' and nature seekers' hub.
Elkanah Lamb had turned the business over to his son in 1889 and
often rambled off on missions to spread the Gospel. Climber-chroni-
cler Frederick Chapin said that Carlyle ran a "charming mountain
inn" where guests enjoyed wholesome food and could sit late into
the evening by the rough stone fireplace talking of the mountains. In
increasing numbers both notable and ordinary people had come to
Longs Peak House to begin their climb of the celebrated Colorado
mountain.

Mills's years of frugality had given him some working capital,
and he now had soil to spade it into for a larger harvest. A reporter

who claimed to know Mills wrote that the industrious youth had already saved $2,000 by the time he was eighteen. Whatever the size of his nest egg, it sufficed for a six-week tour of Europe just a year before his investment in Longs Peak House. Butte had been the source of most of Mills's savings, and he worked one last season there in winter 1901–1902 to bring home money for improvements on his new property.

Mills's trip to Europe in 1900 shaped some of his attitudes about the tourist business and revealed some of his noteworthy traits at age thirty and those of his traveling companion, the sixty-nine-year-old Elkanah Lamb. Passages from Lamb's 1906 autobiography disclose a great deal of bumbling by the two American tourists, woefully inept at dealing with and accepting foreign cultures. The 1900 Paris Exposition — a highlight of their Cook's tour — represented, said Lamb, "the world's genius in the productions and combinations of all things in every department of improvements for the world's betterment." But "who can enjoy an exhibition . . . with two hundred and eighty thousand engaged in French gabbling (for us a meaningless language)? Why not everybody talk the English language? We left . . . in semi-disgust and went to our hotel, retiring instead to dream of home and intelligent civilization." Whatever credit was due for this new high technology belonged, according to Lamb, to "the graces of the Christian system."[1]

In England, Lamb browbeat a waiter into reducing the price of a cup of coffee because the cups were so small. Both he and Mills were voracious coffee drinkers and weren't going to sacrifice their frontier standards. Lamb boarded the wrong ferry over the English Channel, luckily rejoined the tour group on the French side, then got lost a few days later in Paris. He wandered into a steep-sided railroad cut, tripped over the tracks, and narrowly escaped with four trains bearing down. An "invulnerable protestant," he mocked Catholicism (the Vatican was a "superfluous building"). His racial slurs were incessant and crude (A "soap factory . . . ought to be established for the sanitary benefit of such very doubtful humanity"). Then, however, the parson concluded: "Traveling abroad and coming in contact with other peoples, places, and customs, eliminates narrow prejudices . . . widens the horizon of all who travel with ears and eyes open and with receptive minds."

In his introduction to Lamb's autobiography, Mills put some distance between himself and his United Brethren relative. He noted chidingly that Lamb "gives advice excessively," and said he "rarely agree[d] with him on any proposition." He nevertheless praised Lamb as an honorable man whose company is ennobling. As an emerging freethinker, Mills doubtless felt a need to separate himself from Lamb's self-indulgent pieties and Christian sermonizing. And perhaps Mills was not pleased with his own portrait during the European tour — his only appearance in the book.

Identified as "a friend from Butte, Montana" rather than as a family relative and Longs Peak neighbor — an anonymity now preferred by Mills's descendants as well — and not credited with any of the glamour his life had already acquired, Mills even lost his mystique for voluntary starvation. In Rome, where the "dry bread, honey, and delapidated butter did not measure up to the demands of Mills's voracious appetite," Lamb wrote, Mills "asked the waiter, in pathetic tones, with innocent demeanor, 'Could we have a beefsteak?' thus evidencing his animal instincts and abnormality of appetite to the citizens of Rome and the Gentile world in general." What an astonishing revision of the image of the mountaineer who walked up and down the Rocky Mountains on raisins, bark, or on no food at all! There is no evidence that the passage was a spoof, and Mills repeated the performance in a cafe in Venice.

Forced to hire guides for a trip up Mt. Vesuvius, Mills threw a tantrum at his pony guide "using words more voluminous than elegant, mixing semi-expletives fragrant with sulfurous import . . . not only directed against him, but the Italian nation in general." No longer insulated from foreign realities by their Cook's tour, the two now found themselves forced to hire new guides at three different stages of the ascent. Mills was unraveled by the injustice of this extortionary tourist trap and stormed into a government office to assert his rights. The voluble exchange, with not a word understood by either side, is amusing to contemplate. Back on Longs Peak, Mills altered his notion that climbers should always take a guide ("The ideal way to enjoy the mountains is to go without a guide and frequently ignore or go beyond the trail," he wrote in 1905). He simultaneously strengthened his determination to give the guide a positive and useful role through nature interpretation.

Only in immaculate and postcard-pretty Switzerland did Lamb and Mills feel at home. Switzerland reinforced Mills's growing perception of the value of scenery as a national economic resource and the need to preserve it as the foundation of a vacation industry that would yield both monetary and intangible benefits — an important theme that will be discussed later.

Before putting all his eggs into one basket, Mills might have considered branching out in the hotel business. In 1903 he made inquiries about the potential for a successful guide service and hotel at the foot of Mount of the Holy Cross — the peak made famous by its dramatic cross of intersecting snow gullies. Hardy pilgrims came to gaze at it, Henry Jackson photographed it, and Thomas Moran painted it, but — Mills learned — only twenty-three had actually climbed the peak over a sixteen-year period. The mountain was too remote to support a tourist facility.

With a single focus and a decisive sense of direction, Mills renamed his hotel Longs Peak Inn in 1904, began steadily to upgrade its facilities, and advertised the quintessential experience he wanted to give his guests. In the back of his 1905 book *Early Estes Park* he ran the following ad:

> At Longs Peak Inn
>   You will hear the
> Call of the Wild
> Nature will be your neighbor.
> Higher than any hotel in the Alps.
> Above troubleline and near timberline and snow.
> The place to meet Long's Peak
>   and see the Rockies.
> TRAILS to the silent places
> and the heights.
> Evergreens and their rich aroma.
> No consumptives taken.
> The house stands by a mountain
>   brook in a wild flower garden.
> Fringed blue gentians and columbines.
> Comfort and home flavored meals.
> Pine knots blaze in the big fireplace.
>   Enos A. Mills
> Estes Park   Colorado[2]

The "Call of the Wild" had become an appealing catch phrase with the appearance of Jack London's popular novel in 1903. The book's message, portrayed through animals, was that life's sagging

Longs Peak Inn in its heyday, c. 1920. *Denver Public Library, Western History Department.*

vitality could be restored by a return to outdoor values and experiences. Response to that craving in a nation feeling middle-aged after the frontier experience had ended spurred a prolific growth of country inns, dude ranches, and outdoor organizations. Americans physically and mentally worn down by the fast-moving and competitive industrial era turned eagerly to outdoor recreation, and Theodore Roosevelt, president since 1900, epitomized the new rugged vitality. Muir was busy selling the concept of national parks to restore a tired and nerve-shattered American public, while Mills offered an inspirational hospice on the edge of what would later be the national park of his own vision. But Longs Peak Inn, though a nature haven, was not to be a sanitarium, and Mills's advertisement sandwiched a ban on consumptives between his lush phrases in praise of the inn's attractions.

For Mills's guests to discover the tranquil contemplation of nature, they had to leave conventional diversions behind. A poster in the lobby forbade music, dancing, and card playing, while dogs and guns were not allowed on the property at all. Such apparent austerity branded Longs Peak Inn as peculiar and Mills as something of a curmudgeon in Estes Park business circles. But Mills already knew plenty about tourists' vacation habits from his early days at the Elkhorn, from his work at Longs Peak House under Carlyle Lamb, and from writing Estes Park social news for Denver newspapers in the late nineties. He saw people having their vacation fun and returning home unchanged to face another year on life's grindstone. Recreation for Mills went realms beyond card-playing and into that exalted domain of personal expansion that he called "seriously splendid business." There were plenty of other inns offering conventional diversions and there were enough guests unbothered by the Longs Peak Inn's proscriptions to keep the place full. Those who objected left for more familiar surroundings or broke the rules and were asked to leave.

Earl Harding's discovery that he forgot "all dreads, fears, and limitations of life" when Mills guided him up Longs Peak was representative of the transformative experience Mills personally gave to many. And this accolade from a past guest bespeaks the tranquillity of a Longs Peak Inn vacation: "He [the letter writer's friend] said in all his Eastern and European travels he has never struck such a restful place as your inn and its surroundings and influences."[3]

Mills's frequent morning greeting, "Glad you're living?" may have been for some too forced a show of optimism. But on the whole, the Longs Peak host brilliantly carried off his ambition to be a guide in the larger sense, and many came away like Harding feeling "the triumph of high resolve." Among Mills's guests were many of high professional standing — not the sort to take their inspirational cues from a mere zealot. Mills's profoundly sincere commitment to nature stamped him with a fascinating individualism, and it was on the strength of his personality that Longs Peak Inn flourished.

Short of Longs Peak itself, the surrounding mountains offered abundant hiking destinations, and Mills hoped that all would at least see the tumbling brooks, the quiet, bird-filled forests, the graphic frontier of timberline, the stark and delicately beautiful alpine tundra, and "utterly wild" Chasm Lake. Part of the experience he preached was to care for nature as well as to enjoy it, and he set the tone with a plea for protecting wildflowers. A sign on his grounds proclaimed:

You can keep this region a beautiful wild garden.
Spare the flowers. Thoughtless people are destroying
the flowers by pulling them by the roots
and picking too many. Neither the roots
nor the leafy stalks should be taken, and flowers,
if taken, should be cut, not pulled.
WHAT DO YOU WANT WITH AN ARMFUL OF WILD FLOWERS?[4]

Turn-of-the-century nature fanciers were used to bringing home large bouquets of flowers, and could even take Sunday railroad excursions into the Rockies for just that purpose. Thanks to Mills and others, the new morality was getting around. In the Tahosa Valley it was soon taken up by Charles Hewes, a poet and nearby innkeeper. But there were, rhymed Hewes, a few valid uses for carefully picked wildflowers: to "fair adorn the votive vase, the dining hours, blossoms on a maiden's breast, a bridal shower — all functions appropriate to social power."[5] Mills's limited version of that — adorning Longs Peak Inn's dining hours — was a single flower on each table. That simple touch seems for Mills's time to have been novel and widely admired. And the small gesture somehow brought the presence of Enos Mills to each table.

As for the food itself, Mills was a stickler for excellence. The result was a bill of fare "equal to any first class city hotel." Nay, better, wrote one enthusiast. It was "equal in fact to the old farmhouse dinner fare, for on the place is produced the milk, cream, butter, chickens, eggs, and vegetables that satisfy so well your Estes Park appetite." The food was wholesomely American, the quantities adequate for any appetite.[6] Chickens were butchered, plucked, and cleaned by the kitchen staff; meat hung in quarters in a walk-in ice box and was cut into roasts or individual servings. Cooking was done on three wood-fired ranges and in separate baking ovens. Renowned house specialties were fried chicken and raspberry jam. Raspberry jam sandwiches were also part of the box lunches prepared for hikers and sold to nonguests who stopped at the inn to register for peak ascents. The box lunches also contained roast beef sandwiches, raisins, an orange, and a piece of chocolate, and were supposed to "furnish all the nourishment needed on the trip [up Longs Peak] without loading you down." Mills of course still had his raisin gospel, having written in *Early Estes Park* (1905) that "for lunch, everything except raisins may be excluded." His advice did not specify whether a raisin-only lunch should be preceded by a beefsteak breakfast.

In his habitually close supervision of the kitchen — he was a martinet in petty details — he insisted that even flour be left out of the pie crusts. His objections to unhealthful food made him hotly opposed to the rampant abuses in the food industry and a proponent of the federal controls just then being enacted. He lashed out at food adulterers, and in *Early Estes Park* he noted that among the varied political and religious beliefs represented locally were "Agnostics, Socialists, and food cranks." The remark was no doubt a wry reference to himself on all three counts.

Mills liked his coffee strong and served it that way to his guests (strong enough to float a battleship, said one). Many diluted it with hot water. Mills must have craved the chemical boost of caffeine just as Muir did from drinking infusions of strong tea. As for alcohol, Mills revealed little about his personal habits. Longs Peak Inn was dry, but that was not unusual, for prohibition was a Progressive ideal and became Colorado law in 1916. Mills's home state of Kansas was the first state — in 1880 — to write prohibition into its state constitution. Mills nevertheless seemed to have some liking for the stuff. His good friend Irving Hale — a decorated Spanish-American War veteran, a ranking figure in the Progressive Movement, and a friend of President Theodore Roosevelt's — teasingly recalled an inebriated Enos Mills in a 1905 letter:

> I am pleased to receive your letter and to learn that you are jayhawking the jayhawkers in good shape and presumably having a good Christmas time at your old home, but am sadly grieved from your failure to sign the letter that you have apparently not entirely emerged from under the table as a result of that champagne banquet early last week or have gone under the table again under the exhilarating atmosphere of Carrie Nation's district. I hope however that you will thoroughly recover before starting East into regions where they demand a steady aim.[7]

Evening meals at Longs Peak Inn were often cooked and served outdoors, and guests sometimes gathered for marshmallow roasts around a bonfire. Mills led after-dinner walks, often to a nearby beaver pond. On the urging of his guests, he began and finally made a regular tradition of evening fireside talks. Flushed and relaxed from a day outdoors, the guests listened to Mills's firsthand accounts of all-season adventuring in the high Rockies, the marvelous ways of birds and beasts, and sometimes a dab of poetry to round things off. Guests sometimes followed Mills with presentations on science, travel, or literature.

As a vacation gathering spot for prominent people from all over the country, Longs Peak Inn and Estes Park generally could generate impressive fireside culture. Even the local residents had a well-functioning discussion group that Mills rated as a good literary country society. With the guest list at Longs Peak Inn including nationally prominent politicians, judges, publishers, writers, physicians, entertainers, financiers, and professors "as thick as peas in a pod," Mills's talks had to have substance and solid expertise behind their informality. Nevertheless, employees listening from the top of the stairs sometimes had to suppress their laughs as Mills seemed to be "taking in the green Easterners with his 'tall tales.'" But "looking back," wrote one of the inn's employees many years later, "I think he was giving some good talks and knew more than we thought."[8]

Among the luminaries reputed to have stayed at the inn were publishers Russell Doubleday, George Horace Lorimer, and William Allen White; novelists Edna Ferber and Gene Stratton Porter; foreign correspondent and news commentator Lowell Thomas; actors Cornelia and Otis Skinner and Douglas Fairbanks, Sr.; architect Frank Lloyd Wright; surgeons William and Charles Mayo; social activists Jane Addams, Helen Keller, and Eugene Debs (five-time socialist presidential candidate); criminal lawyer, social reformer, and writer Clarence Darrow; oil magnate, philanthropist and national park promoter John D. Rockefeller; New York governor, U.S. secretary of state, and later chief justice of the Supreme Court, Charles Evans Hughes; naturalists Frank Chapman, David Starr Jordan, Vernon Kellogg, Edward Orton, Jr., and Julia Ellen Rogers (but not, to Mills's regret, John Muir, who never traveled to Colorado); and Mary Belle King Sherman, national park promoter, conservation chairwoman, and later president of the National Federation of Women's Clubs. Important acquaintanceships also began at the inn, where, for example, Lorimer met Adelaide Neall, who became his faithful associate at the *Saturday Evening Post* for more than a quarter century.

Other inns had their evening talks, nature walks, and guided trips up Longs Peak as well as their dances, music, and merry making. It was in the nature of Enos Mills to remain a purist and not to see the possibility that dancing could compatibly follow the quiet contemplation of nature or singing follow a peak climb. As Mills's reputation as a speaker steadily grew — he was soon on a national lecture circuit — there was almost a sense that attendance at his talks was compulsory. To skip a Mills talk and travel down the road to a dance at another inn was an unforgivable affront, and legends have trickled down to our time of an irate Enos Mills summarily expelling such frivolously disloyal guests.

Mills also held his guests rigidly to his ban on tipping. Mills and Lamb had been permanently disenchanted with tipping on their tour of Europe, and upon acquiring Longs Peak House Mills had immediately established it as a "non-tip house." If the dining room supervisor saw guests leave money on the table, she gathered it up as soon as they left and returned it with a gentle reminder of the rule. Only twice did Mills accept a tip, both while guiding on Longs Peak. A millionaire who disrupted Mills's entire day and cost him another guiding job, tipped him a minuscule twenty-five cents; and a woman who insisted that Mills had saved her life during a storm prevailed on him — fortunately with humor — to accept $1.00 as the fair price for the value of her life.[9]

Mills's staff — totaling about thirty-five by 1915 — were held to high standards of conduct, but they were not supposed to develop slick professional polish. Male waiters (always students or teachers), supervised by a female dining room boss, carried their trays at waist level rather than over their shoulders. Tree stumps located around the room were their serving stations. They recited the meals' courses — there were no printed menus — and remembered the orders rather than writing them down.

Strict morals governed the help's off hours as well. When two young men and a young woman climbed Longs Peak by moonlight, Mills saw them returning at five A.M. and dismissed them at once. Though a champion of moonlight climbs and a foe of chaperones, Mills would not have his own help putting themselves in morally questionable situations. He did allow the help to have a phonograph in their separate eating and gathering area. The illustrious Irving Hale, after all, had spoken well of these marvelous new devices and had urged Mills to get one for himself.

Some of the inn's publicity included the wry caveat "Conversations with the proprietor extra." It was a jest, yet it signified that

(A)

Celebrities at Longs Peak Inn. Mills with: (A) Film star Douglas Fairbanks, Jr. *Courtesy, Colorado Historical Society.* (B) Labor leader Eugene Debs. *Cunningham Memorial Library, Indiana State University.* (C) Novelist Edna Ferber *(on slide). Courtesy, Enos Mills Cabin Collection.*

(B)

(C)

Mills was both important and busy. He remained closely involved in the inn's daily operations and in the supervision of its personnel and finances. Through 1906 he led dozens of trips up Longs Peak each summer and henceforth he continued leading nature walks and established nature-study facilities at the inn. As a public speaker he soon began traveling widely — mostly in the off season — and he was beginning a productive career as a writer. But he retained, wrote Esther Burnell Mills, "the marvellous faculty of never seeming hurried, of giving the impression that his entire time was at the disposal of his guests. It was as restful to meet and talk with him as to pause on one of his trails under the whisper of the pines." One guest wrote of sitting up on many evenings with Mills until nearly two A.M. — evenings that were "treats" and "more than that, they were inspirations."[10]

After his breathtaking feat of guiding thirty-three parties up Longs Peak in August 1906, Mills turned his energies to other tasks and turned the guiding operation over to one Shep Husted. Husted had come to Estes Park in 1898 and worked as a Forest Service ranger for two years before becoming a professional wrangler and guide. Mills chose his chief guide well, for Husted quickly mastered the art of combining climbing and nature guiding, and in fact became an expert self-taught naturalist. Called by Mills "a prince on the trail," Shep's great genuineness of character was appreciatively remembered by such luminaries as Charles Evans Hughes, Edna Ferber, Otis Skinner, and the Doctors Mayo.[11]

Many other guides learned their trade at Longs Peak Inn, following the standard set by Mills and carried on by Husted. Among them was Mills's younger brother, Joe, who had arrived on the scene from Kansas to help both in guiding and in running the business. In virtually the only reference to Joe in all his published writings, Mills in *Early Estes Park* called Joe the "versatile Beau Bummel [sic] of the guides." "Beau Brummell," signifying a dandy, was perhaps only brotherly teasing, but it signaled a difference in personal style that foreshadowed the serious trouble soon to erupt between them.

If anyone surpassed Mills's diligence as a host, it was Scotch, the short-nosed Collie. One guest wrote:

> Scotch was no less the host than was his master. He welcomed the coming and sped the parting guest. He escorted the climbers to the beginning of the trail up Longs Peak. He kept the burros on the other side of

Mills and Scotch, "co-hosts" of Longs Peak Inn. *Courtesy, Enos Mills Cabin Collection.*

the brook. He stood between the coyotes and the inhabitants of the chicken yard. He was always ready to play football for the entertainment of the guests after dinner. He was really the busiest person about the inn from morning till night.[12]

Scotch was above all gifted, and nearly human in intuitive intelligence. He could open the gate and could play a masterful game of hide and seek, with obvious powers of make-believe. His engaging personality won everyone's heart, and, Mills wrote, "though Scotch admitted very few to the circle of his intimate friends, he was admired, respected, and loved by thousands."[13]

Scotch's daring exploits with Mills supplied material for many a talk and written story, and to those he added some valor on the home front as well. When a toddling baby strayed away, it was found a quarter mile away with Scotch as both protector and pillow. When a young woman wanted to climb the peak alone, Mills agreed but sent Scotch along for security. Overtaken by clouds and darkness on the descent, she lost the route despite Scotch's growling attempts to correct her course. Marooned at an impasse, she hugged Scotch tightly all night to keep from freezing. When found by searchers at sunrise, she confessed that if she had paid attention to her companion, she would have easily made it home.

The heroic dog who saved Mills's life in a forest fire was an exact contemporary of Johnny and Jenny and was briefly larger than his playmate grizzlies. An indispensable fixture at the inn for eight years and a born fighter of fires, Scotch met his end trying to extinguish the burning fuse of a dynamite charge set by a road crew. "He was instantly killed," wrote Mills as the final sentence of his 1916 booklet chronicling the life of this gallant dog. Abrupt endings were often Mills's way of plucking his readers' heartstrings, particularly when tragic outcomes were caused by human negligence and deserved a moment's reflection.

On a late afternoon in June 1906, Longs Peak Inn burned to the ground while Mills was lecturing in Minnesota. The fire was discovered at 5:30 P.M. and quickly threatened to spread to the entire cluster of buildings. The cook and one other person narrowly escaped, with only the clothes on their backs. Joe Mills was at the post office and did not reach home until an hour after the fire was discovered. Well-placed dynamite blasts diverted the fire and saved some of the surrounding buildings. The total loss was $4,500, only $925 of it covered by insurance.

Irving Hale notified Mills of the fire by telegram, and, on returning home, the two exchanged several letters on the disaster. Mills wrote that most of his important personal effects had been safe in his own cabin, but that some of his notebooks, picture books, and 100 large negatives were destroyed, along with 200 copies of *Early Estes Park*. "I am not discouraged," he said. "I still have health, scenery, love of nature, and intense love of life. These should be enough for anyone." A few days later he wrote: "The most startling thing connected with me and the fire is that it effected [sic] me so little. Still, this manner is in accord with my past emergencies. I believe the ultimate result of the fire will be great good for me — development."[14]

Mills told Hale of his plans to start rebuilding immediately, hoping to complete at least the kitchen and dining areas within a month. That much, Hale surmised, would be covered by his insurance, for within recent years homestead cabins had been built for as little as $100. Hale guessed that the outcome would ultimately benefit Mills's business by stimulating him to expand his facilities to meet the demands brought by his own growing reputation.

Rebuilding Longs Peak Inn gave Mills the opportunity to express his deep bondedness with nature in a simple rustic design

(A)

Interior of the rebuilt inn: (A) The famous rustic staircase. (B) The inn's lobby, where Mills gave his popular fireside talks. *Denver Public Library, Western History Department.*

(B)

and to satisfy his always latent artistic urges as well. Throughout the interior he used twisted, gnarled, and fire-burnished logs colored and preserved by their own heat-extracted resin. The split-log stairway rising to the twenty-bedroom upstairs had heavy broken roots for posts and banister spindles made of dwarfed timberline trees. A twelve-foot-diameter tree root whose interlaced segments resembled a huge spiderweb was positioned near a window and cast filigree shadows on the floor. The fireplaces were of rough stone, the furniture handmade and unpainted. The atmosphere, Mills said, conveyed "restful forest aisles," and one guest even noted a nesting robin among the logs near his dining table. "[Mills] will never lack a monument while this lodge stands," wrote one close friend. "Into [it] he threw all his intense energy, all his money, all his fierce craving for self-expression, all his genius, and all his sense of the fitting and proper."[15]

The new inn was solid but not ponderous and had plentiful windows with spectacular views. It "did not frighten the peaks and scenery of the nearby mountains," Mills wrote. "Both the lines and color of this structure allowed it to stand in the little high mountain valley as though it were a cliff . . . shaped by the same slow-acting elemental forces that had shaped the region." Those could have been the words of Frank Lloyd Wright, who about that same year had scanned the Wisconsin hills for a homesite "where the rock came cropping out in strata to suggest buildings." Wright had begun as early as 1894 to insist that nature must supply architecture's basic inspiration. His poetic prescriptions — "architecture [is] something in league with the stones of the field"; "hill and house should live together, each the happier for the other"; "architecture . . . is no less a weaving and a fabric than the trees"; and so forth — were the notions of a kindred spirit that Mills had undoubtedly discovered in his wide-ranging attentiveness to contemporary trends and some personal acquaintance with Wright.[16]

Mills's new promotional literature called the Longs Peak Inn "the most artistically rustic inn in America." The slight sense of oxymoron — that rusticity was a quality consciously contrived rather than native to simple circumstances — did not escape Mills. When he finally got around to describing the conception and construction of the inn in a 1921 magazine article, he stressed that the design avoided both "conspicuous craftsmanship" and "striving for effect."

"Simple lines produc[ing] substantial and pleasing results" was the intent, and what resulted was not so much artistically attained rusticity as "a good combination of the two."[17]

Irving Hale proved right, and Longs Peak Inn grew and flourished in parallel with Mills's own reputation. In 1908 Mills built a ten-room cabin in the same rustic style and called it Forest House. In 1909 he built a three-room cabin for himself and in 1911 a dozen new guest cabins, some with steam heat (for the Boston people, someone said) and some with simpler facilities for lower budgets. In 1912 telephone service came to the Tahosa Valley, and by 1916 Mills had built still more cabins, expanded the inn's living and dining rooms, and added electricity.

The Estes Park area was growing rapidly. A local paper wrote in June 1908 that "there is more building going on in Estes Park at this time than ever before in its history. No matter which way you look, you will see a new building going up, a hotel, a cottage, or a business house." One hotel begun that summer was designed by the master himself, Frank Lloyd Wright. Wright's plans alone convinced the local press that the hotel would be "a part of the beautiful landscape, rather than a mar upon it, as is so often the case with summer hotels."[18] Quite the opposite, and completed in 1909, was the Stanley Hotel, a large white neo-Georgian structure resembling much of the resort architecture of the East Coast. Though the Stanley was candidly unrelated to its setting, it bespoke a refined gentility that was another side to Estes Park tourist life. And its owner, Freelan O. Stanley, was withal an ardent nature lover with whom Enos Mills would find a close and productive rapport.

Mills's calling cards retained the call-of-the-wild theme, which was evidently giving him good mileage. And by referring again to the inn's high-altitude location — "nearer the sky than any hotel in Europe" — he was playing on a popular See America First theme that glorified American mountains at the expense of the famous Swiss Alps. One other promotional phrase was noteworthy: Mills's inclusion of the famous Medicine Bow National Forest among the region's special places revealed his belief that national forests protect scenic beauty and thus enhance the commercial base of the vacation industry. But Mills eventually had his illusions about the Medicine Bow National Forest dashed. As utilitarian uses of the forest began to dominate and to spoil its natural beauty, Mills belatedly joined

Muir in opposing Forest Service policy and practice. Carving an unspoiled national park out of the Medicine Bow National Forest would pit Mills in bitter controversy with both local forest administrators and the whole agency that he served loyally under Roosevelt from 1907 to 1909.

CHAPTER 11

The Snowman: Mills and Western Water

When Enos Mills groped his way back to the Continental Divide from a midcliff ledge where he had plunged on a collapsing snow cornice, he was on official business for the State of Colorado and the U.S. Department of Agriculture. For three winters, beginning in 1902–1903, he bore the title State Snow Observer and was commissioned to measure the mountain snowpack along the headwaters of major watersheds. Known already as the "Snow Man," who appeared out of blizzards at mining camps and isolated homesteads, Mills was now a snowman with official duties. In discharging those duties with his unrivaled outdoor skills, he became a Rocky Mountain legend known to thousands.

The snowman was not merely a curiosity. He was part of the great drama of water that has marked the West's history from its beginning. Even by the turn of the century more water was wanted than was available, and the amount that flowed in summer was seen to depend in large measure on the amount stored in mountain snowpacks. The Newlands Act of 1902 had created what was hailed as the "New West" — a homeseeker's ideal for climate, soil, irrigation, and industry, where hundreds of thousands could settle in areas irrigated by federal reclamation projects and as many more could find employment in consequence of that. Colorado, once thought to be only a mining state, was now producing more wealth from crops than from metals.

Virtually beneath the spot where Mills stood when he regained the Continental Divide after his near-fatal plunge, water would flow half a century later through a tunnel in the state's largest west-to-east diversion scheme. The 300,000 acre-feet-per-year Big Thompson

Project was started in the 1930s under Franklin Roosevelt but was not completed until 1947 — twenty-five years after Mills's death and two years before his rebuilt and rustic Longs Peak Inn burned to the ground and passed into history.

But even where Mills stood on that day in 1904 there were signs of what was to come. Running along the divide close to that same spot was a small ditch built only a summer or two earlier to carry meltwater from West Slope snowbanks to a tributary of the Big Thompson River. The fractionally enlarged Big Thompson flowed through Estes Park and down onto the plains, where the ditch partners took out what the ditch had put in — all according to legislated rules of water appropriation. And off to the northwest Mills could see the course of a larger ditch — called the Grand Ditch — traversing the forested slopes of the Never Summer mountains. That ditch, built in the late 1880s, carried water through another gap in the Continental Divide and still flows today.

Even in the remotest reaches of Wild Basin — one of Mills's favorite grizzly-tracking haunts — three lakes had been dammed the summer before to raise their levels and supply lowland farmers with late-summer water. Wherever Mills wandered in Colorado's high mountains he saw that water was a scarce commodity.

Mills's father might have been one of the early practitioners of irrigation in Colorado had he not had a successful farm to return to in Kansas after he found poor diggings in the gold boom of the late 1850s. Spanish-American farmers had begun irrigation and ditch-building in southern Colorado well before 1850, but a new wave began when unsuccessful miners stayed to farm rather than drift back East. Of the more than 20,000 able-bodied men who inhabited Colorado by 1860, many had farming skills and quickly saw the logic of watering crops with the mountain streams that flowed out onto the arid plains.

By the early 1860s, the tributaries of the South Platte were irrigating food and hay crops for the mining regions. Farther south along the Arkansas River, developments were slower because the great cattle barons still controlled the surrounding lands. During the silver boom of the seventies, new surges of population made demands on agriculture that surpassed the limits of individual irrigation projects, and both cooperation and capital were needed for larger-scale operations.

"The Snow Man." *Courtesy, Enos Mills Cabin Collection.*

Cooperative colonies sprang up as the most successful response. The first and most prominent was the famous Union Colony, founded in 1870 by an intense social idealist named Nathan Meeker, agricultural editor of the *New York Tribune*. He chose the confluence of the Poudre and South Platte rivers — near present-day Greeley — as the site for the colony on the suggestion of a fellow farmer-journalist, William Byers. Savvy about the needs of western agriculture, Byers used his paper, the *Rocky Mountain News,* to advise Colorado farmers about irrigation, and he was eager to see Meeker's experiment succeed.

The Union Colony built a thirty-mile ditch and brought over 17,000 acres under cultivation. As a social experiment the colony flourished as well. Its communal structure contrasted starkly with the feudalistic system of the great cattle barons, whose rule of the high plains in northeastern Colorado was in rapid decline. When Colorado became a state in 1876, it was the first to include principles of water allocation in its constitution. The Greeley Colony provided much of the needed expertise and some of the early state engineers who administered the state's water laws.

The nineteen years of Mills's life in Colorado before his assignment as the state's first snow observer no doubt impressed upon him the importance of water throughout the West. His adopted state — as poet laureate Thomas Hornsby Ferril's poem in the state capitol building would later proclaim — was "a land where life is written in water." In 1889, Frederick Chapin reported in his book *Mountaineering in Colorado* that he could see thirty-five lakes on the plains from Mummy Mountain near Estes Park. Those lakes were artificial reservoirs and were evidence that the normal flow of the rivers no longer met all irrigation needs. Reservoirs were needed to store water from spring runoff, summer storms, and water beginning to be brought over the mountains from the wetter and less settled western slope.

Mills saw cities beginning to compete with agriculture for a share of the water. He saw some farmland turned to alkaline waste from over-irrigation without proper drainage. He witnessed the brief era of dryland farming in the late 1880s, when hardy homesteaders, living mostly in sod huts, grew crops without irrigation on the eastern Colorado plains. He saw withering droughts in the early nineties drive most of them out. And as the climate extremes leveled off, he saw those who stayed establish dryland techniques as a valuable supplement to irrigation, often on the same farm. While assisting primarily the irrigation interests of the state, Mills never forgot the importance of dryland farming and had wise words of counsel for it as a public conservationist in the years after 1906. The greatest issue for Mills, however, was the appalling damage done to Colorado's forest watersheds by mining, timbering, and a seemingly limitless number of forest fires caused by humans. It was that concern that he would carry most prominently into his public years of conservationist activity.

The Newlands Act of 1902 ended a period of frustration for the state, which had tried unsuccessfully to sponsor large-scale water diversion projects and had sought federal assistance since the late 1880s. Popular Teddy Roosevelt was hailed as a hero of western reclamation. "Colorado has the foundation and influences for developing a race of Roosevelts," rejoiced former two-term governor Alva Adams. "This place," he said, "[was] held fallow by divine providence until the new art of irrigation could come along and make [it] the new land of prophecy and revelation."[1]

So it was in the opening years of the New West when Enos Mills strapped on his snowshoes and tramped hundreds of miles through the high mountains of Colorado to measure snow for water resource forecasts. Forward-looking and himself a champion of the developing West, attracted to socialism but more broadly aligned with the Progressive Movement and the ideals of Roosevelt, Mills saw his place in Colorado's water destiny from his vantage point on the state's wintry peaks. The stored water that he measured flowed in summer through hundreds of measuring gates and into thousands of miles of canals and local ditches that had already been established. The Gunnison and Uncompahgre rivers, at whose headwaters he measured the snowpack, would soon be linked by a tunnel, as federal money came to the rescue of a project that had faltered under state funding. Federal projects proliferated throughout the West and would dominate water-planning strategy for the next seventy-five years. But dam building and water diversion schemes would gradually engender environmental opposition. One of the first to object was John Muir, who from 1907 until the end of his life fought a losing battle to stop the flooding of Hetch Hetchy Valley in Yosemite National Park. For Mills, as the Colorado snowman, those controversies did not yet exist. The forest itself was nature's great reservoir, and preserving it was his chief concern.

Mills's employer was Louis G. Carpenter, the state's ninth engineer and head of the country's first college-level irrigation department at the agricultural college in Ft. Collins. Carpenter was an international figure in the water field whose pamphlets had been translated into several foreign languages. He received honors from the French government in 1895 and again at the Paris Exposition in 1900. A scholar of breadth, he was an authority on the Italian Renaissance who cultivated contacts throughout the world and was an expert on Colorado history who later served a term as president of the Colorado Historical Society. He was the erudite translator of da Vinci manuscripts and owned the most complete collection of da Vinci first editions in the United States at the time of his death in 1935. A remarkable man, in short, whom Mills had every reason to admire. In a reverential fragment of an essay, Mills called him the "master of irrigation."[2]

Mills's official reports to Carpenter — written as letters — reveal an earnest and diligent snow observer. They show Mills's delight in being part of a scientific process wherein his penchant for measuring and counting had an application and his vast skills as a mountaineer were called on to the fullest extent. He covered impressive itineraries to get representative snow data, yet reported matter of factly:

> I went from home S.W. four miles and up to an altitude of 10,000 feet: thence from home up the S. Poudre to Chambers Lake: then S.E. to a point on the N.W. slope of Hague's Peak about 13,000 feet: S.W. to ditch camp — Grand — about 10,500 ft., Southward to summit of Specimen mountain then turning west near Poudre Lakes to North fork of Grand-Pacaiic [sic] slope — then timberline on Lead mountain, Richthofen and Lulu pass. From this pass 22 miles southward down N. Fork to Grand Lake: four miles N.E. to Big Meadows then S.W. to Lehman, Coulter, then S.E. to Berthoud Pass and Empire. Total traveled between home and Empire about 170 miles; 70 miles of this was on show shoes.[3]

Keeping track of his wanderings, the press reported during that trip:

> Feb. 19, 1904 — The state snow inspector, Enos A. Mills, came in here this evening after sleeping last night in the woods at timberline on Lulu Pass. . . . On Monday morning, he left the source of the Poudre River and worked his way southward along the Medicine Bow range and the

Continental Divide. Twice he climbed up as high as 13,000 feet and three times crossed the summit of the range. He spent one night in a deserted cabin and one night by a campfire and was caught in a storm yesterday on the summit of Specimen Mountain. With the exception of a slightly frostbitten finger, he is in excellent condition.[4]

Mills roamed extensively through the headwaters of the South Platte and Arkansas, through the high, steep Sangre de Cristo range that separates the Arkansas and Rio Grande watersheds, and through the San Juan mountains where half a dozen major tributaries of the Colorado River arise. He traveled by snowshoe, foot, horseback, and sometimes on narrow gauge trains. Colorado's narrow gauges formed one of the most extensive mountain railroad systems in the world and allowed him to get a quick overview of the snowpack through large areas. Railroad personnel could often tell him how typical the snowpack was, and other local opinions — if he considered them reliable — entered his reports. The winter of 1903–1904 was so dry that the postmaster's well in the mountain town of Alma gave no water for the first time in twenty years. And in that winter Mills made his entire 140-mile trek through the Sangre de Cristo range without once using his snowshoes. When he did travel over deep snow he occasionally used skis but preferred snowshoes, which were easier to strap on his back when he crossed dry areas, rode horseback, or boarded trains.

Mills went over some of the same areas at least twice per winter and sometimes recorded snow depth at the same spots in consecutive years. More often, he measured the snowpack at many locations and then reported averages. He also melted sample snow cores and reported wide variations — six to twenty inches — in the amount of snow needed to yield an inch of water. He included weather summaries for some of his trips and interesting sidelights such as descriptions of hollow air chambers beneath unstable snowpacks and a lengthy period of strong electrical activity in May 1905. The practice of measuring snow depth and water content on key watersheds remains a vital activity in the Colorado Rockies. By the 1970s, the U.S. Soil Conservation Department in cooperation with state agencies was operating more than 100 snow courses and gathering additional data from automated SNOWTEL stations, which transmit measurements to a central recording station.

Mills often inspected forest conditions from horseback and narrow-gauge trains. *Courtesy, Enos Mills Cabin Collection.*

The records are not complete enough to show whether Mills followed specific snow courses and consistently recorded annual and interannual variations. Nor does any official record remain of the trek he said he made along the Continental Divide from the Wyoming to the New Mexico line — a sinuous 600 miles of high-altitude terrain. What is resoundingly evident in Mills's reports, however, is the deplorable condition in which he found Colorado's forests. Wherever he went the picture was the same:

From Lulu to Grand Lake — 18 miles — almost all the bordering forest of the stream has been burned, and I think that fully 50% of the original tree growth of the watershed of the North Grand [now the Colorado] has been burned over.

In the Arkansas watershed:

Ragged trees and scattered growth are all that remain of the once wide and deep forests. . . . Only about 20% of what was growing in 1860 remains.

In the Sangre de Cristo range:

About 20% of the original forest remains and of that only about half is of the original best. Over the shoulder of Sierra Blanca to Huerfano, fire has killed most of the spruce which was once very thick.

In the San Juans:

Use and fire have extensively deforested. . . . Many wide and long areas [are] deforested by fire. . . . The timber [is] scattered and sickly. . . . The best timber has been culled out for use.

And back on his home turf of Estes Park:

Forest fires, slash, and sawmills have stripped the Big Thompson of the greater portion of its forest covering. Below 8,500 feet, there is no forest protection.[5]

In the West, mining and timbering interests as well as many individual settlers opposed forest protection on the grounds that it thwarted development. They waged a bitter campaign against it from the establishment of the first federal reserves in the early nineties. The forests Mills tramped through on his long winter treks were forests under contention, and the battle between opposing forces reached its bitter climax in precisely those same years, 1903 to 1905.

Though the need to preserve forest watersheds required continuous stressing in the timber-ravaged West, it was a principle known from ancient times and forcefully restated in George Perkins Marsh's 1864 book *Man and Nature: or Physical Geography as Modified by Human Action.* Marsh argued that forest cover prevents drought, flooding, erosion, and unfavorable climate changes, and cited the environmentally damaged Mediterranean empires as a graphic example. His influence helped bring about the establishment of the Adirondack Reserve — one of the country's first forest reserves — to protect the watershed that sustained New York State's canal transportation system. Equating forest protection with economic progress was an argument that Muir and other early preservationists rapidly embraced. The state's irrigation interests lay strongly on the side of forest protection, and Carpenter did not hesitate to make that clear from his high position. He wrote, and later repeated in a talk to the influential Denver Chamber of Commerce, that "the preservation of the forest is an absolute necessity for the interest of irrigated agriculture."[6]

Mills undoubtedly recognized the importance of forest watersheds as soon as he knew Muir and had perhaps read Marsh's book long before Irving Hale gave him a copy in about 1905. Despite Carpenter's international fame and focused expertise, Mills, with unflagging loyalty, cited Muir as "probably the greatest authority concerning the relation of forests and stream flow." Later as a public lecturer he often repeated Muir's warning: "Cut down the groves and the streams will vanish." And in his own writings Mills would later call the relation of forests to stream flow "one of the most impressive facts in all nature."[7]

Ranking by now as something of an authority on beavers, Mills urged Carpenter to consider their contribution to maintaining watershed stability. Action was beginning in Montana, the Dakotas, and New York State to repopulate streams with beaver, which had been nearly exterminated throughout the United States by the fur trade which had peaked in the 1880s. Mills wrote to Carpenter that the first settlers in the Leadville area had found, besides heavy forests, as many as fifty beaver dams along each mile of the Arkansas River's high mountain tributaries. The mining boom and fires that reduced 75 percent of the forests to "charcoal ruins" also destroyed the ponds and swamps that stored immense amounts of water. Now, Mills said, the streams "hurry unimpeded away."[8]

The Arkansas in fact hurried away toward Kansas more quickly than Coloradans liked. Forgetting that God established river systems but not state boundaries, zealous Colorado patriots proclaimed that any drop of water allowed to leave the state was a wasted gift of God intended for Colorado's own prosperity. With natural mountain watersheds greatly reduced, Coloradans tried to empty as much of the Arkansas as they could in the lowland agricultural areas. In 1902 Kansas brought suit against Colorado, and the case was heard by the U.S. Supreme Court in 1907. Though each state could control the waters within its own boundaries — Carpenter prepared Colorado's defense of that — the high court also said that no state could dispose of all the water of interstate rivers. That "equitable apportionment doctrine" led the way to interstate water compacts throughout the West in coming years.

Mills said that Carpenter's instructions on hiring him as snow observer included a warning "not to lose my life." Perhaps Carpenter had premonitions or knew about Mills's habitual risk-taking. The mountaineer uniquely suited to gathering the data Carpenter wanted had come close to losing his life a score of times already and would, in fact, continue flirting with death on his snow-observing missions. His fall through a fractured cornice was only the first near miss in that wild medley of events cited in chapter 5. Some of Mills's winter escapades with Scotch — acquired in 1903 — must also have been snow-observing missions, and his winter ascent of Blanca Peak, delirious from drinking poisoned water, was part of a snow survey in 1903–1904. Several other close calls with avalanches and at least one near-drowning are probably traceable to his snow-observing winters as well. Awaiting the arrival of Mills and his reports, Carpenter must have fretted over the press accounts coming in from the mountain towns. One was headlined "Perilous Trip":

Jan. 5, 1903 — A six-day walk of 120 miles over the snow-covered mountains was the trying experience of Enos A. Mills, a deputy of the state engineer's office, while inspecting the headwaters of the Platte. Mr. Mills was recently caught in severe snowstorms, and while groping blindly over the ranges several times narrowly escaped death. The doughty engineer has just reached the city, tanned from exposure, but in good condition.[9]

The poetic rapture that catalyzed Mills's risk-taking probably peaked during his snow-observing winters, and it carried over to his first winter ascent of Longs Peak in February 1903 and his daring descent of the peak's east face the following June. Already feeling the load of his new innkeeping business, he perhaps sensed that his outdoor adventures would soon be curtailed and sought one last time to fill his cup to the brim. He later recalled his snow-observer years as the happiest of his life, a time when poetic living required only a few ingredients. Of a typical day he wrote: "At timberline . . . I built a camp-fire and without bedding spent the night . . . [then] climbed several peaks, took many photographs, measured many snowdrifts, and made many notes in my notebook."[10]

Little wonder that Earl Harding and other summer guests of Longs Peak Inn were so infected by Mills's life-affirming presence and his heady personal-growth resolves. Beneath the wonderful adventuring and scientific importance of his winter job lay his growing self-awareness as a public figure. The summer guests whom he impressed saw in him not merely a daring mountain rustic but also a many-sided expert whose skills were needed in the pursuit of the public good. That acknowledgment gave depth to Mills's self-confidence and later during his lecture tours gave weight to his messages about nature and conservation.

Mills also had direct literary returns from his treks. He began sending articles to Denver publications under the byline State Snow Observer, and although he already had it in his head to be a writer, Carpenter's encouragement may have helped him along. That assumption remained a matter of record thirty years later in Carpenter's 1935 *Denver Post* obituary: "It was while he was state engineer from 1903 to 1905 that he employed the late Enos Mills as a snow observer, was impressed by striking phrases in Mills' factual reports and urged him to write. . . . This encouragement aided Mills to become nationally known as a naturalist and writer."[11]

Mills found an engaging style for popularizing technical subjects. He explained to his readers how snowflakes vary, how snow is distributed around the state, how it accumulates in some places and not in others, how it varies in moisture content, and how avalanches

work and how miners cope with them. He easily found the metaphors that fit his readers' mixed urban and rural backgrounds:

> On the alpine slopes above timber the snows are drifted and redrifted,
> shifting about in the capricious winds like unstable sand dunes before
> coming to a final resting place. But as the snow swirls and eddies about
> its particles break against the ground, grind against each other and
> crush to fine powder against the rocks and cliffs. All this time the wind
> is juggling it about as though it were hay to be dried out, or for the
> purpose of sucking all the juice before letting go of the peel.[12]

These early pieces — usually published in the weekend supplements of Denver newspapers — also captured the flavor of his missions and their high-mountain locale with a particular charm and
raciness:

> One day near Alma some miners mistook me for the promoter who
> had cheated them out of their wages, and I am thankful that my agility
> enabled me to transform the impending tragedy into a rank and fleet-
> ing farce. The old rancher near Eldora amused me so much that I for-
> give him for sizing me up for a bolder character than I am. He took me
> for a horse thief and called me everything except a gentleman. But I
> forgive him, though I do not forgive the Leadville liveryman who sized
> me up for a tenderfoot and gave me a bucker which compelled me to
> amuse the hooting gang not only with rough riding but at the same
> time with a juggling exhibition with bundles, barometer, camera and
> snowshoes. This liveryman will please remember that the sworn testi-
> mony I offered concerning his character in my busy moments, still
> stands. A curious woman opened a package of my undeveloped nega-
> tives in daylight — I hope she will pardon me for exposing my temper a
> little out of focus.[13]

In other passages we see Mills fending off a pack of hostile dogs
with his snowshoes as he walked the streets of Leadville; finding
only a bear trap in the deserted main street of a mining town that
had teemed with 500 inhabitants only a few years before; and shying
away from the only boarding house in a town when he saw a sign
above the door: "This way for prayers."
There is zesty irony in seeing Mills, the successful innkeeper who
in summer catered to a cultured and educated clientele, transformed
in winter to a rank and tattered wanderer who was turned away by

hotels and once asked suspiciously, "Have you any insects on you?" We learn furthermore that Mills, who, in his later writing shrugged off near-lethal experiences as mere "entertainment," did not withstand his dangers and hardships so blithely. His nights by the fire without bedding were often interminably long. Going without food when his rations were used up took its toll. Once, after not eating for forty-eight hours and spending two rough nights by a campfire, Mills confessed that his faculties were so dulled that he mistook a schoolhouse for a ranch house. While his early pieces confess to many blunders, his 1910 story "A Colorado Snow Observer" is by contrast a string of heroic deeds showing Mills in his acquired posture of invincibility. It conspicuously lacks any meaningful discussion of the snow-observing assignment itself.

Regardless of how he presented it at the time or later, Mills craved the experience of living on the edge. He was adamant that his nights outdoors were infinitely better than "the stuffy and life-killing air of the slums." He was not afraid to say that his job, however serious its purpose, gave him an immense amount of fun. And the profound vitality that will always stand as one of the sentinel qualities of Enos Mills was always apparent to the true people of the mountains. When he snowshoed into an isolated cabin near Mosquito Pass, it took the grizzled prospector only one glance to size him up and say, "I'm glad to see one young man who isn't going to hell."[14]

CHAPTER 12

Mountain Folks of the Rockies: Mills Discovers Hidden Heroes

"Not all nights were spent outdoors," the itinerant snowman wrote. "Many a royal evening was passed in the cabin of a miner or a prospector, or by the fireside of a family who for some reason had left the old home behind and sought seclusion in wild scenes, miles from neighbors."[1] The settlers that aroused Mills's greatest admiration were well-adjusted and resourceful people who were harkening to the era's new call of the wild and beginning new lives of self-sufficiency. The old couple near Blanca Peak that nursed him through the night on herb teas were a prime example. He a former attorney general of Kansas and she a physician, these vigorous idealists had tired of public life, built a comfortable home in the wilds, stocked it with the books they had always wanted to read, and checked out from conventional society.

Mills happened onto the cabin of a professor who had taken a year off to free himself from routines and obligations, found himself unable to return after the year was over, and stayed on in his serene isolation to write a book. Another dropout professor had become a sheepherder, wanting pure outdoor simplicity and nothing more. For two young mountebanks, Colorado's wilds offered temporary seclusion while they grew long hair and prepared occult herbal mixtures to sell later in the cities.

As it had earlier in Colorado's history, health-seeking brought new settlers, and the mountains continued to attract a few "strange characters" who "had a history behind them." Mills knew from his early exposure to cowboys to obey the law of the West that respected everyone's private past. But many wanted to talk, including people who were driven into seclusion by grief. Mills said that in

Colorado's mountains there were "an unusual number of strong characters who are trying again," and trying again — for Mills a quintessential opportunity of the American West — signified a brave refusal to go down in defeat or to abandon life's ideals.[2] The stories that came out of Mills's snow-observer years showed him to be as vitally interested in Colorado's mountain people as in the mountains themselves.

"In the scattered homes in the outlying districts," he wrote in a 1904 news weekly, "there are but few whose biography is not interesting, whose lives are not instructive or ennobling." An astonishing number of the homes he saw had good books and pictures, "an aroma of refinement," and a spirit of "sincerity, hope, and repose." Many families were raising healthy, vigorous children and educating them at home. One of Mills's most inspiring acquaintances was the family of Claude E. Street, living above timberline at 12,200 feet. Both parents were college trained. They had opted for a simple mountain life and were making a subsistence living from a small mine. Most of their knowledge of mining had come from correspondence courses. Mrs. Street cooked, read widely, and schooled the boys. When Mills met them she had seen no other woman for nine months. The nearest post office was ten miles away, and the nearest doctor — never sent for — thirty miles. The boys had spent most of their lives above timberline, had no other children to play with, and had never been to school. "Brighter, braver little fellows I have never known," he wrote. "There are but few boys who have so much useful information and so little useless information." These were boys whose parents read to them, talked intelligently to them, and allowed them to explore. They knew the plants, animals, rocks, and weather of their high-mountain world. They were agile on both snowshoes and skis and, with their parents, advocated wildlife protection and had no use for firearms. "The dinner I spent with them was one of the happiest hours of my life," Mills wrote in his profile of the Streets for the *Denver Times* in January 1904.[3]

Another of Mills's mountain heroes was Perlina Zabriski, postmistress at the timberline town of Hancock, whom he featured in a January 1904 article. The fifty-year-old widow lived alone in a cabin and hand carried the mail to many of the miners. Herself a miner and prospector, she was a self-taught expert on minerals frequently consulted by others. She was skilled as a dressmaker, blacksmith, and cook, and sold bread and pies to the miners for extra income.

She was an effective conservationist who organized crews to fight forest fires and had successfully fought a fraudulent corporate take-over of some nearby public lands. In winter she took correspondence courses and avoided cabin fever by going out on her snowshoes and following rabbit tracks. She stayed out for hours, "for exercise and to dream," said Mills, clearly recognizing a kindred spirit. Hardship and a nearly fatal bout of flu had put "the marks of the trail . . . upon her face," Mills wrote, "but in her heart is the love for our race."[4]

Perlina Zabriski and the Street family were surely remarkable people to start with, but the mountains, Mills believed, brought out their best:

> There . . . are character qualities developed here which an environment less favorable to their development fails to emphasize. A fearlessness in the face of danger; a fertility of resource, a quickness of apprehension, a frankness and an open-handed generosity is characteristic of these dwellers among the mountains. Nowhere else among men are these qualities so marked.[5]

That open-handed generosity created an almost universal hospitality that made it easy for Mills to stop at isolated cabins for a meal or a place to sleep. "People almost without room will bravely lodge the traveler for a night and give him true welcome if not comfort," he said.[6] The most touching of his invitations came from two children out getting a Christmas tree one snowy December day. Without even asking their parents, they invited Mills for Christmas dinner, promising him a good meal and a share of the gifts Santa would bring.

When Mills mistook a schoolhouse for a ranch house, the teacher first thought he was a face-blackened desperado, but soon she and the children were sharing their lunches with Mills to revive him from his forty-eight-hour fast. At one cabin a kindly grandmother who invited Mills in thought he was practically a boy. When he removed his slouch hat, she lurched in her chair seeing "how far it was on my head to timberline." Able to joke about his receding hairline — at age thirty-four it was halfway back on his skull — he wrote after meeting and dining with poet laureate Harriet Wason that he had read her work long before he needed hair tonic.

Still hankering for romantic love in his life, Mills was profoundly

moved when a "restlessly happy" but illiterate young man on a
stagecoach asked him to examine his marriage license to be sure it
was correct. "I trust," wrote Mills, "if I ever secure a license that
with it will come the ecstasy which enthused my seatmate. The
pleasantest recollection of this happy young man will cause me to
love this lover forever."[7]

Mills knew, too, the ways of young men making their way in the
raw West, for he had lived among them and been one of them. With
palpable empathy, he addressed the worrying mothers left behind:

> At rural post offices I have often seen advertisements that tell too well
> that some mother's heart is breaking. . . . Young men are often thought-
> less when they are among new scenes with a life of action. Their heart
> is all right, but they forget all about letters. . . . A few for a time miss
> the trail, but they usually turn up O.K. I have seen enough in scores of
> localities in the state to compel me to say, "Mother, tonight your wan-
> dering boy is all right."[8]

Mills's gladness about the sometimes bustling, sometimes
secluded pockets of life in the high mountains extended to the animals who, in their own mute way, helped shape Colorado's destiny.
In Butte he had seen a remarkable sentimental devotion to the horses
and mules in the mines and the other animals about town. A fire
department horse that had survived a mine explosion had free run of
the city, and a bull wandered freely on the town's upper hill. A collie
named Dynamite ate regally at local restaurants, showed up as a
spectator at fires, and rode the trolley to evening baseball games. A
huge white cat named Kelley the Ghost wandered freely through the
passageways of the mines, often scaring workers with his glowing
eyes.[9]

Mills's affection for horses gave him a special interest in the
return horses that Colorado miners rode to their mountainside
mines and then released. He said he delighted in watching them trot
confidently down the precipitous trails, often in the dark and often
in deep snow. He saw return horses hampered by dangling reins or
loose saddles after being released by careless riders. He watched as
one miner was badly kicked trying to intercept a return horse —
trained to be uncatchable once turned loose — and he risked a severe
kicking himself trying to free the legs of a horse badly hobbled by
loose reins. In Telluride he saw a tenderfoot somehow succeed in

catching a return horse and tying it up, thinking it was a stray. Mills listened once as a livery owner inquired by phone to a high mine about an overdue pony, then saw the missing animal straggle into the mine with a flopping horseshoe and continue homeward after a handy miner made repairs.

In the steep and spectacular San Juan Mountains, return horses could be seen hauling miners and supplies thousands of feet up the mountainsides from the valley-bottom supply towns. In those mountains, feared then as now for their deadly avalanches, Mills had a hair-raising adventure with a return horse named Cricket, surviving three perilous days and nights escaping the deep, early snows that had trapped them. On another occasion, Mills said Cricket followed him into a Telluride saloon. He did not specify whether Cricket could not part from her life-and-death companion or whether it was a simple case of a horse in need of a good stiff drink.

Mills wrote later of another adventure with a return horse near Leadville and called it "one of the happiest experiences . . . with a dumb animal that has ever come into my life." Named Midget, the gallant little pony carried him up a pass and gamely followed him when he led the way through deep snow on his snowshoes. She stayed by his side when he put up his tripod to take photos. She seemed curious and attentive as he kept up a running commentary about photography in his usual manner of talking to animals as if they were people. When he finally turned her loose, she made no move to leave, and required a stern command from Mills to trot away. Weeks later, on the snow-observing trip he had begun from Leadville late at night, Mills snagged and broke a snowshoe and took a shortcut cross-country to intercept a trail he knew descended from a mine to Alma. As he approached the trail, he saw Midget, homeward bound. He called her name, and — in defiance of all training — she stopped, left the trail, and came to Mills through deep snow. "How in thunder did you catch her?" asked the livery owner when Mills rode in. "Yesterday Pat O'Brien tried that and now he is in the hospital with two broken ribs." The story illustrates Mills's deep attachment for these plucky animals and his apparent belief that affection can overrule training and instinct.[10]

For the developing naturalist, intrigued by the "biographies" of all living things, the tramp dogs that roamed the mining West added an element of psychological mystery. What extraordinary circumstances, Mills wondered, made these dogs lead a freewheeling and roving gypsy life, attaching themselves to human companions for a while, and then moving on?

Humorist Will Rogers said he got an early lesson about show biz from a tramp dog, and his story dates from the same years Mills was roaming the snowy Rockies. A "sly old spotted dog," Rogers wrote, rode freight trains from town to town and entertained the boys in the saloons in return for coins placed on his nose. "I got to thinking while watching this old dog, how much smarter he is than me," Rogers said. "Here I am out of a job five hundred miles from home . . . and this old dog hops off a train and starts right in making money, hand over fist." The dog — so it appeared — hid his coins, then took them to a butcher shop for a steak or bone. "He always paid for what he got in the line of grub," Rogers insisted. "Pretty soon he seemed to get tired of the town, and one morning he was gone. A railroad man told us later that he seen this same dog in Trinidad, Colorado."[11]

Mills wrote of two tramp dogs, one with what would probably be called today a serious socialization disorder. Lacking human contact in his first weeks of life, the collie seemed unable to adapt to either the world of people or of animals. After much extraordinary wandering and a time spent as leader of a coyote pack, he found his identity on a sheep ranch purchased for him by a wealthy widow.

Mills called the other wandering dog Rob of the Rockies and met him three times in locations far apart. He first met him in the flood-swollen Poudre River, trapped and half submerged in a tangle of willows, barbed wire, and mud. He freed him, and the two continued downstream, dried out at a friendly ranch, then boarded a stage coach together. Mills learned that Rob was a tramp who had been seen over a 200-mile arc from North Park to Cheyenne to Greeley. When Mills finally boarded a train, Rob casually sauntered off, seemingly oblivious to the attachment just formed. That winter, 200 miles away in Leadville, Rob suddenly appeared to rescue Mills from a pack of pursuing dogs. Miners said Rob had been hanging around town for two or three months, aloof from other dogs and from most people, sometimes following ore wagons to and from mountainside mines, and coming frequently to a certain stable to drink. Again Mills lost track of Rob, but met him the following spring 100 miles to the south in the Sangre de Cristo Mountains. The two climbed among the high peaks, and that night Rob crouched closely beside Mills, cringing from the shrill cries of a nearby lion. Next day Mills stopped at a ranch, where Rob befriended a young boy. The family offered handsome payment to keep him, but Mills replied that Rob was free to do as he liked and was not his to sell. Rob stayed on the ranch, but whether he settled down or continued his gypsy life, Mills never found out.

"Besieged by Bears" was the title Mills gave to one of the best of the many tales he heard from the mountain dwellers he visited. Recounting the story in his first major book, *Wild Life on the Rockies,* Mills showed his gift for humor and proved himself heir to the "graphic, earnest, realistic style" he said was "so often possessed by those who have lived strong, stirring lives among crags and pines."[12] The tale is a rollicking saga of three bears bent on entering the cabin of two old prospectors to get at their sugar-cured ham. The bears are persistent and ingenious in their efforts, but never seem — as Mills portrayed them — vicious or dangerous. The prospectors tear up their beds and floorboards for barricades and their mattresses for burning missiles to hurl at the bears. But at last, with the cabin in shambles and the bears clawing their way through the sod roof, old Jason and Sullivan concede defeat and throw the ham out the window.

The fabric of Mills's narratives about the people and animals he met as a snow observer identified him with the concerns of the growing West to a degree not found in his idol, John Muir. Settlements throughout the Colorado Rockies gave Mills a richer mixture of humans and high mountains than Muir had in the granite expanses from Yosemite eastward to the Sierra crest. And Muir's disposition, as already noted, was more fundamentally nature-oriented and people-shy than Mills's. The chronology of Mills's life took him, by his own design, away from his extended periods of wilderness solitude to the world of men, to whom he could bring his message of the great outdoors. As his public ambition accelerated, the fulfillment of personal love would continue to elude him, estrangement would soon drive him apart from his brother, Joe, and personal and political differences would alienate him from his neighbors. But his attachment to the human race remained sincere and deep. His compassion became, in fact, the measure of his vehemence in opposing whatever seemed to threaten humanity's right to a happier and saner life.

Part III

Public Causes, Private Passions

CHAPTER 13

Colorado Forests: "A Picturesque Remnant and Melancholy Ruin"

In a luncheon speech to the Denver Chamber of Commerce in March 1905, Mills reviewed the sad condition of Colorado's forests, citing firsthand information from his winter treks as the state's snow observer. He told the influential gathering — the elite of Denver Progressives — that Colorado's forest is a "picturesque remnant and melancholy ruin of its former grandeur." Only 5,000 square miles remained undamaged of the 36,000 found by Colorado's pioneers. Knowing the chamber's concern for viable water resources, Mills drew graphic comparisons of forest areas containing deep snow next to deforested areas that were bare and dry.[1]

The introduction that brought the snowman to the podium said he had the experience and knowledge "to speak as few men can." And when Mills called for "an end to anarchy in the forests," the chamber nodded in agreement, for it had been on record for nearly fifteen years as favoring legislated protection for Colorado's forests. "No question can be of greater concern to the state than that of its forests," said the chamber, whose motto was to stand not only for the welfare of the capitol city but also of the state at large.

When President Benjamin Harrison set aside nearly 1.2 million acres in Colorado as one of the nation's first federal forest reserves in 1891, the Denver chamber passed a resolution endorsing the reserve and calling for more like it. But most of the state's legislators denounced the withdrawal of forest lands as an insult and an injury to the whole cause of western settlement. From that year on, bitter polarization divided pro- and anticonservation factions in Colorado and throughout the West. The Forest Reserve Act made no provision for regulated use of the reserves and also failed to install any protective enforcement mechanism. Grazing and timber cutting continued virtually as before. Many settlers, indignant over being "locked out," cut the forests with a vengeance, burned them to make pasturage, and even set destructive fires in a spirit of defiant retaliation. Mills knew the extent of forest damage as well as anyone and recorded it in his snow reports. For him and for his receptive audience at the Denver chamber, more forest reserves and more stringent enforcement measures were an urgent necessity.

"In no part of the country," U.S. forester Gifford Pinchot had said in 1898, "were the rights of the U.S. government and its property more disregarded"[2] than in the central Rockies. Pinchot was the leading force in American conservation by 1905 and the architect of forest policy in the Theodore Roosevelt administration. He was a scientific forester, trained at Yale and in Europe. He believed in managing trees like crops: cutting mature trees and replacing them with new seedlings to yield a perpetual harvest of timber. Pinchot had traveled with John Muir and others in an 1896 survey of western forests, but he differed with Muir over the question of opening the reserves to commercial development. Muir and the commission's head, Harvard botanist Charles Sargent, influenced the survey's final report to reflect their views that more forest reserves should be created, but without provision for commercial use. Pinchot entered a dissenting opinion, and the Forest Management Act of 1897 was a clear victory in his favor. It opened the reserves to regulated commercial use and inaugurated the era of scientific conservation that Pinchot would dominate for more than a dozen years.

Pinchot, who had earlier admitted to Muir that sheep grazing badly damages rangelands, was now backing it in the reserves. In Muir's own hallowed Sierras, 200,000 of the "hooved locusts" were turned out to graze. Muir broke relations with Pinchot, and Sargent retired in bitter disappointment. Seeing in Pinchot an ambitious empire builder, Sargent wrote to Muir in 1902, "There is no one but you and I who really love the North American trees."[3]

The ideological split between use and nonuse — utilitarianism and preservationism — persists today. Utilitarianism is technologically and economically based, places function before beauty, and cites national security, national efficiency, job growth, and — in theory — egalitarian distribution as its bases. In practice, resource extraction is dominated by special interests that reap profits at the public expense. Preservationism cites nonmaterial values as the greatest good to be gained from undeveloped public lands. Its motivating values are sanctuary for the human spirit, a national heritage of lands unchanged since the nation's beginning, and the right of nature and its creatures to have some areas free from human domination.

A few settlers, especially those concerned about protecting the watershed, backed Pinchot and the new scientific forestry as a needed remedy to forest destruction. But most settlers and the many exploiters of the forest were as opposed to controlled use as to no use at all. They saw Pinchot not as a benefactor who had opened up the reserves to a long-term balance of use and regeneration, but as a self-serving and militant eastern "czar" who was denying westerners their rights. The great era of strife in Colorado's conservation history revolved not around the Muir-Pinchot dichotomy but around the belief that even Pinchot's prescription for the reserves was militantly restrictive. Settlers and legislators alike claimed the federal government was thwarting the state's development. They saw themselves as government tenants rather than as settlers "building a free America."

Pinchot, a staunch Progressive, believed conservation was a social necessity that would promote democracy and protect individuals against exploitation by monopolists. His conservation "dealt . . . first, last and all the time with human beings," said his widow, much later. He made frequent visits to the western states to explain his program, but won converts only slowly. He continued to be called an "alien bureaucrat," an "eastern hypocrite," a "dictator of the forest," a "wicked forest king," and a "fanatical zealot." Profiteers who hid behind the settlers' outcry of "freedom for the West to develop without restriction" fueled the defiant resistance for their own ends.[4]

A few concerned conservationists had begun organizing in Colorado as early as the mid 1870s. They warned the settlers that many who were destroying the forests neither lived in them nor cared for their welfare; they were in the business of destruction, for sheer profit. Conservationists united more cohesively under the Colorado State Forestry Association in 1884 and rallied around Pinchot's programs before and during the Roosevelt presidency. When Roosevelt came to office in 1901, conservation foes naively hoped that he would understand their concerns and abolish the reserves. But Roosevelt was already an active conservationist who had helped establish the reserves in 1891. He had enacted far-reaching conservation measures as governor of New York. As president he announced that firm and swift action was needed to prevent a national disaster. By 1901, roughly half the timber in the United States had been cut and four-fifths of the remainder had passed from public to private hands. Minerals had been squandered, many birds and mammals approached extinction, and vast amounts of agricultural topsoil had been blown and washed away.

Roosevelt acted quickly to increase the reserves and to enforce their regulation. Frustrated by continued opposition to the reserves, he appointed a Public Lands Commission to travel through the western states in 1904 to survey public opinion. The commission was headed by Pinchot and Reclamation Director Frederick Newell. It met in Colorado in January and August 1904. The January meeting, held at the Denver Chamber of Commerce, was dominated by the furious denunciations of conservation foes. The August meeting followed the same course. The arguments of local conservationists were not heard until late on the second day and, as before, were hooted and booed. But the presidential election was fast approaching, and in November Roosevelt was voted to a second term by a landslide. So great was his popularity that both senators and all three representatives elected in Colorado were Roosevelt supporters despite their opposition to his conservation policies.

Roosevelt had not yet established any new reserves in Colorado, but starting in May 1905 he created eleven before the year was over. They included the watersheds of nearly all Colorado's major river systems, and their total extent of 8.8 million acres astonished even those who had campaigned for them. One of the first to be set aside, in May 1905, was the 1.5-million-acre Medicine Bow Reserve (later named Roosevelt National Forest), which included public lands around Estes Park and Mills's Longs Peak Inn. In the same year, Roosevelt moved jurisdiction of American forests to the Department of Agriculture and made Pinchot their sole administrator under the Forest Transfer Act. By 1907, Roosevelt had established three more Colorado reserves.

Mills's 1905 talk to the Denver Chamber gave no political context to the forestry controversy, and mentioned no alliances pro or con. He made no mention of the chamber's role in the controversy's dramatic history, nor of the events that had transpired in those very halls in the past year. He mentioned none of the groundwork —

including a vigorous petition campaign — laid by the Colorado State Forestry Association, of which he and the chamber were both members, for the tremendous wave of reserves about to be established by Roosevelt.

Perhaps Mills wanted to portray himself as the simple man from the woods who told in graphic terms of the forest damage he had seen. He wore his mountain clothes and stood, said one observer, "like a sturdy oak among many trees." Yet he came across not as a mountain Jeremiah but as a civic-minded Coloradan and a businessman with a stake in the economic value of forests to tourism. His 1900 visit to Switzerland had convinced him of tourism's vast earning potential, and that, he told the chamber, promised to become the most profitable of Colorado's industries. "But a tourist hotel located in a sheep pasture . . . [or] in a forest fire desert will not hold its guests," he warned.

Mills did not make clear whether he believed a hotel *would* hold its guests if located in a forest logged, grazed, and mined according to governmental prescription. Was there a conflict between the vacation industry's need for quality scenery and the demands of sanctioned forest uses? Mills seemed for the moment to be ambiguous or naive on the subject. He said blithely that forests "supply water for the farmer, timber for the miner, lumber for the cottage, wood for the hearthstone, Christmas trees for the children, climate for everybody and scenery for us all."[5] If he thus supposed that forests could be all things to all people, he would in time change his mind. Muir never believed that resource extraction and scenic preservation were compatible and refused even to use the word "conservation" once Pinchot had appropriated it to title his program. But Mills in 1905 called the reserves "a thing of beauty and profit."

Mills may have failed to foresee the full impact of utilitarian forestry because he viewed fire as a greater threat. He told the chamber that "fires have damaged the forests five time the extent of use and of all enemies." Later he decided that insects are a greater threat still. In 1905 he saw the forest reserve system principally as a guardian against fire. Trained fire-fighting rangers patrolled the forests, posted fire notices, and levied fines against those who caused fires. In a magazine article a year earlier Mills had called the work of those rangers "a wonderful preventive of forest fires."[6] If the fire problem could be solved, perhaps the forests could, in fact, meet the needs of all users simultaneously.

Mills seemed to assume, though, that some forests would be harvested in orderly fashion while others would be left alone. He invoked the turn-of-the-century nature fad in telling the chamber, "People are feeling the call of the wild. People want the wild, wild world beautiful. They want the temples of the Gods, bits of the forest primeval, the pure and fern-fringed brooks." In the San Juan and Medicine Bow regions — and probably elsewhere — he hoped eventually to see national parks carved out of the forest reserves. Little did he suspect how strenuously the U.S. Forest Service would resist removal of "bits of forest primeval" from its cash-crop tree farms to create national parks.[7]

Why, in any event, did Mills align himself publicly with Pinchotism fully eight years after Muir had broken with Pinchot, and why from 1907 to 1909 did Mills serve as an official publicist for the Forest Service? The reasons are complex but consistent with the course of Mills's life; though he remained a steadfast Muir disciple, he perceived Muir through the public compromises Muir was forced to make and through the Sierra Club's own limited vision of its founder.

Mills had, first of all, a dispositionally greater interest in the concerns of the growing West than Muir. He had been a health-seeker, miner, cowboy, and homesteader; he had assisted in the development of Colorado's water resources and was now an entrepreneur in the state's burgeoning vacation industry. While Mills saw romance in the settlement of the West, Muir saw the settlers as an invading horde of destroyers, "gnawing like beavers, and scratching for a living among the blackened stumps and logs, regarding the trees as their greatest enemies." Many historians agree. "The idealized yeoman farmer," writes G. Michael McCarthy, "was in reality a grasping, ambitious entrepreneur, more interested in exploiting the land for his own needs than in creating a stable civilization."[8]

Though Mills saw plenty of those grasping settlers, his view was colored more by the new breed of settlers brought by the back-to-nature movement — settlers such as the retired couple near Blanca Peak, the Street family, and Perlina Zabriski. Settlers in general were for Mills courageous, resourceful, and blessedly fulfilled in their destinies. He thus readily accepted the egalitarian slogans of Progressive conservation: "fair to all," "strictly democratic," and "efficient." And he said of himself: "I was drawn to the philanthropic side of the forest."

Mills's fellow conservationists in the Colorado State Forestry Association were concerned primarily with the economic welfare of the state and were thus far closer in spirit to Pinchot than to Muir. They never advocated a policy of nonuse for the reserves and rarely voiced aesthetic concerns, believing nonuse would be as damaging to the state as unmanaged use. Louis Carpenter and others in the irrigation field with whom Mills associated were likewise solidly behind Pinchot. The Roosevelt administration had won wide acclaim in Colorado through the newly established reclamation program, and to all with an interest in water resources, the administration's forestry policy was an inseparable partner.

Muir conceded for a time that he could not advocate preservation against all use and that impression must have stuck with Mills. As president of the Sierra Club, Muir wrote in 1895: "It is impossible, in the nature of things, to stop at preservation. The forests must be, and will be, not only preserved, but used. . . . The forests like perennial fountains may be made to yield a sure harvest of timber, while at the same time their far-reaching uses may be maintained unimpaired."[9] That was exactly the spirit of Mills's 1905 chamber speech. Like Aldo Leopold later, Muir was disgusted with the actual practice of tree farming, and he always opposed grazing on public lands. But his 1901 book *Our National Parks* contained some of his earlier essays that condoned utilitarian forest management and politely praised Pinchot. Though Muir had severed relations with Pinchot by 1901, Mills's reading of *Our National Parks* gave him an easy basis for thinking of the reserves — the real subject of Muir's book — as parklike places allowing practical uses as well.

Whether by 1905 Mills was more a Progressive or a socialist, he found abundant political rationale for scientific forestry in both. Utilitarian forestry was claimed as a central ingredient of Roosevelt's social agenda, and socialist party platforms were remarkably similar. It was a natural socialist goal to enlarge the public domain and to conserve and develop natural resources for the use and benefit of all the people. Both Progressives and socialists pushed for scientific forestry, reclamation of swamps and arid lands, dams for water storage and hydropower, conservation of topsoil, minerals and oil, and the development of highways and waterways for transportation. Both, furthermore, placed a premium on technology. Some historians say that applied science was in fact a stronger impulse behind conservation policy in the Roosevelt era than its social agenda. Conservation leaders tended to be technically trained experts whose professional loyalties isolated them from grassroots public concerns. While Muir disliked the domination of man by technology and foresaw the inevitable tendency to seek technological solutions to all problems, Mills always retained an optimistic streak of technological utopianism.

Mills may have also trusted the business rationale of Progressive conservation to an extent unthinkable to Muir. Good business sense was the efficient partner of applied science in the management of natural resources, and Roosevelt proclaimed that "the National Government shall proceed as a private businessman would." While Roosevelt's trust-busting assured Mills and many others of watchful government control over business, the Roosevelt presidency in fact cemented government-business alliances to an unprecedented degree. The primary outcome of Progressivism, say some historians, was the power acquired by business interests to steer government policy in their favor. For Muir the business rationale of Progressive conservation was greed wrapped in flimsy camouflage; for Mills it contributed to "efficiency" and saved "vast sums of money to the nation."[10]

Muir hoped and Mills believed that Roosevelt's own values would protect the forests' nonmaterial assets. Roosevelt felt a deep kinship with Muir when the two camped together in Yosemite in 1903, even though the president was already well along in his programs to develop the nation's resources. Roosevelt "was a preservationist by instinct and avocation," notes historian Stephen Fox, "but a politician by vocation." Muir hoped Roosevelt's love of nature would eventually prevail over Pinchot's influence. Instead, Pinchot brought utilitarian conservation to its full development during Roosevelt's second term after gaining full charge of the administration's conservation interests through the Forest Transfer Act of 1905. "If the president had vacillated on public-land questions before 1905," says conservation historian G. Michael McCarthy, "after that time he did not. . . . Pinchot's ideas became Roosevelt's ideas, and all were quickly and efficiently translated into conservation action." Mills, who praised Roosevelt for knowing the forest not only "with the eye of a scientific forester and patriot and economist, but with that of the forester of sentiment," remained faithful to the conservation gospel throughout the Roosevelt presidency. Because of his faith in Roosevelt, Mills only slowly let go of his belief that the forests could remain places of beauty while meeting the nation's material needs.[11]

Of all the differences between Mills and Muir, the greatest was that Mills never questioned the basic premise Muir had confronted as a young man: Should man exercise dominion over nature? Muir rejected the anthropocentric view that dominated all of Western civilization. Perceiving the interconnectedness of all things, he denounced "Lord Man's" arrogance in seeing the cosmos as a creation made for him and placed at his unlimited disposal. That denunciation contrasted sharply with Pinchot, who said, "The first duty of the human race is to control the earth it lives upon." The depth of Muir's personal experience in the Sierras and the way he sought to comprehend nature as an organic whole through immersing himself in its processes led him, argues Michael Cohen, to a religious view of the cosmos as sacred. Only through a reverence for the whole earth and all its creatures would humanity stop its self-justifying expansion and its use of every last resource as a commodity. Muir anticipated today's growing belief that civilization separate from nature and its balanced processes is no longer tenable.[12]

Though Mills had a deep love and reverence for nature, he did not develop Muir's religious perspective for man's relation to nature. Mills differed from Muir and yet felt allied with him in exactly the same way that Muir's own Sierra Club did. Like Mills, its members were limited in their vision by the Progressive Era's reformist perspective. They were mostly professional-class men, often members of chambers of commerce, Protestant, moralistic, eager to eliminate corruption in politics and to improve society without challenging its basic structure and power relations. They found no ideological conflict in supporting Pinchot's utilitarianism to meet the nation's practical needs while promoting national parks and outdoor recreation to satisfy "higher values." Neither Mills nor the Sierra Club saw that even if intentions are good, civilization's appetites will always demand more.[13]

Though the Sierra Club did not comprehend Muir's deeper vision, it championed him as an inspirational nature prophet now at the height of his fame. And Muir, in turn, was forced to public compromises that obscured what he stood for on deeper levels. To win public support for unspoiled nature and national parks, he needed to appeal to mass sentiment. Once scornful of tourists, he now accepted them less critically, for he needed to believe that anyone could learn to appreciate nature, profit from exposure to it, and want it preserved. His 1901 *Our National Parks* was really a book about the beauty spots of the forest reserves that he wanted to become national parks. He described all thirty-four reserves and urged people to visit them and vacation there — competing, in essence, with the spoilers. "If every citizen could take one walk through this reserve, there would be no more trouble about its care," he wrote. "Only in darkness does vandalism flourish."[14]

Both Muir and the Sierra Club encouraged the development of roads, trails, and overnight accommodations to get people to those places of beauty. In 1905, Muir even advocated a road through Yosemite's Tenaya Canyon — one of his own inviolate temples. To further entice people outdoors, the Sierra Club began a program of outings with camp-outs at inspirational spots where Muir and other naturalists held forth on the wonders of nature.

Getting people into nature, inspiring them, and restoring them physically was precisely what attracted Mills most and was what he took for Muir's central message. It was in fact a derivative ideal of Muir's — no less admirable in its own right — but subordinate to his whole-earth ethos. Mills would for the remainder of his career preach nature's benefits to humans while reflecting only loosely on the need to preserve nature for its own sake. He did not examine man's place in the cosmos, and though he voiced isolated concerns such as the loss of wildlife habitat, he did not worry about the final outcome of "Lord Man's" dominion. He adopted the notion that nature is good medicine to restore "human efficiency" and to return people to the cities better able to resume their jobs. Mills would later preach as the chief value of the national parks the making of better men and women, and while speaking only hastily of wilderness values he would speak constantly of getting the parks ready for the people. He overlooked the possibility that without a deeper adjustment of values, humans restored by nature to full efficiency will add their efficiency to the very system that destroys nature.

To those aspects of Muir he understood, Mills gave considerable depth. On his nature walks and talks at Longs Peak Inn he was able to instill a deep sense of wonder for the outdoors that took many of his guests into new dimensions of appreciation. His own profound experiences as a solitary mountaineer enriched his ability to inspire, and his example showed, as Muir's showed, the possibilities of wild nature for human growth and self-improvement. His seriousness of purpose, including even his injunction against dancing and music at the inn, would have appealed to Muir, who disliked and discouraged frivolity on Sierra Club outings.

If Muir's public compromises hid his radical nature from Mills, it must also be said that Muir's deeper vision remained unfinished and ultimately confusing to his followers. Muir failed to develop a comprehensive vision of civilization harmoniously integrated with nature. Adopting tourism and recreation as the only antidotes to resource development, he remained arrested in wishful thinking that public sentiment for beauty could preserve the world intact. He failed to work for an ethic that would help man engage in a living relationship with the earth, and, in the words of Wendell Berry, "dissolve the boundaries that divide people from the land and its care."[15] Mills was too much a man of action and too little a man of reflection to complete Muir's vision. Seeing the need for practical measures to stop outright abuse in the treatment of America's resources, he found wise-use conservation reasonable and fair. Some of its shortcomings became apparent to him later and led to his antagonism toward the Forest Service. Others would remain for future generations to articulate.

Mills's talk to the Denver chamber was a spectacular success, described by magazine editor J. A. Maguire as the finest appeal for conservation he had ever heard. Both Maguire and Mills stated erroneously that it was Mills's first public speech, and Maguire had sat nervously in the audience until he saw that Mills was off to a good start. Mills later wrote Pinchot that he had first attempted a forestry talk in San Francisco in 1891, given his first good forestry talk in Kansas City in 1895, and given frequent talks throughout Colorado from 1900 to 1905. G. Michael McCarthy's detailed chronicle of the conservation controversy in Colorado from 1891 to 1907 reveals, however, no presence of Mills in the many town meetings and newspaper accounts of the bitter debate over the forest reserves. Much of what he said to the Denver chamber in 1905 would have brought angry boos from the settlers in Colorado mountain towns, where Pinchot met noisy opposition to his explanations of wise-use forestry. We can guess instead that Mills focused mainly on the ravages of the state's forests by fire — his earliest concern and the one he was most qualified to present.

Had Mills taken part in those small-town debates over federal forestry, he might have been in a strategic position to soften the resistance of the obdurate settlers. Unlike the cultivated and Yale-trained Pinchot, who was always considered an eastern intruder, Mills was mountain-bred, rustic, self-taught, and known for his rugged exploits. Though eager to convey nature's "poetry" and given to flourishes like "fern-fringed brooks," he could also speak the language of miners, cattlemen, and homesteaders. While strongly advocating the reserve system, he wrote reassuringly in 1904 that if "vast reserves [are] made, cattle will not be put on short rations, no mine will be closed and not a single sawmill will need to stop, and the price of wood and lumber would not be increased."[16]

Whether or not Mills presented such ideas in public talks, he appears to have channeled most of his early conservation efforts in the work of the Colorado State Forestry Association. He was a valued member who could convey his first-hand knowledge of the forest to influential Progressive leaders within the organization — men such as Irving Hale, a personal friend of Roosevelt; Edward Costigan, a Progressive candidate for governor who fought against public corruption and special interests; Ellsworth Bethel, a noted botanist and teacher; and William B. Kreutzer and Henry Michelsen, professional foresters with distinguished records in the Forest Service. A letter to Mills from the association's president, W.G.M. Stone, expressed hope that the next legislature would create the position of state forester and said that Mills would be the man to fill it. "That is what you must be and the state will not do itself justice till you are," wrote Stone.[17]

Mills supplied data and photographs for candidate reserve areas and wrote at least two pamphlets for the association. In one of his pamphlets, adapted from a talk he gave to the association in January 1907, Mills said that within the last two years a majority of Coloradans had finally come to accept the reserves. In a strong vote of confidence for federal conservation, Mills said: "I believe this marked change in public opinion has been brought about chiefly by methods of the Forest Service officials — their explanatory way, the square-deal spirit at all times manifest, the civility and the calmness, the firmness and the fairness with which the Service met every issue won out and I think won permanently by convincing the opposition."[18]

Seen at a distance, Mills correctly sensed the drift of the times despite momentous events to the contrary. A month later, in February 1907, anticonservationists from western states forced a bill through the U.S. Senate shifting the power to create or enlarge forest reserves from the president to the U.S. Congress. Fearing a loss of unreserved timberlands to land grabbers, Roosevelt proclaimed twenty-one new reserves and enlarged twelve more before the new law went into effect. Anticonservationists were stunned by Roosevelt's swift and retaliatory doubling of the reserves' total extent. They "turned handsprings in their wrath," said Roosevelt. Colorado's legislature called for a convention of representatives from all western states to discuss the president's outrageous action.

The storminess of anticonservation rhetoric reached an all-time high at the June 1907 Public Lands Convention. But conservation foes failed to dominate the convention's resolutions committee and hence failed to convince the world that the whole West was "in a condition of revolt." Many newspapers insisted that far more people supported the Roosevelt administration's policy than opposed it, and they criticized the intemperate tone of the insurgents during the convention. "Whatever its effects," writes McCarthy, "the Denver Lands Convention was a watershed in the history of the conservation conflict in the American West. . . . Though the anticonservationist movement there was not dead, it would never again be as strong and as vibrant as it had been in the past."[19]

Substantial force, Mills noted in his pamphlet, had been wielded by women's clubs in Colorado in turning the state's majority sentiment in favor of forest reserves. Fifty-five women's clubs in the state had held forestry meetings with large public attendance. "And having the ballot [in Colorado]," Mills said, "they can . . . [also] emphasize their convictions at the polls."[20] Women furthermore exerted a positive influence on their children and were thus a key to the attitudes of oncoming generations. It was to these vast national resources of public opinion — women and young people — that Mills turned most of his attention as an official conservation spokesman for the Roosevelt administration from 1907 to 1909.

CHAPTER 14

Champion of Trees: Mills Lectures the Nation

Denver, Colorado, January 7, 1907

My dear Mr. President:

I wish to take the liberty and pleasure of introducing my friend, Mr. Enos A. Mills of Estes Park, Colorado — Guide, Snow Inspector and Forester — with whom I have spent many happy days, and who is equally entertaining and instructive on the trail and platform. He is an enthusiast on Nature and especially forestry, and has done splendid work in lecturing on this important subject throughout the country — largely at his own expense, and is attending the meeting of the American Forestry Association in Washington. I am sure you will enjoy talking with him.

Very sincerely yours,
Irving Hale[1]

Mills handed the letter to Theodore Roosevelt at the Forestry Association meeting later in the month and a few days later wrote Hale about meeting him: "Mr. Pinchot had introduced me but I was glad to give him your letter. . . . He delayed business for a time to talk with me . . . [and] was really glad to honor your letter. . . . When I told him your conduct was good he laughed. He was well but was carrying much weight."[2]

Roosevelt and Pinchot quickly sized Mills up as a valuable resource for the massive publicity campaign for Progressive conservation that they were carrying on with strong backing from the press, a blizzard of governmental bulletins, and massive private mailings. Mills had started traveling and lecturing throughout the country in fall 1905, and his efforts had already attracted Pinchot's attention. At about the time Mills met the president, Pinchot told the press that his work was "of incalculable value to the national department." An official letter dated January 23, 1907, appointed Mills as a forestry agent with a salary and traveling expenses, leaving him free to arrange his own speaking engagements. The Denver press, swelling with pride, said:

> The creation of the position and title for Mr. Mills not only is a fitting reward for his ability and service, but an honor to the state which he loves so well. . . . With such enthusiastic forces and Roosevelt, Pinchot, and Garfield [Secretary of Interior] boosting the forestry game, and Enos Mills talking about it, tremendous results are to be anticipated.[3]

Mills's speaking career before his governmental appointment had been impressive. Following his March 1905 talk to the Denver chamber, he had inspired the Colorado state convention of the Federation of Women's Clubs with a talk they called "the most beautiful and inspiring message that had been sent out over the footlights of that small stage since the club was established."[4] That fall, Mills had traveled from Colorado to Kansas City, Memphis, New Orleans, Pittsburgh, Columbus, and Chicago with many intermediate stops to give upwards of sixty talks, mostly without remuneration and often paying rent on lecture halls. In spring 1906 he was off again, lecturing first in Butte, where some no doubt recognized the former miner, and ending in St. Paul, where he addressed the national biennial convention of the General Federation of Women's Clubs (GFWC). With some of the country's most influential women in the audience, Mills's stellar performance assured him a constant flow of invitations all over the country. He left St. Paul with over two dozen engagements already in his datebook.

"I went to St. Paul chiefly through your efforts," he wrote to Hale. Hale modestly replied that Mills's own success at the Colorado women's convention had sparked his invitation to the national convention. The correspondence between Mills and the well-connected general left no doubt, though, that Hale opened many doors for Mills. He had suggested to women's clubs that they print tickets and brochures to promote Mills's talks, and had sent letters to friends publicizing Mills's talks in the Denver area. Asking for donations to help cover Mills's expenses, Hale wrote, "I feel no hesitation in presenting this matter to friends, not only on account of the public

Robust and confident: Mills on the lecture circuit, c. 1908. *Denver Public Library, Western History Department.*

importance of the cause but the knowledge that you will thoroughly enjoy Mr. Mills's address and views."[5]

Hale also reviewed drafts of Mills's speeches. Mills wrote out his talks and sent both outlines and text to Hale. Urging Hale to be rigorous in making suggestions, Mills said earnestly, "I want to be effective." He was still tentative about his stage presence, having written in fall 1905 that on one occasion "I did not seem to get the range of my audience." He said he "called reserves into action," "shelled the woods," and "when nearly out of ammunition, . . . ceased firing." "Then the audience surrendered unconditionally, to my great relief." Under Hale's guidance, Mills quickly learned that effective audience persuasion was a goal demanding a speaker's full "arsenal."[6]

As his confidence grew, Mills wrote more frequently of his improvements than of his doubts. And he clearly thrived on the challenge. In November 1906 he wrote Hale that he had had "audiences of excellent quality and four times more than a thousand." He had found a vital new field of activity in which he could apply both his knowledge and his love of nature. Asked by a reporter why he had thrown himself into lecturing with such zeal and at his own expense, Mills replied enthusiastically, "I want to save the forests." Moreover, he said, it was "fun — a pure joy."[7] With Longs Peak Inn as his transition from the solitary ways of a mountaineer to the public man, he now made auditoriums his place of adventure and persuasion his chief means of expression. Mills felt alive, happy, and useful.

By the time the Roosevelt administration hired Mills to represent the Forest Service, his confidence and sense of mission were unstoppable. It was of course natural for Pinchot to proceed with caution in sending out a relatively unknown quantity under the banner of the Roosevelt administration. But, after three months, Mills was notified that Pinchot wanted him to continue. Mills replied that whether or not he was a federal agent, he would continue lecturing, "for the sake of the cause." But he knew that an official title gave him more clout, and sensing the importance of his position as a hand-picked representative of the president, he added, "I am trying to be extremely careful not to stir up trouble."[8]

Pinchot had good reason to be reassured, as high commendations followed Mills wherever he went. General William J. Palmer, a powerful Colorado industrialist, wrote Pinchot on February 16 praising Mills's lecture and thanking Pinchot for sending him around the country. A southern college president wrote:

> He gave us new ideas as to the value of trees and showed how we may cooperate with all the forces now at work not only to preserve forests but also to grow more trees. . . . [It] was altogether the best talk on the subject I have ever heard. You may be sure that Mr. Mills has left a very happy impression on all who heard him. . . . It gives me great pleasure to write these things about your representative; he is doing great work.[9]

As a federal lecturer Mills addressed women's groups, schools, YMCAs, business and commercial organizations, service clubs, press clubs, libraries, conservation associations, farmers' groups, and occasionally churches and seminaries. But his preferred audiences and the ones he addressed most frequently, were women and children. Women, he wrote to Pinchot, can "spread an idea around like the grip."[10] When federal legislation created the Inland Waterways Commission, for example, the GFWC was ready with a mailing of 1,800 letters and 50,000 pamphlets supporting the commission's work. Founded in 1890, the GFWC was the strongest organization of women in America, with membership topping one million by 1914. It exerted a strong influence on American institutions, ideas, customs, public administration, domestic practice, morals, education, and culture. Conservation became one of its roughly dozen branches of activity, and through its effective networking at local, state, and national levels, it was a powerful force in mobilizing public opinion and in sharing the trench work of public campaigns. In Colorado, women's organizations led the successful campaign to establish Mesa Verde National Park in 1906. In the East they played a key role in saving Niagara Falls from commercial exploitation and in preserving the Palisades region of the Hudson Valley. They campaigned for national forests in both the East and West. GFWC activists also pressed for pure air and water, and their influence on proper sanitation during construction of the Panama Canal led to a sanitation record that was called a model for other nations.

In a society dominated by male thinking and values, women had a vital relevance to conservation. Mrs. H. L. Hollister, president of the Colorado Federation of Women's Clubs, told a national irrigation congress:

Women's work and conservation are largely the same thing whether by right of citizenship or only by moral suasion. She must stand for the things that mean most to humanity: conservation, life, health, love, happiness, children and home; working for an education that shall instill into our youth an active conscience, a clean comprehension of life and its responsibilities, an intelligent understanding and love of nature that counts it a dishonor to take from her without paying tribute and making a just return.[11]

The sentiment was broadly Progressive. But loving nature, paying tribute to nature, and paying back what is taken from nature bespoke a partnership with the earth closer to the spirit of John Muir than the patriarchal outlook that dominated utilitarian thinking. Muir's thinking had gained that useful feminine component through the influence of Jeanne Carr, a personal friend of Ralph Waldo Emerson's. Viewing nature as a living spirit, she helped Muir to trust his own growth away from nineteenth-century norms into a view of the cosmos as sacred. Though Mills did not follow Muir into a biocentric and religious vision, he instinctively knew the importance of women in the conservation movement. That gave him a kind of bridge to Muir, even while he promoted the Progressive conservation gospel. Mills even hoped women would seek professional careers in forestry, and said, as early as 1906, "A woman with capacity for detail, with a knowledge of chemistry, mathematics and botany, with a genius for directing and a love of nature could make herself a power in the department."[12]

What is remarkable, in fact, about Mills's talks to women's groups is that even though he covered the essential points about utilitarian conservation, much of what he said was not utilitarian forestry at all and could have been said by Muir. When he addressed the GFWC in St. Paul, he did not talk about timber harvests or board feet, but began with the simple declaration "This is a beautiful world." He urged women to write their congressional representatives to save the California sequoias from logging. "These splendid evergreens with their historical lore and unequalled grandeur have amplitude and poetry enough to enrich the ideals of the world," he said in an openly preservationist declaration. He challenged national priorities by asserting that saving those trees would cost only a third as much as a single warship. And he anticipated a much later wilderness ethic by asserting that one does not necessarily need

to see natural treasures to want them preserved. It suffices "to simply know that on the sublime Sierra [the sequoias] still grandly
wave," he said.[13]

As he enumerated the uses of the forests, Mills gave no more
prominence to material than to nonmaterial values. Forests suppress
floods, store water, provide wood for lumber and fuel, but they are
also places "made for hunters of dreams," he said. He quoted Walt
Whitman's claim that all great poems and heroic deeds are conceived
in the open air; he praised artistic uses of wood for furniture and
musical instruments; he underscored the value of fruit and medicinal
trees, and drew a portrait — drawing on Byron's poem "Darkness"
— of life impoverished by the destruction of forests. He spoke of the
globally uniting spirit of Arbor Day and said he hoped someday the
pine tree would be the universal flag of a peaceful world. He always
stressed planting trees more than cutting them — up to fifteen
planted for each tree cut — and hence created a desire for trees
standing rather than trees felled. But despite these deep preservationist currents in his talks, he differed from Muir in settling for nature
cultivated by man rather than left alone by man: "Primitive people
and pioneers could depend upon wild products. . . . Civilized people
must domesticate and improve all plants and animals used. A complete domestication of all birds and trees is now necessary. Germany
and Japan are giving all trees the care that we bestow upon the apple
and the orange."[14]

Mills wove his outdoor adventures into his talks both to entertain and to evoke sentiment. He told of his wanderings through the
mountains and forests as a boy, of his intense happiness when the
world was young, when eating didn't matter, and when the storms
and snowslides were sometimes "deadly in earnest." He spoke of
campfires, of roaming the peaks by moonlight, of sleeping under
trees so high it looked as though the "silver braid" of stars could
become entangled in them, of the caress of summer rain on his
cheek, and of waking to find "dear flowers bending over to watch
my face."[15]

For such effusions of sentiment to work — even by the standards
of Mills's day — Mills needed considerable skill as a speaker and a
convincing presence. In reviewing Mills's St. Paul draft, Hale evidently knew Mills already possessed both. The message that Mills
wanted to evoke was that trees are mankind's truest and most faithful friends, inseparably linked to our "most sacred hopes and

needs." Mills, like the women he addressed, stood for the broadest urges and needs of civilization. He told Pinchot that in presenting information on forestry, he wanted "at the same time to awaken a deep and lasting interest in the subject."[16]

The same applied to children. He had told the Denver chamber in 1905 that "if there are to be forests, there must be forest sentiment. Sentiment is formed in childhood." Mills reached young people through talks at schools, YMCAs, and other youth groups, often contacting them in cities where he was already booked for evening talks to adults. He held the attention of his young audiences with entertaining anecdotes that included his many encounters with bears as a youngster. At a Chicago Latin school where the boys were tired from a long day, Mills began at once by talking rapidly, moved forward over the stage toward them, jumped off the four-foot edge of the platform and walked backward up the stage steps without a break in his narrative. From then on he was ensured of the boys' attention. A biographical sketch of the Western writer-historian Jay Monaghan tells of his hearing a talk by Mills in Philadelphia, where Mills made a fire by rubbing sticks together. "In the process [Mills] set a flame burning in one of his young auditors that was never to be extinguished."[17]

Mills encouraged schools to give prizes for essays on conservation and got women's clubs to sponsor them. He urged state governments to follow Colorado's example of letting school children vote to select state flowers and state trees. In Wisconsin, at least, he succeeded, and, on Arbor Day in 1908, the children voted in the state tree. He urged school boards to introduce conservation into school curricula, and Louisiana, prompted doubtlessly in part by his many talks there, became the first state to undertake that step. Mills urged older students to investigate careers in scientific forestry. At Northwestern University, where his talk prompted a large number of students to write off for USFS career bulletins, a university publication said, "No lecture . . . has ever had more immediate returns than Mr. Mills's on forestry."[18] At a teachers college in Georgia, 500 students training to be teachers turned out to hear Mills address the need for conservation education in schools. He preached the same message to women's clubs and teachers' organizations and let them follow through with their own influence. At the college level, he urged establishment of chairs and departments of forestry.

Mills maintained his grueling schedule, ranging as far as New England in fall 1906, across the deep South and the northern states in spring 1907, east to Kentucky and west to Washington in fall 1907, through the South, New England, and the West Coast in spring 1908, through the South again in fall 1908, and through the South, Midwest, New England, and the West Coast in spring 1909. He traveled thousands of miles by rail. In 1910 Mills wrote a colleague in the Colorado Forestry Association that he had given 2,118 addresses, speaking at least twice in each state and many times in most states, with up to four tours through most states. During the peak of his activity he was receiving seven requests a day for talks, and in one area of Alabama alone, twenty organizations clamored for him to speak. Sometimes the schedule was too much even for the tireless Mills. "[He] was pretty well played out when he arrived today and excused himself from lecturing at the school buildings," wrote the Shreveport *Journal* on February 14, 1908.

The sizes of Mills's audiences ranged from gatherings in private homes, court houses, union halls, and churches, to auditoriums holding over a thousand. Women's groups often opened their talks to the public and preceded them with posters and press announcements. The Charlotte, North Carolina, *News* noted that "the large and cultivated audience which greeted Mills was the flower of the thinking people of Charlotte." A poster announcing Mills's talk at Carnegie Hall billed him as "an able speaker and master of his subject."

Mills wrote to Pinchot shortly after he became a federal agent that people knew very little about forestry, that the idea of national forests was still unfamiliar, and that, because of strong anticonservationist sentiment, particularly in the West, "the name Forest Service is one which falls unpleasantly on the ears of most people."[19] He said government pamphlets were still needed in large numbers, and he often carried stacks of Pinchot's own pamphlet, *The Conservation of Natural Resources* (USDA Farmers' Bulletin 327), to hand out after his talks.

The peak of Mills's lecturing activity in 1908 coincided with the zenith of Progressive conservation in the Roosevelt administration; Mills's most frequent talk was "Our Friends the Trees," in which he explained the almost limitless benefits of forests to the nation. He showed that a third of all American wealth derived ultimately from its forests. He expounded on the theme that sound conservation

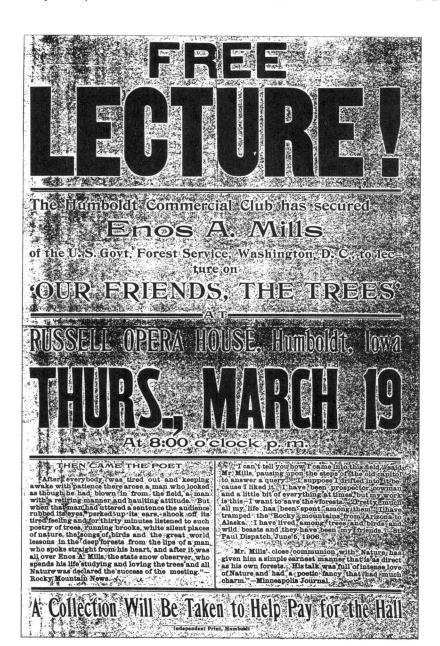

Advance billing, Humboldt, Iowa, 1908. *Mills Papers, Denver Public Library*

practices underlie sound civilization generally. He traced the history of forestry back to ancient China and Japan, in Germany from the time of Frederick the Great, and in Switzerland, where one stand of forest had been yielding an undiminished crop for six centuries. He still called fire the greatest enemy of forests but now spoke openly of the ruthless slaughter of unregulated lumbering. He related deforestation to floods, air pollution, drought, the spread of disease, the growth of slums, and the ultimate decay of civilization. He said that because of upstream deforestation, more silt was flowing into the Mississippi than was being dug from the Panama Canal. The money spent on flood control levees should be used for upstream tree planting instead, he said. The same arguments applied to the vast network of inland waterways, which cost the federal government millions in dredging to keep free for transportation.

Mills told Floridians that cutting too many pines would cool the climate and endanger the orange industry. He said that the French method of turpentine extraction from pines should be used to avoid killing the trees. He told audiences in farming areas that 20 to 40 percent of all agricultural land should be planted with trees to help stabilize climate, control erosion, and provide bird habitat. Birds would in turn reduce tree and crop damage from insects — a matter of immense monetary importance. He discouraged converting forests into commercial assets, but urged rather that people plant trees as an investment, as a farmer sows his grain. He said planting trees in Nebraska and Kansas had made some arid regions agriculturally productive again, and that in areas of marginal precipitation forest protection can save crops in dry seasons by reducing evaporation. He supported dryland farming as a necessary adjunct to irrigated farming in the West and said it was intimately related to proper forestry practices. Forests can be planted as to make every field a harbor, he lectured. He paid high tribute to Pinchot and praised the work of the USFS in combating forest fires and diseases and in developing methods of creating healthier and faster-growing timber stands. He knew his subject so well that he could speak for two hours without a script.

One of Pinchot's major publicity efforts was to reassure the public that conservation does not mean locking up resources, that "the first principle of conservation is development, the use of the natural resources now existing on this continent for the benefit of the people who live here now." Mills, even while dwelling more on planting trees than on harvesting them, also assured his audiences that conservation did not mean nonuse. Rather than removing them from use, national forests make them more useful, he said. "Forestry is cooperation with nature." He said that raising trees like crops in fact goes nature one step better by bringing them to maturity faster. "Scientific forestry may be called intensive farming with trees as the crop," he explained. Even Christmas trees, he said, serve as a useful reminder of the benefits of the forest. "The more Christmas trees there are in the homes, the more lessons taught of what those trees are and do for the country . . . the more good will come to the forest," he said. He had absorbed the Pinchot orthodoxy well, and faithfully reproduced it in his own idiom.[20]

Early in the game he illustrated his talks with lantern slides — a suggestion from Hale — and one paper reported that both Mills's lectures and pictures had "attracted wide attention in all parts of the U.S." Sometimes he showed a quick sequence of slides illustrating good and bad forestry practices, but more and more he abandoned pictures in order to concentrate on his words. He sprinkled his talks with epigrams he hoped would stick — folksy tidbits such as "Keep your farms out of your rivers if you want to keep your rivers"; "Forest destruction is national suicide"; "Dr. Woodpecker is the chief surgeon of the forest"; and "No bald-headed man ought to shoot birds that catch flies and mosquitos."[21]

Mills added new anecdotes to his talks: the suspicious prospectors at Buchanan Pass who followed him as he examined and talked to trees; his vivid adventures as snow observer in the wild Colorado mountains; his escapades with Scotch; his habit of eating only once a day in the wilds, learned from the Indians; and a rich assortment of lore on birds, trees, and animals. His account of dissecting a huge fallen pine in southwestern Colorado and reading its history from its rings and scars was immensely popular — so much so that the governor of Georgia took Mills home after the lecture and woke his wife and daughter to hear Mills repeat it. Through his accounts, Scotch became a national celebrity along with Mills, and newspapers sometimes ran separate stories of their adventures.

In an age when outdoor themes had new and fresh appeal, Mills's combination of ruggedness and lyricism gave him good mileage. People saw that his prowess as a woodsman came from his knowledge and love of nature, rather than from a he-mannish determination to subdue nature. He satisfied Americans' nostalgia for the pioneer experience by telling them they could find a deep relationship with nature wherever they lived, but he urged them to correct the mistakes of the pioneer past. Mills's combination of fact, mood, and advice added up to a strong message of hope for the nation, that it could regain vigor by practicing conservation according to its broadest principle: humane common sense.

The press delighted in covering Mills's talks and quickly gave him national prominence. They called him "one of the foremost exponents of the new profession of forestry in the U.S.," a "distinguished scientist," "a naturalist of the highest order," "one of the most original students of nature of the present day," "a man in whom the scientist is blended with the artist," and "a person who sees with the heart as well as with an accurate eye." They commented on his simplicity and immediacy, but also on his fervor, which "dazzles like a forest fire on a mountain ridge at night." They called him "conversant to the finest shade," and said that "his words were simple but his thoughts pungent with reason." They said, "His eloquence partakes of the ruggedness and altitudes of his native hills," and that he "outclassed every other lecturer on the subject."[22]

The press doted on his eccentricities, his simple dress, his frugal diet, his preference for a handful of raisins to a sumptuous banquet. They were curious about his bachelorhood, and some called him the hermit of the Rockies. Learning little about his private life, they commented on his reticence: "He is long on enthusiasm but short on autobiography." They liked his personal appearance, which matched his character. One paper said his face showed the effect of blazing sun and bitter wind and that he had the nose of the pioneer and the clear, blue eye of the man of the open country. His hair, it said, was gone in front and long behind and gave him the odd appearance of wearing a wig that has slipped. Not suprisingly, Mills picked up colorful titles such as Professor Mills, Dr. Mills, and Colonel Mills to add to The Honorable Enos A. Mills that he earned as an official government representative.

The Denver press eagerly claimed Mills as a native son, citing his service to the state and his inspiration to the forestry movement. An admiring writer who later moved to Estes Park said of him, "The great movement toward the conservation of natural resources is one of the epoch-making events in the history of the United States; and of this movement Enos Mills is the inspired prophet."[23] That writer even asserted that Mills was the equal in stature to Pinchot, and had arrived there without Pinchot's advantages of wealth and influence. But for all their hyperbole and frequent treatment of Mills as a novelty bred in the womb of nature, the hundreds of press accounts showed a consistent theme: Mills was a vital force in American conservation. He was justly remembered in Colorado's 1976 Bicentennial history as the conservation publicist who "found an admiring audience of millions."[24] Mills had achieved his goal of "being effective," and scores of his hosts, besides writing to Pinchot of Mills's great service, gave him gratifying assurances that his influence would carry forward directly into the political process. Mills was widely viewed as a sower of seeds, and Pinchot could have wished no more from his official representative.

The climax of Mills's lecturing career came in January 1908, when he was the principal speaker at the convention of the Appalachian Forestry Association in Atlanta. The timing coincided with the campaign for the Southern Appalachian and White Mountain Forestry Reserves (HR 10454) — one of the first tests of Congress's willingness to designate national forests after having removed that power from the presidency. Now, more than ever, the establishment of protected forests required public pressure. As he lectured through the South in early January, he geared his talks to this crucial issue with the constant reminder, "Congress is at your command." He sparked letter-writing campaigns and inspired some towns to pass municipal resolutions supporting the bill. Roosevelt was campaigning from the sidelines and had written the president of the Appalachian Forestry Association stressing the need for national or state forests all along the Appalachian crest. But Mills was the warrior on the scene, mobilizing grassroots support. If ever he was a direct ambassador of the president, it was now.

The Atlanta convention was jammed with delegates from over a dozen southern states. Pinchot and Roosevelt both sent telegrams. Even at this convention with an immediate political goal, Mills spoke "with deepest interest . . . as the lover of nature and trees and birds." In urging strong concerted action to influence Congress, Mills "brought out the more intellectual and aesthetic phases of the subject and directly appealed to that better human self . . . which reaches out for closer contact with nature." Mills drew from his versatile kit of fact and mood, then waxed poetic to end his speech with a utopian prophecy of conditions after fifty years of enlightened forestry practices.[25]

Errant knight in defense of the nation's forests. Mills was the convention's star performer. *Mills Papers, Denver Public Library.*

In tones distinctly reminiscent of Bellamy's *Looking Backward,* Mills said the Forest Service in fifty years could report that the national forests were now universally accepted and producing greater wood crops and revenues every year. Former desert areas such as the Dakota badlands and the Nevada desert were now forested and would soon be yielding paying crops too. Forest fires and floods had been virtually eliminated, and farms, now sheltered by trees, were more productive. People, brought increasingly outdoors by "tree-love" and "excellent and artistic systems of roads and trails," had become healthier. The national forests were wonderlands of peaks, canyons, flowery dells, and wooded wilds, visited by large numbers of both Americans and Europeans. Birds had become tame through universally friendly treatment, and "one of the pretty common pictures in the forest [was] children and birds playing together." Forests had taken their place as a strong influence on American arts and letters, inspiring "immortal poems" and filling "many grand books with [their] strength . . . and . . . majesty."[26]

Mills received a standing ovation. Two of the conference organizers wrote Pinchot praising his performance, and Pinchot at once wrote back to thank and congratulate him. Pinchot saw the meeting as thoroughly successful and was impressed by the wide support forestry was gaining in the South. The press cited Mills as being one of the most influential in bringing about the needed awakening.

But events were transpiring that should have begun to tell Mills he had pitched his tent in the wrong camp. In May 1908, Pinchot organized a governors' conference on the conservation of natural resources to publicize the concept of resource management on a scale never before attempted. He invited the governors of all the states and territories, each with three advisors; every member of Congress; the nine Supreme Court justices; Roosevelt's cabinet; the Inland Waterways Commission; the presidents of sixty-eight scientific, academic, civic, legal, industrial, agricultural, and commercial organizations; the editors of twenty-one prominent periodicals, as well as representatives from the press and forty-eight "general guests" (mostly governmental agency chiefs) and five special guests — altogether over 1,000 attendees. In his keynote address, Roosevelt called the gathering "a meeting of the representatives of all the people of the United States called to consider the weightiest problem now before the Nation."[27]

But those "representatives of all the people of the United States" did not include John Muir and other leading preservationists who by now were a considerable force on the American conservation scene, with a large public following. Pinchot had carefully orchestrated the conference planning to exclude Muir, whose vision of man's right relation to nature was beyond the ken of Progressive conservation. Robert Underwood Johnson, Muir's publisher and himself a vocal preservationist, wrote to Pinchot of the glaring omission of Muir. Still Muir was not invited. The participants were instead geologists; chemists; electrical, mechanical, hydrological, mining, transportation, and waterway engineers; utility managers; economic planners; scientific foresters and lumbermen; forest product manufacturers; stockmen; agricultural and irrigation experts; manufacturers from industries using natural resources (and what industries did not?); prominent businessmen, including Andrew Carnegie; the railroad magnate John Mitchell; and labor leader James Hill. They were there not to talk about beauty or a sacred cosmos, but about "this great material question of our time."

That great — and by now well worn — question was the imminent depletion of the nation's natural resources — its forests, coal, iron, oil, and gas. The country had squandered them in a reckless pursuit of wealth, and now its very safety and continuance were at stake, said Roosevelt. The critical time had arrived to inventory the remaining resources and to work as a unified nation in rationing their use. It seemed like a belated conference agenda coming at the end of Roosevelt's second term. But whatever lessons the governors had missed in eight years of Rooseveltian conservation, the conference, Pinchot believed, now drove home. It gave the governors "a conviction of national unity that had never dawned on them before," wrote Pinchot in his autobiography.[28]

Had the wisdom existed, the time would have been ripe as well to understand what the preservationists had to say and to urge that grand gathering of movers and shakers to seek a balance between material, cultural, and spiritual goals. But of over 100 speakers only three mentioned nonmaterial uses of resources. While the conference was ostensibly planned around the governors, it remained the conference of technical experts it was planned to be before the idea of inviting the governors was conceived. A Florida representative discussed plans to drain the Everglades and turn them into plantations. An Iowa delegate boasted that "no rugged mountains with [Iowa's]

borders mock the civilizing hand of man." The president of the
National Association of Manufacturers regretted that "every hour of
the day and night horsepower representing many million of units is
thrown away at the cataract of Niagara."

But two speakers, J. Horace McFarland, president of the American Civic Association, and George F. Kunz, president of the American Scenic and Historic Society, who could not — perhaps for
diplomatic reasons — be excluded from the conference, used the
opportunity to speak out strongly for scenic beauty as a vital
national resource. They stressed the social consequences of urban
and rural beauty, and argued that patriotism and love of country
depend primarily on that beauty. They deplored the appalling ugli-
ness of American cities, the unsightly railroad thoroughfares, advertising signs nailed everywhere on trees, waste dumps from factories,
mines and quarries, dead fish along large stretches of the polluted
Hudson River — all blights that could be corrected by regulative legislation and all things that should come under the jurisdiction of a
national conservation policy. The final message of both speakers
came down to national attitudes and priorities. America's crass com-
mercialism must not engulf the conservation movement. The nation
must grow up and decide to be a civilized country where commercial
development is not the sole standard of progress.

If those views startled the audience momentarily, they had no
lasting effect. No mention of scenic preservation made it into the
governors' declarations that summed up the conference. Not even
the simplest principles on which preservationists and utilitarians
might have agreed, such as steps to mitigate environmental damage
during extraction of resources, came out of the conference. The
spirit of the conference's opening prayer persisted to the end: "The
harvest field is ready and Thou are pleased to send us into the harvest."[29]

Pinchot, locked single-mindedly into his own vision, saw the
conference as a possible "turning point in human history." He called
it an event that "drove home the basic truth that the planned and
orderly development of the earth and all it contains is indispensable
to the permanent prosperity of the human race." As such, he said, it
even provided a basic foundation for permanent world peace. For
him the conference's strength was in treating the management of natural resources "not as a series of separate and independent tasks but
[as] one single problem." Yet he did not understand the simple

notion that cultural and spiritual values are part of that "single problem," and that the "permanent prosperity of the human race" requires something beyond material well-being. Johnson, who attended the conference as a member of the press, complained that the national conservation leaders in their obsession for efficient use of the environment were little better than the exploiters they purported to replace. He excoriated the conference for having claimed that "beauty, healthfulness, and habitability of our country should be preserved and increased," while in fact the country's conservation leaders "have not even shown a cordial . . . interest in safeguarding . . . scenery." McFarland confronted Pinchot bluntly, saying the conservation movement was being weakened by its failure "to join hands with the preservation of scenery," and in 1909 he published an influential essay called "Ugly Conservation."[30]

It was time for Mills to recognize that his own declarations about the beauty of nature, the higher values of forests, the ideas he shared with McFarland, Kunz, and Johnson about the economic value of scenery, and the benefits of the outdoors to an overworked society, had been excluded from the nation's official conservation agenda. Mills may have attended the conference on a press pass — he told a New York audience on May 11 that it was his next destination — but he was not an official participant. He was precisely the man who could have told those thousand obdurate utilitarians the single most important lesson of his talks in every state of the union: What sells conservation to the masses is the promise that forests, though managed for utility, can remain places of beauty if beauty is maintained as a carefully safeguarded goal. Mills was given no opportunity to tell the conference that or anything else about how conservation ideas were being understood and acted on at the grassroots level. Nor among those "representatives of all the people of the United States" did women have a voice. The president of the GFWC was invited to attend but not asked to speak. And Roosevelt's keynote address spoke to men only: "Governors of the several states, and gentlemen," he began.

Mills never stated whether he knew about the intentional exclusion of Muir or how little the conference cared about what McFarland and Kunz had so passionately argued. This important moment in history may have passed Mills by, for he wrote in seeming innocence in 1915 that "the White House conference of governors recommended that 'the beauty . . . of our country should be preserved and increased'" — exactly what the conference had failed to recommend. Mills continued for another year as official Forest Service spokesman, optimistically spreading the conservation gospel as before. He did not update his talks with any material from the conference, and he did not ruffle the Forest Service's feathers by publicly opposing the Hetch Hetchy Dam proposal in California. Hetch Hetchy was now a national cause célèbre, with legions of conservationists rallying behind Muir in opposition. McFarland was campaigning vigorously for Muir, as were Johnson's *Century Magazine* and many other prominent national magazines. Johnson called Roosevelt's failure to stop the dam a blot on his administration. Senate testimony, he said, had clearly shown that other sources existed for the water. Apart from McFarland's mention of it, the Governors' Conference had completely avoided the issue of Hetch Hetchy, and Muir said afterward, "Pinchot is ambitious, never hesitating to sacrifice anything or anybody in his way." If Pinchot was uneasy that McFarland was arranging many of Mills's speaking engagements, he continued to receive reassurances from Mills's hosts that he was ably representing the Forest Service's cause.[31]

It is not clear at what point Mills began to shed his illusions that national forests would uphold scenic and recreational values. Did McFarland — whom Mills knew well — help him comprehend that it was only wishful thinking to suppose another fifty years of Forest Service administration would make "majestic wonderlands" of the national forests? Hadn't Mills seen the actual results of cutting? And did he think that cattle grazing on the national forests would leave "flowery dells"? Did Mills not see that the agency he represented had no use for beauty and that Pinchot could not "see beyond the end of a lumber pile"? Mills, perhaps subtly and innocently, began to speak about national parks as well as national forests as places of beauty and recreation. And Pinchot, who deeply distrusted the national park movement, could not tolerate pro-park propaganda from his Forest Service representative. Mills may also have drifted toward favoring the transfer of national forests to the states. In his Atlanta speech, in fact, he projected that in fifty years "the greater portion" of the nation's four billion acres of commercially earning forests would belong to the states. Pinchot correctly feared the transfer of the forests to the states as a scheme by which private interests would soon gain possession, and he tried to lay the transfer idea to rest at the Governors' Conference. If Mills naively suggested transfer to the states — an idea he too should have opposed — Pinchot would have wanted him quickly silenced.

But those rare deviations from the party line are scarcely perceptible in the continuing press accounts of Mills's talks and cannot be taken as an attempt to undercut Forest Service policy. Notified that his "services [were] no longer required, effective at the termination of April 30, 1909," Mills gave his last talk on April 28 and said nothing inflammatory. Pinchot preceded the termination notice with a polite letter explaining that "the educational work of the Service in connection with women's clubs has practically been completed," a plausible assertion since the Forest Service was winding down its speakers' program anyway. Perhaps sensing he had been eased out, Mills said later that he had in fact resigned in October 1908, to be effective the following May, and he reminded Pinchot of that in a 1912 letter. But nothing in Pinchot's termination letter or in the official termination notice indicates any response to an action initiated by Mills. Had Mills resigned over any ideological differences, it is unlikely that Pinchot would have allowed him to continue speaking during those seven months, in which he gave 161 talks in thirty-one states.[32]

Mills had in any event reached a necessary stopping point. It was not a schedule anyone could maintain indefinitely, and press accounts were commenting on his need to return to Colorado for a rest after five years of nearly constant work in the forestry cause. Mills had, furthermore, found time in those busy years to write a book, check the proofs at Houghton Mifflin in Boston, and bask in a new source of national acclaim. And at home he was at last getting a taste of what grazing under Forest Service leases really meant: Cattle grazing on the surrounding national forests began wandering onto his own unfenced property, chewing their way right past his signs that read RESERVED FOR FLOWERS. The problem would soon escalate into bitter feuds with both his neighbors and the Forest Service, and would dog him for the rest of his life.

CHAPTER 15

Mills at Forty: Books, Politics, Domestic Strife

Mills's career passed easily from lecturing to writing. His 1909 *Wild Life on the Rockies* gave the same message of an invigorating and life-affirming outdoors that had swayed his lecture audiences. The book was not and did not need to be a work of reflection. The same glad phrases that rang out from the podium echoed through the book: "This is a beautiful world"; "enter the forest and the boundaries of nations are forgotten"; "it may be that some time an immortal pine will be the flag of a united and peaceful world." With the hint of a pun in the book's title to signify both the "wild life" of Mills's rugged living and the wildlife he saw, Mills devoted three of the book's twelve chapters to his daring adventures as a snow observer and the majority of the rest to animal lore.

Scarcely pausing to describe the snow observer's significance to western water management, Mills told about living in the snow, surviving falls, and riding avalanches. No matter what the danger, the message was positive. "I breathed only by gasps, and my heart became violent and feeble by turns," he said of the "electric atmospheric waves" that once held him in their grip. "But since I have felt no ill results, the effect of the entire experience may have been beneficial." With those kinds of assurances, Mills replaced conventional warnings that the mountains "don't care" with rhapsodic assertions that "nature is one of the safest and most sanitary of places." It is, he claimed, a blissful sanctuary from the "death-list" of urban perils.

Mills's adventures with Scotch and with the return horse Midget gave testimony to the deep bond between man and animal. His account of guiding eight-year-old Harriet Peters up Longs Peak bespoke the same between adult and child. And his genial surveys of

Rocky Mountain birds and flowers echoed Muir's sentiments about the affinity between humans and all of nature. To whom else besides Muir could Mills have dedicated his first full-length book?[1]

Several of the pieces in *Wild Life* had appeared previously in magazines. And when Mills published his second book, *The Spell of the Rockies,* in 1911, twelve of the eighteen stories were magazine reprints. The books and most to follow were thus loose collections of miscellany rather than sustained works of prose. As a magazine writer, Mills gained broad readership and immediate income. Magazines publishing his popular essays then and in years to come included the *Saturday Evening Post, Atlantic, Harper's, World's Work, Collier's, Craftsman, Country Gentleman, Country Life, American Boy, Youth's Companion, Outlook, Muncies, Cosmopolitan, McClure's, Recreation, Sunset, Physical Culture,* and the magazine sections of numerous newspapers. The short vacation season at Longs Peak Inn made supplemental income desirable if not imperative, and Mills said at least as late as 1914 that writing helped make up deficits from the inn. Through his books Mills achieved a more enduring literary reputation, taking his place as a nature writer published by Houghton Mifflin along with Burroughs and Muir. It must have been a dream ardently pursued.

The *Spell of the Rockies* built on the success of *Wild Life* and increased the number of spine-tingling adventure stories that had proved so popular and had brought a compliment even from Gifford Pinchot in an otherwise businesslike correspondence when relations between the two were at best cordial. Mills's first two books laid claim to his genre of outdoor adventure: daring what few others dared, surviving against all odds, pursuing danger for the sake of the poetic inspiration.

Other essays reprinted in *The Spell of the Rockies* from the *Saturday Evening Post* presented most of the forestry material from Mills's lectures. He told Pinchot in a 1912 letter that lecturing was his main contribution to the forestry movement, and that these essays were a representative summary of what he had said. But they differed strikingly from his lectures in abandoning any mention of wise-use forestry or the Forest Service. There was no doubt about what Mills wanted to have remembered and not remembered as his contribution to American forestry. The four essays showed Mills's skill in making technical subjects interesting and a matter of importance to a large lay audience. His balance of the poetic and practical,

rehearsed and rewarded at the podium, served him well as an interpretive nature writer. His essay on forest fires, the book's lengthiest,
takes the reader into a burning forest:

> Up the shallow forested valley below me came the flames, an inverted
> Niagara of red and yellow, with flying spray of black. It sent forward a
> succession of short-lived whirlwinds that went to pieces explosively,
> hurling sparks and blazing bark far and high. During one of its wilder
> displays the fire rolled forward, an enormous horizontal whirl of
> flame, and then, with thunder and roar, the molten flames swept
> upward into a wall of fire; this tore to pieces, collapsed, and fell for-
> ward in fiery disappearing clouds. With amazing quickness the splen-
> did hanging garden on the terraced heights was crushed and blackened.
> By my promontory went this magnificent zigzag surging front of flame,
> blowing the heavens full of sparks and smoke and flinging enormous
> fiery rockets. Swift and slow, loud and low, swelling and vanishing, it
> sang its eloquent death song.[2]

And with a telling series of verbs Mills sums up the "bald facts"
of how "fires make the Rocky Mountains still more rocky":

> Most Rocky Mountain fires not only skin off the humus but so cut up
> the fleshy soil and so completely destroy the fibrous binding that the
> elements quickly drag much of it from the bones and fling it down into
> the stream-channels. Down many summit slopes in these mountains,
> where the fires went to bed-rock, the snows and waters still scoot and
> scour. The fire damage to some of these steep slopes cannot be repaired
> for generations and even centuries.[3]

Mills's dramatic skill made the still rampant problem of fires a
true-life matter rather than an abstract statistic. As a naturalist he
told his readers how he reconstructed the causes of fires. As an
adventurer he told the bizarre tale of eating from a fire-roasted deer
carcass and leaving the rest to a waiting grizzly. And as a committed
social reformer, he told of sitting under a rock shelf in the remains of
a burned forest to reflect on the "injustice and enormous loss" they
caused.

Mills's prose was sincere, enthusiastic, and uncomplicated. He
sought consciously to be understandable by everyone, and from the
beginning his books appealed to readers of all ages. His first-person
narratives presented him as a genial guide who described the wonders

of nature and related his own adventures with enthusiasm and some-times modest understatement. Mills the narrator was good-natured, idealistic, and mild-mannered, but excitable when appropriate. His heroic deeds inevitably glorified him, but not at the expense of his message that nature can be a place of self-attainment for everyone. Mills's tendency to personify nature provoked a warning from one reviewer that he was "near the danger zone" of fictionalizing nature through anthropomorphism, but his 1913 work *In Beaver World* soon proved his capacity for a more sustained documentary style.

With the publication of *Spell* in 1911 and the revision of his pamphlet *Early Estes Park and a Guidebook* that same year, Mills's published output reached a total of five or six dozen essays ranging over the subjects of natural history, forestry and conservation, adventure, travel, local history, local color, and opinion — the last mostly as letters to the editor. He was at heart a journalist, both as a reporter on nature's doings in the back woods and as an editorializer with messages suited to the age's meliorative taste. Since the late 1890s, when he had gathered resort news in the Estes area at one-third cent a word for three Denver newspapers, his writing career had been subject to the tastes and requirements of his editors. "Give the names of the most important tourists only," instructed his editor in 1896. And "give me a vigorous story on forest fires," said Walter A. Dyer of *Country Life* in 1910. He received regular correspon-dence from some of the country's big-name magazine editors, such as George Horace Lorimer of the *Saturday Evening Post* ("looking forward to seeing you at the publishers' dinner") and Walter Hines Page of the *World's Work* ("delighted with 'Thousand Year Pine'").[4]

Mills's revision of *Early Estes Park* in 1911 brought up to date the pamphlet he first published in 1905 at his own expense through J. A. Maguire's *Outdoor Life* Publishing Company. Maguire, who helped launch Mills's speaking career, had also published his first bona fide magazine story, an account of the western painter E. S. Paxton, in 1902. The 1911 edition of *Early Estes Park* chronicled the park's history from its earliest settlement to the progress brought by Freelan O. Stanley, whose arrival in 1903 Mills called the epoch-making event in the history of Estes Park. Stanley was a man of wealth and influence, who with his brother Francis had cashed in on a photographic patent and then developed the famous Stanley Steamer automobile. When he came to Estes Park from Massachu-setts he was reduced by tuberculosis to less than 100 pounds. He

responded at once to the high, dry mountain air and quickly perceived the tangible benefits of climate and the drawing power of
scenery and tourist services.

When Stanley opened his luxury, eighty-eight-room hotel in
1910, Mills wrote, "This large and adventurous investment required
nerve, good business sense, the capacity to see the recreation needs
of the future, and showed great confidence in the future of Estes
Park." The business world took note and the resulting publicity, said
Mills, "greatly hastened [Estes Park's] development." Though some
of Mills's vision about how people should experience nature rubbed
off on Stanley, the hotel was largely an accommodation for gentry
and was strikingly different from Longs Peak Inn and the area's
other log and stone lodges. Three new specimens of the latter had
opened their doors in 1910 alone, while Stanley opened an annex —
the Stanley Manor — a year after the hotel to accommodate over-
flow. Estes Park easily drew enough guests to fill all available accommodations, with the number of annual visitors reaching 50,000 by
1913. Tourists, "a potential wave of prosperity," had "splashed into
the park," exactly as Mills had predicted.[5]

With only a small amount of state help, Stanley rebuilt the road
from Lyons to Estes Park for his twelve-passenger Stanley mountain
wagons. The steamers covered the stretch in one and a half hours
and soon replaced the four-hour stagecoach. Representing the side of
Progressivism that believed in putting capital to work for civic
improvements, Stanley gave funds for the school and town water
system, and land for a seven-acre park. And the munificent entrepreneur supplied the town with electricity from his hotel's generating
plant. Other businesses were sprouting along street-front lots created in 1905; the first among them were a bakery, butcher shop,
laundry, photographic studio, shoe repair, and livery. By 1910 the
village had a population of 400 and a school, church, volunteer fire
department, and municipal utilities, including a telephone exchange.

Progressivism in Estes Park also found expression in the Estes
Park Protective and Improvement Association (EPPIA). The name,
though prosaic, expressed exactly what Mills thought man's relation
to nature should be: to protect it and to improve it for the betterment
of humanity. Led by Stanley as president and C. S. Bond as secretary
(whom Mills admired as a "live wire" and man of strong convictions)
the EPPIA sponsored road and trail construction, built a fish hatch-
ery, and encouraged game and flower protection. Bighorn sheep and

deer soon became so plentiful that Mills wrote cheerfully in 1911 that they could again be seen "delightfully near the roadside." In 1914 Stanley helped fund elk imports from Yellowstone to restore the local herd.

The EPPIA broadened the language of Mills's flower protection signs at Longs Peak Inn to serve the whole area. The notice ended with the reminder that the association was the valley's watchful conscience: "Those who pull flowers up by the roots will be condemned by all worthy people, and also by the Estes Park Protective and Improvement Association."[6]

Estes Park had become a thriving resort nestled amid scenery of incomparable beauty, aware of its destiny, defining and shaping its future with vigor and optimism. Its name took on new significance, for though "park" is a geographic designation in Colorado — meaning an open valley surrounded by mountains — the region now had aspects of a man-made public park as well. It was a park in the spirit of those illustrious Frederick Law Olmsteds — father and son — who preached that parks should restore people, raise their hopes, reduce crime, and breed individual and social efficiency. An Olmsted admirer, Mills believed too that parks were "society's safety valve."

As a resort, Estes Park was by definition a retreat, far from the world's cultural epicenters where twentieth-century genius was striking out in new directions, some too modern for most of the world to comprehend even today. There were, doubtless, among the park's sophisticated summer clientele, those who could name the artistic avant-garde from Picasso to Pound, Stravinsky and Proust. Some could discuss the discovery of chromosomes, the importance of vitamins, technological developments in lighting, photography, and radio, the precursors of plastics, and New York's first skyscrapers. A few, perhaps, could hold conversation on the theory of relativity. Many of the well-to-do vacationers were acquiring those beguiling new gadgets such as electric irons and toasters that were fast breeding a consumer society. There were doubtlessly some who owned shares in the 112 corporations now controlled by three men that had an assessed value greater than all the property of the states west of the Mississippi. Some were bound to have favored and others to have opposed America's now well practiced habit of defending its foreign investments with troops. And there must have been more than a few who saw the conditions brewing for the war that would permanently change the world's outlook.

It was time, if Mills still had the radical views of a socialist, to take stock of where society stood after the immensely popular Roosevelt presidency. If Progressive conservation had turned out to be something he could no longer support, what about the rest of the Roosevelt agenda? Though there was nothing in Estes Park to mar the lustre of Progressivism — no minorities, strikes, slums, urban crowding, dirt, or factory smoke — it was not far, even to places in Colorado, where employers were saying with impunity that widows of workers killed on the job would receive no compensation. Workers continued to labor under long hours, low pay, and severely substandard and often lethal working conditions. Tens of thousands died every year from job-related accidents, Roosevelt's critics charged. A quarter of a million children ten to fifteen years old continued to be exploited under nearly slavelike conditions in factories, mines, and mills. When a march of children was organized to dramatize their plight and present their case to Roosevelt personally, he refused to see them. Critics deplored that neither Roosevelt nor Taft did anything to stop the murderous riots against racial minorities and the constant lynchings of blacks. Debs and other socialists pointed out that the wealthy class was growing wealthier in staggering proportions, while enlisting the law and military force against the working class. Where was Roosevelt's "distributive justice"? And why did socialism continue to grow during his presidency? Roosevelt, many historians say now, was deeply conservative after all, and events during his two terms reflected that.

The muckraking writers not only exposed abuses but also pointed to the need to change the whole system: Progressivism was a sham. Upton Sinclair, Theodore Dreiser, Frank Norris, and Jack London all espoused socialism in their impassioned novels of social abuse. Eugene Debs, occasionally retiring to Estes Park to renew his strength, galvanized crowds with his oratory, and might, when they met in 1913, have given Mills a personal lesson in what was wrong with the times. But that keen-witted writer Edna Ferber, an occasional Longs Peak Inn guest and literary acquaintance of Mills's, may, on the other hand, have grafted onto Mills some of her boundless admiration for Roosevelt. For her, as for millions of others, Roosevelt was precisely the man who "dispelled . . . the cynical assumption that there was one law for the rich and another for the poor."[7]

With the capital-labor conflict nevertheless intensifying, Debs helped found the Industrial Workers of the World (IWW) midway in Roosevelt's presidency. So sweeping a consolidation of labor was an enormous threat to established interests, and they attacked it with a vengeance through the press, the courts, the police, the army, with mob violence, and by the denial of constitutional rights. Throughout the Roosevelt era and into the Taft presidency, violent class struggle continued and socialism flourished. In 1910 a socialist congressman was elected, and a year later seventy-three cities had socialist mayors. In the presidential election of 1912, Debs won over a million votes, the largest showing ever for a socialist candidate. A useful but missing piece of information would be to know how Mills voted in that election: for Taft, who was proving friendly to the cause of national parks, now Mills's chief preoccupation; for Roosevelt, who had defected from the ultraconservative majority of the Republican party and now led the Bull Moose ticket, but might have continued the indifference to scenic preservation exemplified at the 1908 Conference of Governors; for Debs, at the peak of his popularity and a hero of the oppressed; or for Wilson, who was unpredictable in his limited understanding of the outdoors but warned that after twelve years of Roosevelt and Taft the wealthy few controlled the government more than ever in an economic system grown utterly "heartless."

We can guess, though at risk of oversimplification, that Mills voted for the candidate he thought would be most likely to favor the Rocky Mountain National Park proposal now in the works. Though he took parks to be a broad social issue in their own right and an absolute necessity for a healthy society, little evidence remains of his views on other social issues. Isolated radical attitudes would crop up in his public statements in coming years, but outdoor causes transcended them and may have gained their broadest support through their nonpartisan appeal. Mills remained a reformer rather than a revolutionary. His pronouncement that "any normal person under fifty [who] cannot enjoy a storm in the wilds . . . ought to reform at once" exemplifies his quickness to frame even outdoor issues in reformist terms.[8] A broadly and wisely conceived park movement, from the local to the national level, became virtually his sole political issue, and he would see its benefits as little short of a national panacea.

When Mills left government service as a public forestry lecturer, he rejoined the ranks of impassioned amateurs who carried the banner for the preservation of nonmaterial values. Now a foe of the Forest Service, he saw national forests as at best a necessary evil. They had become for him the vulgar opposite of national parks, and raising trees as crops was little different, he said, from "raising hogs." Cutting quotas allowed woodsmen to "fell [trees] by the thousands to keep numerous sawmills at work." A national park, by contrast, has "a more important place in the life of every man, woman and child in the land," Mills said, "for [it] suppl[ies] the finer, the greater, things in life." Rangers in national forests were narrow specialists who issued grazing permits "to the detriment of the native wild flowers"; those fit for the "noble work" of the national park profession, on the other hand, understood the principles of forests, recreation, and education, combined the abilities of artists and teachers, mastered the details of natural history, and could transmit their "knowledge in an understandable form to the benefit of visiting multitudes." Of course national forests and national parks should at last come under separate management, for they represent, said Mills, "radically different" land-use principles.[9]

Mills could not wholly abandon an acknowledgment that those bureaucratic tree farms had a place in the nation's well-being. But, though a businessman himself, he relegated them to the harsh, almost sordid world of business. "They are plainly and severely a business proposition," he said. Mills remained, in fact, curiously ambivalent about the wholesomeness of business for the rest of his life. Once agreeing with the "business sense" applied to national forests, he was now appalled at the result. As a park crusader he was more quick to denounce the Forest Service than the national forests themselves; as a Progressive he continued to believe, almost to the word, what McFarland put succinctly in 1912: "The primary function of the national forests is to supply lumber. The primary function of national parks is to maintain in healthy efficiency the lives of the people who must use that lumber."[10] That ethic, itself profoundly utilitarian, was not one that would teach Americans a broadly based love of land either through using it or preserving it. If Mills appeared in a few statements to repudiate the whole utilitarian frame of reference, he in fact moved only incrementally away from it. He would remain, as a promoter of parks and tourism, an apostle for the necessary development to make scenery "usable."

Mills began to spearhead the campaign to establish Rocky Mountain National Park as he turned forty, and he needed the wisdom to know that in the cause of preserving and promoting nature, the political landscape was complex. Pinchot, though congenitally unable to see the value of beauty and recreation, upheld the proclaimed Progressive pledge to protect society against corporate exploitation of natural resources. When he charged that Taft's interior secretary, Richard A. Ballinger, was toadying to special interests in the leasing of Alaskan coalfields, Taft fired him in anger. If Mills took secret delight in that, his own dislike of corporate power must have caused him to admire Pinchot as well. If Ballinger had his seamy side, he was, however, proving friendly to the cause of national parks. He had drafted a bill to establish a parks bureau and looked with favor on the Rocky Mountain National Park proposal. Taft, too, seemed to favor a separate bureau to administer national parks, and he asked just the right person to help investigate the matter: Mills's friend J. Horace McFarland. McFarland called in Frederick Law Olmsted, Jr., a champion of national parks who had crusaded with him to save Hetch Hetchy and Niagara Falls. Olmsted saw in Ballinger's ideas for separate administration of the parks an unsavory bias toward special interests. Ballinger was perhaps a friend of the park cause for the wrong reasons. But when Olmsted proposed regulatory language to protect the integrity of national parks, Ballinger surprised the preservationists by accepting it. McFarland, now Mills's closest ally, was in many ways his opposite as a person: an urban gardener who grew roses and played organ at church services, a conservative Republican with a deep fear of socialism and anarchy.

How would Mills handle this complicated world of allegiances and motives? Saving nature and making it available to the public was not a democratic, republican, or socialist cause. Allies came from unexpected places, and were perhaps only allies on single issues. The world did not consist of simple rights and wrongs, and required strategy, compromise, and pragmatic alliances. As Mills threw himself into the park battle, many saw in him not a flexible savoir faire, but a growing rigidity, a refusal to compromise, and a quickness to denounce opposing views as wrong. His would be a politics of passionate energy and headlong confrontation. He would show an almost ferocious tenacity of purpose, an undaunted fighting spirit, and the faculty of creating enemies, even of his closest allies.

It did not, however, require political confrontation to bring those traits to the surface. Combat began on Mills's own premises and in his own family in the sad and permanent rupture with his brother Joe — a story that can be only approximately reconstructed from fragmentary evidence. Joe Mills (1880–1935) came to Colorado in 1899 as a student at Colorado Agricultural College (CAC) in Fort Collins, and as an athletic prodigy he starred in virtually every contest of football, basketball, baseball, and track.[11]

In 1903, Joe spent a year living near Enos at the foot of Longs Peak. He immersed himself in hiking, camping, and nature study, both with his brother and alone. It was their first real time together, for Joe had been only four when Enos left home in 1884. He eagerly learned what Enos eagerly taught him. Enos was in his own mountaineering prime and accomplishing some of his most daring feats. It was his creed and his gift to teach others. Joe was an able subject: bright, willing, and perhaps flatteringly deferential. Could Enos have fancied himself in the exalted role he imagined Muir had held for him twelve years earlier?

Success followed Joe wherever he went. He held in quick succession coaching or player-coaching jobs in two Ft. Worth colleges. There he earned all-Southwest honors in football, introduced a new set of football rules, and published an article about them when they had proved their worth. By 1908 his talents were in such demand that he received five college-level coaching offers and an offer to play professional baseball.

By helping his brother at Longs Peak Inn in the summers of 1906 and 1907, Joe enabled Enos to begin his speaking career while still developing the young business. The financial records of those summers carry Joe's signature, "Enoch J. Mills, Manager." But he was now a grown man, and if he once accepted the role of kid brother, the urge and need for autonomy was overdue. He, too, was an energized high achiever who perhaps felt eclipsed by Enos's rapid rise to national fame. Joe matched his athletic talent with charm, style in dress and manners, a knack for public speaking, and budding literary aspirations. There was perhaps nothing Enos did that Joe could not potentially do as well.

When Joe arrived at Longs Peak Inn in summer 1908 he had something Enos did not have: a beautiful new bride. He had married Ethyl Steere, a Ft. Worth lawyer's daughter, just a month before. The couple spent their honeymoon at the homestead cabin Joe had built

Joe Mills in his homestead cabin, c. 1903. *NPS photo*.

and occupied in 1906 a couple of miles down the road from Longs Peak Inn. According to a later account from Joe's side of the family, Enos was furious that Joe had married. While the young couple should have enjoyed encouragement from Enos, they labored under his deepening grudge, and the young bride was deprived of a normal and happy relationship with a brother-in-law she could have greatly admired.[12]

The possibility that Enos's bachelorhood was troubling him deeply and leaving a hole in an otherwise abundant existence is underscored by two utterances he made at virtually the same time in 1906. In one he said with evident bravado, "I have the mountains here, and the flowers and birds . . . I need no woman to love me here with these." In the other he said with terse resignation, "I am a bachelor and sorry for it." Usually reticent about his personal life, he confided again several years later, "I have no cause for unhappiness unless it is that I am not married." And far from being a substitute for love, nature, he confessed, was precisely what he wanted to share with a mate.[13]

Approaching middle age, doting on children, and at a ripe age for parenthood, he doubtless craved children too. He said that guiding eight-year-old Harriet Peters up Longs Peak was not only his most memorable climb but "the happiest moment of my life." Perhaps even his relationship with Joe contained an element of sublimated parenting that, with Joe's autonomy, turned to the pain of abandonment. In the recollection of some, Enos had a need to keep Joe "indentured," and the phrase found most frequently in the scanty references to the brothers' relationship was Joe's need to "break away."[14]

A complete rupture occurred in summer 1908, probably over the construction of a small cabin to serve as a way station at timberline on the Longs Peak trail. Joe, the story goes, had it halfway built when Enos intervened with an order from the county to stop construction. Enos then finished the cabin and called it his own. Connected by phone to Longs Peak Inn, Timberline House was used for the next seventeen years for overnight climbing parties and rescue work. *Enos Mills of the Rockies* says with circumspection not that Enos built the cabin but that he "opened" it in 1908. Had Joe begun the cabin, not as an agreed-on project for the inn, but with plans to use it for a guiding service of his own? Or was the quarrel simply a rivalry for the honor of conceiving and completing the project?

It was, in any event, a sorry episode, which can have only been the outward sign of deeper problems. Whatever the private details, the split was painful and irreparable for both. Joe took a coaching job at Baylor University that fall, and an article welcoming him called him "one of the most vigorous athletic men and elegant gentlemen in all the country." Enos at the same time was being lionized in the national press for his deep sensitivity and poetic love of nature. Joe retired from coaching in 1911 and returned to Estes Park, where he and Ethyl opened the highly successful Crags Hotel in 1914. In parallel, but never together, the brothers remained a vital force in Estes Park's development. Some of the summer guests who knew them both — guests of the stature of Clarence Darrow and Irving Hale — began to divide their stays between Longs Peak Inn and the Crags. In Estes Park's historical memory there remains a lasting polarization over the rupture. Joe is remembered as a man of easy charm and grace, Enos as a man by turns kind and irascible, gentle and egotistical. The Crags was a lively social center where the guests were "never allowed to spend a slow time"; Longs Peak Inn was the nature lover's retreat, "austere but bouncing with life [and] sparkling conversation."[15]

In 1926, four years after Enos's death, Joe published an autobiography of his youth, describing primarily his experiences at the foot of Longs Peak in 1903–1904. Called *A Mountain Boyhood,* the book portrays a youth rather younger than Joe actually was at the time. He did not hesitate to take liberties with his material to portray the thrill of mountain adventuring he had experienced. Joe substituted "Parson Lamb" for Enos as the source of knowledge about nature and woodcraft, though, like Enos, he never acknowledged that Lamb was a blood relative. Lamb had a substantial knowledge of the outdoors that both brothers drew on, but it is Enos who stands behind the facade of Lamb as the fountain of information to which young Joe turned with his eager questions. Despite the pain of estrangement, Joe's book returns to an unconscious acknowledgment of the gift of outdoor knowledge he received from Enos. And what Joe purported to have discovered or learned for himself is in an astonishing number of instances identical to what Enos had discovered and learned for himself.

Both brothers reported that they graduated from carrying immense amounts of equipment to practically nothing; from a reliance on firearms to an insistence on carrying none; from using blankets at night to using no source of warmth but a fire. Both learned to subsist on little more than raisins for days at a time and often fasted entirely. Both stressed that they had climbed Longs Peak and camped out in the Rockies in every month of the year. Both said they had followed the Continental Divide from Wyoming to New Mexico. Both escaped from certain death innumerable times under similar or identical conditions, and both claimed that through all their perils they were never afraid. Both had a penchant for falling. Both fell through a cornice at virtually the same spot on the Continental Divide, landed miraculously on a midcliff ledge, worked their way back to the ridge, descended the other side, followed a frozen stream, and fell through the ice.

Both brothers said they spent their happiest days at and above timberline, described it in the same way as a strange and fantastical place, and followed it along mountain slopes for many miles. Both built their own cabins and at once began conducting extensive observations of beavers in the near vicinity. Both learned to become acquainted with wildlife through a combination of patient stationary observations and the curiosity to follow everything of interest. Both believed that animals spend a significant amount of time in leisure activity, that beavers can be downright lazy, and that animals regularly "pay social visits" to their neighbors. Both indulged a romantic idealization of pioneers but learned to be skeptical of the natural history proffered by old timers. Both learned from their own experience not to believe in folkloric assumptions about nature.

Both brothers disliked predation, especially the killing of deer by lions, and both tried at times to foil lion attacks. Both were grizzly fanciers and said the grizzly came to interest them more than any other animal of the wilds. Both wrote admiringly of grizzly intelligence and came to the conclusion that grizzlies can reason. Both had been led to assume from accounts of the Lewis and Clark expedition that grizzlies are aggressive, and both, in their first encounters with grizzlies, fled home in panic, sure they were being pursued. Both went on to conclude from their own experience that grizzlies are unaggressive and mind their own business. Both followed grizzlies extensively and both reported the results of following a grizzly for the first few days after it emerged from hibernation to see what it ate. Both described in detail how they alone captured and brought home the grizzly cubs Johnny and Jenny.

A degree of similarity in the outdoor methods and adventures of the two brothers might not be surprising. Experience often suggests its own solutions, and as seasoned mountaineers they were bound to develop some of the same skills and attitudes. High intelligence and curiosity in both brothers could have bred similar habits of nature observation. The capture of Johnny and Jenny was a joint enterprise reported separately by each brother after the break. Each brother — and especially Enos, with his far longer outdoor career and many more books — reported experiences the other did not.

But the astonishing similarity between the two brothers' attitudes and adventures far outweighs those differences. *A Mountain Boyhood* comes close to serving equally well as the youthful biography of Enos as of Joe. Did Enos, who had twenty years to explore the wilds, have the boyhood Joe craved and had to cram into little more than a year? Did Joe therefore complete — consciously or unconsciously — his own aspirations by drawing from the wealth of his brother's experiences? There were even times when Joe's intention became Enos's accomplishment. Joe had long wanted to repeat Elkanah Lamb's descent of Longs Peak's east face and "planned secretly" to do it; but it was Enos in June 1903 — when the two brothers were together and on good terms — who without announcement accomplished it. Joe did not say that Enos did it, because Enos was absent from his book. But in that feat as in all those that made Joe the hero of his own book, there is an implied acknowledgment and emulation of his older brother.

The fusion of identities has a still more peculiar twist: While Enos always insisted on being taken seriously and did not realize that his constant predicaments often made him appear foolish, Joe was willing to play the clown in episodes that seem overtly farcical. Enos was at times silly without meaning to be; Joe was at times silly by design and with a touch of self-effacement. While still a user of firearms, for example, Joe could never hit his target. Once he gave up and felled with stones the grouse that had patiently sat on an overhead branch watching him haplessly discharge his pistol. And once after emptying his pistol and his whole ammunition belt at a wounded coyote without hitting it once, he fell savagely on the beast with a stick. With obvious self-irony Joe said he turned to using a camera because he could never hit anything with a gun. Enos took up a camera as a matter of principle and perhaps because Muir preached it. Joe was a likable buffoon when he crept along a ledge toward a bighorn sheep, his eye glued to his camera lens, stepped out into thin air, and landed with infallible Millsian luck in the top of a spruce tree. He was likable but scarcely believable when he startled a bighorn lamb with the click of his camera, was dislodged by the falling lamb, lost his camera but caught himself on a bush, then climbed to the bottom of the cliff and carried the dazed lamb to a resuscitating bath in a cold stream.

Joe was the consummate athlete, Enos the artistic woodsman. Joe was the frank Westerner when he admitted that in capturing Johnny and Jenny he had first trapped and then killed their mother. Enos was the purist, claiming no part in the mother's death and saying that he "came upon" the orphaned cubs. Joe allowed his readers to accept the possibility that he was often spinning yarns; Enos was ever serious, always insisting that truth in all matters pertaining to nature was imperative. *A Mountain Boyhood* thus goes beyond the interlocked biography of both brothers to a revelation of how Joe differed from Enos and to what he felt his own essence to be.

Of all the passages in the book that fuse the identities of the two brothers, none is more apparent than the matter of credit for working to establish Rocky Mountain National Park. By the time Joe wrote *A Mountain Boyhood,* Enos's reputation as "the Father of Rocky Mountain National Park" was firmly established. Yet Joe wrote that, discovering that the region's wild and unspoiled character would vanish unless it were protected, "I set out to see what could be done about it . . . and [that] the most permanent and effective protection could be procured by getting the government to preserve it as a National Park." After that astonishing suggestion that it was he who started the ball rolling, Joe was careful not to claim too much. "I found others as concerned as I," he continued, and in the ensuing political battle, "men of vision prevailed" against opposing interests.[16] Enos, though not mentioned, was irrefutably one of those men of vision, and once again Joe could not help acknowledging the brother he repudiated. In some obscure way the bond between the brothers could not be broken. In those painful years of estrangement, when Joe could not even force himself to go near Longs Peak Inn, he did not follow his brother's enemies into their vindictive opposition to the national park. Joe believed in the cause that his brother led, helped it succeed, and was present at some of the victory celebrations.

In 1910, the first year Enos Mills appeared in *Who's Who,* even the death of his dog Scotch elicited eulogies in the nation's press, while the death of his father the same year was noted only locally in Linn County, Kansas. There, perhaps not so incidentally, divisions lurked elsewhere in the Mills family. When Ann Mills disbursed the modest proceeds of her late husband's estate among her children, she expressly excluded Sarah and Horace, who had shirked financial obligations to her and perhaps displeased her in other ways. Enos and Joe appear, however, to have both remained in her favor, and she is known to have visited them at least once in Estes Park after their rupture.

The beginning of Enos's personal difficulties with Joe and others coincided with his rise to national fame. In the vicinity of Longs Peak Inn, neighbors estranged from Mills expressed dismay over his change of personality. Their former friend seemed to have become arrogant, self-righteous, and self-serving. Mills's friend Robert W. Johnson, who confessed that he scarcely saw Mills during his last eighteen years, acknowledged in his 1924 memoir the possibility that fame had "somewhat turned his head." But he hastened to add that "no man is conceited till he over-estimates himself," implying perhaps that Mills had earned a high opinion of himself through his equally high achievements.[17]

As a celebrity, Mills, who described himself in his earlier days as "young, wise, and impertinent," frequently discarded conventional manners in the pursuit of his own image. Notified, for example, that he was expected to wear evening dress for a talk at a social event, he sent in his place, says a later account, "a Negro waiter, attired in evening dress, with this note: 'Here's the full dress. I will be unable to attend.'" If he was pleased with his clever sarcasm, Mills badly overlooked his dehumanizing use of the black waiter to convey it. When, under similar circumstances, he offended the *Saturday Evening Post's* George Lorimer and his wife, Alma, by announcing he would not attend a dinner in his honor if he had to wear evening dress, the tables were turned. "Wear what you like," Alma assured him, as she began already to plot her revenge. When Mills showed up in a neat business suit, he found the Lorimer house decked out ranch-style and the other guests dressed in western costume. "Mills found himself decidedly overdressed," records Lorimer biographer John Tebbel.[18]

Though Mills often offended others, he was quick to take offense himself. And his abrasiveness, if innate, was perhaps intensified by use. As a man promoting public causes, Mills appeared to see himself as a force for principle, consistency, and rightness in a world that lacked all three. He aspired to a kind of heroic nobility, and Eugene Debs, who met him in 1913, found just that quality in him. "He's the most noble soul I've ever met," wrote Debs — despite the bitter recriminations against Mills he may have heard on the same Estes Park visit from the deeply pained Elkanah Lamb and Charles Hewes, now avowed Mills enemies. Surviving correspondence from Debs and others shows that though quarrelsome with some, Mills was capable of deep and lasting friendships.[19]

Did Mills wear different faces for different people or was the same man judged oppositely by friends and foes? As we will see, Lamb, Hewes, and others became locked with Mills in a repetitive flipflop of victim and persecutor, played out first against the background of the campaign to create Rocky Mountain National Park. From now on, Mills's personality would be present as a controversial element of his public career, allowing his opponents to attack his causes as aberrations of his own character. Seen today, it was perhaps profound ambitiousness that put Mills so easily into conflict with others. And it was pure stress, some believe, that took its toll on his life at so early an age. At age forty, however, he could still weather stress in huge amounts, and his greatest battles and greatest glories still lay ahead.

CHAPTER 16

The Battle to Create a National Park

A crowd of 3,000 cheered to the telegrams from President Wilson and Interior Secretary Franklin Lane, read aloud by Enos Mills, master of ceremonies for the dedication of Rocky Mountain National Park (RMNP). The festivities on September 4, 1915, began with a coffee reception, band music, and school children singing "America." Then followed a procession of dignitaries called by Mills to the podium for five-minute speeches. The stunning outdoor setting was Horseshoe Park, the flat resting place of an ancient glacier, now a sun-filled meadow traversed by an oxbow stream and a road under construction toward the Continental Divide. Excited spectators had come by horseback, automobile, carriage, and foot. Two cars en route had plunged into the Big Thompson River, but without tragic consequences. A university president and personal friend of Woodrow Wilson's tried to hike from Grand Lake over the Continental Divide, lost his way, and was never seen alive again.

A crude government movie camera recorded the flapping of the flags and the festive banner as sharp winds brought in a shower. Reporters jotted on their notepads that clothes but not spirits were dampened. For Mills, who preached that nature is our friend in any weather, the shower was as appropriate as sunshine. And for him the pine trees were flags as much as those of cloth, their brisk waving symbolic of the hope of international unity. It was an occasion that united the concerns of humans and nature by proclaiming a park for human enjoyment under terms that would protect its scenic beauty forever. The crowd joined in singing the national anthem with a patriotic fervor rivaling that of the Fourth of July — and fittingly so. For as Mills and J. Horace McFarland had preached in promoting the park, patriotism requires love of land, and what better way to inspire love of land than through our national parks: scenic treasures and public playgrounds that could be admired and shared by all. National parks were the very stuff of democracy.

Rocky Mountain was the nation's thirteenth park and the one most accessible to mass tourism. It would soon attract more visitors than Yellowstone, Yosemite, Glacier, and Crater Lake National Parks combined: 51,000 in 1916, more than doubling to 120,000 in 1917; 170,000 in 1919, 20,000 of them arriving in automobiles. Adventurous visitors could explore 358 square miles of high mountains that included seventy peaks over 12,000 feet, eighteen over 13,000 feet, and 14,255-foot Longs Peak, the mountain now synonymous with the name of Enos Mills. On his famous survey of the West, Ferdinand van Hayden had called the Longs Peak section of the Continental Divide the most rugged in Colorado. And to him as to Isabella Bird, and later to Enos Mills, all the scenic ingredients were arranged in "perfect artistic effect." Forests draped the peaks' lower slopes like robes, climbing until battered and tattered at the frontier of timberline; hundreds of species of wildflowers graced the meadows and gave exquisite color to the most extensive tundra areas of any national park. The wildlife population was already recovering from earlier depredations and offered to the patient observer those endless magical moments that Mills had begun portraying in his books. Scores of alpine lakes told the stories of their creation by glaciers and their future destiny as alpine meadows. Snowfields, brooks, waterfalls, remnant glaciers, and moraines created settings ranging from the gently tranquil to what Mills still delighted in calling the "utterly wild."

Photographs of Mills taken at the dedication show his characteristic intensity combined with a look of almost immeasurable determination. It was a look that said he had more on his agenda. And even as he praised all who had cooperated to bring about the park, he announced his determination to extend the park southward to Pikes Peak, at least quadrupling its size. He knew that to do so would reopen the six-year battle he had just endured. For the key to gaining approval of the park dedicated that day had been to reduce its size to a third of his original vision.

The park acquired minor additions during Mills's lifetime, and it underwent over a dozen boundary revisions in the next half century. The Indian Peaks Wilderness brought under protection wild lands

"The proudest moment of my life." Mills at the dedication ceremonies. *NPS photo.*

Mills at the park dedication with *(left to right):* Robert Sterling Yard, Colorado Senator Edward Taylor, Mary K. Sherman ("The National Park Lady"), and Colorado Governor George Carlson. *NPS photo.*

south of the park that had been in Mills's original park proposal — but not until 1978. September 4, 1915, remained the high point of Mills's career and the greatest single triumph he would ever enjoy. As a federal lecturer he had campaigned for a cause he later deserted. And though he would probably have come to embrace the idea of undeveloped wilderness, he would have fought bitterly to prevent the Indian Peaks from being administered by the Forest Service, now his implacable and permanent foe. National parks remained the center point of Mills's life, and protecting their integrity would be his next cause. It was a cause that would unleash his fury on the administration of the park he had just helped create — the park of which he was, and still is, called "the father."

Mills eagerly accepted the title "Father of Rocky Mountain National Park" and used it himself. By 1916 it was attached to his name in *Who's Who.* It has remained virtually intact in the several generations of prose describing our national parks. It was commemorated in stone on a roadside marker placed by the Daughters of the American Revolution in 1982. One DAR member wrote, "It was through the dogged persistence of Enos Mills that millions have been able to use this famous area for pleasure and study. Mr. Mills's single-handed efforts produced a bill that was passed in 1915."[1] "Dogged persistence" is abundantly true; "single-handed" is overstated. Mills was phenomenally dedicated, tireless, and powerfully effective. At times he was counterproductive. His contribution must be seen in the context both of his individual personality and the larger struggle for definition of the national park system that took place simultaneously.

Mills's own versions of the campaign focused on his adversaries more than on his allies, many of whom he neglected even to mention. One account, in the 1917 edition of *Early Estes Park*, begins with his proposing the park idea: "In 1909 Enos A. Mills commenced to urge that about six hundred square miles of the surrounding region be made the Estes National Park and Game Preserve." Mills had in fact called for a park of 1,008 square miles coinciding with the boundaries of a game preserve suggested by U.S. Forester Herbert N. Wheeler. Wheeler had been asked over a year earlier to discuss with the Estes Park Protective and Improvement Association (EPPIA) how it could enhance the area's tourist potential. "I said if they wanted more tourists, it would be well to create a game refuge," Wheeler recalled in his characteristically pragmatic way. But it was not a casual suggestion, for Wheeler had already created a game preserve in western Colorado to restore depleted species and would later create the first Forest Service game preserve in California. He suggested an area twenty four by forty-two miles surrounding Estes Park and hoped to extend the eastern boundary of the national forest to lower elevations to protect migrating herds in winter.[2]

The EPPIA liked Wheeler's idea and unanimously adopted it at its annual meeting in September 1909. But a week later Mills went public with his national park proposal, which stressed the already extensive recreational use of the area and threats to its scenic beauty from sawmills and grazing.

The EPPIA — Mills was still a member — soon backed the park proposal, while Wheeler began to push more energetically for his. Historical shorthand has called the original idea for RMNP the Wheeler-Mills proposal. But the game preserve suggested by

Wheeler would have been administered by the Forest Service and permitted timbering, grazing, and mining to continue. A national park would remove land from Forest Service jurisdiction and protect it against the utilitarian applications Mills now found so distasteful. How, Mills said, could the Forest Service, with its single-minded emphasis on use, administer an area whose primary resource was scenic beauty?

Mills was no less a booster for the vacation industry than the rest of the EPPIA, and commercial ambition was part of the fertile soil that took and nourished the park idea. But had Mills not acted, the EPPIA would have just as eagerly gone forward with Wheeler's idea. Mills wrote later that he had envisioned a park in the Estes area in 1891 when he worked on a summer Geological Survey crew in Yellowstone. Discovering a spot that reminded him of home, he thought, "Why not a national park of the Longs Peak region?" Fifteen years later — in fall 1906 — he showed McFarland photographs of the region and McFarland said too, "Why not a national park?" But if the idea was given its first serious consideration late at night in McFarland's Mountain View, Pennsylvania, press room, it slumbered unannounced until Wheeler made the first move. Wheeler said in fact that Mills publicized the Forest Service game preserve while still a federal lecturer under Pinchot before 1909, then changed the idea to a national park on the suggestion of Mary King Sherman. "She was a power in the GFWC and spent much time at Longs Peak Inn and greatly influenced Mills," Wheeler recalled. When Wheeler asked Mills "to desist on the park idea," Mills replied that "he would continue to talk park, as his friends had advised him to do."[3]

Whether or not Mills needed prodding to bring forth a park proposal, enough precedent existed for him to have done so much earlier. Parks had been suggested at Pagosa Springs in 1877, the Pikes Peak region in 1885, the Flattops area of western Colorado in 1889, and the Royal Gorge in 1906. Women's groups had begun work in 1886 to protect the Indian cliff dwellings at Mesa Verde and had led the successful campaign to establish Mesa Verde National Park in 1906 — a campaign to which Mills had lent support. And in 1903 Mills expressed hope that the Uncompahgre area of the San Juan Mountains would someday become a national park.

Mills might have also been slow to act because the Estes region did not need national park status to attract large numbers of visitors.

Its accessibility and natural beauty had already brought a brisk tourist trade. Mills was perhaps at last aroused to action by his growing sense of the value of parks as a social institution and the conviction that scenic beauty must be protected both from misuse by visitors and the depredations of the Forest Service. He continued to believe that national park status was not needed for the mere sake of stimulating tourism — a position taken by park opponents as well. As late as his testimony to the House Committee on Public Lands in 1914 — just before passage of the bill — he said, "I do not agree . . . [that] we need the name 'national park' for that region. We do not. The region has supreme merits of its own that have brought people there already . . . faster than the people can take care of them."[4] Opponents had said all along, "Why then make it a national park?" And Mills had said, "to protect it and develop its scenic resources for public use." That formula — fostering public enjoyment and at the same time keeping scenic resources intact — became the governing principle of the National Park Service, created at last in 1916.

When the EPPIA endorsed Wheeler's game preserve proposal, it did not question whether keeping the area "in a state of nature" was compatible with Forest Service control. But Mills's proposal, referring to areas of forest misused and ruined, "humming saw-mills," and "cattle in the wild gardens," was an undisguised expression of his antagonism to Forest Service control. He could not yet, on the other hand, claim with certainty that all such activities would cease in a national park. No uniform policy existed to exclude them in parks, and each existing park had its own set of rules.

There was, nevertheless, enough of a precedent in the parks to suggest that the trend would increasingly shift toward excluding resource extraction. Timber, mining, grazing, and hunting interests routinely opposed park proposals as an invasion of their rights. Settlers feared that their properties would be confiscated or their access to watersheds cut off. To diminish those fears, the EPPIA sent out both letters and flyers with a modified version of Mills's park proposal buttressed with reassurances that "the regulations and changes which a national park would bring would not interfere with any business nor injure anyone. . . . No property is to be bought or sold; mining and prospecting are to continue as at present; fishing is to go on as now; timber-cutting is to continue under Forest Service regulations and grazing is to be restricted to local stock."[5]

Not so, said the Forest Service. If a park were created, it would probably pass under Department of Interior jurisdiction, with prohibitions on grazing, timbering, mining, agricultural development, and water rights. So don't raise false hopes in trying to sell the park idea to settlers who want to retain those rights, the agency's statement implied. But "please," said its author, A. F. Potter, in a letter to Mills, "do not construe this as an argument against the creation of a National Park." Mills took that as a howling example of bureaucratic hypocrisy and published Potter's letter in his subsequent accounts of the park campaign.[6]

The Forest Service's position was in fact complex, contained internal ambiguities, and evolved during the course of the park campaign. Initially the agency continued to push for a game preserve, pointing to the good it had already done in the area. It allowed timbering and grazing but regulated the stockmen and sawmill operators according to its rules. Wheeler had been admired for the professional standard he set by standing up to rule-defying sawmill operators. The Forest Service was successfully fighting forest fires and sponsoring dam construction on high mountain lakes to benefit farmland irrigation. To brighten its public-service image it gave Wheeler funds for building several trails and a fire lookout atop Twin Sisters Peak. It appeared to have the best interests of Estes Park tourism in mind by suggesting a game preserve. And since its jurisdiction of the surrounding public lands had not stopped the growth of the Estes vacation industry, it could convincingly claim it was a valid partner in the area's flourishing development.

Backing parks was for the Forest Service diplomatically risky with western constituents but ultimately necessary in the interagency turf battle. The USFS was at a point historically when it needed to show that it promoted vigorous use of the forest's material resources. Accused too long of "locking up" resources, it could not now afford to appear as an accomplice in just that. Rumblings about Forest Service restrictions still reverberated throughout the West, and Pinchot, now president of the National Conservation Association, still feared the whole national forest system could unravel. Pressures continued for Congress to abolish the national forests and turn federal lands over to the states. But as the inevitability of parks became increasingly apparent, the Forest Service needed to back them in order to qualify as the administering agency. Its strategy became one of favoring parks but opposing a separate agency to run them.

At the local level, administrators like Wheeler were slower to get that message and were at first so engrossed with the idea of harvesting trees that they were blinded to other values. Their training was also strongly geared to fire suppression, particularly after the scourge of fires in 1910 that burned nearly three million acres in Montana and Idaho — a year still remembered in forestry circles and not equaled even by the great western fires of 1988. Rangers, Wheeler said, didn't want people to use roads and trails, for fear they would set the woods on fire. Mills himself had written earlier that most fires are caused by careless campers and had praised the work of patrolling rangers. To Wheeler's generation of rangers, parks, with their masses of incendiary tourists, were a threat to the precious commodity of timber.

Most commentators agree that the Forest Service was the park's primary opponent in the early part of the campaign and that it organized much of the local opposition. In January 1911 Mills wrote to McFarland that the Forest Service chiefs in the Denver office were pushing the state legislature to condemn the park idea and to endorse a game preserve under its control. Mills was certain the Denver office was taking its marching orders from Washington. McFarland, furious, said he would go to the president if necessary. He had harsh words with Pinchot and with Pinchot's replacement as Forest Service head, Henry Graves. Both, he found, had mistaken and "deeply negative ideas" about national parks; both considered a pending bill to establish a National Park Service a plot against the Forest Service. McFarland soon wrote Mills that he believed he had succeeded in bringing Graves "out from under cover and made him . . . ashamed" about his attitude toward parks. Graves denied issuing any instructions for local Forest Service action against the park proposal and agreed to cooperate with Interior.[7]

Mills, however, believed otherwise. He charged that "an aggressive and conspiratorial" Forest Service used every means "to suppress and blackmail into silence any opposition to its methods." He accused it of deliberate misrepresentation of facts and harassment of park promoters — chiefly himself. In June 1911 he sent a letter to Graves via McFarland:

Last summer the supervisor of the Colorado National Forest [formerly Medicine Bow] allowed more than three hundred head of cattle to have access to this territory [Longs Peak trail] yet it is doubtful if ten would

find sufficient grass on it. Of course these three hundred head not finding sufficient grass . . . grazed elsewhere and this elsewhere was mostly
on my land. Against this injustice I have repeatedly protested to your
supervisor [Wheeler] in vain.[8]

Wheeler's memoirs, though frank about many other controversies, do not mention the grazing quarrel with Mills. They show a
strong concern with problems of overgrazing throughout his career,
with notations in later years that many areas were more valuable for
wild game and tourists than for grazing. Wheeler nevertheless distinctly disliked Mills and may have dealt harshly with him or looked
the other way while his subordinates did. In November 1911 Wheeler
was sent to California on an eighteen-month assignment, perhaps to
quiet down the controversy. At some point before or after that, he
was called to account by his supervisors for his public outspokenness against the park. To them he "repeated what [he] had said all
along that [he] saw no reason for the park since the Forest Service
was taking care of the area and [they] hoped to open it more for the
benefit of tourists. However if the opinion was general that [they]
should have the park, [he] would say no more about it." With that
Wheeler claimed to have withdrawn from the controversy.[9]

McFarland, who had received assurances that Graves was not
directing local opposition, began to fear that Mills could undo his
diplomacy. Graves "cannot afford to have you, with your national
reputation and your well-known park knowledge, calling attention
to deficiencies in the management of the Forest Service," he warned
Mills. "We have got to work with him."[10] Graves quieted the waters
by sending Mills and McFarland letters similar to one he had sent
earlier to the Sierra Club: He did not oppose national parks in principle, but until a national park service bill had cleared Congress to
define exactly what national parks were, the Forest Service must
withhold its approval of Rocky Mountain or any other park proposal.

That was a safe stalling position for the Forest Service and one
that it held consistently. It had in fact originated with Interior Secretary Richard Ballinger. When McFarland approached him about
drafting a RMNP park bill in 1910, Ballinger had replied that it was
first necessary to study the national park question as a whole. And
instead of drafting a RMNP bill, he soon drafted a park service bill.
President Taft followed the same line, telling McFarland's American

Civic Association that a bureau was needed charged "distinctly with responsibility" for park management. The campaign for RMNP thus appeared to be thrust into lockstep with the park service campaign, and McFarland conceded that "the further interests of establishing parks are being better advanced . . . [by] this proposed Bureau, than in any other way."[11]

Each time a park service bill was drafted, it died in Congress. How much the Forest Service pulled strings behind the scenes to kill it remains conjecture. Pinchot's bitter feud with Ballinger, resulting in both their dismissals by Taft, is bound to have caused him to see any Ballinger-sponsored bill as a plot to undermine the Forest Service. Graves, trying to head off the formation of the park service, made his pro-park position public and instructed his subordinates not to oppose or appear to oppose parks. He was angered by the hectoring and misplaced accusations of Mills that he opposed parks. But Mills did less to breed distrust for the Forest Service than its own contradictory support for the Hetch Hetchy dam proposal in California. That support gave the public a clear signal that the Forest Service could not be trusted to protect scenic treasures against development. Even the publicizing of recreational opportunities in national forests by a paid publicist could not polish the Forest Service's image enough to make its case for putting parks under its jurisdiction.

Mills held to the simple and increasingly outdated belief that the Forest Service opposed parks categorically and would do anything to prevent them. He said the agency "kept out of sight, worked through others, and supplied munitions from ambush." He alleged that he mysteriously lost his right to receive mail at the Estes Park post office and had to apply to make Longs Peak Inn a post office with himself as postmaster. He alleged that the inn's water pipes were cut several times and that phony lodging reservations were made by guests who never appeared. Mills took the harassment badly. Early in the conflict — in September 1910 — he was taken to court for physically assaulting Arthur Cole, a member of a ranching family that Mills accused of conniving with the Forest Service to overrun his unfenced property with cattle. Found guilty and given the maximum fine, Mills was not exonerated, said the press, by his national reputation or his standing as a citizen.[12]

Three months before that humiliating defeat, Mills had been publicly denounced by his neighbors. A notice printed in one of Denver's leading papers said:

We, the undersigned, all of the neighbors residing within a mile and a half of Longs Peak Inn (the hotel owned and managed by Enos A. Mills), view with apprehension the activity of the said Mills in an attempt to have this neighborhood included in a national park. We fear the prominent part he is taking in said movement may be thought to entitle him a place in the administration of said park, if created, and we feel that any authority he may acquire over our property or the surrounding region will be used to our detriment.[13]

The signatures given were E. J. and J. J. Lamb, Charles H. and M. M. Levings, Charles E. Hewes, Dean Babcock, H. Bittner, Harry G. and Rosa G. Cole, and Mary C. Kirkwood. So even old parson Lamb had turned against his younger relative, fearing, like the others, some abusive power that Mills could exert over them. Hewes, a Longs Peak Inn employee at the time the Mills brothers parted ways, said the problem stemmed from Mills's personality: National fame had changed him to a militantly opinionated egotist.

In summer 1911 some or all of the same neighbors, with Hewes as their secretary, issued a flyer opposing the park. Naming no one but Hewes, they called themselves the Front Range Settlers' League (FRSL). Mills's later account charged that the Forest Service incited the league's organization; one of its members was, in fact, a ranger living in nearby Allenspark. The flyer's arguments were not framed explicitly around Mills but were weakened by that underlying bias. They supported the Forest Service but unwittingly undermined it as well. In opposing the idea of a game preserve included in Mills's park proposal, the flyer also cast a bad light on Wheeler's proposal. In maintaining that two-thirds of the proposed park, presently under Forest Service jurisdiction, were being controlled more efficiently than most national parks, it helped call attention to the neglect of other parks and the need for a special park agency. Worse, the flyer argued for state control of public lands — the very thing Pinchot had been battling for years as the ruse of powerful private interests to gain control. And arguing that a park bureaucracy would be "irksome and disagreeable," the flyer asserted that "it would be shortsighted policy to further segregate any portion of the state under the control of an administration 2,000 miles distant." But the Forest Service was also controlled by an administration 2,000 miles distant and was already viewed as "irksome and disagreeable" throughout much of the West. Those were in fact arguments thrown ad nauseam at the Forest Service since its beginning. In wild ignorance of Colorado's recent history of forest destruction, the flyer also asserted that a national park was not needed to protect scenic beauty since "Colorado citizens from earliest times have conscientiously treasured and conserved its natural beauties." And last but not least among the flyer's flaws, some of its language betrayed the league's personal fear of Mills. "To menace the homes, interests and local autonomy of these people is a cruel and intolerable action on the part of the park promoters," it said.[14]

Mills charged that the FRSL tried to appear as a large organization and that "countless letters on [its] stationery . . . poured forth addressed to newspapers over the country, to individuals of prominence, and to members of Congress." "Six are the most members ever claimed for this organization. It may possibly have had three," he wrote. And, in fact, the FRSL refused to reveal its membership even to Congress, thus compromising much of its credibility.[15]

Both sides indulged in character sniping, and Mills wrote of the FRSL even after the park battle had been won, "Not one of these . . . has ever been known to do anything for the public welfare." Lamb had answered Mills's earlier attacks in his 1913 *Miscellaneous Meditations* — his "farewell volume to his time on Earth." Obviously deeply hurt by Mills, he responded in the only way he knew how: with pompous rectitude:

> My reason and only apology for delineating the personal status and special characteristics of my immediate neighbors as above, is to refute certain unjust insinuations and intimations, that our community was below par, lacking in moral and mental makeup and void of manly dignity and those harmonious relations demanded by society in this age of the world's history. While I endeavor to restrain a drastic spirit and utterly condemn unrighteous language used towards any one, yet I feel under mental and moral obligations to vindicate our neighborhood from such unjust aspersions as those which have obtained in the minds of some who are too quick to decide adversely regardless of that intelligent and true information which is easily to be obtained of any one or any neighborhood . . . .[16]

Lamb's descriptions of the valley's neighbors (most were residents only part of the year) sought to make clear that all were people of integrity and stature. Mills, through omission, was the exception. Bittner was a successful attorney. Charles Levings was a prominent civil engineer, a leader in the development of Chicago's park system, and a literary friend of Eugene Fields's and James Witcomb Riley's. His son Mark and nephew Dean Babcock were both talented artists who had trained at academies in the United States and Paris. Mark was a prominent Chicago architect, Babcock a painter living year-round near Longs Peak Inn. The Levings family had provided the valley with a new telephone link to Estes Park. In 1908 Babcock had written the panegyric that called Mills "the inspired prophet of the conservation movement" and the equal of Pinchot. For him to sign a public denunciation of Mills two years later bespeaks a drastic reversal in Mills's personal relationships. Virtually all the Tahosa Valley residents had once admired Mills and enjoyed his friendship. The most tragic break was with the Lambs. "Be the truth known," lamented Hewes with some piety, "Mills's loss of the friendship and esteem of Mr. and Mrs. Lamb is, to my eyes at least, a frightful calamity, and can only be explained by an inexplicable change of character since his absurd egotism led him estray [sic]. He has himself told me that he received the first inspiration and love of nature things at Mr. Lamb's fireside when he first came to the vale a little fellow in skirts."[17]

Hewes was Mills's most colorful and implacable enemy. A poet, devout and mystically inclined Christian, and widely admired innkeeper, he was, according to Lamb, "bright beyond the ordinary." Another called him the "nearest Christlike character I have ever met," while another said he was capable of "vile cursing." Lamb called Hewes's mother an intellectual of "queenly dignity." Exactly Mills's age, Hewes worked at Longs Peak Inn in 1907 and 1908 under Joe's management, mostly driving a stage to and from Estes Park. His Hewes-Kirkwood Inn rivaled Longs Peak Inn as a starting point for peak and nature tours. Hewes grazed cattle to supply his guests with fresh dairy and leased some of his pastures to tenants. Mills may have attempted to curtail his grazing rights or block his acquisition of additional land. Hewes wrote appreciative verse about nature and local events. He kept a detailed personal journal, worked on an autobiography, and labored seventeen years on a huge epic poem that he finally published himself in 1941. A wide-ranging spiritual and intellectual history of mankind, *The America* revealed a searching attempt to understand life through poetry, hinted of a blighted romance from which he never recovered, and gave one line, perhaps in a spirit of rapprochement, to Enos Mills's achievement as a nature writer.

Mills's neighbors were thus people of intelligence and attainment, most from backgrounds more privileged than his, who could easily find fault with his self-acquired knowledge and the unevenness of his behavior. Mills had public fame beyond any of them, but they had admirers of their own and were probably capable of swaying others against him. But their opposition to the park ultimately betrayed their own ideals. All were nature lovers and some had commercial interests similar to those of the EPPIA. Probably not one of them, if alive today, would want the park abolished. Hewes's later poems praised the park's beauties if not the park as an institution. Babcock soon became a ranger-naturalist and then assistant park superintendent. Old Elkanah Lamb died in 1915, just after passage of the park bill.

In fall 1912, Interior Secretary Walter Fisher — Ballinger's replacement — sent chief U.S. Geographer Robert B. Marshall to Estes Park to see if the area warranted consideration as a national park that Interior could back. Hewes sent Marshall a letter before his trip arguing against the park and spoke to him personally during his visit. But Marshall wisely delayed all interviews until after he had toured the proposed area himself. Then he interviewed widely to compare what he heard with what he had seen. He talked to Mills, Hewes, Governor John Shafroth, Governor-elect Elias Ammons, Denver Mayor H. G. Arnold, the Denver chamber's national park committee chairman Frederick Ross, Senator Thomas Patterson, and James Grafton Rogers — the young Denver attorney who would write the park bill. Scrupulous in his objectivity, Marshall refused all favors, including an invitation from Mayor Arnold to be his guest on a trip through Estes Park. *Enos Mills of the Rockies* records incautiously and almost certainly incorrectly that Mills paid the whole bill for Marshall's trip.

Marshall was overwhelmingly in favor of the proposed park and expressed himself with an exuberance rare in an official governmental report:

> There is spread before the eye a gorgeous assemblage of wonderful mountain sculpture, surrounded by fantastic and everchanging clouds, suspended in an apparently atomless space. At first view, as one beholds the scene in awe and amazement, the effect is as of an enor-

mous painting, a vast panorama stretching away for illimitable distances; gradually, this idea of distance disappears, the magnificent work of nature seems to draw nearer and nearer, reduced apparently by an unseen microscope to the refinement of a delicate cameo. Each view becomes a refined miniature, framed by another more fascinating, the whole presenting an impressive picture, never to be forgotten.[18]

In the three months between Marshall's visit and the issuance of his report, the press and the public waited with baited breath. He had not tried to hide his enthusiasm and had left Denver with encouraging hints. He said the area "was one of the grandest views anywhere in the world," and that if his report was favorable it would be a "Christmas present." After the report was out and enthusiastically hailed by park supporters, Marshall said, "After having seen that glorious country, I could not say less."[19]

Marshall cited accessibility as one of the most important attributes for the park's success. "It will assume a much more national character than any of the existing parks," he noted. Still lacking guidelines applicable to all national parks, Marshall recommended allowing dead timber to be harvested but leaving living timber for watershed. Prospecting and grazing should also be permitted but would be naturally limited in scope. If Marshall was cavalier about allowing extractive activities in a national park, it was largely because he thought that none had significant potential. There was little timber of merchantable grade, and the heavily mined Front Range mineral belt stopped at about Ward. Marshall recommended boundary reductions from 1,008 to slightly over 700 square miles to exclude active mining areas. Use provisions nevertheless became controversial, and were modified through successive revisions of that bill. Marshall's boundary recommendations also excluded significant areas of private land. The government, he said, should swap lands with remaining property owners surrounded by the park. That controversial provision — called lieu land — was later struck, and the park, like most others, was established with islands of private inholdings.

A jubilant Enos Mills wrote Muir about Marshall's report and with renewed confidence sang out, "You have helped me more than all others; but for you, I might never have done anything for scenery." Muir wrote back with words Mills treasured for the rest of his life: "I always feel good when I look your way: for you are making good on a noble career. I glory in your success as a writer & lecturer and in saving God's parks for the welfare of humanity. Good luck & long life to you."[20]

Despite the surge of energy and prestige Marshall's report gave to the campaign and despite Mills's joyful reference to it in his letter to Muir, his accounts of the park campaign failed — astonishingly — to mention either the report or Marshall. And even more conspicuously absent from all his accounts was James Grafton Rogers, author of the park bill and president of the young Colorado Mountain Club (CMC). Mills had prodded Rogers in summer 1911 to form the CMC to support mountain recreation, nature study, and conservation, along the lines of the Sierra Club. Though Mills may have thus conceived the idea for the club, he told Rogers he had no time to help organize it or to hold office. Rogers rose to Mills's challenge. Within a month he had publicized the club idea in the newspapers and received a strong show of interest. The club's kickoff meeting was in April 1912. Needing Mills's presence to give the event prestige, Rogers wrote him, "We cannot form a club without you." Mills could not attend but sent a letter of support. So important was his name to the new club that it voted to "consider him present" at the organizational meeting.[21]

Taking the RMNP campaign as its first public challenge, the club set about providing much-needed geographical information about the area, researching questions about boundaries, inholdings, acreage, and — following a suggestion from Marshall — finding meaningful names for the many unnamed peaks.[22] The new CMC also established links with other outdoor clubs such as the Sierra Club, the Mazamas of Portland, the Seattle Mountaineers, the Prairie Club of Chicago, and the Appalachian Club. Mills had already learned the effectiveness of outdoor clubs in the American conservation movement, saying that they could "accomplish wonders" when united on specific issues. Rogers himself was well connected in both Colorado and Washington, D.C. He was a 1905 Yale graduate, got his law degree in Denver in 1908, worked in the state attorney general's office in 1909–1910, and was now a law professor. His law partner, Morrison Shafroth, was the son of Colorado governor John Shafroth, who became a leading democratic senator in the Wilson administration.

Rogers worked hard and suffered many bruises in drafting and redrafting the park bill. Following the ideas of Marshall's report, his first draft allowed for timbering, mining, grazing, and the lieu land provision to acquire private inholdings. The bill was submitted to the U.S. House and Senate on February 6 and 7, 1913, accompanied by a supporting resolution from the Colorado state legislature. The bill was not reported out of committee. Resubmitted to the next Congress a month later, the bill drew an unexpected response from the Forest Service. "This, in my judgment, is going exactly in the wrong direction," Graves wrote to Rogers. "[It] makes the policies of use and development now in effect on the National Forests applicable to National Parks." Sounding more like Enos Mills than like the Forest Service, Graves continued, "A National Park should be an area of exceptional scenic character, and one requiring a management wholly in the interests of the protection and development of its scenic beauty." B. F. Galloway, the acting secretary of agriculture, confirmed Graves's opinion: "The bill does not follow language set forth in any previous law establishing a national park. It would [be] a park in name only."[23]

The Forest Service's position was consistent with its new strategy of espousing park values in order to vie for the jurisdiction of all parks. And, short of that, yielding a few parks with high standards of scenic quality, the Forest Service could pursue its utilitarian goals throughout the rest of its huge domain without further pressure from preservationists. It had tried in fact to maintain that the scenery in the proposed RMNP was "of a commonplace character and not at all fitted for park use." "This in face of the fact," Mills wrote in his later account, "that during 1913 this region was visited by about forty thousand people." For Rogers the use provisions were simple strategy: thinking, as Marshall had, that there were few marketable resources in the area anyway, he included utilitarian language solely as window dressing "to satisfy out local kickers and to silence the oppositon here." His aim, stated frequently in his correspondence, was to get a bill passed and then to work at once for stricter protective measures. Mills, distrustful of the strategy, began to suspect that Rogers was waffling because he was ambivalent about the park itself.[24]

Rogers meanwhile had tried to conciliate the Forest Service over the touchy matter of Enos Mills. Calling Mills his "very close friend," he confided to Graves that he thought Mills was doubtlessly being overemotional in his charges of Forest Service complicity to block the park.[25] But as more of the public voiced doubts about the

Forest Service, Rogers, too, began to wonder, and he, too, publicly criticized Wheeler. He asked Graves for his explicit endorsement of the park to assure the public of the Forest Service's good will. Graves again backed into a neutral corner, declaring that although he favored the park in principle, the bill's utilitarian aspects prevented his endorsement. Interagency diplomacy also dictated his waiting for endorsement by Interior before backing the bill, he said.

Rogers laboriously revised the bill for resubmission in October 1913. Graves now wrote him, "It seems to me that you have worked out a bill which will admirably meet the various requirements of the situation."[26] Indeed, the Forest Service might at this point have approved a 600-square-mile park rather than the 358-square-mile park finally passed by Congress. Interior was now the snag, and Secretary Lane — Fisher's replacement in the Wilson administration — though also favoring the park in principle, raised nagging details that still had to be worked out. An eighth of the total recommended acreage was still in private holdings, and Lane asked for further boundary reductions to exclude them.

Meanwhile the CMC was maddeningly slow in some of its public efforts. Whatever channels it may have pursued informally, it failed to adopt a public resolution favoring the park until two years after its founding meeting. It took nearly two years to appoint a park committee and another three months to elect its chairman. The resolution finally adopted in April 1914 — when passage of the bill was likely — was so innocuous that it could have been easily adopted earlier. A single assertion may have caused the delay: only after the proposed park boundaries had been repeatedly trimmed, could the club say with certainty: "[It includes] almost exclusively high tracts of alpine and subalpine territory . . . without lumbering, agriculture, mining or other possibilities comparable to its value as a scenic, scientific, and recreational ground." That was a safe formula that had worked elsewhere. Backers of Glacier National Park — whose campaign had just preceded that of RMNP — had said, likewise: "[The Glacier area] is too rugged for agriculture and too arid for grazing. . . . It is of no use to commercial man, but as a playground for the people, there is nothing anywhere to equal it for scenic beauty." Until official park policy existed, parks were best won by being limited to terrain where the conflict between use and preservation was essentially moot — a theme examined in detail by historian Alfred Runte.[27]

To Mills, the CMC's delay was certain evidence of Rogers's connivance with the Forest Service. He wrote to McFarland in December 1913 that Rogers had purposely held up the club's endorsement. Then, five months later, more exasperated than ever, he wrote Rogers a searing letter, condemning his actions as club president in handling the park proposal and protesting "against [his] further conniving with the Forest Service." Saying that Rogers had "shown only contempt" for Mills's evidence of the Forest Service's eight-year record of opposing *all* park proposals, he said, "I can no longer remain silent while the President of the Colorado Mountain Club exhibits the Forest Service on one shoulder and the Park on the other." He ended, however, not with condemnation but with "a last effort to arouse you . . . to frankly cooperate . . . in securing the . . . Park."[28]

Rogers wrote back at once that he would answer Mills's charges in detail after he consulted with other CMC officers who had shared his policy decisions. But he never wrote the follow-up letter. A week after Mills's attack, Rogers warned the Denver chamber that Mills "seems exceedingly jealous of his own part in the campaign for the Park and very suspicious of everybody's motives but his own." He agreed with what must have been an earlier statement by someone in the chamber that Mills's "ferocious attitude" toward his opponents had diminished his effectiveness as a park campaigner. He believed indeed that Mills could fly into destructive behavior: "[He] can do those who hope for the park and even the chamber considerable harm if his feelings are hurt."[29]

Though Mills had originally chosen Rogers as an ally in the park campaign, there may have been incompatibilities from the start. Recollecting the campaign later, Rogers said that through all his exhausting work Mills had not "gained an inch" of forward progress. That "exhausting work" had begun with Mills's tour through Colorado in early 1911 to marshal broad popular support. That fall he traveled east, giving addresses in major cities along the way, and at the annual meeting of the American Civic Association, where he shared the podium with Interior Secretary Fisher, Senator Reed Smoot of Utah — a staunch backer of the Park Service bill — and President Taft. He stayed in the East until spring 1912, meeting with outdoor organizations, conservation societies, and other potential backers, working the whole time at his usual high intensity. Before the campaign was over he had spent six to seven thousand dollars of his own money. Rogers's tendency to minimize Mills's efforts, historian Patricia Fazio notes in her excellent study of the park campaign, "was near-sighted — and ungenerous," because "it could be argued that Mills had gained Rogers and the Colorado Mountain Club, McFarland and the American Civic Association, Muir and the Sierra Club, Mary Belle King Sherman and the General Federation of Women's Clubs, George Horace Lorimer and the *Saturday Evening Post,* Frederick R. Ross and the Denver Chamber of Commerce, Freelan Stanley and his EPPIA cohorts, and a lengthy list of magazine editors and writers."[30]

Though Mills wrote Rogers cordially about other matters four months after his searing attack in May 1914, the relationship was never again the same. His later accounts of the park campaign, failing to mention even the name of the man who drafted the bill, must be reckoned as vindictive. The CMC's role generally, which Mills also failed to mention, was valuable enough to cause one later park superintendent to remark that without it, "there would not be a Rocky Mountain National Park." Rogers's own account of the campaign, written in 1965, gave equal credit to Mills, to the Denver chamber led by Frederick Ross, and to the CMC. Remembering Mills's "fiery personality and small bald figure" over the span of fifty years, Rogers generously forgot old quarrels and said, "My admiration and even affection [for him] have not faded." CMC's seventy-fifth anniversary history (1987), perhaps believing Rogers's credit to Mills had been too generous, downgraded Mills's role to "work[ing] with . . . members" of the club which "led the effort" to create the park. But the reference is only fleeting, and the club history attempts no analysis of the park campaign, dwelling little even on Rogers's role.[31]

An element of the campaign that is not controversial was the staunch support of the news media. Lionized by the press as a forestry spokesman, Mills had a ready ally for his new cause as he traversed the country promoting the park. The *Denver Republican,* an early backer of the forestry movement, now showed a forward-looking sentiment for parks: "Let the next step be to put [this Colorado wonderland] side by side with Yellowstone and Yosemite where it belongs as a government park to be enjoyed by the whole people."[32] Papers along the Front Range — in Denver, Colorado Springs, Pueblo, Boulder, Longmont, Loveland, and Ft. Collins — joined the chorus, and the valiant little *Estes Park Trail* added its boosterist fervor. Major East Coast papers joined in, and big city papers in the Midwest spoke to readers who would supply the majority of vacationers to the new park. Influential magazines also added their voice for the park and for national parks generally. They included *National Geographic, Century, Atlantic Monthly, Forest and Stream, Colliers, Country Life in America,* and the *Saturday Evening Post.* Mills wrote scores of magazine and newspaper articles, and Mather, soon to be assistant secretary of interior and then the first National Park Service director, wrote an article favoring the park that was included in the record of the House committee hearings. Interior's support of the park had its own internal journalist.

Rapidly gaining fame as a nature writer, Mills wrote two more books during the campaign as well. Two chapters in his 1913 *In Beaver World* promoted the park (as had two chapters in his 1912 *Spell of the Rockies*), and two more appeared in *The Rocky Mountain Wonderland,* printed just after the park was approved. The latter book's chapter, "The Conservation of Scenery," was one of Mills's most comprehensive and balanced statements on the differences between national forests and national parks. With a few exceptions ("trees to the forester mean what cattle do to the butcher"), he moderated his anti–Forest Service rhetoric to a balanced discussion of preservationism versus utilitarianism, the economic and "higher" values of scenery, and the importance of a vigorous park program to the overall national well-being. He said with a wisdom still needed today, "If scenery is to be saved, it must be saved for its own sake, on its own merits; it cannot be saved as something incidental."

Throughout the campaign, local supporters maintained an active role, balancing and ultimately outweighing opposition forces. Popular Longs Peak guide Shep Husted, speaking for the "old timers" of the area, wrote directly to President Taft, hailing him as a fellow native Ohioan and wishing that he could descend with him into one of the craters on Specimen Mountain (Taft weighed over 300 pounds). The EPPIA worked steadily for the park and Stanley may have helped to fund Mills's publicity tours. Men's and women's service organizations, county boards of commissioners, realty exchanges, and other regional organizations joined the snowballing campaign. Joe Mills, now an accomplished speaker, won friends for the park, largely among church and business groups.

Though never directly involved with the RMNP campaign, John Muir provided an energizing presence. He encouraged Mills in several letters between 1910 and 1915 — including the one in which he said, "I glory in your success" — and expressed his sympathy with the complexity of the struggle: "Strange that the government is so slow to learn the value of parks." To each letter Mills responded that it was Muir who gave him strength and inspiration. Exactly a month before Muir died, in December 1914, Mills wrote to him: "It is the work you have done that has encouraged me in all that I have accomplished & in the big work that I am planning to do." McFarland also drew sustenance from Muir. He met him for the first time, probably in late 1911, and wrote Mills, "I had a holiday with him that I shall never forget. He is a marvellous man."[33] Muir died on Christmas Eve, 1914, one day after the RMNP bill had begun its hearings before the House Committee on Public Lands. Robert Marshall interrupted his prepared testimony to eulogize Muir:

> As you probably know, gentlemen, while we are talking about creating another park, the flowers he loved so dearly are placed on the grave of that wonderful man, John Muir, the Father of National Parks. I received a great deal of my inspiration for outdoor life, and what it means to the people, from my close association with him for some twenty-odd years, and I feel that even now, Mr. Chairman, while we are considering this measure, it will be a great courtesy to the memory of that grand old man if you gentlemen unanimously recommend the creation of this park.[34]

By the time of those hearings the Forest Service had cooperated with Interior to work out boundary details. Mills continued to believe its compliance was a smoke screen. He wrote in August 1914 — ignoring McFarland's advice — "Everyone . . ." now "wants this Park — except the members of the Forest Service, who are behind the scenes at Washington trying to defeat this worthy measure. For five years the Forest Service has insidiously used all the machinery of its office to prevent the establishment of the park. It is still trying to prevent this. . . . Let no one be deceived by the hypocrisy of this political machine." McFarland was losing patience and wrote to Mills in December, "Your splendid work is being discounted because of the hostility toward the Forest Service. . . . I do not trust the Forest Service any more than you do, but I do not want to let my feelings in that direction handicap the possibility of doing something for the National Parks."[35]

Though Mills's scrappy behavior was increasingly disturbing to his own allies, it did not diminish his importance as a spokesman for the park at the House Committee hearings. Colorado Senator Taylor introduced him as "one of the noted naturalists, travelers, authors, and lecturers of this country, who has made a great study of this question and has lived in the park for a great many years and knows almost every foot of it, and is probably better qualified to speak on this park than anyone."[36] The two sessions of committee hearings on December 24 and 30, 1914, were the final and successful steps in the park campaign. Mills was in high-level company, testifying at the first hearing along with Colorado Governor-elect George Carlson and Senator John Shafroth. Speakers at the second hearing were Senator Charles Thomas, who had already guided the bill through the Senate, Robert Marshall, and a national park official, Mark Daniels. The Front Range Settlers' League, still refusing to reveal its membership, was represented in abstentia and had been largely discredited.

Following the second hearing, the committee recommended passage of the bill with an annual funding of $10,000 for the new park, the lieu land clause removed, and a few other adjustments. Congressman Taylor then skillfully maneuvered it through the House on January 18, 1915, and President Wilson signed it into law on January 26th. Supporters exchanged jubilant congratulations, the town of Estes Park honored Mills with a reception, and McFarland, the well-bred Christian and gentleman, praised him for the very virtues many had found him lacking: "Your success is surely a matter of personal persistence and tactfulness. . . . [That] you are going to leave, I think, mighty few sores anywhere, is a great credit to you." But sores there were, and Mills's relationship with McFarland would eventually lead to bitterness as well.[37]

Nor was Mills finished bashing park opponents. "Immediately following the creation of the park," his later account reads, "the Forest Service set about trying to prevent the securing of appropriations for it, and to this end incited a letter-writing corps to write Congressmen, urging that the park territory be given over to the charge of the Forest Service."[38] Though his account failed to state that the National Park Service bill, passed in 1916, assigned park jurisdiction explicitly to Interior, he proved to be correct in his fears that the Forest Service would persist in trying to co-opt the park system. In the tension over that threat, Mills's relationship with the new Park Service would soon begin to deteriorate. It was an agency he himself helped to conceive, plan, and promote, meeting at least once in Washington with California Congressman William Kent, McFarland, Marshall, Yard, Olmsted, Albright, the writers Emerson Hough and Herbert Quick, and Gilbert Grosvenor, editor of the *National Geographic*. The sessions were crucial to the formative thinking for the proposed Park Service at a time when even such basic questions as grazing in the parks were still under debate.[39]

Mills's growing testiness no doubt stemmed both from nervous strain — he quipped to McFarland that the park campaign had added "a few convulsions to my brain"[40] — and from his conscious adoption of a fighter's stance. His historical sense had always persuaded him that people with vision and ideals are misunderstood and suffer persecution but are vindicated in the end. Press accounts inferred just that, as they called Mills "the man who combatted opposition from his own dooryard to the legislative chambers of the national capitol, [and] never let go of the idea." A cartoon at the time the park bill passed showed even the mountain peaks smiling proudly at Mills and declaring, "I always knew you were all right, Enos."[41] The personal harassment Mills alleged during the park campaign may have pushed him toward a belief in conspiracy that he generalized to a view of government as a self-serving machine capable of any amount of treachery. Once aligned against the Forest Service, Mills failed to see the changes to which it was forced during the campaign and to see that beyond a certain point its opposition did not matter.

Whatever the cost in personal strain and deeply ingrained mistrust — soon to fester again — Mills took the park campaign as a salubrious experience. In March 1914 he wrote to a judge of his acquaintance, "I am hammering away hard — and enjoying life." He called the victorious campaign the "most strenuous" but also the "most growth-compelling" event of his life. He was doubtlessly buoyed through it all by his awareness that he was himself a heavy slugger in a big-league contest. And at the end he had a tangible and glorious reward: a park universally admired and the rich praise of the press for having brought it about. Mills proclaimed in his dedication speech that it was the proudest moment of his life. Far from being damaged, his fame reached new heights, and with new fame grew his confidence in his right to assert it. The death of

(NPS photo.)

Muir, furthermore, had perhaps left him with an inkling that he would step into the shoes of that great man whom he called the "Nestor of National Parks." His friend Eugene Debs gave him reason to believe he had. "You, my dear Mills, who are his only successor," Debs wrote, "alone realize the vast wealth of legacy he left to mankind."[42]

CHAPTER 17

From Park Publicist to Park Critic

Publicizing the national parks and their new agency kept Mills on the elite park-support team until feuding began to separate him from it by mid 1917. Just before quarreling with Park Service chiefs Stephen Mather and Horace Albright, he was one of their leading spokesmen at a 1917 national park conference and published a 500-page book, *Your National Parks,* that both praised Mather and foreshadowed the coming conflict. At the five-day conference in January 1917, Mills shared the podium with lawmakers, educators, editors, businessmen, clergymen, philanthropists, and leading conservationists from all over the country. The proud father of his own national park, Mills gave talks on Sequoia Park and "Parks for all the People," chaired a workshop on recreation in national parks, answered questions on the training of park guides, entertained the conference goers with his famous bear stories, and helped organize a banquet for Mather after the conference.

The event was Mather's and Albright's timely introduction of the new Park Service to top government and business circles and to their own growing constituency of supporters for scenic preservation. Because the Park Service Act, passed only five months earlier, had not yet brought tangible funding for the agency itself, the conference was also an appeal, said Albright, for the parks' desperate need of attention. Restrictive funding ceilings handicapped individual park development, and the whole park system had no secure place in the federal power structure. The two-page Park Service Act stated no agency missions or management principles beyond a general charge to promote parks and regulate their use.

But the conference gave clear evidence of the progress of scenic preservation since the time Pinchot had ignored it at his 1908 Governors' Conference. Supportive senators and congressmen now stepped forward to speak out for protecting and maintaining the nation's scenic treasures. Beauty was recognized as a money-earning commodity, an agent of social utility, and, for most, a good in its own right. "Let [the parks'] mission be to stimulate and promote the higher and better instincts of men," said Scott Ferris, chairman of the House Public Lands Committee. Let them uplift the spirit, invoked a minister. And let them inspire the arts, said the head of the National Gallery against a backdrop of distinguished paintings of national park scenes arranged for by Mather himself. Let Americans vacation in these great American parks rather than in Europe, urged the railroads and the tourist industry. And let the people fly to the parks in airplanes, said the flying Orville Wright. So the conference went, with dozens of others helping to fashion the broad appeal of the park movement, which it continues to enjoy today. Ideas traceable back to Thoreau and Muir, now clad with Progressive notions of public utility, at last found broad political support. Mather's gift was to guide those ideas into official governmental policy.[1]

Mather was an imaginative salesman, alternately energetic and incapacitated by fits of depression. Even before the Park Service was formed, he had hired Robert Sterling Yard to help him publicize the need for parks and an agency to regulate them. The former newspaper colleagues launched a publicity campaign for the parks that the news media quickly joined with force and pride. Not the least among those who spurred them on was Enos Mills. Introducing Mills to the national parks conference, Mather said that he had been "absolutely unselfish" in "his stirring up of the leading papers of the country to a realization and to a proper enthusiasm for the parks."[2]

In issuing its own propaganda, the Park Service matched the Forest Service during the Pinchot era. Yard wrote and sent a booklet, *Glimpses of Our National Parks,* to 117,000 influential people. He surpassed that with an impressively illustrated *National Park Portfolio* that was put on every desk in Congress and mailed to a list of 275,000 potential park backers compiled by the GFWC. Mather contributed from his own pocket to fund the *Portfolio* and got the railroads to contribute $43,000 more. The railroads spent hundreds of thousands of dollars on their own publicity brochures, using the national parks to advertise travel excursions but advertising the parks at the same time. They offered special excursion packages, teamed up to link their routes through several parks, and helped develop park facilities. Courting both the railroads and the auto travel industry, Mather promoted road construction in and to the parks, hoping to link them with excursion routes or to send cross-country travel their way.

Mather was a self-made millionaire who could convincingly portray the parks as prime opportunities for private enterprise. He managed the parks themselves like businesses, just as Interior Secretary Lane said he should, and just as the Forest Service managed the national forests. He showed that the parks could attract as large a business constituency to profit from the park facilities and concessions as the national forests attracted to profit from extracting resources. Albright went out to chambers of commerce with a speech entitled "Parks are Good Business," and Yard published an article called "Making a Business of Scenery."

Mills pushed the business theme too. He had preached it to the Denver chamber in 1905, applied it to forestry as a lecturer under Pinchot, and tailored it to his RMNP campaign. His 1915 essay "The Conservation of Scenery" extolled the cash value of tourism and its superiority to revenue from natural resources. With Switzerland his still well-polished model, he said the Alps produced annual tourist revenues of more than $10,000 per square mile, while the Rocky Mountains were being "despoiled by cattle and sawmills" for only a "few dollars a square mile." The United States could have a tourist industry "many times as productive as our gold and silver mines," he said, provided the parks were "made ready" for mass visiting. They could not yet accommodate even a fifth of the Americans who took their vacations abroad. In *Your National Parks,* he urged his readers to lean on Congress for adequate park funding. He said he wanted the NPS director to be able to say, "Your national parks — our matchless wonderlands — are now entirely ready for millions of travelers." If we supply the parks, he added, the people themselves "will help us to build a vast travel industry." Related economies would benefit as well. Park travel would bring jobs and income to the railroads, auto makers, hotels, guide services, clothing manufacturers, travel book and souvenir industries, and local farmers supplying resorts with food.[3]

Enticing accommodations and recreational facilities at the parks promised to breathe new life into the See America First slogan.

National pride had already elevated American scenery to privileged status as the equal of or better than European scenery. But before 1915, Yard said, the standard scenic destinations remained the Alps and the Canadian Rockies. With home travel stimulated by the national parks and by the war's closure of Europe, Americans — who prefer to "buy the best" — could at last discover their own treasures. Both Yard and Mills indulged lavishly in superlatives to describe the national parks. Yard called the Grand Canyon the world's "hugest and noblest example of erosion"; Mills called it the "greatest inanimate wonder in the world." Yard called Hawaii's Hauleakula the "hugest living volcano"; Mills called it the "chief scenic attraction in the world." Mills continued a Rocky Mountain tradition already sixty years old by asserting that the Rockies surpassed the Alps. "The mountain sheep," he said, "is as interesting . . . as the chamois," and "the fair phlox dares greater heights than the famed edelweiss." He called Pikes Peak — still on his park-planning agenda — a "peak for the multitudes," and said, "It has given mountain-top pleasure to more people than any other fourteen-thousand-foot summit of the earth." It was the place where Kathryn Lee Bates had stood enraptured as she wrote the words for "America the Beautiful." And Bates, another veteran of vacations in the Alps, had exclaimed with seemly patriotism that Pikes was the "most glorious scenery" she "had ever beheld."[4]

As a spokesman for the multitudes, Mills neglected the more obvious virtues of American mountains, which had already been discovered by some writers to be a national asset immune to comparisons with Europe: their vast regions of rugged and solitary wilderness. Though his adventure stories gave plenty of wilderness flavor, his national-park propaganda sold the See America First theme almost solely through its appeal to mass tourism. And Mills continued to preach that all the natural beauty contained in the parks would be for naught unless it was "made ready" for use.

Mather set out to do just that. He supplemented the skimpy government budgets with private money of his own, adding to the salaries of some of his staff and funding developments such as the Tioga Pass road in Yosemite. He was a master at cultivating personal contacts for both political support and funding donations. He continued his practice — begun when he campaigned to create the Park Service — of taking VIPs on saddle trips through the parks to let nature state its own case for the park movement and to let the fellowship of men in the outdoors graft their loyalty to his cause. Senators, Congressmen, writers, and businessmen — some of whom had never seen a national park before — saw America's natural wonders firsthand and experienced the inspiration of outdoor living that Muir and Mills knew was irresistibly persuasive. The converts returned to Congress, the press, and the boardrooms of business ready to help sponsor legislation for needed park improvements and ready in many cases to become benefactors themselves. Horace Albright's private fishing trips with Calvin Coolidge and Herbert Hoover bred a taste for parks in two future presidents. By 1919, park funding began to improve; influenced by Mather's personal allies, Congress learned to trust his judgment so highly that he could himself suggest most of the legislation affecting national parks.

While cultivating new bases of support, Mather held on to loyal allies such as conservation clubs and the GFWC. He backed local organizations such as the Save the Redwoods League and promoted the formation of state parks to extend park consciousness and his own good image to local levels. He helped create the National Parks Association (NPA) as a nongovernmental voice for park advocacy, and Yard became its first head in 1919.

Under Mather the parks developed roads, trails, campgrounds, lodging, sanitation, and recreational facilities. Rangers replaced the armed troops that formerly guarded the parks and learned to cater to tourists' needs. They stocked streams and lakes to ensure fishermen a good catch. They eliminated predators to increase deer, elk, and sheep populations, and set out salt licks and even fenced enclosures to concentrate animals for viewing. They helped tourists to photograph wildlife and cut roadside windows in the trees to open up scenic vistas. They developed sites to encourage popular all-season activities, which came to include tennis, golf, swimming, skating, skiing, sledding, summer concerts, plays, and all manner of evening entertainments. In RMNP, rangers provided a backcountry cabin and obligingly packed in supplies for winter outings of the Colorado Mountain Club. Mills's hope that national parks would become all-season playgrounds was well on the way to fulfillment.

Mills shared with Mather a belief that tasteful and "artistic" development in the parks made humanity's imprint on the natural surroundings acceptable and even desirable. Both cited the rustic lodges built by the Great Northern Railroad in Glacier Park as models for other parks. Balance and harmony had surely been achieved when animals grazed unafraid on one side of a picture window while admiring tourists watched from the other side. But the heavy emphasis on recreation in the parks introduced tension into the pro-park coalition. While the profitability of park facilities was attractive to most of Congress, Secretary Lane, and to the tourist industry, the preservationist wing of the coalition was becoming disaffected: Parks were becoming human zoos and their natural settings little more than painted backdrops for entertainments that could take place anywhere. As head of the National Parks Association, Yard quickly grew critical of Mather's administration and steered the new organization to the position that the parks "were best where modified the least." He could not countenance what was happening in places like Yosemite valley, which by the mid twenties had a Coney Island atmosphere. A typical evening's entertainment included music and vocal numbers performed on a lighted bandstand, amusing stunts (Yard called one of them "flagrantly vulgar"), bears under bright spotlights gorging on garbage (called "swell swill" by the emcee), and dance music droning late into the night. "So far as my sympathies are concerned," Yard wrote, "the valley's lost."[5]

Mather held his coalition together by developing facilities in concentrated areas of high use and keeping the park hinterlands wild. He vetoed Albright's idea for a cable car into the Grand Canyon and planned for certain areas such as an eastern extension of Sequoia Park to remain roadless. On balance, however, Mather may have trivialized the park experience, for he comprehended parks neither in terms of ecological integrity nor in terms of Muir's spiritual vision. Michael Cohen relegates Mather to the category of, "flat, tasteless bureaucrat."[6] In the forward development of American wilderness awareness, Mather handed the initiative back to the Forest Service and its new generation of thinkers centered around Aldo Leopold. Yard in time shifted the NPA's support to the Forest Service, relieved that it, at least, did not allow bear shows and tawdry entertainments.

The stern master of Longs Peak Inn would have been as dismayed as Yard by the gaudy spectacles in Yosemite valley. And in *Your National Parks* and elsewhere he openly condemned feeding garbage to bears. But the parks remained in his vision so much an institution for the people that he did not explore in any consequential way the ramifications of mass visitation. His quarrel with the

Park Service would not be over depriving nature of its rights but over depriving people of theirs.

Though Mills called the parks as great a blessing for the protected wildlife as for humans, their real function was to serve people. Without parks, he said, "all that is best in civilization will be smothered." "To save ourselves, to prevent our perishing, to enable us to live at our best and happiest, parks are necessary." He invoked heady epithets for parks such as "magic realm," "the directest approach to the fountain of life," "the richest and noblest heritage of the nation," and "islands of safety in a riotous world." He admonished that "the beautiful is as useful as the useful," and promised that these magnificent playgrounds would "keep the nation hopeful and young." Following forest trails would teach the general lesson of finding one's way through life. Matchless breeders of character, the parks would teach both adults and children the traits of sympathy, courage, kindness, individuality, sincerity, wholesome self-reliance, efficiency, and love. "I feel certain that if Nature were to speak," Mills said, "she would say 'Make National and State Parks of your best wild gardens, and with these I will develop greater men and women.'"[7]

Those greater men and women would, in turn, add to the nation's efficiency. Returning from vacations "glad to be living," the citizenry would accomplish its duties "with happiest hands." Parks would also foster democracy, class understanding, teamwork, and peace by bringing together easterners, westerners, capitalists and laborers, "in the happiest of circumstances." Parks, like nature itself, recognize no prejudices, "no flags of hatred," he said. And what he once said of forests, he now said of parks: "It is but little less than folly to spend millions on forts and warships, on prisons and hospitals, instead of giving people the opportunity to develop and rest in the sane outdoors." "It may be," he said elsewhere in *Your National Parks*, "if we quit shooting animals on one side of a Park boundary-line, that we shall in due time become sufficiently civilized to stop killing people on the other side of a national boundary-line." Mills's boldly declared pacifism harkened back two years to his speech at RMNP's dedication ceremonies; avoiding the decorous platitudes that might have sufficed for the occasion, he said: "Heretofore we have celebrated the launching of battleships, the barbarous slaughter of a weaker people, . . . The nation that prepares for war ultimately bleeds to death. Preparing for war has never failed to cover a land with blood — and ruins. With the winning of this park, Peace won a victory."[8]

Mills's growing fame as a naturalist and writer gave him authority to portray the national parks as the quintessence of all that is best in nature. His hyperbole was an idiom his readers knew and understood. His outspokenness was part of that idiom and expressed a hope for vast improvements in a world he wanted to become flawless. If he seemed to play fast and loose with high-minded rhetoric, he nevertheless wrote with sincerity and force. Mills's real product was social health and he sold it with almost evangelistic passion. He could say what he wanted to say because he was a voice that always spoke from outside the system, unrestrained by bureaucratic protocol. His zealous arguments, far from being detrimental to Mather's cause, served it well, just as his podium rhetoric had added the spice of native wisdom to Pinchot's cause. As a nongovernmental voice, Mills could proclaim better than Mather that the Park Service director should be a cabinet-level post. He could sell the national park idea in the broadest social terms by asserting that "the supreme triumph of parks is humanity." He could sound simultaneously fanciful and plausible in hoping that the anniversary of Yellowstone — the world's first national park — would someday become an international holiday of peace and good will. Mills's idealism was rooted in healthy common sense, and in claiming so vast a role for the parks he was making a strong and relevant statement about social values generally. Proclaiming, for example, that parks are a greater force for peace than warships, he was pleading, as activists do today, for the nation's return to sane priorities.

The first-person hero of Mills's adventure stories sparked his readers to find new levels of experience in the parks. He was quick to see the emergence of a new class of vacationing Americans who had left the year-round commitments of farm life for urban jobs with paid annual vacations. Preaching the active and growth-building use of leisure time and adult play, he urged park visitors to ignore the weather and come when they could "stay the longest." He told them to regard storms as nature's "vigorous building environment," and admonished with Progressive zeal, "If any normal person under the age of fifty cannot enjoy being in a storm in the wilds, he ought to reform at once."[9] Though he recommended bringing a raincoat on park visits, he also wanted people to get wet. Had not Thoreau once said that being cold and wet can be as rich an experience as being warm and dry?

One of Mills's most characteristic themes as a park publicist was that nature is safe — and safer of course than the civilization he wanted to cure. The back-to-nature enthusiasm of Mills's era had done much to erase superstitious fears of the wilds that had their roots among early pioneers facing an unknown and overgrown continent and in the Judeo-Christian belief that the wilds are Godless places where the soul becomes confused and lost. But residues of those fears remained. "Being afraid of nature is like being afraid of the dark," Mills said, pointing to the essential irrationality of those fears. Like Muir, he endeavored to show that civilization, not nature, was where the dangers lurked. His 1909 *Wild Life on the Rockies* had contrasted the safety of the outdoors with the "death list" of urban perils such as fire, automobiles, street-cars, and banquets. He insisted that wandering snowblind for three days through the wilderness had frightened him less than his narrow escapes from automobiles. He confidently told his mass readership that getting lost was only a temporary inconvenience that could be prevented by simple common sense; that a night outdoors was good for body and soul; that starvation in the wilds was "unlikely"; and that a fast of a few days was beneficial anyway. Those were by now standard Millsian themes, meant, perhaps more to shape attitudes than to be taken literally by tenderfeet from the city.

Probably the most uniquely Millsian theme publicizing the safety of the outdoors was the good effect of high altitude. As a guide and innkeeper in the nation's highest state, he had a practical need to develop that theme. His own guests, noted Edna Ferber in her autobiography, often reacted to the 9,000-foot altitude of Longs Peak Inn with insomnia, pounding hearts, and swimming heads. Oxygen levels at that altitude are about 40 percent lower than at sea level and the thin air is furthermore wrung dry of over half its moisture. Today, the Colorado Heart Association warns that although adjusting to Colorado's altitudes is relatively easy, symptoms in the unacclimated can include heart palpitations, headache, nasal congestion, coughs, flatulence, fatigue, intolerance to exertion, nausea, insomnia, diarrhea, restlessness, shortness of breath, and more severe problems, such as high-altitude pulmonary edema.

Mills preached that the "ill effects of altitude are mostly imaginary" and sworn to by "the anaemics who stay at home." He believed that many, arriving in Colorado with a fear of altitude gained from hearsay and outdated beliefs, talked themselves into getting sick. They should promptly talk themselves back out of it, he insisted. "Anyone in normal health who fears the altitude can not be acquainted with Mental Science," he exhorted. Altitude also tended to deal its blows to those who deserved them. Those included the "bilious," those careless about their diets, and "those who celebrated the climb the night before it was made." With a well-turned pun, he said that "feeling the altitude would often be more correctly expressed as feeling the effects of high living." Altitude, in short, was "the scapegoat for a multitude of sins."[10]

Mills cited the findings of a British-American scientific study of altitude conducted on top of Pikes Peak in 1911. The study concluded that, under normal exertion, high altitude is not a cardiac risk factor. He quoted with evident satisfaction the Pikes Peak study's conclusion that reduced oxygen levels often induced a sense of well-being.[11] The reserved, he had often noted himself, became talkative and confiding, and acquaintances ripened "with amazing rapidity." The friendships and romances Mills saw blossom on the slopes of Longs Peak had not only the inspiration of the setting to thank but also the physiological effects of rarefied air.

Yet another theme Mills pushed as a park publicist was that visitors had nothing to fear from wild animals. He attacked the long traditions of fear and hatred for wolves and lions, saying that virtually all accounts of attacks on people were fabrications. Wolves, he said, had never attacked him, while dogs, their civilized brethren, often had. In defense of lions, he brought for a witness Theodore Roosevelt, who said that "it would be no more dangerous to sleep in woods populated by mountain lions than if there were so many ordinary cats." Mills called the black bear "infinitely less dangerous than the old hen with chicks."[12] And he took pains to portray the good behavior of unprovoked grizzly bears. Mills and his contemporary William Wright popularized and defended the grizzly in books of remarkably similar character and content. Both cited a host of other authorities, including the famous naturalist William Hornaday, who, as early as 1904, had come strongly to the defense of America's greatest beast.

Mills believed that the protection of animals in national parks would improve the relationship between people and animals that "appear to desire human society." *Your National Parks* expressed that kind of Edenic vision, noting that "birds and animals are hoping and waiting for friendly advances on our part." The protected park preserves would promote mutual acquaintance and allow people to discover the heretofore "underrated . . . mental powers of animals" and their wide range of emotions.[13]

The parklands surrounding Longs Peak Inn were briefly a publicized Garden of Eden with a real Eve when a twenty-year-old coed named Agnes Lowe donned a leopard-skin robe, waved farewell to a crowd of 2,000, and disappeared into the wilds to spend a week with nature. At the departure ceremony on August 6, 1917, reporters photographed the modern Eve shaking hands with Enos Mills. Barefoot, with waist-length hair and a soft smile, she wore a look of benign innocence. Mills, clad in a suit coat, knickerbockers, and boots, scrutinized her as if wondering if she was remotely capable of such a feat. Of course it was possible, of course he had done it many times, of course nature was the safest place in the world. But could she really manage? Should he give her some last-minute advice? Next to Mills stood park superintendent L. Claude Way, uniformed, upright, military in bearing. He appeared to like the pretty face but to wonder what lay behind it. When Eve departed, Mills accompanied her a short distance into the woods.

She emerged after a week in perfect health, received a mailsack that included sixty-four marriage proposals, and soon disappeared into obscurity. But the press let out the grimy secret: It had been a hoax from beginning to end. What sort of publicity stunts, asked a fuming Horace Albright from Washington, was the park getting into? Superintendent Way had to explain that he had been duped into participating in the deception. As soon as Mills — probably innocent of the ruse — left Eve, a ranger had spirited her to a cabin elsewhere in the park, then brought her back after a week for her grand re-entry to civilization. Way contritely protested that, after the dust settled, greater interest in the park and more visitation would be the result.[14]

Eve's stunt, even though a hoax, was richly symbolic. It was a reminder that the unspoiled wilderness preserved in national parks *was* an Eden where precivilized purity could be rediscovered and relived. And in a more American sense, parks were a new kind of place where people could rediscover their own pioneer heritage. That idea was important enough for Mills to use as the theme for his preface to *Your National Parks*. With the frontier gone, he said,

Mills wishes "Eve" good luck; Superintendent Way at far left. *Lulie and Jack Melton Collection.*

national parks allow the pioneer in each of us to act once more and to "rebuild the past." Reviewing the lives of some famous pioneers, he extolled the bygone era as a time not of sacrifice but of "selection" — freedom to choose — and a life of abundance away from the crowd — from "the enemies of sincerity and individuality." The theme of an unspoiled American heritage remains a potent argument for both park and wilderness protection today.[15]

As support for parks grew, education and research emerged as additional reasons for keeping them unspoiled. Yard's own preference as a publicist had been education from the start, and he included that function in his official title. Perhaps on Yard's advice, Mather appointed a commission to study education in the parks and subsequently formed an official educational advisory board for the Park Service. He established museums at Mesa Verde in 1918, at Yellowstone and Yosemite in 1919, and at other parks soon after. When Albright drafted a set of policy objectives for the Park Service, Yard helped him articulate the importance of parks as resources for education and scientific field research. Nature programs and museums in the parks should highlight each park's unique natural history, he said, and candidates for future parks should be "distinguished examples of typical forms of world architecture."[16]

Yard organized his 1919 *Book of the National Parks* on the theme of "world architecture," and he sought "to add the intellectual pleasure of comprehension" to the "almost wholly emotional" experience he saw park visitors limited to. He confessed his dismay with a tourist who was thrilled by the view of Yosemite Falls principally because she could add it to her list of other spectacles: the world's tallest building, longest railroad, largest lake, and biggest department store. "I am not condemning wonder, which, in its place, is a legitimate and pleasurable emotion," Yard instructed gently. Yet "she was conscious of no higher emotion than the cheap wonder of a superlative." Yard hoped the national parks would teach a series of stories that would make people open their eyes to all the rest of nature's stories. "I invite you," he said, "to a new and fascinating earth, an earth interesting, vital, personal, beloved, because at last known and understood."[17]

Precisely that same spirit pervaded Mills's *Your National Parks*, which preceded Yard's book by two years and was acclaimed on its appearance as the standard introduction to the new park system. Mills, the outdoor guide par excellence, added a chapter on outdoor education to the book, in which he called nature "the teacher of teachers" and parks "the greatest of schools."[18] His individual park chapters sought to convey both understanding and love for the parks. Like Yard, he wanted visitors to see the parks as more than collections of curiosities, to discover their mysteries and subtleties. In his Yellowstone chapter he described the protean manifestations of water in rivers, lakes, geysers, springs, and mudpots, and as an agent of erosion. He described the park's amethyst forest as a story laid down in layers as interesting as the archaeological layers of Troy. His Yosemite chapter told of the region's famous stream and ice sculpting, but delved with equal enthusiasm into the Sierra's flora and fauna. His Rainier Park chapter taught the rudiments of glacial mechanics and climatic responses, then dwelt lyrically on the park's incomparable wildflowers. His Mesa Verde chapter offered appreciative speculations about the vanished inhabitants and praised their architecture, masonry, and artwork. And his Grand Canyon chapter dealt at length with the fascinating mechanics of river erosion.

Your National Parks was published in June 1917, two months after America's entry into the war. It was an ambitious work, with six chapters of empassioned pro-park advocacy following his accounts of the individual parks and monuments. A ninety-five-page park travel guide, compiled by a collaborator, Laurence Schmeckebier, followed Mills's main text. Mills's pitch for national parks was explicitly political in his chapter "Park Development and New Parks," which opened with a "Platform for Park Promoters." He praised Mather for bringing orderly planning and businesslike management to the parks. He urged citizen pressure to shake loose adequate appropriations for every national park, enlargement of a few parks, and "prompt creation" of several others. He warned that each new park proposal would have "powerful, insidious opposition." Just as he had urged young men and women to seek forestry careers several years earlier, he now sought to recruit to the park movement people "who are willing to serve a noble cause."[19]

Mills urged "eternal vigilance" to help the Park Service and to keep it "absolutely separate from the Forest Service or any other organization." Still fearing a Forest Service coup of the national parks, he stacked up three lengthy quotations (by Stewart Edward White, Frederick Law Olmsted, and John Nolan) stressing that national park and national forest management must remain separate. Despite his by now obsessive distrust of the Forest Service,

Mills's fears had substance. They were fears that preoccupied Mather and Albright too — fears that perhaps more than anything else spurred them to forge political alliances, enlarge their base of support, and clearly define their agency goals. In a recent study of Park Service policy history, Ronald Foresta says, "There can be little doubt that capture of the Park Service's charge and its extinction as an independent bureau were important goals of Forest Service leadership during the first years of the Park Service."[20]

Pinchot had helped force the Park Service into being through his intolerance of noncommodity uses. The loss of Hetch Hetchy in 1914 and the public's association of Pinchot with the dam proposal seemed conclusive proof that the Forest Service could not be entrusted with scenic preservation. Conversely, the rhetoric of social utility that the preservationists developed in response to that loss showed their desperate realization that beauty alone could not survive in the contest of the "greatest good." Defending scenery as a business asset was their strongest argument and was given a boost by burgeoning park visitation during the war years. The broader value of parks — what Mills called their "large dividend to humanity" — also acquired tangible focus in the war years. McFarland's influential shift of preservationist rhetoric from "pleasure and adornment" to "service and efficiency" served its purpose well in the war years too, for the health-building environment of the outdoors could now be seen as contributing to the country's industrial might by providing "men as well as minerals." Robert B. Marshall went so far as to suggest that if America were pulled into a war, young men who had "built up their bodies by lying next to nature . . . will be able to meet the physical needs of a strenuous field service."[21]

If the war in a perverse way justified the man-building power of parks, it also threatened the parks with new invasions for natural resources. Using the war emergency powers as an excuse to exploit park resources, food producers proposed slaughtering Yellowstone elk and buffalo for war meat, and sheep interests sought to graze tens of thousands of sheep in Yosemite, Glacier and Rainier national parks. Lane, who had favored the Hetch Hetchy dam and was an easy target for utilitarian persuasions, approved grazing in Yosemite but then reversed his decision under public pressure. Herbert Hoover, head of the Food Administration at the time, turned down the callous Yellowstone proposal and sided with Albright to defeat grazing in Rainier and Glacier parks. When Seattle area residents called the bluff on sheep interests by offering their front lawns for grazing, Lane got a clear message — one he received personally from Mills as well — that the public would not tolerate brazen exploitation of the parks in the guise of "national security."

But under Henry Graves the Forest Service posed a new and increasingly serious threat: It began to close the gap on the differences that distinguished the Park Service and Forest Service as separate agencies. The Forest Service began building campsites; restricting grazing in selected areas; leasing land for summer homes, hotels, and recreational facilities; and issuing internal bulletins on recreational management. At the Grand Canyon — not yet a national park — it built its own tourist facilities. Graves could assert with increasing emphasis that the continuance of separate agencies was inefficient, and he argued the point explicitly in a 1920 article. As a "functional competitor," notes Foresta, the Forest Service was becoming the most dangerous kind of rival. If it could unify the management of all public lands and appropriately designate areas for resource extraction, recreation, and strict preservation, it could offer something the Park Service could not.

Albright condemned the Forest Service's "monstrous recreation campaign" and tried with Mather to force the rival agency back into the narrow utilitarianism of its own earlier definition. Mills's lengthy distinction between Forest Service and Park Service functions in *Your National Parks* served the same end. Rather than condemning the Forest Service outright, he acceded its necessity if kept properly in its own sphere. But he had no prescription for reforming the Forest Service as a strictly utilitarian agency. Even honoring scenic values was no longer a redeeming quality if the Forest Service was to stay put in its own bailiwick.

Despite Mills's praise for Mather in *Your National Parks,* the book betrayed irritations that would fester to gaping wounds. While Mather openly promoted the use of concessions to provide visitor services and facilities in parks, Mills openly criticized them as "a bad feature in any park." Mills's business arguments for parks seemed to stop short at the park boundaries, and the concessions that Yard — while still a loyal Matherite — described as "partners pulling together" were for Mills profiteers at the public expense. "Why should private concerns reap profits by exploiting the visitors to National Parks?" he asked. He praised Palisade Interstate Park for running successfully without concessions and dedicated the book to

George Perkins and William Welch, "whose statesmanship, energy, ideals and courage are making the Palisade Interstate Park the greatest park in the world." Mather must have felt more than a little pique that the definitive book on the new national park system by a famous author praised a state park above any national park and that the statesmanship recognized was not his own. Mather probably also saw his leadership impugned by Mills's suggestion that a Board of National Park Commissioners be created to exert "absolute control over the National Parks."[22]

About the time the book was published, Albright visited Mills in what he later described as a "difficult, unpleasant meeting." Mills came down on the much younger Albright over the matter of concessions in a way that Albright interpreted as self-interest. "He . . . wanted to ban all transportation and lodging concessions while still retaining his own inn and his other property in the park," Albright recalled. And in a complaint becoming increasingly common, he added, "His adamant attitude seemed to leave no room for reasoning."[23] In fairness to Mills, Albright failed to distinguish between existing inholdings in the parks — such as Longs Peak Inn, just incorporated in an eastward boundary expansion — and profit-making concessions brought into the parks after their formation. And Mather would not escape the criticism in later years that his concessions were more interested in profits than in true park values.

Mills also battered Albright over the timidity of the Park Service in fighting for new additions to RMNP. Congress had approved boundary adjustments that added forty square miles that February, but both Mills and the Park Service had their eye on the scenic stretch of Continental Divide stretching south to Arapahoe Peaks, the Neversummer Range northwest of the park, and the Mt. Evans area west of Denver. Of the three, only the Neversummer Range ever became part of the park — many decades later. The proposed southern extension became the Indian Peaks Wilderness in 1978, while the Mt. Evans addition was fought to its conclusion at once and ended Mills's relationship with Albright.

Mills advocated an open fight to add Mt. Evans as a free-standing park annex. Albright, seeing the difficulty of plucking 100,000 acres from the middle of a huge forest reserve, favored delicate negotiations behind the scenes. It in fact became official policy to investigate possible park annexations jointly with the Forest Service "in order that questions of national park and national forest policy as they affect the lands involved may be thoroughly understood." Albright had drafted that policy himself, along with twenty-two others, to define the Park Service's agency mission.[24] He circulated the draft to Yard, McFarland, Kunz, Marshall, and the Sierra Club leadership for suggestions; if he had once thought of including Mills, the unpleasant encounter at Longs Peak Inn changed his mind. Mather approved Albright's draft, sent it to Lane, and received it back from Lane as his official mandate in May 1918. Albright had probably already begun following the policies he invented.

Albright's preference for closed-door meetings brought criticism later in his career and was contrary to the professed spirit of the Wilson administration that "government must, if it is to be pure and correct in its processes, be absolutely public in everything that affects it." For Mills, already inflamed and suspicious, and blaming Albright also for delays in removing park funding ceilings, the absence of a publicly visible battle over Mt. Evans was sure evidence that Albright was using his official position "to screen the insidious work of the Forest Service." He attacked him in a searing letter to Lane, calling him a "menace to the entire cause of the National Parks." Lane's quick defense of Albright did not appease Mills, who charged a few weeks later that Albright was a "crook" who had "sold out to the Forest Service" to further "his own cheap political interests." Albright, deeply hurt, drafted a reply to Mills and planned to confront him personally during a visit to Colorado in fall 1918. Then he decided not to mail the letter and to ignore Mills during his visit. While Mills fumed and waited in vain to be contacted, he received a pungent letter from Mather defending Albright and dismissing Mills's charges as slander "not even worth discussing."[25]

After spending several days personally examining the Mt. Evans area, Albright strongly recommended it for park status. But Graves fought it with his powerful lobby, won, and quickly made Mt. Evans a Forest Service recreational area. Today it is a primary tourist destination, with protected wildlife herds and the country's highest auto road. Though Albright's diplomacy failed to secure Mt. Evans for the park system, he and Mather won more battles than they lost, and created — mostly from Forest Service lands — some of the most renowned parks, including McKinley, Zion, Bryce, and the Grand Canyon. The Forest Service continued its recreation campaign, but the Park Service survived and grew. Mills was seen as a troublesome meddler who in his hatred for the Forest Service had "tried to fan up the interbureau rivalry into something even hotter." So concludes Mather's biographer, Robert Shankland, who saw Mills both as a key figure in spreading national-park sentiment and one of the West's "most combative characters." In the ensuing dispute over the RMNP concessions, Shankland says, "Mather found himself down at the far end of the target range with Joe and the Forest Service" — "the two sorest ulcers on Mills's psyche."[26]

CHAPTER 18

Mills vs. Monopoly: "The Acme of Human Tyranny"

On August 16, 1919, Enos Mills sent a car from Longs Peak Inn on a tour into Rocky Mountain National Park (RMNP), intentionally violating a ban on all commercial travel except that granted to a single touring franchise. Park superintendent L. Claude Way, cued by Mills himself, was there to intercept the car and order it out of the park. It was an almost staged and for the moment politely acted drama by which Mills hoped to force a test case in the courts. Since May, when the franchise began, he had assailed its injustice. He said the Park Service had chosen the concession without competitive bids, public hearings, or disclosure of the terms of the contract; that it violated the terms of the park's creation; and that it put tourists, local residents and local merchants at the mercy of a conniving and price-rigging monopoly. A scant four years after he had proudly dedicated the park, Mills was seeking legal action against it.

The rhetoric of Mills's worst enemies now reverberated in his own. In 1911 the Front Range Settlers' League had said, in opposing creation of the park: "Those merchants and storekeepers who have established lines of trade with the people of the region view with concern and alarm the possibility of trade and traffic privileges farmed out and licensed to strangers by a park administration." Mills now said: "This autocrat — the Director of the National Park Service — is farming these parks out to monopolies. All the resources of these parks, which afford a living to numerous resident local people, . . . are given out to monopolies, over which the public have no control and which the public cannot remove."[1]

Mills said the monopoly threatened to "wreck" the local economy. Its direct effect on him was that he was barred from transporting

Mills's opponent in his last public cause. *NPS photo.*

his own guests from Estes Park to Longs Peak Inn, which sat on private land surrounded by park territory. Eight other hotels, similarly situated, faced the same problem. All outlying hotels inside or outside the park were vulnerable to losing business when coach drivers steered tourists to hotels — the Lewiston in particular, Mills charged — favored by the franchise. Nor could any hotel take its guests on scenic tours into the park — a restriction particularly irksome to Freelan O. Stanley, whose business operation at the high-class Stanley Hotel included squiring loads of tourists through the park in his elegant Stanley Steamers. Most affected were the independent jitney drivers who hired out their services individually and now faced a cancellation of their seasonal livelihood. The business they formerly shared at rates set by their own competition was now given exclusively to Roe Emery's Rocky Mountain Parks Transportation Company. Emery already had a transportation franchise in Glacier National Park and had competed with other operations locally since 1916 while awaiting approval of his franchise application.

Tourists in private cars were not affected by the monopoly and accounted for 85 percent of the park's 170,000 visitors in 1919. But that still left 25,000 captive to Emery's monopoly and to its high prices — doubled, Mills contended, over the competitive rates of previous seasons. He charged that multitudes had been deprived of visits to the park by the high prices alone. He implied economic class discrimination. And tourists able to afford private cars faced exploitation too: They were soon — it appeared — to be charged a five dollar park entrance fee and were already required to yield right-of-way to franchise coaches on park roads. Emery wanted the roads uncluttered, Mills said, in order to maximize his travel volume and profits. The final and perhaps greatest threat was to property owners with cabins in the park. Access roads built by the county, the state, or their own toil were now guarded by uniformed rangers. To get to their own homes in hired cars they had to ride in Emery vehicles; and with entrance fees imminent — though in fact there were none for twenty more years — they feared having to pay toll charges for their own cars on their own roads. The transportation monopoly was, in Mills's view, a tyrannical weapon against the people. It had replaced motor services that supported the local economy, prospered through the all-American principle of free competition, and met everyone's needs with good service at good rates. Mills saw his ideal of "parks for all the people" being torn apart by a militaristic and monopoly-serving bureaucracy.

Park Service director Stephen Mather, who had created the controversial monopoly policy, was undaunted by the furor it was causing in more than one national park. It was a policy he had begun in 1915, defended at the 1917 national parks conference, and included in the May 1918 policy directives that define major national park philosophy even today. Under its terms, he was systematically forcing hotel, food, camping, and transportation concessions into mergers or out of business in order to abolish what he believed were the squalor and confusion of services competing for limited tourist dollars during the short park seasons. Rival businesses fought for profitable operations and neglected unprofitable ones. They cut corners to maximize their profits and often rendered shoddy service. Competing drivers waited hungrily for tourists at train stations and assailed them with a noisy confusion of offers. One tourist in Yellowstone alleged that two of them tugged at him until his coat ripped apart. Land space in the parks was consumed by the offices, garages, and utility areas of multiple companies. Most of the companies closed down as soon a peak-season profits tapered off; almost none provided services in winter. In RMNP, congestion on the limited roadways was cited as an additional reason for reducing the number of commercial carriers.

Though some aspects of park administration laid down by Mather soon alienated conservationists, the apparent intent of his concession policy was to make the parks run smoothly. He had a patrician's taste for class, and he indisputably loved the parks. He wanted them to present a tidy image to the public and to the VIPs whose support he needed to keep the fledgling park system alive. If he was a businessman who might have defended the right of unrestrained entrepreneurship, he also had a corporate executive's instinct for eliminating competition. And he was a businessman now in government office during an era of strong business-government collaboration. With admiring overstatement, a modern follower of Mather calls it "one of the great ironies of American history," that "Steve Mather, free enterpriser par excellence, decided to establish a regulated monopoly system for the national parks."[2]

The official line was that the parks were an inappropriate setting for competing concessions. And the exclusive franchises that replaced them were akin to the regulated monopolies adopted by many cities for telephone, power, and trolley services. Some economists called them "natural monopolies." Mather called them "public-utility services," and avoided the word "concession" in his annual reports. Part of the bargain of those utility services was profit sharing: In return for the privilege of doing business in the parks, they gave a cut — around 25 percent — of their profits to the park. Those profits could then be put to work for park improvements. It was more of what Yard, while still a loyal Matherite, called government and business "pulling together."

Mather never fully achieved his goal of consolidating each park's hotel, food, transportation, camping, livery, and trail-guide services into single monopolies. He had to fight multiple businesses already in place — many defiant and determined to blast him out of office. Some had strong allies in Congress; all cited the canons of competitive free enterprise. The greatest controversy was in Yellowstone, where concessions were deeply entrenched and well connected politically. To their defense came two senators and a congressman, all with friends operating concessions. Senator Walsh of Montana said that anyone who wanted to run any sort of concession should be allowed to do so.

Mather nevertheless pushed his program forcefully. By 1917 he had cut transportation and hotel operations in Yellowstone to single but separate concessions. He combined the camping companies and stripped them of their transportation business. By 1924 he had consolidated everything in Yellowstone except the general stores and a few minor services. But in Yosemite, where the Curry Company flourished and the Yosemite National Park Company was faltering, he propped up the underdog with a personal loan of $200,000 rather than letting it die and prove that there was only enough business for one. "Indiscreet," says park historian William Everhart of the loan. Indiscreet indeed; and it characterized the kind of erratic behavior that Mather, alternately hyperactive and incapacitated by depression, brought to his high office. It complicated relations not just with volatile characters like Mills, but also with his own second-in-charge, the loyal Horace Albright. Mather's inconsistencies showed all the more that, in his hands, park policy was elastic. He used his charm, power, and diplomatic skill to shape it to his personal vision. To implement his concession policy, says Don Hummel, a veteran concessioner, he "[used] whatever means proved workable, persuasion when possible, tyranny when necessary."[3]

It was Mills who most acutely felt the policy as tyranny. And because of it, more than anything, Mather's own standing with Mills plummeted from hero to villain in the short span from 1915 to 1919 — hastened, of course, by his defense of Albright in 1917. It was an almost worshipful Enos Mills who wrote a personal profile of Mather to accompany Mather's first article, "The National Parks on a Business Basis," in April 1915, after taking control of the parks. Mills's profile ran opposite Mather's title page and portrayed him as an outdoor lover, park enthusiast, and intimate friend of John Muir's, who would "bring to these neglected parks that which they have not yet had, — a strong, sympathetic, and constructive administration." Mills's personal praise went even higher in a letter to the magazine's publisher. He called Mather the "most human man I ever knew," and said he was "calm yet enthusiastic, always level-headed, always keen for the main issue." He was a man who modestly helped "everyone who he thinks deserves it."[4]

What bitterness and sense of betrayal seized the heart of the man who five years later saw Mather as a heavy-handed autocrat who controlled the lives of the local villagers while using his propaganda machine to spread news of his beneficence. "The Director of the

National Park Service," Mills wrote, "is not chosen by the people and cannot be removed by the people. . . . It makes [him] a king and gives him the protection of the monopoly. . . . [This is] the very acme of human insolence and tyranny. . . . Any individual who seeks to rule people without their consent should be at once branded as an incompetent or a schemer."[5]

At the midpoint of that period — in early 1917 and before the Albright feud — Mills was still praising Mather formally but not hiding his opposition to concessions. With Mather presiding at his talk "Parks for All the People" at the 1917 national parks conference, he denounced concessions as profiteering enterprises that exploit the people. The people should run the parks that they themselves own, he asserted. McFarland told the conference in even stronger terms that the government should run all services within parks as cheaply as possible, and without profit. "The very fact that it is good business for [the concessions] makes it bad business for the people," he said.[6]

Mather, quite to the contrary, had said in his 1915 article that what makes good business for the concessions makes *good* business for the people:

> The Government must do its part to make the national parks as cheap and as attractive as possible to the people, in order that the people, by coming yearly in great numbers, may make business profitable for the concessioners.
> The proposition appears complicated. To some it may seem impossible. Yet it is only, after all, an every-day business problem. Its solution is increased business. Bring enough people to the parks and charges will decrease, while the concessioners, after sharing profits with the Government, will be far more prosperous than ever.[7]

In 1915 that logic must have appealed both to Mills's business instincts and to his own desire for mass visitation. He was as convinced as Mather that park visitation could be raised tenfold, and he identified keenly with Mather's intention to "get America's scenery ready to be seen." But as soon as he saw that Mather wanted to convert concessions into exclusive franchises, he took up the opposition. Both men, ironically, expressed business principles — Mills through competition, Mather through consolidation.

When Mills said that "the people" should run park services and McFarland said "the government" should run them, they might have meant equivalent things. In practice, they did not. McFarland, though a conservative Republican, wanted business out of the parks and meant literally that government should do the job: municipal governments for city parks, state governments for state parks, and Uncle Sam for national parks. They could offer rock-bottom prices to the public because the government "can buy in the cheapest manner, . . . has indefinite credit . . . pays no rent or taxes . . . and needs no profit." If the government can be trusted to send the nation's mail and run the Army and Navy, it ought to be trusted to provide beds, food, and auto stages in the national parks, he said.[8] Mills, on the other hand, meant by "the people" not the whole people operating through their government — as he clearly implied in his earlier socialist utterances — but instead local merchants operating through the free enterprise system. He stressed consistently that traffic and business in the national parks should be "truly regulated" through free and open competition. That position, despite the fury of his polemical assaults, was as soundly American as anyone could have wished in a time of intense wartime and postwar Americanism.

Mather said after Mills's talk that he found the idea of parks "run by the people" "particularly interesting." He said he had thought about it often but did not say what he had concluded. He conceded, however, "I hope the time will come when the Government will conduct all the facilities for the people in the parks; but that time is probably some years ahead." But it was not then, or ever, Mather's agenda to do so. It was not seriously considered until Interior Secretary Harold Ickes brought it up in the Franklin Roosevelt administration, and it remains unrealized even today. Mather sought always to make parks an enticement to business and to protect the businesses he selected against competition from others. His formula to keep costs to the public low and profits to concessioners high by maximizing business volume remained his gospel.

Twice in the two weeks after Mills sent his car into the park to provoke a confrontation, Way offered explanations and compromises he hoped would lay the matter to rest. In a letter to Mills he explained that Emery's rates were higher because he had to absorb losses from mandatory operation in all seasons and in bad weather when ridership was low. He promised to review and adjust the prices, if necessary, after the first year. He said that if the jitney drivers would operate under those same conditions (most, being only seasonal operators, could not) they could resume operation with competitive prices under a fixed ceiling. Hotels on private land in the park, including Longs Peak Inn, *would* henceforth be allowed to haul their own guests or to hire other companies to haul them if Emery's schedules didn't fit. He reminded Mills that tours into the park were in any event permitted if not for profit. Was he hinting that hotel owners could offer their guests free tours or tours at break-even rates and recover costs in other ways? Mills was not, in any case, appeased or moved to cooperate. He refused to meet with Mather, who came out from Washington to explain concession philosophy to Denver and Estes Park businessmen. He was bent on eradicating the handpicked monopoly that was linked by what he believed were obscure deals to the park bureaucracy. He was determined moreover to make RMNP a test case to challenge the monopoly principle throughout the park system and probably saw his strategy weakened if he bought into conciliatory local terms. But he failed to move the debate to the new level set by Way's significant compromise offers. He failed ever to say what Way's offers were and that he *had* resumed hauling his own guests to and from Estes Park. He doggedly persisted in criticizing the original evils of the monopoly: doubled prices, inferior and discriminatory service, damage to the local economy, and hegemony over the people.[9]

In early September of 1919 Mills filed a complaint against Way in U.S. District Court, claiming his "common right as a Colorado citizen to travel over the park roads." He cited language from the RMNP bill that protected his rights as an inholder: The government, it said, could not exercise control over private inholdings or "the full use and enjoyment" of those inholdings by the owners. The U.S. attorney convinced the judge that Mills was misinterpreting that language and moved to dismiss the case. "The whole subject is within the exclusive control of the Department of Interior," said the judge.[10]

Before and after that, Mills and some of the jitney drivers had continued driving into the park, hoping to provoke additional litigations. Washington warned Way to go easy, for the Park Service feared a major test case in the courts. It wanted first to strengthen its hand by gaining legal jurisdiction over the state and county roads in the park and hoped to do so over the winter of 1919–20. Instead, that issue alone became an endlessly thorny and complex one that would drag on for years. With jurisdiction undecided, the park in summer 1920 became a battleground where defiant jitney drivers, determined to stay in business, became aggressive activists. They distributed business cards and erected billboards advertising their services. They recruited tourists to sign antimonopoly petitions. They drove to the park boundary with loads of tourists, demanded entry, and were rejected with much hullabaloo. They encouraged their annoyed passengers to complain to their hotel management, the Park Service, and to Washington directly. Jitneys drove into the park past unguarded entry points, while rangers with binoculars tried to record the violations for future prosecution. A driver named Charles Robbins sought repeatedly to provoke his own arrest. Way, hearing of a plot by Robbins, Mills, and others to pounce on any arrest with an assault charge, kept his rangers in check. Robbins at last filed suit anyway, claiming his right to travel freely, "without molestation." In follow-up litigation his attorneys received assistance from the state attorney general's office and in turn represented the state in a suit filed against the Park Service. One of them briefly described the legal controversy up to 1924 in the memorial edition of Mills's *Rocky Mountain National Park*.

So long as the Robbins case remained undecided, the jitney drivers were emboldened even more to flout the park's rules. Some entered the park by threatening to run down the guard rangers. One was pulled from his car by an exasperated ranger when he appeared to be reaching for a pistol but was in fact reaching for his handbrake. The car's passengers, two suitably proper ladies, swore to the ranger's guilt and he was convicted and left by his superiors to pay his own fine. Visually, the affair must have resembled silent-movie slapstick; yet it was noisy, grim, and often ugly on both sides. It was another chapter in the chronicle of defiant westerners fighting government bureaucracy run from Washington. Way had to enforce a policy that he was given, whether he liked it or not. And though a majority of locals agreed with that policy, the park's days of innocence were gone and the character of the place changed. The "people's playground" had become an institution with rules that took uniformed officers to enforce. By the end of the next summer, Way was drained and abruptly resigned. He felt he had faced vicious and irrational adversaries and at times feared for his life at the hands of the jitney drivers, who taunted him with insults and were often said to be "in a killing mood."

Charles Robbins lost both his own suit and a countersuit by the government forbidding any unauthorized entry into the park. Mills, faring no better in court, saw the lack of legal recourse as the work of a political machine. He turned, consequently, to what he knew best: writing and speaking. He traveled and spoke in many cities, wrote to local and Washington politicians, prodded conservation groups to make their own inquiries, wrote editorials in newspapers and magazines, and got editors as far afield as Boston, Houston, and St. Louis to follow suit. In a string of articles from August 1920 to the end of 1921, Mills maintained an angrily polemical tone. He spoke without restraint of conspiracy, saying both that the park served the monopoly and that the monopoly served the park. Either way, it was an evil mixture of business, bureaucracy, and political machinery, with the Park Service supplying the police force. Mills alleged local corruption in a secret partnership between Emery and the Lewiston Hotel Company to force all other hotels out of business and absorb their holdings. He said the plot was backed by the Denver Tourist Bureau, the Denver Civic and Commercial Association, and several prominent Denver businesses; all conspired, he said, to suppress public discussion and press coverage of the issues. Mills also continued to pound on the secrecy of the franchise contract despite availability of that contract for public scrutiny. He refuted the Park Service's concession policy in all national parks, citing especially Yellowstone, where his old adversary Horace Albright had been installed as superintendent in July 1919.

Mills's attack came from deep within his psyche. He saw the monopoly policy as undemocratic in the most fundamental sense. It summoned to mind all the evils of monopoly he had inherited and internalized and which were so widely denounced during the Progressive Era. Nor did the public utility analogy provide any guarantees against corruption. Much of the turmoil in Denver politics that Mills witnessed around the turn of the century revolved around corrupt alliances between office holders and franchised utility companies. Mills attacked this new monster at his doorstep with all the zeal of a knight taking on the dragon of Standard Oil. In anguished insistence on the country's founding principles, he harkened back to the Declaration of Independence, saying, "This monopoly utterly [sic] violates the fundamental principles for human government laid down in the Declaration of Independence. It allows a few people to govern the majority without the consent of the majority." He attacked Mather as an unelected official, immune to correction or influence by the people, who was using taxpayer money to run a renegade agency. He was a usurping "dictator" who declared his own rules superior to the laws of the land. And as evil as the dictator's untouchable powers was the bureaucracy that served him. "Bureaucracy is a failure and a curse," Mills wrote. "It feeds a horde of politicians. It has the means to conceal its tyrannies . . . and its large powers for rewards and punishments give it a silencing dictatorship over the local people."[11]

The monopoly controversy was the worst kind of case for Mills to have been involved in, for everything hinged on interpretation. The rights of inholders seemed indisputably clear in the RMNP act: "No lands located within the park boundaries now held in private, municipal or State ownership shall be affected by or subject to the provisions of this act." Yet the judge said Mills's interpretation was wrong. And the judge who threw out both his and Robbins's suits was the same judge whom Mills had praised for rendering a landmark decision that established natural beauty as a legally defensible value. Mills seemed staggered by the realization that he lived in a country where the courts, depending on time and place, could decide virtually anything. It was a country where in his own lifetime, a Supreme Court justice had said, "It is the unvarying law that the wealth of the community will be in the hands of a few." Mills might have remembered back to his early exposure to Edward Bellamy's classic in which — in its most famous and telling metaphor — the masses of humanity are harnessed to a coach that carries the wealthy, pulling it along a sandy road in unrequited toil. If the injustices of monopolies had heretofore been an abstraction in Mills's world, they now hit home with full force. For him, as for Bellamy, monopoly was the ultimate tyranny against the people, debasing them more than anything else in history.[12]

Roads were furthermore central icons in Mills's imagination as "thoroughfares of freedom" and thus as a symbol of democracy. He had said in his 1903 defense of socialism that the people must own and administer roads for their own protection. He had said as a park advocate that roads are the key to getting people into the life-restoring outdoors. And he had said as a booster of road improvement that good roads are "one of the most reforming influences of the day." Now, opposing the monopoly, he invoked the spectre of sweeping totalitarianism. "If public roads are not free, then private property is not safe, and life and liberty are menaced," he warned. Mills worried, and Governor Oliver Shoup soon began to worry with him, that if the government could control county and state roads in RMNP, it could just as easily control roads over all the national forests within the state and hence regulate the majority of the state's east-west traffic. Conceivably the Forest Service — capable in Mills's view of any treachery — could even ban the public from all its public lands. Perhaps the same could happen to any other roads — "even the streets of Manhattan" — where the government could arrogate jurisdictional powers.[13]

Road control thus loomed for Mills as a step toward enslavement of the population — a step taken by the heavy-heeled boots of "Prussianized" public officials. Freelan Stanley, who backed Mills throughout the controversy, also stressed the breach of fundamental democratic principles, saying, "There is no problem confronting the American people today so serious as the transportation problem." Stanley said that during his nineteen years in Estes Park he had paid $40,000 in taxes and donated another $15,000 for roads in and to the present park but was now denied the full use of those roads. He said the 1917 park annexation had brought private lands into the park and now exercised control over their roadways. The inholders had not at the time sensed any threats to their rights because they had put their trust in the protective clauses of the park's enabling legislation.[14] Now, added Mills in one of his articles, the park threatened to encroach even farther into the Estes Park region "to [further] wreck the private property holdings."

In representing the transportation controversy from Mills's standpoint, *Enos Mills of the Rockies* points to the obedience of the local population and the fear of resistance that characterized the postwar years. Of all the chapters in the Hawthorne-Esther Mills biography, "The Last Stand" is the one most clearly not meant for young readers and the one most concerned with defending Mills's reputation. The chapter is noteworthy because it states a coherent and appealing case on Mills's behalf and because it describes a public campaign that Esther Burnell Mills experienced at her husband's side as a newlywed and young mother. It was a campaign, furthermore, that she continued after Mills's death in 1922. Her narrative has the immediacy of her own observations, shares both the biases and sense of outrage of her husband, and reveals her feelings of loss as Mills became consumed by a cause greater than the cause of home and family, which could have finally given him surcease from a decade of public crusading. "It is tragic to watch the heroic struggle of this one man for his ideal, but it is also inspiring," she wrote. That sentiment remained undiminished in her 1959 foreword to a reissue of *Early Estes Park,* in which she portrayed his "gallant fight" and "unselfish devotion" to park ideals.[15]

It cannot be guessed how much support Mills might have gained for his cause in different times and with a different power structure at the top. But though he reacted to and was surely in part a victim of the age's hysteria, he was in some measure part of that hysteria himself. His rhetoric was incendiary and often exaggerated. He stressed principles at the expense of specifics and testily refused to supply specifics when pressed. And by equating Mather with the German kaiser, he not only invoked the image of a hated and feared dictator, but — whether he knew it or not — indulged in the era's epidemic habit of red-baiting. For part of the confusion of that confused postwar period was the mistaken belief that the Bolshevik movement was a spinoff of German aggression. Early in the game — in fall 1920 — McFarland, whose patience with Mills had nearly reached the breaking point before, confronted him head on: "I think your course tends toward the belief that you are somewhat unbalanced. . . . All this slop about Prussian invaders, transportation monopolies, and other things you do not like does nothing for you and only discredits the parks you really love. Can't you cut it out Mr. Mills?" Mills answered angrily that he had long since learned that McFarland was no longer a fighter [Where *was* the McFarland who had opposed concessions?] and probably didn't even want to know the true facts of the monopoly controversy. Another ally — who had tolerated Mills's excesses during the park campaign — was now on the chopping block. In was an ally whom Mills in one generous moment had ranked with Muir and Shakespeare as his "favorite inspirations" and to whom he had dedicated one of his books.[16]

McFarland fired back that Mills was "dead wrong" in his attitudes and that his "violence" was undercutting his own "great work" and adding to the vulnerability of the Park Service and federal conservation generally. "You cannot possibly maintain as one single American that you are always right and everyone you criticize always wrong, nor can you possibly sustain an attitude of continuous objurgation and scolding with any expectation that you will be taken seriously," McFarland warned. Within a year, in fact, the new Interior secretary, Albert Fall, came to Estes Park to notify the people that he would himself abolish RMNP if the concession flap

POLITICIANS AND PROFITEERING IN NATIONAL PARKS

Poor Service and Overcharge Under "Supervision and Control"

Park News Suppressed and and Censored

Private Property Wrecked Through Blackmail and Discriminatory Service

A PRUSSIANIZED PARK SYSTEM

Mills's flyers attacking concession policy revealed his anguish and fear of government conspiracy. *Courtesy, Enos Mills Cabin Collection.*

didn't stop. With him came a high Union Pacific executive who added that, if park status were lost, "further attention to this region [by the railroads] would necessarily cease." Bullied into submission, the Estes Park Chamber of Commerce, which had not passed any resolution on the controversy, went on record in favor of the concession and condemned "the trouble a few persons have sought to stir up."[17]

If Mills was a crusader close to losing control, Fall was a model of corruption who has been described as the worst Interior secretary in United States history. The Park Service itself cringed at the thought of having him for its new boss. From the moment Harding nominated him for the office, "gloom settled over all of us,"[18] Albright recalled later. They were soon embarrassed by Fall's desire to create a national park in New Mexico with his own ranch in the middle — a plan Mather managed through skillful maneuvering to dispose of. When caught cheating on grazing restrictions on national forests surrounding his ranch, Fall said the Forest Service would "rue the day" it interfered with private enterprise. He tried to turn the tables on the Forest Service and incorporate it into the Department of Interior in order to restore full exploitation of forest resources. And as a "superpatriot" — a term widely used — he advocated annexing Mexico, currently wobbling with internal difficulties. Fall resigned in 1923, and in 1924 a Senate investigating committee discovered he had received huge sums from oil millionaires for granting leases on federal oil reserves without competitive bidding. The Teapot Dome scandal was one of the most sordid in United States history, and Fall, indicted for conspiracy and bribery, was the first cabinet officer ever to go to prison.

Fall's example underscores in retrospect the danger of Mather's own self-appointed privilege of granting concessions without competitive bidding. Because he often recruited businessmen he knew personally to develop park concessions, he had to impose on himself the highest integrity to avoid the reality or the suspicion of cronyism. Roe Emery, who accompanied Mather on a reluctant trip to inspect Fall's proposed national park, must have also seen in Fall a sobering reminder of how easily power can be abused. The alliances between Emery, the White Automobile Company that supplied his cars, the railroads with which he collaborated in package tours originating in Chicago, the Lewiston Hotel where tour guests stayed and many of

the Park Service social events took place, created a web of interlocked interests that could have raised suspicions in many besides
Mills.

It was predictable that Mills's own neighbors, who had opposed
him by opposing the park, now opposed him by favoring the
monopoly. Most had no motor services of their own to defend and
said they preferred Emery's reliable service to that of the independent jitney drivers. And it was perhaps now predictable, though it
stemmed from conviction rather than spite, that Mills's estranged
brother Joe should oppose him too. Soon after Mills took on the
transportation issue in August 1919, the Estes Park Hotel Men's
Association appointed Joe, its secretary, to survey the membership
and to summarize opinions and suggestions about the concession.
The enmity between the brothers was doubtless a polarizing force
but may also have worked to suppress debate. In the wake of
Mather's visit in September 1919, Joe distributed twenty-six ques-
tionnaires, followed by personal letters, and received none back.
"We inferred from this, of course," wrote Way confidently, "that
conditions were satisfactory." Was it silent and cowardly acquies-
cence? Enos Mills was sure it was. "As well to ask," he wrote in
1921, "why were so few people in Germany opposing the Kaiser? It
is not safe to do so." But Way thought Mills misjudged the hotel
men, insisting that they were "not the class of men who could be
intimidated."[19]

In spring 1921, Mills and his colleague, hotel owner and writer
Clem Yore, unsuccessfully promoted a "taxpayer's ticket" that made
park policy a primary issue in a mayoral and city council election.
Yore had fared better in the lowland cities where, in January 1920,
he succeeded in getting the commercial clubs and chambers of commerce in all seven cities from Boulder to Greeley to condemn the
monopoly and to set their congressional representatives against it. In
May 1921 Mills addressed the Denver Civic and Commercial Association, making charges, which though refuted by Way and by
former Denver Tourist Bureau chief Fred Chamberlain, prompted a
full investigation by a special committee. Its October 1921 report
charged Mills with a "propaganda [campaign] of vilification and
untrue statement pursued . . . with unrelenting virulence through
writings, interviews, lectures, correspondence with Congressmen,
public bodies and prominent officers besides every other form of
publicity known to disgruntled spitefulness." It cited numerous

instances in which Mills had distorted the facts and charged that he refused to supply proof of any of his claims.[20]

Two years earlier — in November 1919 — said the report, Mills had applied for his own transportation franchise — an allegation that could have exposed him as hopelessly hypocritical if it meant that he had applied for exclusive, that is, monopolistic, rights. That, however, seems scarcely possible, and the report risked no such claim. In November 1919 Mills's case against the monopoly was pending in court, and he was on record publicly that monopolies in parks were illegal. Had he applied for exclusive rights, Way could at once have caused him major public embarrassment. Nothing of the sort happened, nor is the subject mentioned in any of Way's monthly reports. Mills could not, furthermore, have even faintly supposed that the Park Service would cancel Emery's twenty-year contract and transfer it to a militant adversary and court opponent.

Mills's application was instead a defiant and calculated attempt to crack open the monopoly. Applying for a franchise to *compete* with Emery as a legitimate and bonded operator could open the way for others to follow. *Enos Mills of the Rockies* raises and dismisses the charge that Mills "wanted the transportation monopoly himself, and hence was fighting it." "If," the book asserts plausibly, "Mills had been looking for a money-making proposition, he would not have chosen that one . . . [which] was at the antipodes of all to which he had devoted his life." Indeed, Emery himself had not, even as late as 1921, realized a profit on the franchise. And even if Mills had subcontracted for some of the equipment for a full motor-coach operation, he would have been involved in a huge capital venture. In spring 1921 alone, Emery acquired twenty-five new ten-passenger vehicles to meet growing travel volume. The implication that Mills wanted some or all of the road business for himself has nevertheless entered Park Service history, both in Robert Shankland's biography of Mather ("Roe Emery had the transportation rights tied up; Mills wanted to get at them") and in John Ise's history of national park policy ("When Mather gave exclusive transportation rights in Rocky Mountain to someone else he incurred Mills' bitter animosity"). A lengthy examination of the controversy by historian Lloyd Musselman fails, curiously, to comment on this crucial detail.[21]

Mills's expanding business interests are another source of doubt about his integrity in the transportation controversy, though they, too, warrant some qualified defense. On the eve of the park bill's passage in 1914, Mills undertook three new business ventures in apparent anticipation of increased park travel. He opened a restaurant in Estes village, purchased land and established a hotel called the Horizon northeast of Estes Park, and purchased private land within the proposed park boundary for another hotel "in the style of Longs Peak Inn" — clearly banking for the latter on the rights of inholders to use and develop their properties. What Mills sought to develop outside the park was nothing more than the kind of development that national parks were supposed to stimulate in local economies. That point had been stressed by the whole raft of pro-park advocates, Mather and McFarland included. Mills was an ambitious entrepreneur, but an entrepreneur expanding his assets in the normal and sanctioned American way.

Development on inholdings was a touchier matter, and the stage for conflict had been set even before the park was formed. In the December 1914 hearing at which Mills testified before passage of the park bill, the House Public Lands Committee asked him: "If the Government should take this thing over and try either to make a resort of it or to control the hotel privileges, and so on, for the general benefit, would you not have the people on these privately owned patches competing with the Government?" "Not necessarily," answered Mills. Since hardly any of the landowners had thought of developing their properties for their scenic assets, he explained, "there would not be in any sense competition along that line."[22] And so the matter slid by. But Mills almost surely saw the strategic potential of inholdings (which his own Longs Peak Inn became in the 1917 park expansions) to capture an important fraction of the park's tourist trade. And soon, especially after those 1917 annexations, the growing number of facilities and services on inholdings hinted of a future resembling the cluttered concessions on park land that Mather wanted to prevent. Unable to do that in RMNP, he was trying — it appeared to Mills — to drive the inholders out by wrecking their businesses. He was cutting off their lifelines by controlling passenger and freight services on their roads. He was allowing Emery's drivers to divert their guests to other hotels, and he began plucking off other mainstay resort services, such as horseback riding and trail guiding, and putting them into exclusive franchises as well. Mills's belligerent response, swollen by overreaction, was in part an anguished cry of pain at what he felt was his extreme vulnerability as an inholder. Secretary Payne's charge that Mills "was acting not

Enos Mills, father and public man, 1921. *Courtesy, Enos Mills Cabin Collection.*

with the high motives of patriotism but in the selfish interest of his own commercial enterprise" failed to register the simple and painful fact that Mills may have feared for the future of his renowned Longs Peak Inn.[23] It is loss of business, or even fear of lost business, that invariably brings a howl of protest from any American businessman; Mills's defense of his own interests was no different. Nor was it anything less than predictable for him to protest that jeopardy to free enterprise was jeopardy to American and personal liberty. But his failure to stick to and prove specific charges in fair debate colored his case with the suspicion of ulterior motive. Even the Commercial Association report said that his opposition to the monopoly would be a respected opinion "if in maintaining it, he would confine himself to the truth and to reasonable deductions from proven facts." Repeatedly provoking disbelief in his own integrity was the fatal flaw in Mills's public style, allowing his genuine concern for broader issues to be mistaken for self-interest.

Attacked by high officials like Payne and by the Sierra Club, of which he was a member, Mills was increasingly discredited but the more convinced of conspiratorial machinery throughout the whole system. Isolating him as a lone and cankered voice of dissent, the Park Service, Mills insisted, tried to control the press against him. He once said that even the Secret Service was involved, and he charged that one of the "Prussian spies" aligned against him was "a prominent club woman" — perhaps his once close friend and park advocate Mary King Sherman.

As always, Mills had an uncanny talent for retaining substantial and vocal support. In 1921, while the controversy was at its height, Arthur Chapman published his booklet *Enos A. Mills, Author, Speaker, Nature Guide,* which documented Mills's career and widely varying achievements with newspaper quotations from the last two decades. If Mills drew some of his strength from self-image — which he clearly did — Chapman's book gave him a flattering mirror in which to gaze and regather his forces. It reaffirmed for him that the park he now battled was the noble creation of his own prophetic and crusading spirit, and that it was a park now in need of rescue from its corrupt masters. Chapman's section on the monopoly battle cited supportive editorials, such as one from the Houston *Chronicle* that said it "wishes to endorse, in every particular, the stand taken by Enos Mills. Probably no man knows more about our national parks than he. Probably no man is more interested in them from a purely disinterested motive." Another, from the St. Louis *Post Dispatch,* proclaimed that Mills was a courageous crusader against social injustice generally: "Most of us submit tamely to injustice, feeling ourselves powerless to do anything about it," it said. "Our old friend Enos Mills is not like the rest of us. There is nothing meek about him. . . . He is a wonder. . . . None of us who are of the meek is a wonder. None of us will ever drive greed out of a national park or anywhere else. None of us will ever arouse public opinion to correct anything. It takes a man like Enos to do that." An impressive number of newspapers took up Mills's cause and were in turn frequently castigated by Mills's opponents for naively reproducing his "propaganda" and "utter falsehoods" without checking the facts.[24]

Mills had learned in the park battle that tenacity is all, and, with positive assurances from his supporters, he could once again see himself as a prophet of uncompromising integrity. He had embraced as a virtual motto for his life Whittier's challenge to "attach yourself to a noble cause and to stay with it till you win." He was always fortified by his historical sense that great crusaders must usually fight alone. He had for his most recent example his own John Muir, who in the battle over Hetch Hetchy in his last years had lost many of his supporters and was defamed in much the same way as Mills was now. With his battle lost Muir had written, "The present flourishing triumphant growth of the wealthy wicked . . . will not thrive forever. . . . We may lose this particular fight, but truth and right must prevail at last."[25] Where Muir had lost, Mills still hoped to win. Pretty soon now, predicted the St. Louis *Post Dispatch,* thanks to one man hurling himself headlong at the foe.

Encouragement materialized in the form of a suit filed by the state of Colorado against the Park Service in August 1922 over the key issue of road jurisdiction within the park. Over a year earlier, Mills wrote, Governor Shoup had "respectfully contended that the State of Colorado possesses under the Constitution of the United States complete jurisdiction over all of the highways within the State, regardless of whether or not such highways extend over any part of the public domain or over any national forest or national park of the United States." Mills, at that time, had cited claims by the governor that "by a conservative estimate at least 10,000 visitors were excluded from Rocky Mountain National Park through the [monopoly's] inadequate service and excessive charges." Mills, according to Esther, offered to help pay the state's costs in the litigation, a claim that is, in fact, plausible. The next month Mills suddenly died, but he had been confident, apparently, that the case would be won. "It was well for [him]," Esther wrote, "that he could not foresee the seven years more of legal and legislative controversy which were to ensue before the citizens of Colorado succumbed under the pressure from Washington, and relinquished their own and the nation's rights to personal liberty in the national parks of the State." And well it probably was, for what followed after Mills's death was a legal nightmare and a series of power moves by the government that would have kept his energies and emotions tied up for the rest of the decade.[26]

Three weeks after Mills's death, Charles Robbins, despite assistance from the Colorado attorney general's office, lost an appeal of his case in U.S. Circuit Court of Appeals. In 1923 a federal court dismissed the state's suit against the government, but in 1925 the Supreme Court ruled that the suit had been wrongfully dismissed. The case was now eligible to be tried on its own merits, but the Park Service was confident it could win. In 1926 Colorado suddenly dropped its suit under threats from the government that the park would lose its operating budget and cease to exist. The government flexed its muscles by withdrawing $140,000 in scheduled road funds and $500,000 in ad hoc road funds. With unprecedented cooperation, the Forest and Park Services jointly promoted a southern expansion of the park to Arapahoe Glacier west of Boulder. Mills, who had so ardently wanted a bigger park, would have probably led the opposition against it, seeing the most sinister implications in the cooperation between the two agencies, both "evil," and their partner Roe Emery. The broader public — beyond Estes Park — was now more favorably disposed to the Forest Service than to the Park Service and believed that Emery's transportation company was pushing for the park expansion to further its own interests. The plan, then and several times subsequently, failed.

In 1924 the solicitor of the Department of Interior confirmed the granting of preferential rights to park concessioners, and in 1928, the year Mather died, Congress gave his regulated monopoly policy the status of law. It specifically allowed concessions to be granted without advertising or competitive bidding. Mills's charge of autocracy was at last rendered moot by due process of law. In 1926 the park's eastern boundary was adjusted to eliminate much private land, including Longs Peak Inn, and Mills's grievances as an inholder were at last resolved too.

Final resolution of the controversy now depended on Colorado's ceding jurisdiction over roads in RMNP to the government. James Grafton Rogers, whom Mills had accused of Forest Service connivance in the park campaign, drafted legislation in 1927 for the state to take that action. Emotional debate ensued all up and down the Front Range, with water, mining, and states'-rights interests most opposed. "What would Enos Mills say, were he here to raise his voice?" wrote one newspaper.[27] Washington continued threatening to abolish the park, and again withheld money for park highways. By 1928 Colorado businesses were swinging in favor of ceding jurisdiction. Joe Mills, as president of the Estes Park Chamber of Commerce, campaigned for it extensively, stressing the practical reality that the government could develop roads the state could not. The vacation industry, and hence the state's prosperity, had more to gain than to lose.

Another year passed, and with the government still threatening to end all appropriations for the park, the Boulder *Daily Camera* said the people must adjust themselves to the fact that "we are living in a different age than that in which Enos Mills conceived the idea of a national park."[28] Joe and Esther Mills gave opposing testimony before the Federal Relations Committee of the Colorado House of Representatives. A month later — in February 1929 — the state legislature passed the bill ceding jurisdiction. Esther found the action "inconceivable." With that cession went the state's rights of "police power," she said, and that should have required a state constitutional amendment. As soon as Colorado ceded, Albright unfurled a $1.75-million, ten-year road plan including construction of the now-famous Trail Ridge Road.

Monopolies were now legal, roads were built, tourism flourished, and so did private inholders, who by 1930 were operating forty-five hotels, lodges, and campgrounds on their "patches" within the park. Far from being "wrecked" by park policy, the proliferating businesses on inholdings threatened the park's natural environment and at last their own profitability. The whole region in fact — in and outside the park — was overbuilt and heading for serious economic decline even before the calamity of the Great Depression. Albright, now the Park Service director, announced in 1930 that he wanted to phase out all concessions in the park except

Emery's transportation concession — still on its contract — and to rely on businesses outside the park to provide visitor services. The park began its long and laborious process of buying up inholdings and returning the land to its natural state. For sentimental reasons, the people of the region reluctantly let go of the old places where they had spent some of their best hours, and the process was punctuated by contradictory delays in which some of the purchased facilities continued as concessions under government contract. Time, economics, the pervasive influence of the automobile, and the rise of environmental concerns all changed the conditions that had pitted Mills against the bureaucracy in charge of his beloved park. But concession policy has continued to plague the Park Service. It has been described as the most controversial aspect of national park management and the "nemesis of every park superintendent." "Concessionaires holding long-term monopolies at national parks are reaping tens of millions of dollars in excess profits": That opening pronouncement of a May 1990 news story is telling evidence that we have inherited much of what bothered Mills seventy years ago.[29] His early challenge to park concessions — fought fiercely and not always wisely — remains historically important as a battle of principle; it links him to the concerns of conservationists today who share his fear of increasing corporate control, not just of park policy but of the Park Service itself.

CHAPTER 19

The Final Years and Early Death

Red-haired Esther and dark-haired Elizabeth arrived at Longs Peak Inn wearing long skirts and high black shoes, their city attire contrasting with the sporty dress becoming common at western resorts and marking them as "a bit quaint" and "old fashioned." "They were gentle, unassuming girls," observed Katherine Garetson, an adventurous woman in her late thirties who had begun homesteading nearby two years earlier. "They were enjoying the first experience they had ever had of outdoor life and the West . . . [and] although they came for a short vacation they fell in love with our country as I myself had done, and Esther, at least, was destined to 'take root.' "

Esther was twenty-seven that summer of 1916 and Elizabeth — Bessie to many — was twenty-nine. They had heard about Longs Peak Inn from a lecture Mills gave in Cleveland the previous fall, a lecture probably charged with more than a usual amount of his enthusiasm, for he had just dedicated Rocky Mountain National Park and was full of victory and high hopes for the park movement. He invited his listeners to come to Rocky Mountain, to the Inn, and to his nature study center at the inn. The Burnell sisters came. And they were being, said Katherine Garetson with light irony, "introduced to Nature." The sisters, she declared, were "the most eager pupils Enos Mills ever had."[1]

Esther soon packed away her city clothes and was romping over the hills in knickerbockers, her eroded health returning as the tensions of eastern life ebbed away. Nature was working its curative magic on her, just as Mills had told his countless lecture audiences and readers it would. After studying at Lake Erie College in Cleveland and then taking up interior decorating at the prestigious Pratt

Institute in Brooklyn, she had begun a career as a consulting decorator for the Sherwin-Williams Company. But she had loved her job so much, Mills later wrote, that she had worked herself into a nervous breakdown. If that was so, she was well prepared to understand the driving passion and relentless work pace of her future husband, who though always rejecting the work ethic, could exhaust himself through overwork.[2]

When the vacation was over, Bessie returned to her job teaching math in California, but Esther was not ready to leave. She had abandoned her old life and was ready to follow new dreams and opportunities in the West. The most compelling of those dreams was to homestead, and now, if ever, was the time to do it. She stayed on a while at the inn doing part-time secretarial work for Mills, beginning a professional association with the famous man she would later marry. Typing copy for his drafts of *Your National Parks* exposed her to potent concentrations of his ideas about the benefits of outdoor life. And when she was not typing, she was living those ideas, shouldering her knapsack and roaming by day and night, sun and moon, through the bounteous world around Longs Peak Inn.

Mills, perhaps already attracted and not wanting to lose her, proposed a continuation of the secretarial arrangement through the winter. But Esther was not casual about her dream of homesteading, and for now it came first. It did not mean, though, that she would drop out of sight. Katherine Garetson had filed on her 160 acres only two miles from Longs Peak Inn only two years earlier. Perhaps, in fact, Esther could join Katherine, someone suggested. But Katherine, though taking a liking to Esther and soon to be her fast friend, wanted her solitude, for she was working out things in her life, too. Esther invited an artist friend from the East to join her, but failing to entice her, discovered a common attitude: Now that homesteading no longer served a pioneering function, it was regressive, an intentional denial of what the pioneers had sacrificed so much to make possible. Who would homestead now? So Esther decided to meet the challenge alone.

Fortified by the persuasive body of Millsian doctrine which she eagerly absorbed, Esther stood her ground with skeptics, even among the guests at Longs Peak Inn. The matrons were alarmed by her long solitary rambles, the more so by her explanations that she was looking for land to settle. No, it was not silly idleness, she could say forcefully, nor an intentional throwing away of one's life. As for the severing of a career path, that had taken care of itself. No, the outdoors was not dangerous, she said with both learned conviction and growing practical experience. Nature "was the safest place in the world . . . free from limitations of fear or worry," she said, mimicking Mills, but knowing already that the ideas were valid. Still, she confessed, it took more courage to counter the objections of friends and relatives than it did to homestead itself.[3]

Mills, she later recalled, neither encouraged nor discouraged her plan. Perhaps she suspected quite early that his neutrality was an ambivalence centered on her: He must have both admired her plans and wanted her to stay at Longs Peak Inn. Two winters earlier he had helped give Katherine Garetson the courage of her convictions by letting on that it was perfectly normal for a young woman to homestead. Katherine had in fact had — even with a companion — a tough first winter, and said she might not have gone through with it if she'd known what was in store. Now she could relive all she had experienced by sharing and watching Esther's experience. The two of them took "glorious hikes" to look at unentered tracts of land. And they went over plans for Esther's cabin ("forty different ways of building") and discussed "the minutest details of food and utensils and clothing." A "deep impression was made upon me by watching this other girl from a city go through what I had known," Katherine wrote. "Indeed, there was so much . . . that my heart was wrung for my old self."[4]

Esther chose land four miles west of Estes Park near the rim of Horseshoe Park and near MacGregor Pass, the low point between Castle and MacGregor mountains. She could look up the Fall River Valley to the snowy headwalls of Mounts Chapin and Ypsilon, and see portions of the Fall River road, still in construction by convicts toward Grand Lake over the top of the Continental Divide. Nearby were Horseshoe Inn and Fall River Lodge, both accessible by road but slumbering in winter. Much of Esther's land was steep mountainside, some of it leading to a sheer granite cliff and some forested with a mix of pine, spruce, and aspens. But a gentle meadow fronted her cabin site and would soon yield to cultivation under the requirements of the homestead law. At an altitude of 8,000 feet, she would enjoy milder winters than in the lofty Tahosa Valley a thousand feet higher and fourteen miles away.

Having chosen her site, Esther made out for Denver one fall day to file on her homestead papers at the land office, take her oath, pay sixteen dollars, and receive her instructions for eventually "proving up on her claim." Fate had arranged for Enos Mills to be on the same Denver-bound train, just setting off on an eastern speaking tour and apparently not informed of Esther's progress over the last few weeks. So she was staying, he learned, and not retreating from the early onset of winter. No indeed, for this, as Mills would later write, was a woman who knew her mind. And soon she was back at her claim, supervising hired help in building her cabin, pitching in vigorously, and designing and building much of the furniture. She helped to shingle the roof and could, rumor soon had it, shingle as fast as a man. Esther Burnell was capable and confident, shirking no task in her way. She belonged to that new breed of homesteader that Mills, the wandering snow observer a dozen years earlier, had admired and written about: intelligent, civilized, and idealistic; following not the lure of riches but of happiness; accumulating little, and reducing life to its meaningful basics. Meaningful basics for Esther included painting and writing, "knowing how to walk and enjoy it," setting out a feeding table for the birds, watching the deer and mountain sheep pass on a nearby game trail, and planting potatoes on the meadow outside her front door the following spring. The homestead would be called "Keewaydin" — the place visited by the northwest winds, the winds of home.

As Esther began her winter of solitude, Mills was at the peak of his career as a spokesman for the park movement. But he was yet a bachelor and probably not even acquainted with his five-year-old niece Eleanor, born to Joe and Ethyl in 1911. How often did his thoughts turn to the young homesteader at Keewaydin during that winter, as he told his eastern audiences of the glories of the West and its power to create new life? And how much did thoughts of her enliven his statements at the parks conference in January 1917 that women can meet the challenges of the outdoors as well as men? While she was still typing for him that first summer, he had seen her go off hiking and camping by herself, and had listened eagerly to her reports of activities at the nearby beaver colony. And now, in winter, she regularly walked four miles into Estes Park for mail and supplies and often returned home after dark. That was better, she said, than staying in town to while away a winter evening playing cards. And it was better yet — when she was warned about bears in the vicinity — to walk through the night in hopes of seeing one of those bears. Mills's later portrait of Esther imagined her camping and sitting by her fire, "thinking such thoughts as a lone outdoor woman thinks." He saw in her a "creative and courageous young woman with refreshing enthusiasms . . . colored with high ideals," yet with seemly reserve — more reserve, in fact, than he had expected in an art school graduate.[5] Mills must have hoped her thoughts sometimes turned to him that winter of 1916–17, and to him as a person, not just as a public figure. Would she, if and when the time came, take him seriously as a suitor approaching the age of fifty while she was not yet thirty?

On Christmas day, 1916, when Mills must have been in or on his way to Washington, D.C., for the parks conference, Esther and Katherine Garetson met in the snowy woods halfway along the sixteen-mile distance separating their homesteads. They had agreed earlier to meet that day but had had no opportunity to reconfirm their plan. Each, heading toward the rendezvous point, thought the other had surely forgotten the plan or accepted other holiday invitations. And then all at once they met. "I didn't think you would come," they exclaimed in unison. The two women "acted like mad-caps" in those snowy woods, and they declared with pagan gusto — never mind that Esther was a minister's daughter — that their celebration was a "tribute to the God of Winter." And Katherine who less than half a year ago had pronounced Esther "not well," now saw her in radiant health. Her lush red curls blended with the red of the fire against the white backdrop of snow, and her lively eyes were "the exact tint of her hair." "She looked wonderfully pretty," said Katherine, "animation transforming her into a beauty."[6]

Esther continued to prosper in body and soul, wrote a poem about her happiness, and by spring had a charming cabin ("five rooms, all pretty") to show her visitors. She was putting in her potatoes when Mills rode up on his pony. Esther showed him around her place. She showed him a letter from her artist friend back east who had not come — a letter candidly and urbanely neurotic, that clearly contrasted the world Esther had left with the one she had now. She led him up Castle Mountain, and there, sporting about like a boy, he forgot all the concerns of his public life. Perhaps on that day, a courtship began in earnest. Esther showed him some poems and stories, and he encouraged her to continue writing. They agreed that he would read her stories and she would continue typing for him. The hazard of mixing courtship — or even just friendship — with criticism seems not to have spoiled the process. Mills was probably gentle in his suggestions and Esther eager to accept the judgment of a writer of secure reputation. And for her it was exciting that thick packets passed between them — packets, she said, that looked like a "voluminous correspondence."

Esther's life was grist for Mills's own literary mill. As the unnamed homesteader in "The Development of a Woman Nature Guide," Esther embodied exactly what Mills wanted to portray about people making their way creatively through life. She had "secured leisure" — a step Mills found crucial to personal growth — and had used that leisure "to develop steadily since the day she arrived." She handled her life "artistically" in the way she "accumulated experience and information." Though her nervous breakdown was the result of being "in love with her job," any steady job, Mills took the occasion to say, cut off the possibility of personal growth. Mills insisted, like a later French existentialist, on "constant self redefinition and the chance to be the architect of one's own fate." Mills also portrayed Esther's "wide sympathies" and "universal thoughts" that gave her potential for transcending herself and serving others. She had already read some of Mills's writings about nature guiding and knew how vital a social function he believed this creative new profession filled. He assured her that she was a natural to take it up, and would find all of her gifts put to full use. Though "The Development of a Woman Nature Guide" is an account of Esther's homesteading, it shows what Mills made explicit many times: Explorers, homesteaders, and aboriginal natives all acquire the detailed knowledge and love of land that makes them the best guides for others.

Cheerful and supportive toward all Esther did at Keewaydin, Mills nevertheless continued to betray his ambivalence at her being so far from Longs Peak Inn. At last he displayed his affection openly — and publicly — at a meeting of the Estes Park women's club, which he addressed in May 1917 and to which he contrived to have Esther invited. His subject was the goldfinch romance, the study of avian courtship and family rearing that in its later written version fairly gushed with sentiment. Mills's eyes fell often on Esther as he told it, and she may have blushed. The other women saw and approved of the connection, smiled as Mills dashed to sit beside Esther afterward, and then left the two goldfinches alone. The written story clearly reads like a courtship statement, and its anthropomorphism bears the marks of its persuasive intent. If Mills took liberties with scientific objectivity, the context was perhaps excuse enough: It helped him win a young and handsome wife. Esther responded to his sensitivity of character and to the ideals of love and marital devotion he portrayed.[7]

Soon after that, Esther must have made her spectacular solo snowshoe trip from Estes Park over the Continental Divide to Grand Lake and back by another route — an accomplishment that brought her acclaim on both sides of the divide. Spring goes well into June at those altitudes, and in the last days of long and brilliant sunshine, flowers were springing up beside the retreating drifts. Within nine months after coming west, Esther had acquired not only health and strength but also the considerable mountaineering skills to accomplish what few men had. Nothing could have been more appealing to Mills, and it can be supposed that the attraction between them was one of likenesses rather than opposites.

Sometime after that came another event that stuck in Esther's mind over the years to 1935, when she coauthored *Enos Mills of the Rockies*. It was an afternoon at Keewaydin spent talking, a quiet afternoon of intellectual exploration that belongs to every true courtship. They talked, she said, about books and writing. Mills had brought a copy of *Your National Parks,* just out, and the young woman could see and hold the book she helped prepare and whose ideas had proved to be so valid for her own life. Esther was becoming part of Mills's world.

Bessie came for the summer and the two sisters moved to Longs Peak Inn. Both trained to be nature guides in the national park, and Bessie took over much of the nature program at Longs Peak Inn, especially the Trail School, Mills's committed experiment in alternative education. The Trail School had developed gradually over the years, was entirely informal, and was geared mostly to children. It was so informal, Mills said, that it was "little more than a name, plus results." The name was entirely appropriate, for the trail was one of Mills's principal metaphors for living, learning, and growing, whose rich possibilities he had expanded to a whole chapter in *Your National Parks*. The school was in session, he said, "whenever children wandered over the trail, free from academic chaperonage":

> There is no organization, no staff; no opening, no closing. It has no courses of study, no set times for study, no set tasks, no grade cards. The children follow any interest that appeals, and when it appeals.

They are never asked to pursue anything distasteful, in fact, any given subject or for any given period. There are no recitations and no examinations. Competition, as ordinarily known, does not exist.[8]

Mills instinctively knew the way to children's hearts and minds and had set the tone for his Trail School as early as the late 1890s, when he said a group of boys and girls had appeared at his cabin and asked him to take them to a beaver colony. "Stepping softly and without saying a word," Mills said,

> we slipped through the woods and peeped from behind the last trees into a grassy opening by the beaver pond, hoping for a glimpse of a coyote or a deer. Then we examined the stumps of aspens recently cut by the beavers. We walked across the dam. We made a little raft of logs and went out to the island house in the pond. Then we built tiny beaver houses and also dugouts in the bank. We played we were beavers.[9]

The Trail School's facilities were the whole outdoors and the nature room at the inn, with its carefully selected specimens and books. Outdoor specimens were not to be collected aimlessly and then deposited and forgotten. The books had to be by real naturalists. There were no textbooks and emphatically none of the children's books that warned of bears eating bad children or promised fairy rewards for good children. Mills, and soon the capable Bessie as well, took the children out by day and night, in fair weather and foul, up into the clouds, along streams to their sources, and along the tracks of animals. The children counted the flowers in a circle the size of their own height, and learned to examine each object with all their senses — to look at, touch, smell, and taste the bark of a tree, for example. They learned what they could about the outdoors blindfolded. They drew maps. They pretended to be animals, explorers, or aboriginal people faced with finding food in the woods. They learned in all they did to focus on what was immediately at hand, to learn each object's story, evolution, and relation to its surroundings.

Interest was the "master teacher." And love, as John Burroughs had said, was "what made the knowledge stick." The children entered a world of real and palpable things that ignited their imaginations far more than the movies many had been addicted to or the chimerical fantasies of legends or fairy tales. They were working and learning without realizing it, Mills said. And when they needed facts from books, they eagerly sought them. The task, and the rare gift, of the teacher was to guide the children to needed information "in an appealing way" in order to maintain their immense and innate appetite for learning. Mills wanted to set the children's imaginations ablaze to make the world an exhilarating and inexhaustible wonderland in which they sought, discovered, and digested the facts their own curiosities demanded. In the evening when the children discussed their experience, the teacher's task was to comment in a way that increased their interest and inspired them to go back and look for things they might have missed. "Surely, the opportunity of one's life is to listen helpfully when a child is talking and to answer happily his eager questions," Mills said.[10]

Though free to follow their own interests without academic structures, the children developed systematic mental habits and observational capabilities superior, said Mills, to those of adults. They learned to use their senses, to accumulate facts, to think, and to reason. Following their own drive to learn, they frequently imposed upon themselves a strenuous voluntary self-discipline. Their minds "grew like a wild garden"; and their imaginations developed through contact not with "life-wasting mental mirages" but with real things. With learning came a maturing of character as well. The children's interests naturally broadened, they acquired "universal feelings," and they naturally developed "democratic actions and habits."[11]

Mills's Trail School was a significant educational experiment, and his essays "Children of My Trail School" and "Longs Peak Trail School and Nature Guiding" were serious statements that brought together the ideas Mills had accumulated on the subject all his adult life.[12] The importance of nurturing healthy sentiments about nature in children came across clearly in his 1905 address to the Denver Chamber of Commerce and both motivated and informed his subsequent forestry addresses to women's groups and schools. At root, Mills was as ardent an educator as he was a reformer. In "Children of My Trail School" he called attention to the ideas of Charles W. Eliot, the grand old man of American education, who pronounced against the serious failure of contemporary schooling to create healthy and clear-thinking minds, to train the senses to record accurate observations, and to teach children to determine facts and weigh evidence. Of the postwar mentality, Eliot wrote and Mills quoted:

There has been an extraordinary exhibition of the incapacity of the American people, as a whole, to judge evidence, to determine facts, and to discriminate between facts and fancies. This incapacity appears in the public press; in the prophecies of prominent administrative officials, both state and national; . . . and in the almost universal acceptance of people . . . day by day, of statements which have no foundation and of arguments the premises of which are not facts or events, but only hopes and guesses.[13]

In his most pessimistic moods, Mills believed the inadequacies of the educational system were compounded by outright conspiratorial forces that sought to keep the public in the dark about the facts of the outdoors. In revealing passages from his 1919 essay "Censored Natural History News," he asserted that governments and priesthoods in all ages propagate lies and superstitions to maintain social control. In the domain of "natural history news," the censorship "begun a few generations ago, has developed to near exclusiveness of facts. Those censoring appear wholly unacquainted with their subject, and therefore . . . give to the public such selected nature lore as it can be trusted to know and still remain loyal to public institutions."[14]

Mills's fear that a citizenry unregenerated by outdoor exercise and unenlightened by the influence of outdoor ideas would become increasingly obedient to despots shows the extent of his belief in the social importance of nature. He never said exactly who was generating this "insidious enemy propaganda" that tried to cow the public into avoiding outdoor experience and the democratic ideals it bred; but his fear of social enslavement was never far below the surface, and he warned that nations that pursue such a course are bound to perish. Feeling misunderstood and persecuted himself, Mills believed that an uninformed public maligns and hunts down its own best citizens. "Bears," he said, "like all strong and desirable citizens, are constantly assailed with attempts at character assassination."[15] With such pronouncements, Mills revealed that nature remained for him the yardstick for human and social behavior: As we understand and deal with nature, so we understand and deal with ourselves. "Censored Natural History News" is Mills's strongest statement about the need for truth and accuracy in all matters pertaining to the outdoors, and sets the standard against which his own writings must be measured.

In that same frame of reference can be seen the vital importance Mills ascribed to nature guiding. A "noble profession" that he hoped would become common and valued throughout the country, nature guiding was the channel through which Americans would reestablish contact with the outdoors, with themselves, and with the ideals of democracy and internationalism. Nature guiding was to the whole nation what the Trail School was to the children gathered at Longs Peak Inn, and the national parks, he believed, could be for both children and adults the greatest of all outdoor classrooms.

Mills found a stirring example of the redemptive influence of nature in a road crew from the state penitentiary that he visited sometime in the war years, when so much else, including his courtship, kept him busy. His observations of the convict camp near the Royal Gorge in southern Colorado reflect an ultraprogressive political cast and an assertive departure from mainstream social values. He expressed high admiration for the convicts, who lived in an orderly democracy with their own elected officials and codes of honor. And he saw them not as criminals but as victims of past errors, about which no one needed to inquire. Working with little supervision and granted a high degree of self-determination by an enlightened warden, they had gained self-respect and — in today's argot — "empowerment." They had shed much of their bitterness and acquired both health and knowledge, a result, Mills said, clearly in contrast to that of punitive incarceration, from which a person "usually comes . . . in broken health [and] hatred in his heart — a far more undesirable citizen than when he entered prison."[16]

Mills was quick and eager to see the connection between the convicts' positive outlook and their wholesome outdoor life. He found the men "efficient and manly" and "less quarrelsome, considerably cleaner and far less vulgar of speech than the men in any camp that I had ever worked in." An earlier stay of a full week, in which he had worked, dressed, and been taken for one of the convicts, had perhaps given him the firsthand experience he needed for his claims about the good influence of nature on convicts in *Your National Parks*. When some petty thieving occurred in the camp, the elected chief of police called the men together and made a short speech that ended with his expression of confidence that there would be no more of it: "You may continue to leave your chests open and your things lying about as before, for we are not and have not been a set of thieves." Rehabilitated toward "safe and sane citizens," the inmates inspired Mills to assert that the combination of outdoor life and self-determination could "avoid the building of so many prisons, asylums and hospitals and actually make vacant much of the room in those already existing."[17]

Social themes continued to occupy some of the conversation at Keewaydin, where Elizabeth Burnell, on sabbatical leave for the winter of 1917–18, had joined Esther and where Mills must have visited as often as he could. With teaching and nature guiding a theme of interest to all three, there was continued talk of the misguided direction of American schooling and its pernicious facility for "extinguishing the wonderlight of imagination." And there was the Great War, which despite Woodrow Wilson's resisting efforts, the United States had now entered. Mills was described by one of his friends as an "absolute abhorrer of war," and pacifism, as we saw earlier, was a conviction he attached to his national parks ideology.

The summer of 1918 brought the two sisters again to Longs Peak Inn. Bessie continued to lead the Trail School, to guide Longs Peak ascents and camping trips, and to give some of the inn's fireside talks. Both sisters received certification to work as nature guides in RMNP, some of the first women in the country to earn that distinction. Of the two, Bessie appears to have been the more prominently active, while Esther, who later portrayed herself as having been drawn closer to Mills through "walk[ing] his trails, assist[ing] in his far-flung projects, his writing, his speaking tours, [and] his battles to preserve nature," was now in a serious relationship that would soon lead to marriage.[18]

On August 12 the marriage took place in a simple ceremony at Mills's homestead cabin across the road from the inn, with only Bessie and a few other associates attending. Neither Mills's mother nor Esther's parents were present, and no available correspondence indicates what wishes they might have sent: whether Esther's parents encouraged or discouraged her marriage to a man considerably older than herself, whose nationwide fame was tempered locally by a sizable component of controversy; nor whether Esther's father, the Reverend Arthur Burnell, found Mills's saucy pokes at organized religion cause for alarm. Katherine Garetson said that the wedding sent a ripple of excitement through the valley, but Longs Peak Inn guests hoping to witness it were disappointed. Privacy was Mills's usual choice in personal matters, as Esther noted more than once in *Enos Mills of the Rockies*. But the fact was at least public: The

Longs Peak bachelor, whose romantic fortunes must have long been the subject of speculation, at last had a bride, a bride indeed who had made her own mark on the local community. Among the hundreds of letters and telegrams of congratulations that poured in, the one Esther said she liked the best was "Though the Mills of the Gods grind slowly, they grind exceedingly fine." The setting for the wedding at Mills's homestead cabin was a fitting one for the two Midwest transplants who had both homesteaded and found their way to health and self-definition in this glorious part of the world. Describing the happiness of his marriage to his friend Philip Ashton Rollins, Mills said later, "All the great happinesses of my life have seemed to center around that little cabin that I built in boyhood."[19]

Not far from the homestead was Mills's roomier log house, now enlarged to accommodate his bride and enlarged soon again for the baby born the following spring. Esther described their first fall and winter together as a quiet and happy time, the first winter in many that Mills did not travel. Mills, the loving foster father of orphaned bluebirds over thirty years earlier and the symbolic father of a national park, would soon become a real father with a real child on whom he could lavish his parental emotions. If he followed the model of the goldfinches, he was a solicitous and caring husband, preparing the conditions for Esther to spend her pregnancy in the warmth and contentment of her nest. And with the hectic winter schedule in abeyance, Mills was given the opportunity to be available and happy throughout the winter, and productive in his writing: By spring, two new books were ready. The flu epidemic that reached the United States in 1918, killing 500,000 at home and 20 million worldwide, did not touch the secluded couple in the high Colorado valley. And the war seemed for the most part far away and far below. Even Edna Ferber, always in the thick of things, found escape from the cares of the war at Longs Peak Inn, where she was now a regular summer guest. Of course the deception that the war did not exist was selfish, she confessed, but for a brief moment in time it was an allowable deception. And at Longs Peak she found writing, "ordinarily such a slow and painful process," a "merry occupation," her "words com[ing] with ease" and her "characters leap[ing] into life."[20]

The Armistice came in November 1918 and sparked delirious celebrations throughout the land, only to be followed by the confused postwar era, which would be the setting for Mills's feud with

Esther, Enda, and Enos Mills, 1920. *Courtesy, Enos Mills Cabin Collection.*

Happy times with daughter Enda, 1920. *Courtesy, Enos Mills Cabin Collection.*

the Park Service. Less than a month before Roe Emery's franchise began operation and less than four months before Mills's first confrontation with Superintendent Way, Enda Mills was born. She arrived on April 27, 1919, six days after Muir's birthday and five days after Mills's. Mills, who had never forgotten his favorite Longs Peak client, eight-year-old Harriet Peters, and had given her a chapter in his latest book, now had a girl who could give him all the delights Harriet had. His own childlike simplicity in the natural world was something he could soon share with a growing and blossoming child. Esther described Mills as a happy and devoted father, and photographs captured happy outdoor scenes of father and child. The smile Esther found so contagious replaced the worried and tense look Mills wore in some photos at the same time. Esther spent much of her time with the child outdoors, too, and wrote a poem that Enda must have treasured later in life. Toddling with her teddy bear as a two year old, Enda was a nature guide showing teddy the secrets of the outdoors. It was a poem full of natural charm about a child Mills was destined to enjoy for only three and a half years — years in which home and family had to compete with the transportation battle and the harsh feelings, loss of friends, frequent traveling, and constant stress that were its remorseless by-products.

Those same three and a half last years of Mills's life were years of confusion and contrast everywhere. Depression, unemployment, wage cuts, strikes, and the crushing of strikes came with the industrial slowdown following the wartime boom. Corporate power, partially checked during the Progressive Era, rebounded with a vengeance. As the red scare swept the country, labor leaders were imprisoned. Yet labor remained a defiant force, expressing deep contradictions in the nation's psyche. Eugene Debs, serving his term in the Atlanta federal prison, won the hearts of his 2,000 fellow inmates and ran for president from his prison cell in 1920. The Ku Klux Klan exerted unprecedented influence over the politics of many cities, including, by 1924, Denver; and counterforces, such as the American Civil Liberties Union, began to form and marshal their constituencies. America — said many — disgraced itself by refusing to join the League of Nations. And fascism began taking root in Germany and Italy by the early twenties.

Besides all that, the guests at Longs Peak Inn could talk of the new fiction of Willa Cather, Theodore Dreiser, Henry James, Sinclair Lewis, Gertrude Stein, and Edna Ferber; of new lights emerging, such as Scott Fitzgerald, Ernest Hemingway, and John Dos Passos; of the verse of T. S. Eliot, Ezra Pound, Conrad Aiken, Robert Lowell, Carl Sandburg, and William Carlos Williams; of the dramas of Sherwood Anderson and Eugene O'Neill; of H. L. Mencken's inquiry into the American language and John Reed's report on the Russian revolution; of surrealism, Dada, and cubism; of Tin Pan Alley and Dixieland; of the comic genius of Buster Keaton and Charlie Chaplin; of Will Rogers's humor and his debunking of Hollywood trash; of Babe Ruth's home runs and Jack Dempsey's knockouts; of Emily Post's book of etiquette and hemlines raised to the knee; of the first airmail letter service and daylight savings time; of prohibition and bootlegging; of women arrested for picketing to vote and of women finally given the vote; and of the beginning of a decade of reckless buying that would end with the great Wall Street crash of 1929.

It is difficult to imagine Mills's life so troubled by the transportation controversy at a time when so much else in his life had come to full fruition. People came, said his friend Rollins, literally by the hundreds on summer afternoons to chat on the wide porch of Longs Peak Inn with "the man whose work they admired or to pay homage to one whom they regarded as a personage." Mills's manager, Emerson Lynn, who had come to Longs Peak Inn as a driver in 1917, said that though Mills was ridiculed by some and hated by some, he was "loved by those who knew him best." The inn was thriving and had achieved just what Mills wanted: comfort, restrained elegance, and a unique blend of restorative calm and intellectual vitality — in Lynn's words, a "unique and piquant flavor." Edna Ferber's later autobiography praised the individual "log cabins de luxe hiding beneath their rough exterior hearts of gold in the form of steam heat, bathrooms with hot and cold water, log-burning fireplaces and comfortable mattresses." Mills's addition of more cabins and the amenities he had installed from 1913 to 1916 had paid off and allowed him to extend his season to six months. The electric generating plant added in 1916 added immense convenience for staff and guests. The lobby and kitchen, both doubled in size the same year, increased capacity, atmosphere, and efficiency. And the huge new fireplace, assembled stone by stone at about the same time Esther was locating her homestead site, had become the lobby's visual and social focal point.[21]

When Mills visited the convict camp in the Royal Gorge he noticed with his instinctive and habitual alertness that mountain sheep in the rugged canyon area stayed near the blasting zone, apparently safe from their shier enemies, the mountain lions. "True to their nature," Mills said, "the alert mountain sheep early discovered this zone of safety and promptly took advantage of it." It was a nice observation, one that exactly characterized Mills's brand of natural history — to discover how each species and individual within a species deals with life and its unexpected opportunities. An abundance of that kind of observation filled the five books that followed, from *Your National Parks* in 1917 to his death in 1922: *The Grizzly, Our Greatest Animal* (1919); *The Adventures of a Nature Guide* (1920); *Waiting in the Wilderness* (1921); *Watched by Wild Animals* (1922); and *Wild Animal Homesteads* (1922, published in 1923).

Mills brought to a culmination his conversationally informal but richly informative essays on natural history, offering portraits of deer, bears, lions, coyotes, wolves, antelope, mountain goats and sheep, pikas, prairie dogs, and squirrels. Three essays dealt with animals' remarkable olfactory talents ("nose craft"), others with winter survival and animal play, and others with timberline trees, avalanches, lightning and thunder, mountain winds, fossil hunting, and channel carving by rivers. He told his stories of tramp dogs, mountain horses, prospectors and even tracking a wily western outlaw. Mills's opening piece of *Adventures* was his still-famous "Snow-Blinded on the Summit," his *pièce de résistance* in the adventure genre, which despite serious flaws continues to captivate readers and to define Mills as a memorable figure in the history of adventure narrative. Half a dozen essays in the same volume traced his development as a naturalist from a youth learning to "watch and wait" at Lily Lake to the maturation of his concepts of nature guiding and outdoor education, the social utility of nature, and his prickly observations in "Censored Natural History News."

The Grizzly, Our Greatest Animal, one of Mills's most famous books and one of his own favorites as well, belongs with his 1913 *In Beaver World* in a separate class of work dealing with the natural history of a single species. The grizzly volume resembled and took note of another popular work that appeared in 1909, William H. Wright's *The Grizzly Bear.* The two works are often mentioned together historically, both, according to grizzly expert Frank C. Craighead, Jr., "making a valuable contribution to the meager body of knowledge about the great bears" available in the early part of the century. Though both were rich compilations of observations

and facts about the grizzly, neither was a systematic scientific trea-
tise, and Mills's work, especially, can be described best as an affectionate portrait of a friend whom he knew and loved well. Opening
with the contemporary plight of the grizzly watching the settling of
the land by humans, attracted to them by his intense curiosity but
driven from their midst by "yells and bullets, . . . dogs, guns, poison,
and traps," Mills shows the grizzly taking refuge in sanctuaries like
Yellowstone Park and from that safety coming forward again "eager
to be friendly with man." Mills hopes the grizzly can divine the
spark of improved attitudes toward him — perhaps "catch[ing] the
echoes of discussions which are telling that he has been misunderstood, that he is not a bad fellow!" Mills's stunning portrait of a
grizzly excavating a marmot den "like a powerful, careful, thought-
ful man," sets a tone of dignity and respect for a species as worthy as
our own that continues throughout the book.[22]

Describing the book as being "drawn chiefly from my own experiences with grizzly bears in the wilderness," Mills covered the subjects of the grizzly's territory, diet, hibernation, and rearing of the
young; his own adventures trailing grizzlies without a gun; extraordinary instances of grizzly "sagacity," play, and curiosity; historical
accounts of earlier grizzly observers; and grizzlies tamed as pets,
including his own cubs Johnny and Jenny. A more formal chapter
described the history and classification of the grizzly, including the
now outdated brown bear taxonomy of the famous C. Hart Merriam. Mills's presence in the book was not one of a death-defying
adventure seeker, nor of a sentimentalist, despite his obvious affection for the grizzly. It was rather one of a man who had lived most of
his life in grizzly country, seeking to learn as much as he possibly
could about the bear, looking for every sign of their presence, tracking them, watching them with binoculars, accompanying hunters,
talking with ranchers, and reading the accounts of others. The book
contains an abundance of personal experience presented in almost
reportorial style without special effects. And it is a book clearly set
in the American West in the second decade of the century, with the
setting defined by a species whose fate is in transition. In his final
chapter, "Will the Grizzly Be Exterminated?" Mills returned explicitly to the precarious fate of the great bear, arguing its benefits to the
human race and pleading for its legal protection through at least
restricted hunting. He said that as a destroyer of pests, the grizzly
("a walking mousetrap") more than compensates for his occasional

predations on livestock. But far more important — as throughout Mills's value system — the grizzly's inspirational values are what make his demise unthinkable. Having established the magnificence of the grizzly as *the* great species of the wilds, endowed with powers, abilities and character traits worthy of everyone's respect, Mills by the end of the book could say without exaggeration that the grizzly's qualities provide us with the "supreme mental stimulus of the great outdoors," and that "the imagination will be alive so long as the grizzly lives." The book's combination of advocacy, deep appreciation, and intuitive feel for the grizzly's true essence makes it perhaps Mills's most appealing work for modern readers. Mills had found his mature voice as a nature writer, and the three volumes that followed — all similar in content and style — rank along with his grizzly volume as his best works of natural history.

The prolific author's constitution began a steep and irreversible decline when a minor accident in the New York City subway in January 1922 dealt him a rib-cracking blow to the chest. The irony of an accident in the city befalling an apostle of nature has drawn comment from nearly all who have written about Mills. But by his own reckoning it was the statistical choice of fate, for it is in cities where dangers lurk and in nature where they are absent. The real irony underlying the accident was that Mills needed cities and cities needed Mills. For it is city dwellers who need and crave the outdoor message most of all and are in turn its most influential backers. Mills's constant travel to cities was the unvarying lot of the outdoor crusader.

He picked himself up from the train wreck and continued with his business. And if America's mightiest city could not smite him dead in a single blow, neither did it deliver the blow with vengeance. It was an anonymous incident beneath the street, unnoticed even by the city's great daily paper. But Mills suffered more of a trauma than he first thought, and trauma combined with stress laid him open to illness. Soon after the accident a flu virus found in him an unresisting host and took up residence in the man who had once boasted, "I'm never ill, never." Mills was ill and weak all winter and spring, his once bounding stride reduced to a slow trudge, his shivering frame huddled beneath a coat and hats where once he had worn none. His neighbors noticed a different man. In May he confessed to a friend that he had been too miserable to answer his letter properly and still could muster only a brief reply; in August he was still too weak to accompany a visiting biologist to the nearby beaver ponds. Yet on a short walk with the publisher Russell Doubleday he "opened [Doubleday's] eyes to the wonders of nature," causing him to "realize the poetry in [Mills] . . . inspired by the spirits of the woods and the mountains."[23]

Esther, writing of his illness thirteen years later, confirmed that after a few weeks of rest, he recovered "some of his former energy and all of his usual enthusiasm." She said that in summer he attended with usual solicitude to the needs of his guests. He resumed his fireside talks. And he smilingly waved aside their offers to look after themselves so he could look properly after his own needs. But Esther's version of Mills's last months revealed, like others, that Mills could not escape his life of extraordinary stress and the further assaults on his health that it brought. He was locked in a death struggle with his demon of governmental monopoly. It was a struggle he could have walked away from had moral conviction not ruled his life and held him on the battle line. At summer's end a severe abscess required tooth extractions and jaw surgery. And simultaneously the old nemesis of cattle marauding his unfenced land flared up and pumped new choler into his ailing system.

As the transportation controversy appeared to be taking a hopeful turn, Mills faced a new round of negotiations about the problem that had bedeviled him off and on for over ten years. This time Charlie Hewes's grazing tenants were the Kerrs, and the Kerrs, Mills said, were "the cat's paw" for deliberate harassment by the transportation monopoly. They drove their cattle from Hewes's barren pastures onto Mills's lush meadows. They threatened violence to Mills's men who drove the cattle back off. And one of Kerr's men assaulted one of Mills's men with a gun. Mills himself, sometime earlier, had been pistol whipped by a drunken stockman named Billy Welch and carried home unconscious in a wheelbarrow. And so it went: a range war on one square mile of land. Mills, badly in need of rest, calm, and time with his family, could not and would not escape turmoil. Why did the cattle wander onto Mills's land rather than onto the surrounding national park lands? Of course, said Superintendent Roger Toll, grazing is prohibited in the park. But "since the State has not ceded jurisdiction of the area to the National Government, your recourse against trespassers is the same as though the park boundaries did not exist." Cede jurisdiction of the "area" and not just the roads? Was that a slip, a sign of deeper intent?[24]

Mills never found out. In the middle of the night, a week after his latest letter to his attorneys about the Kerrs and their cattle, he slipped from conflict into the boundless neutrality of death. His departure was simple and unceremonious. He mingled with the guests on the night of September 20, went to bed at 10:00, woke up in distress at 2:30, and was dead by 3:00. Esther had summoned a physician staying at the inn, but Enos Mills could not be saved. Blood poisoning had stopped his heart.[25]

Mills's vessel for passage to what he once called "the mysterious horizon" was not a hollowed out tree or a simple box. It was a large coffin, which, though resting fittingly on two tree stumps in the inn's lobby, glistened like a mirror on its polished silvery exterior. If it was incongruous for the simple man of the woods, it was a reminder perhaps that he was a man of worldly causes and worldly attainments as well. The coffin rested at the foot of the stairs where Mills had stood for his countless fireside talks, and the man who had "slept beside a thousand fires" now lay beside his last fire. There must have been a period of silence before the funeral guests arrived, with the reflections of the fire's flames flickering over the coffin. And then there was the shuffling sound of 300 guests filling the lobby and overflowing onto the porch outside. Half a dozen of the very old sat and the rest stood for the short ceremony. Present were John Cleaver, age ninety-three, who had accompanied Dunraven into the valley in 1872; Louis Pappa, an ancient Indian cattleman; some of the James family, Mills's first employer at the Elkhorn; the wife of Abner Sprague, Mills's longtime friend who had named a lake for him; the painter R. H. Tallant, whose deceased wife Mills had touchingly eulogized eight years before; Freelan Stanley, faithful to Mills throughout the transportation controversy; C. H. Bond, an Estes civic leader probably torn in both directions by the controversy; Alfred Oberg, Mills's loyal Swedish cook and winter caretaker for over twenty years; multitudes of other friends and admirers; men and women of other nationalities and races who had worked for Mills over the years, and returned, said the news reports, to pay their respects. Death, Mills had always said, was the huge egalitarian force, taking all and uniting all, a receptacle of democracy even larger than nature.

Emerson Lynn reported that Joe Mills was invited but did not attend. Of Mills's estranged neighbors, Charles Hewes, at least, put in a gentlemanly appearance, but recorded the event without comment or emotion in his personal journal. Yet fear and superstition, always part of Hewes's response to Mills, lived on in his imagination. A lone raven, he said later, had circled over the valley for hours on the day Mills died, and those birds "of ill omen" had taken up residence in the Longs Peak region, where they had never been seen before. If the Tahosa Valley wars continued on as a battle of symbols, Mills loyalists might be said to have deserved an easy victory: The raven is both respected in many Native American traditions as a primal creative force and regarded by modern biologists as one of the most advanced of all avian species. The arrival of ravens, if true, can be said to have been a glory rather than a stain upon the valley.

The funeral service was conducted by the prominent Denver juvenile judge and Progressive reformer Ben Lindsey, a longtime friend of Mills with whom he had often shared the lecture podium. Mills's instructions had asked for no hymns or other music; no sermons or passages from the Bible; and no eulogy. The judge spoke briefly and read briefly: Muir, Burroughs, Tennyson, Mills. And then six pallbearers bore the shining coffin over the road to the grave site, blasted, it was said, from solid rock next to Mills's homestead cabin. A child sobbed to Judge Lindsey, "What will the mountains do without Mr. Mills?" But the mountains, accounts of the event suggest, responded with glory. As the coffin started its descent, dark storm clouds moving over the face of Longs Peak were torn aside and golden rays of the setting sun poured through the great notch in the summit ridge. The 300 guests watching the burial at a distance from outside the inn turned to see the brilliant effect. And when they turned back, Mills was gone, as if he had ended his own story the way he had ended the story of Scotch: lunging toward a blaze one moment, gone the next. Into the grave with Mills went a shower of September aspen leaves, strewn by the twelve who had brought him there. And some perhaps remembered that Mills had written, "Oh, that every life might end as gloriously as an autumn leaf."[26]

As the earth closed over Mills's grave, south-flying birds were feasting high up on the tundra where the kinnikinnick, currant, wintergreen, blueberry, and bunchberries, gone for days or weeks in the lowlands, were at last ripe two miles above the sea. It was the great festival, Mills had said, by which "they close summer, begin autumn, and anticipate the winter."[27] It was an exhilarating annual gathering of life, from the last insects to a dozen varieties of birds, some resident, some on the wing; to the chipmunks and squirrels and bighorn sheep; and to the preying eagles, coyotes, foxes, and lions — a chain of food and a fabric of life all gathered in that setting of "strange beauty and wild magnificence" between the forest below and the bare rock of Longs Peak above.

Part IV

Mills Today:
A Modern Critique

CHAPTER 20

Romantic Hero in a Real World

Looking back over the whole of Mills's life and work, we find that his private and public images both found expression in the literary persona of his books, but that both perhaps drew their inspiration from public tastes and trends. As a snow observer he first discovered himself as a figure of public interest who showed that the no-longer-pioneering West still needed brave and resourceful men. The snow-man with slouch hat and charcoal face lent adventure to work, and linked new western themes in an appealing combination of raw action and civilized purpose. Simultaneously, Longs Peak Inn required him to develop the style and gifts of a host. The style that naturally fit was the prototypical nature guide with a lodge in the woods; the most crucial gift — a convincing presence. Mills's sophisticated clientele would not have responded to an indecisive performance, and he met their expectations by becoming as accomplished in his sphere as they in theirs. His fireside talks, his excitable arm-waving to get people outside looking at things, his moral injunctions, and his petulant expulsion of disobedient guests made him a memorable version of the true man of nature.

By 1907, as he toured the country in the service of the president, he had a ready-made persona for the press to glamorize. He added to it a vivid stage presence that was native and rustic, good natured and optimistic. He gave his message and his image a broad appeal that spoke to all, for the good of all. Reaching the heart of America was exhilarating work and a profound fulfillment for a self-made man. His public was his mirror, and its smiling approval told him that he was a chosen one, destined for greater things. In the quick and successful transition to writing, Mills put his persona directly into the pages of his books. In his 1909 *Wild Life on the Rockies,* his first-person narrator was rugged and picturesque: "At one of the big mining-camps I stopped for mail and to rest for a day or so. I was all 'rags and tags,' and had several broken strata of geology and charcoal on my face in addition." He was the companion of danger: "Down I tumbled, carrying a large fragment of the snow-cornice with me." He was competent and analytical: "9,728 trees upon an acre. They were one hundred and three years of age . . . soil and moisture conditions were excellent." He was appreciative: "I had long admired this ever-cheerful, ever-spreading vine . . . had often stopped to greet it, . . . had slept comfortably upon its spicy, elastic rugs." And he was poetic: "The world is flushed with a diviner atmosphere, every object carries a fresher significance, there are new thoughts and clear, calm hopes sure to be realized on the enchanted fields of the future." Even Scotch was part of the persona: "He gave a few barks of satisfaction and started with her up the trail, carrying himself in a manner which indicated that he was both honored and pleased."[1]

As Mills's narratives take us from flowers and nesting birds to the tops of rugged mountains, he is a guide and companion of just the sort we would want to have on a real outing. Like Muir's first-person narrator, Mills's presence gives immediacy and palpable realism to the scene, distinguishing it from the painted-canvas scenarios of earlier travel writing. Mills's persona is usually subordinate to the subject matter and not intrusive. Yet the cumulative impression of his appearances in the narrative casts him unmistakably as a man of agreeable disposition and happy enthusiasms, shorn of the fractious tendencies of his real-life character. That is not to say, however, that the literary Mills was a wholly artificial creation. The narrator of the stories closely resembles Mills as he was when actually guiding people outdoors. And in that agreeable persona is something of what we all feel ourselves becoming in the outdoors: simpler, untroubled, optimistic. Nature, Mills's stories helped to show, is the place where we can be what we want to be. His first-person narrator was thus both a self-interpretation and an interpretation of the outdoor impulse in the postpioneer era. Like Whitman on a more epic scale, Mills grew into the image of what he believed his age needed and wanted. The persona of his books worked, and for the most part worked exceedingly well.

What it failed to depict, because his genre was in no way self-exploratory, was how nature shaped and prepared him to function among people. Because he was high strung and acutely sensitive, his life could have furnished a dramatic instance of the distance that must be traveled from the natural to the civilized, from the solitary to the social. Though those transitions should have been central issues in his life, he neither wrote about them nor perhaps even faced them privately. His books tell us time and again that nature prepares us to return as better men and women to our ordinary lives, but they show nothing of the process, nor of the struggle for integration that should have been his own. When, between 1905 and 1908, he began to clash with those close to him, he could escape to a hero's welcome in the nation's lecture halls. The nervous intensity that made him privately irritable made him publicly vibrant. He had that vibrancy in his own Longs Peak Inn as well, but that was a setting, perhaps like the nature of his books, that ensured him an unchallenged brilliance. His reprisals to guests for hobnobbing at lodges whose owners he disliked indicates what may have been his need for a selective frame of reference to protect his own image.

The National Park campaign was the first major test of Mills's ability to manage himself in complex public negotiations. But nature, it soon became clear, had not prepared him to argue his points calmly and dispassionately. He came to the bargaining table not with the commanding presence of the grizzly — the animal he liked most — but with the snarls and arched back of a wildcat — the animal he liked least. He rarely, moreover, came to the bargaining table at all, for the instinct he never overcame was to deal with his opponents through unilateral condemnation. His denunciation of the Forest Service, though direct and explicit, was not followed by detailed negotiations. The complexities of deciphering and influencing that troublesome agency were left to McFarland and Rogers. And while they labored for understanding, Mills, the naturalist who could sit for a week to watch wild animals, lost first patience and then trust.

The strength that Mills perhaps did bring from the woods to the public arena was an unflagging stamina and a refusal to be defeated. Right or wrong, he was a formidable foe. His public persona as a man of nature was, moreover, attractive enough to sway the public with an impassioned message of personal and social health bestowed by nature. Applied to the park campaign, it was publicity more than politics, but publicity that nevertheless fed into the political process. In the transportation controversy that pattern was even more evident. Embattled and shorn of many allies at home, he won support for his cause primarily in those areas where he could defend and embody the principle itself. He was victorious when the persona known through his books was given final authority in public questions. The *St. Louis Dispatch* editorial cited in Chapter 18 epitomized that triumph, telling its readers of Mills's holy wrath and his oracular wisdom. Its conclusion, "It ought to be as Enos says it ought to be," expressed the political status Mills sought: revered and unchallenged as the man whose vision had been purified by nature, and whose passions, if boiling over, had been driven there by the injustices he opposed.

It is a perhaps troubling yet deeply interesting dimension of Mills's character that he wanted to conduct his public business through his idealized persona, and to a degree succeeded, yet broke repeatedly out of it in angry outbursts. Through all his public campaigns Mills felt a rage against those who did not take him for the noble and simple man of his books. How dare his neighbors drive their cattle onto the meadows of the man who had taught the nation to love flowers? How dare the Forest Service try to block the park plans of the man who had so ably shown their value to the nation? And how dare, subsequently, the Park Service sponsor the venal transactions of monopoly in the park he had created? Mills's rage was the rage of wounded innocence. And the more he retreated into the purity of his principles, the more rigid those principles became. Called on to argue frankly and in detail, he frequently refused even to meet. And the more righteous he appeared to his enemies, the more they looked for his own inconsistencies and faults. A great deal of Mills's public anger, including his refusal to answer countercharges and his frequent boycotting of meetings, seemed to stem from a frustration that his rules were not the rules of the rest of the world. He appeared never to have reflected on his public behavior, which some would say lacked essential maturity. Even one of his ardent admirers referred to his "princely ego" and his destiny of being "peculiar among men and little understood."[2] Nobility is the quality Eugene Debs and others also found in Mills; but its liability is its assumption of entitlement, and that, to his detriment, Mills seems never to have outgrown.

Mills's example tells us perhaps that nature — large, diverse, and ultimately neutral — does not transform all men in the same way. Its function, as Mills at times recognized himself, is to develop in us what is already there. Mills's immersion in nature prepared him not to integrate himself into the world of men but to return as a dissenter; not to acquiesce, but to fight. He was a hard and desperate fighter for whom winning, as in a clash between predator and prey, was the sole aim, and compromise a remote possibility — as even Judge Lindsey said at his graveside. There was something in Mills of Rousseau, who returned to the world of men but was driven out and hunted down; of Thoreau, who preached disobedience to unjust laws; of Muir, who shouted biblical epithets at the destroyers of nature's temples; and of Abbey, who wrote of blowing up dams and spiking trees. Mills was no more a political animal than any of these and his mind was perhaps less advanced; but as much as any of them he was a dogged and single-minded crusader for what he believed in.

If nature supplied the theme for Mills's persona, the limitations of that persona perhaps restricted his depth as a human being. What his persona lacked, if we can verge on a clinical interpretation, was the suppleness to function as a versatile intermediary between his inner and outer lives. Mills appears to have attached his ego so rigidly to his created image that he sacrificed both wholeness in his inner being and flexibility in his external relationships. Moral outrage expressed through his high-principled persona served as well to inflate his ego. He not only lost allies but seemed to want to lose them. Each in turn became unworthy of his support. Even after McFarland warned him, "You cannot possibly maintain as one single American that you are always right and everyone you criticize always wrong," Mills went on scolding and maintaining he was right, and losing allies. To McFarland concerning the park monopolies, we recall that Mills wrote bruisingly, "I doubt if you even want to know."

Mills not only wanted the persona of his books to represent him in public negotiations, but may have escaped to it through his writing to find a place of safety and self-esteem. Portraying himself as a happy and uncomplicated man in nature, he could dwell in a world that he had mastered both physically and emotionally. He could recreate the wildness of his young manhood, in which no other human interfered with or even saw his adventures. He could remember — or imagine — that though nature tested him to the utmost, it never defeated him. And he could believe that out in that wild remoteness the animals were his universal and uncritical friends. Mills's adventure tales are of special interest because they go beyond the guided excursions of his nature stories and, by featuring Mills himself, put his created image most graphically on display. But the hero of those stories is a stereotyped hero who, though regionally distinct and equipped with authentic skills, was reduced virtually to a set of conventions. Mills's predictable fearlessness and indestructibility suggest simple self-gratification rather than any pursuit of self-discovery. His heroics took him away from the enrichment that nature offers to a sacrifice of his own potential wholeness. Mills's heroic persona strikes us today as the most obvious but least successful expression of what he wanted to be. It was a persona of wishful thinking that he could — understandably — not successfully translate back to the public arena.

As stories, Mills's adventures rely on a limited repertory of situations, centered mostly on calamity. Mills's hero was a brave but often bumbling romantic who made many foolish but exciting mistakes, whose chief source of adventure was rescuing himself from trouble of his own making, and some of whose feats border on the preposterous. Mills surely overlooked these less than glamorous aspects of his heroism. And they show a considerable mismatch between the hero that must have served his own needs and the one that needed credible historical status. Mills's hero probably stemmed in part from a mistaken emulation of Muir. Mills went his master one better in ruggedness and audacity but failed to comprehend that for Muir the essence of adventure was spiritual discovery, not escape from calamity. Muir, we noted earlier, fell but once and was badly chastened; he was caught in an avalanche once and never again risked a snowy death by crushing and suffocation. And while Muir was himself subject to the superficial vanities of mountaineering — he was both proud and competitive — he wrote his narratives, argues Michael Cohen, neither to congratulate himself nor to say explicitly what he had accomplished. Mills's narratives were explicit about his accomplishments, and his self-conscious attempts to avoid boastfulness were themselves boastful. Mills evidently did not know that Muir distinctly disliked the kind of daredevil episodes he wrote about and that Muir probably considered accident proneness a sign of separation from both nature and self.

The possibility of fabrication in Mills's adventure tales has been raised and contrasted with his stern insistence on fidelity to fact and as a matter of explicit social importance. In returning to that subject now, we must first distinguish between Mills's stupendous feats and those of the yarns of nineteenth-century storytelling that formed a popular literary genre at midcentury and were still part of the western tradition of "stuffing the tenderfoot." Outlandish fabrications were amusements rather than lies, said William Wright; and adding humor, local color, and deliberate exaggeration was part of the art. One Colorado editor passed off Pikes Peak as a volcano, and a signal officer at the weather station on its summit convinced tourists that there were corpses buried in the snowbanks. It was easy humor and the fun was in gulling a gullible audience. Mills could spoof in this lighthearted vein too, once telling a party of Easterners, for example, "about jumping into a pile of snow on top of [Longs] Peak and coming out at Chasm Lake." Like many western writers he also passed on stories he heard from others, making no claim for truth or fiction. Such was his story "Besieged by Bears," the account of prospectors fending off bears trying to get at their sugar-cured ham. That story is genuinely funny and has been praised as a prototype of a kind Mills could have successfully developed. A few other of his stories, mostly on frontier themes, form a separate category within his writing not dealing with his own adventures. Mills knew the wily ways of the yarn spinners and the exaggerations of the "stretchers," and he told his readers to take with a grain of salt even the wildlife observations offered seriously by old-timers. The scientist in him knew that in the realm of nature observations, fact is prone to errors of bias, judgment, and superstition.

About his own adventures, however, there is never any sense that he wanted to be taken as a teller of tall tales. At no time past or present have his reviewers read him that way. Though he experienced his adventures in isolation and earned his fame solely on the basis of his own testimony, he made it explicitly clear, when asked, that what he wrote he had first experienced.[3] If he falsified, he may have internalized his stories to such an extent that he believed they were true. He was apparently confident enough of his credibility that he exercised none of the cautiousness needed by all adventure writers to avoid straining the credulity of their readers even with provable facts. So confident was Mills, indeed, that he wrote without hesitation that not once — amazing enough — but twice, lightning demolished the tree next to the one he had climbed; that a rock he dislodged set another in motion that broke in half a tree in which a bear cub perched and took the top off the tree to which the bear fled; that in edging away from some menacing bees, he butted into a bush and stirred up more bees, fled those, fell over another bush, and nearly landed on a skunk, which, unleashing a volley of spray, missed him but stopped the pursuing bees. The last of these episodes might have been offered as Munchausenesque farce and was in fact told with humor; yet Mills meant the facts to be taken at face value and presented them in one of his essays debunking falsehoods.

If there is an answer to the riddle of Mills's credibility, it may lie in his notion of imagination, which, he believed, could see beyond present facts and present circumstances to their logical extensions:

> The normal [i.e., healthy] imagination . . . is based on realities; it . . . sees the logical and natural results or developments in advance and pictures glorious changes through natural growth or evolution, and never by magic or enchantment. . . . [It] is a combination of information and inspiration. . . . [It] deals ever with cause and effect; [it] *can expand, extend, or create the probable continuation of facts* [italics added].[4]

Such a resourceful use of imagination was fostered in children in the Trail School and was the basis for what Mills called more broadly "the poetic interpretation of facts." It gave him his conviction that imagination is the highest intellectual faculty. Because it is logical and obeys the laws of causality, Mills appeared to take it as a valid tool of science and its revelations valid forms of the truth. The notion was by no means his own invention. It had abundant antecedents in nineteenth-century thought and art, and will concern us in relation to Mills's achievement as a naturalist as well.

For his adventure tales, the notion gave him an easy justification for what can in simplest terms be called poetic license. If he was sure something was possible, claiming he did it was but a "poetic extension of fact." His story of out-skiing a pursuing avalanche, leaping forty feet over a gully in the process, may, for example, have been his imaginative extension of what skiing was in 1900 to what he believed it could ultimately be. In terms of relative velocities, the chase he described was highly unlikely. Mills stood at the worst possible spot when the slide started: at the top of the gully through which the entire accumulation of the mountain's snowy amphitheater above him would funnel. Unable to ski off to the side at once, Mills raced down the gully ("bristling with ten thousand fire-killed trees") ahead of the slide that from the snow conditions he described could have attained speeds above 50 mph. His head start can have given him only moments to reach the shelter of the side gully that saved his life. The story, like many of Mills's, almost succeeds: the topography, cloud motions, his standing bivouac, and his cautious descent the next morning, followed by the explosive release of the avalanche, have a convincing ring. The chase itself works well as a story: Time is drawn out as the speeding slide gains on the speeding Mills. We see a tiny man in a steep gully pursued by masses of snow. We see with clarity each obstacle he must dodge or leap, and can appreciate his lucid moment of suspended time high above a clump of trees as he leaps. But the basic fact of the chase suggests extrapolation of a lesser event — an imaginative "extension of fact" that is adequate for an untrained audience but not for a knowledgeable audience. Insofar as an expert modern skier could have outrun the avalanche, the story meets Mills's conditions for "truth" and does no harm to its readers except in compressing history by half a century. The fact that even today only under the best and luckiest of circumstances could a skier have escaped the slide he described reduces the validity of his imaginative attempt.

"Snow-Blinded on the Summit," Mills's most famous adventure story, provides the most crucial test of his factual authenticity. It was published late in his career and ensured him a permanent place in adventure lore. The adventure was Mills's greatest test and his last word on survival, for blindness afforded him the opportunity not only to use his woodcraft skills, but also to engage the faculty he most admired: the imagination. Converting the story from its original version in *County Life* magazine to its final form in *Adventures of a Nature Guide,* Mills added this paean to the imagination:

> The compensation of this accident was an intense stimulus to my imagination — perhaps our most useful intellectual faculty. My eyes, always keen and swift, had ever supplied me with almost an excess of information. But with them suddenly closed my imagination became the guiding faculty. I did creative thinking. . . . Any one seeking to develop the imagination would find a little excursion afield, with eyes voluntarily blindfolded, a most telling experience.[5]

Being about the power of imagination to save his life, the story — by Mills's own standards — should be a seamlessly convincing presentation. Yet, astonishingly, it is shot through with claims and circumstances that provoke skepticism in any experienced mountaineer today. At best it raises questions that Mills should have anticipated and taken pains to answer.

With numerous details in the story lacking or unsatisfactory, the most likely verdict must be that Mills neither made the journey nor succeeded in imagining it in any depth. A true firsthand account should have been richer in practical details and in psychological insights; it should have needed none of the miraculous coincidences in which it abounds. If Mills did make the trip or some lesser version of it, the story, like some of his other adventure tales, suffers from *seeming* fabricated. Indeed, if offered as a fictional account in the first place, it might have been said to lack the kind of realism that even made-up stories require. Some — by no means all — of Mills's heroic accounts make us grant too many times that truth is stranger than fiction. It is not the severity of the tests that is implausible. Many well-documented accounts from his time and ours are far more harrowing. The problem lies rather in the details of the events themselves, which fail to withstand scrutiny.

Mills was clearly not writing for an informed audience; but neither, it appears, was he always writing to inform his audience. Since his mission was to dispel myth rather than to create it, it is an inconsistency of rather odd proportions — one probably not possible had his audience and editors been more demanding. Mills's adventure tales show his apparent susceptibility to corruption by the popular magazine genre; to that we should add that the problem was probably compounded by his drive to market large quantities of material produced late at night after taxing days under other pressures.

It could be argued on both literary and practical grounds that it does not matter whether Mills actually experienced his daring feats if he failed to convey what they were really like anyway. In none of his hair-raising episodes, that we noted earlier, can we truly grasp how close he came to death or what it really meant. And little can be truly instructive when so much depends on chance and rare circumstance. His fearlessness, always blithe and taken for granted (when snowblind he was "only moderately excited" and said "the possibility of a fatal ending never even occurred to me") removes him as a human model to identify with and learn from. He explored none of the emotions that confront us in predicaments of our own making: despair and self-reproach for having gotten there in the first place; a futile wish for another chance; hope for a miracle and the dread realization that none might come; a debilitating panic that until mastered can paralyze all rational action; alternating hope and loss of hope; dread of the sheer exertion that survival, if possible, will demand; an exhausted wish to succumb and have it over with; fear of death and acceptance of death; thoughts of loved ones and what friends and the news will say. Considering none of these, Mills easily and cheerfully met his challenge, seeming indeed glad to be there ("delightfully eager they [my fingers] were as I felt the snow-buried trees"). His analytical problem-solving is easy and almost airy, like rock climbing moves executed on a small boulder. Here, as elsewhere in his work, his idiom of understatement fails to imply its intended depth. Had he explored through his own example how each of us must confront our own unique psychology, he would have plunged far more meaningfully into the realm of human accomplishment under extreme duress — whether or not his adventures were literally true. And he would thereby have established a more realistic basis for the valuable lessons he wanted to portray: The more we learn the less we fear; the less we fear, the greater are our chances for survival; the more we trust nature, the more we discover in it the needed resources for coping.

We can never be certain what Mills did and did not actually experience. There are, to be sure, extreme personalities in every generation who risk everything and accomplish the near-miraculous — or die trying. We cannot dismiss the possibility that Mills was one of those and that he was blessed with as much luck as skill. That he has been doubted by some is a matter of record. One has said, "It was well known that Mills overstated his experiences." Another has called him an outright liar, but a liar who used his fabrications to get support for national parks. A third called "a lot of Enos's stuff . . . pure fiction" and said the snowblind story was "all plum crazy." Mills's enemies in the Tahosa Valley appear — predictably, no doubt — to have been unanimous in their opinion that he fabricated much of his material, and they even contemplated publicly exposing his "lies and falsifications." A modern chronicler of Colorado mountaineering, William Bueler, records that "exaggeration and imprecision were no strangers to his voluminous writings." Robert W. Johnson, who vouched for the authenticity of Mills's 1903 descent

of Longs Peak's east face, though not for the manner of his descent
as described by Earl Harding, saw tantalizing hints of a deeper and
more complex Mills under the surface persona — a man able to feel
fear and perhaps compulsively obsessed with mountaineering; a man
who stood intoxicated on ledges waving his arms in the free air, perhaps on the brink of losing control. And while Earl Harding
accepted Mills's explanation after the descent that he was "just out
after some pictures and slipped into some water," Johnson learned
from him that after he got off the mountain he had to roll in the
snow for several minutes to relieve the awful tension. That is the
Mills we wish he had himself explored — a man both more believable and more interesting. That Mills chose to let Harding's highly
romanticized account stand as the official version of his descent, and
even reprinted it in his later versions of *Early Estes Park,* leaves no
doubt that he readily accepted superhero status.[6]

His acceptance of Harding's hyperbole is moreover a reminder
that much of his persona may have been a response to public taste.
Mills's mind and habits were highly eclectic, and throughout his
writings are traces of the currents of his times that he might have
drawn together to create his own image. His striking individuality
may, paradoxically, have been the result of a highly imitative personality, more sensitive to, and molded by, public approval than by his
own inner sense of self. He was in a sense a popular artistic creation,
a self-conscious and self-sculpted Pygmalion. The possibility is not
by itself objectionable. It is one way to lead a life, and we all to a
degree reflect elements of our times in our personalities. But in fash-
ioning his persona to fit a broad public taste, Mills had only to satisfy an adventure-hungry appetite, gullible in its avidity to find
outdoor heroes and to be edified by their lofty attainments. The public, we recall, eagerly swallowed the hoax of Eve, disappearing into
the wilds near Longs Peak in her leopard-skin robe. And in Maine
four years earlier, a similar stunt had made Joseph Knowles a
national hero, cheered by thousands when he returned to civilization
and soon wealthy from selling 300,000 copies of his book.[7] Mills
likewise had an easy audience, and for everyone who doubted his
adventures, thousands believed them. He did not need to delve into
any self-exploration to create a hero who won public acclaim. And
not needing to, he apparently did not bother to.

Mills's trademark as a spokesman for the life-sustaining vigor of
play is characteristic of the kind of trait he made seem like virtually

his own invention, but in fact it was widely in vogue throughout the Progressive Era. And in borrowing themes, Mills may at times have come close to borrowing the words to express them. His invocation of play to explain his winter ride up the gales of Longs Peak may, for example, have been modeled on a passage by Julius Stone that he knew and later quoted in *Your National Parks:*

> It takes on many forms and numberless variations, this thing called play. Its appealing voices come from far and near, in waking and in dreams; from quiet, peaceful places they allure with the assurance of longed-for rest; from the deeps of unfrequented regions they whisper of eager day-and night-time hours brimming with the fullness of heart's desire, while bugle-throated, their challenge sounds forever from every unscaled height.[8]

And here is Mills two years later, clearly imitating and clearly stepping out of his folksy idiom to wax eloquent:

> Irresistible is nature's call to play. This call comes in a thousand alluring forms. It comes at unexpected times and sends us to unheard-of places. We simply cannot tell what nature will have of us, or where next. But from near and far, ever calls her eloquent voice. In work and in dreams she shows a thousand ways, suggests the presence of wonderlands yet unseen. She pictures alluring scenes in which to rest and play; in mysterious ways she sends us eagerly forth for unscaled heights and fairylands. Of these she whispers, or of them she sounds her bugle song.[9]

The superior awareness brought by blindness was another theme that Mills made his own, and though it lacked the obvious link to Progressive Era culture that play had, he may have been attracted to it through a great hero of that era, Helen Keller. Mills both knew and quoted her 1902 autobiography, which portrayed deep nature appreciation without sight or sound. Mills gave blindness a progressive — and admirable — educational function by using blindfolding in his Trail School to acquaint children with their tactile and intuitive universe. He had, furthermore, at least three role models for blind survival in the wilderness and two likely sources for his idea of a winter trek snowblind. When he was a young man, a blind Indian in British Columbia had guided him several miles along a mountain stream. A mining friend from Cripple Creek told him about going blind from exhaustion, being found by soldiers lost on the prairie, and guiding them back to their fort from the landmarks they described to him as they carried him on a stretcher. And Mills knew the story of Truman Everts, an inexperienced city man separated from the Washburn-Doane Yellowstone Expedition in 1870, who survived for thirty-seven days as blind as one can be from losing his glasses: He mistook a pelican for a rescue boat. Everts epitomized for Mills sheer tenacity to survive.

Of the two likely sources for Mills's own snowblind trek, one was an account of two trappers who lost their sight crossing the Continental Divide near Estes Park in 1899. Mills cited the episode in his *Early Estes Park* but never described the remarkable similarity of its circumstances to his own: The trappers were almost blind when they reached the summit; Mills became completely blind at the summit. The trappers came to a deserted cabin after wandering all night; Mills came to a deserted cabin after two nights filled with mishaps. On easier terrain the trappers tried following a road but lost it; Mills came to a road but took a wrong turn and nearly fell into a mine shaft. The trappers came at last to a ranch with a barking dog; Mills came to a homestead and was greeted by a child. The second possible source is an account called "Snow-blind" in a 1904 issue of *Outdoor Life,* the magazine of his friend J. A. Maguire in which he had also begun publishing. Three themes in that story closely resemble those of Mills's: groping for trees, working slowly along a stream course, and confronting a hole in the ice.[10]

Given Mills's fascination for blindness, its relevance to his theory of imagination, and the many models he had, it is tempting to conjecture that he invented or forced some version of an actual blind adventure to culminate his outdoor career and to ensure himself a special place in Rocky Mountain lore. His passages glorifying blindness in "Snow-Blinded at the Summit" make clear how extraordinary an opportunity he believed his temporary blindness had given him. And the story, fact or fiction, *has* helped to immortalize Mills as one of Colorado's most intrepid mountain adventurers. A story that seems to be a misfire by even moderate standards of accountability, has an uncanny ability to create, in many readers, romanticism's willing suspension of disbelief. Perhaps, after all, the story's naiveté is its greatest attraction: It assumes a world in which the miraculous *can* happen.

That possibility returns us to that major theme of Mills's life and of his artistic search for self-definition: his desire to be and to project himself as "poetic." In earlier chapters we saw Mills, the mountain romantic, swept irresistibly away by nature's call to his icy adventures, to his eerie feelings of being the first person on an aboriginal earth, to his profound delight in everything around him. There was a genuine poetic sensitivity in his ability to experience life. His poetic orientation, furthermore, offset his exaggerated posture of fearlessness and placed him clearly outside any tradition of he-man literature. Though a need for masculine reassurance may have in part motivated his risk-taking, what he clearly wanted to portray was the wild romantic, rugged and daring for the sake of the poetic reward. The full realization of Mills's romantic longings could perhaps occur only in the realm of the imagination, and much in his writing makes us want to accept that romanticized world uncritically, with no demands for factual accountability.

Let us conclude that though he could not convincingly explore his own outdoor experiences, Mills at least announced a world of dreams and possibilities that set the exalted awareness of danger against civilized stagnation, that legitimized play and risk-taking as valid forms of experience, and made nature's poetry the pathway to personal freedom. If he bent fact to fit mood, he overran his own principles, but he lacked the art to make that error truly pernicious. Mills's mistakes are both obvious and easy to forgive, because they make so clear what he wanted life and the world to be. To read him as a man of longings and fantasies embodied in a great rhapsody to nature is perhaps not what he intended. But it is what he often wrote. He was a utopian romantic for whom nature was utopia and a social romantic who yearned to give nature a place in human affairs.

Mills lived before antiheroes replaced heroes. He submitted to nothing that oppressed him, crawled for no one, and never whimpered with shame or fear. His ego was large and proud, but large and proud in the manner of heroes bent too grandly on a purpose, and destined, through that flaw, to fall. Early death perhaps spared Mills an extraordinary fall. It left deep issues and contradictions in his life unresolved. It left him the unfinished product of what he tried to be. But it also left the ideals of that unfinished man clearly visible. And those ideals speak to us as forcefully as they did to his own generation. They transcend his artistic shortcomings and the truth or fiction of his stories, allowing us to reattach them to our own outdoor world and our own social concerns. Virtually every critic of Mills has said: "The spirit was there." Let us therefore, says one of the eloquent interpreters of our modern ecological dilemma, hold on to that spirit to help restore our connection with the natural world. Let us, says essayist Bill McKibben, "blow on such sparks as the splendid essays Enos Mills has left to us."[11]

CHAPTER 21

Enos Mills the Naturalist: A Vanishing Breed

An Enos Mills admirer wrote that, when John Burroughs died in 1921, Mills inherited his place as the greatest American naturalist. Though Burroughs did not consider himself a true naturalist if that meant contributing original knowledge to the advance of science, he was revered as a natural philosopher and a nature lover with "powers of intuitive, truthful, and sympathetic observation joined with a love of expression." Mills would have eagerly accepted those words to summarize his own career. As "all-purpose" amateur naturalists, both Mills and Burroughs belonged to a vanishing breed, replaced by specialists in the new age of the expert. Most were biologists rather than broadly informed naturalists, and most studied preserved specimens in the laboratory rather than living creatures in the field. When young Mills first thought of becoming a naturalist, Darwin, who radiated "a vision of the entire living world," was a scant decade dead. But the broad thinkers of Victorian science who came in his wake could no longer keep up with technical details. And Louis Agassiz, America's dean of naturalists, who had taught the "art of truly seeing," had in the end been judged irrational. Mainstream biology had embarked on the long road of reductionism, understanding life by dividing it into smaller and smaller parts, and leading in our time to molecular biology, the discovery of DNA, and the controversial triumph of genetic engineering.[1]

Mills's first acquaintance with John Muir came at a time that Theodore Roosevelt, disappointed by the indoor preoccupations of a once-exciting field, called "a sad time for natural history." The truth, however, was that the need for field studies was greater than ever as science faced the full implications of Darwinism for animal behavior and the relationship of all organisms to their environment. The environment was, in fact, what Ernest Thompson Seton aptly called "the mould in which each species was cast." Muir's example showed young Mills that he did not have to get a Ph.D. and dissect frogs to learn about nature. And he saw in Burroughs's already plentiful books — Muir's were to come later — that nature was an inexhaustible source of things to love and discover in one's own personal way. Muir's and Burroughs's influence combined to give Mills a genre and world view to step into. And with most professionals busy in their labs, some even eschewing the study of animal behavior as mere "twaddle," amateurs had a useful role to play in watching wild nature in its living daily activity. That, we have seen already, was where Enos Mills's greatest interest and talent lay. "He approved," said his friend Philip Ashton Rollins, "of the scientists who endeavored to discover how animals were built; but, for himself, his interest was to learn how animals acted."[2] Though a self-taught amateur, Mills contributed some original field observations that entitle him to historical notice. He did so by following his own inclinations and his own curiosity. He became in his time a quintessential naturalist for the Rocky Mountains, known by scientists, with whom he could converse fluently; some came to his famous inn and even sought his advice on the best locations for their own field studies.

Becoming a naturalist in the era that defined nature in bureaucratic terms as a supply of raw materials for development, Mills heeded Muir's urgent call for a view of nature that kept alive our fundamental sense of identity with all of creation. Mills was part of science and separate from it, a custodian for its connection to humanity and a keeper of a broader vision of nature that slumbered in orthodox science. He was part of a tradition that sought to understand the whole of nature by being active and live in it. He engaged his emotions in what he observed rather than detaching them, following the tradition of Thoreau, who said that "a man has not seen a thing who has not felt it." He sought essences more than details, again following Thoreau, who said he could "learn all he wanted to know about a hawk by watching it fly and did not want to know the length of its entrails."[3] He belonged to the tradition of Emerson in believing that a naturalist must be motivated by love, and of Whitman, who believed that natural history must have poetic inspiration.

Even among professionals, a few "naturalists" still roamed the outdoors. Some, like the eminent Theodore Cockerell in Colorado, had a specialty but knew a "good deal about a great many things"; he kept a constant connection to Darwin with a portrait of the great man on his office wall. The remnant breed of naturalists included collectors and taxidermists, zoo and museum curators, field biologists where they were still needed in agencies like the U.S. Biological Survey, pioneers in ecology and the study of animal behavior, hunter-naturalists, artist-naturalists, and writer-naturalists or "literary naturalists," the category that best describes Burroughs, Muir, and Mills. If Mills filled Burroughs's shoes for the brief period until his own death in 1922, it was not that he was greater or lesser than this diverse assembly of men and women. He was simply one of them, and famous too, succeeding as he said Burroughs and Muir had in "interpreting the story of nature so that all may read and understand."[4]

Love of nature implied a desire for truth, for the demand of love not to misunderstand was as strong as the demand of science not to miscalculate. Amateurs therefore agreed with professionals that nature study at any level had to be correct. Rebuking those who strayed into error or fantasy, Burroughs began a much publicized attack on "sham natural history" in 1903, charging nature writers William J. Long, Charles G.D. Roberts, and Ernest Thompson Seton with reporting preposterous feats of animal intelligence and dexterity. But he went too far in dismissing the possibility that animals can learn at all, and remained, despite his deep love of nature, attached to a mechanistic view of animal behavior that dominated much of the era's biological thinking. Captive late in his life to works such as Jacques Loeb's *The Mechanistic Conception of Life,* Burroughs grew increasingly rigid in resisting revolutionary ideas that were challenging the predominant mechanistic viewpoint. While the majority of biologists dissected and tested animals in laboratories, or at best watched their behavior in zoos, some were convinced that animals are creative organisms whose behavior is inseparable from their environment. Others insisted that animals possess a variety of behavioral and learning abilities as surely the result of evolution as mere morphology. Two new sciences, ecology and ethology, were forging bold new directions during Mills's own active years as a naturalist.

Seton, whose extensive training as a naturalist was unknown to Burroughs when he included him among the "nature fakers," did not retreat from his ideas, which he believed were based on solid field observations. Historian John Henry Wadland has taken considerable pains to show that Seton's animal stories were his vehicle for reporting behavioral observations at a time when they seemed radically new. Recovering his dignity quickly — and confronting Burroughs in person — Seton won high acclaim from the scientific community for his 1909 *Life Histories of Northern Mammals*. Yet into that two-volume compendium of widely gathered data on each species, Seton wove the same ideas about their behavior for which he had been attacked. Wadland argues that the true importance of Seton's *Life Histories* today is their contribution to early insights in the field of ethology. And both Wadland and Ralph H. Lutts, author of a 1990 book on the nature faker controversy, believe that much of the conflict and rancor surrounding it were due to the uncertain state of science itself.[5]

The stigma of nature faking remained a threat to careless writers throughout Mills's life, and it was to his advantage to maintain a safe distance from the tainted genre. His own denunciations of bogus natural history served no doubt as a reminder to his readers that he stood on the side of full authenticity. But despite the risk he incurred, Mills took a stance near the radical end of the spectrum on matters of animal behavior. His portrayal of the forest as a dynamic community of animals — responding to their environment and to each other, often forced by circumstances to exercise their "wits," to modify instinctive patterns with resourceful invention to meet the unexpected, and learning through experience, curiosity, and play — was a bold departure from the mechanistic view of Burroughs and the scientific majority he followed. Mills clearly anticipated the modern view that animals' ability to learn may be more important to their survival than inherited instinct. He went even farther, announcing in his first book and never retreating from his conviction that animals have "intelligence" and can "reason" — despite the frequent charge that the "reason school" of natural history belonged to the degeneracy of nature faking, and despite numerous articles by Burroughs refuting animal "reason."[6] Mills's observations of animal behavior show that he had at least some acquaintance with principles being taken seriously by progressive zoologists when William Morton Wheeler first put the term ethology on the map in 1902. Those included learning through experience, experimentation, and cultural transmission of knowledge between generations; the importance of sociability, communication, and mutual aid in survival; ritual, dominance, and territoriality; posturing, pretending, play, and curiosity; "enjoyment" of leisure time; various expressions of emotion; and at least rudimentary forms of morality, including some sense for the "rights of others." The notion that standards for human morality can be found in nature was an idea widely discussed before Mills's time and traceable not only to Darwin but to scientists and philosophers before him clear back to the Greek Stoics.

Mills's quite evident view of the wilds as a format for a harmonious and morally sound democracy is, in its historical context, not surprising, and it stems no doubt from his own simultaneous immersion in nature study and the social concerns of the Progressive Era. Nature in much of Mills's writing bears the stamp of his own contemporary tastes and prejudices — a slant that was on the whole expansive rather than narrow. His woods express the fullness of life that was the central plank of his social platform. They brim with vitality, joy, playfulness, progress, and good citizenship; their creatures are curious, creative, responsive to new challenges, and often avid for self-improvement. Mills longed for a society like that of nature, "gentle and genuine, all artistic and inspiring." What he prized in nature he preached for humanity, and what he found flawed in nature he judged in reverse by human standards. Otters and jays won his highest praise for their quick-wittedness and joie de vivre, while porcupines earned his occasional criticism for their dull-wittedness and lack of interest in play. Minks and weasels might have ranked as high as otters and jays were their characters not flawed by cruel bloodlust. Mills was indeed never quite comfortable with a naturalist's tolerance of predation as a morally neutral process, and he joined Roosevelt and others in denouncing what he took to be the lion's wanton slaughter of excess game. He favored Ben Franklin's choice of the natively shrewd wild turkey as a national symbol in place of the raptorous eagle, except that the character of the male turkey was tarnished by vanity, boasting, polygamy, and indifference to raising the young. Such anthropomorphic strains in much of his writing — especially his earlier writing — place it in territory strictly forbidden by orthodox biology. But the real root of his anthropomorphism was, like Seton's, an instinctive belief that animals and humans differ only in degree. That in turn was a response to his generation's no longer avoidable attempt to understand behavior in Darwinian terms as something that, like physical features, developed through evolution. His deepest anthropomorphic assumption was that nature "cares" about humanity's well-being and offers both moral guidance and an open invitation for humans to become part of its society.

Nature in Mills's writings thus ceaselessly gestures to us to be its companions. The birds and animals, fundamentally trusting and confiding, "crave our acquaintance." And "knowing that wild folk play and that they have a home territory," Mills wrote, "brings them strangely close to ourselves." From the bluebirds who adopted Mills as a youth to a stunned woodpecker he revived in his hands, to a powerful grizzly piling rocks like a worker in overalls, Mills expressed a deep and pervasive affinity between man and nature. Mills the naturalist, who discovered that nature's path is unfailingly one of self-improvement, speaks as Mills the moralist in urging us to rejoin that evolutionary principle. Getting back into the biological stream both requires and develops our highest evolutionary potential. It makes us more, rather than less human; peaceful rather than aggressive; and creative rather than destructive. That, it appears, was for Mills the deepest message of evolution.

Spending more time in the field than many professional biologists — if they went outside at all — Mills knew that without persistent and often repetitive work an observer gains only a "traveler's impression" of any species. His most serious application of that principle resulted in his relatively early (1913) *In Beaver World,* which presented both facts gleaned from other sources and what are undeniably original observations of his own over a twenty-seven-year period. The book brought some inevitable charges of nature faking for ascribing reasoning ability to the beaver, but it also presented, according to one reviewer, "facts [that] will make the 'instinct school' do some hard thinking."[7] Praised far more than it was criticized, it was called a worthy successor to Lewis Henry Morgan's classic 1868 work, *The American Beaver and His Works,* and was by Mills's own accounting his most ambitious work of natural history. His other sustained work on a single species, his 1919 grizzly volume, discussed in Chapter 19, is a close second to the beaver volume, disadvantaged only by the fact that the mobile and elusive bear afforded Mills a less reliable source of long-term systematic data than the beaver colonies close to home.

Mills watched beavers long and carefully enough to see the work of individual animals improve with experience; to record individual differences in ability and alertness; to see failures as well as successes;

to discover differences in the forms and methods of building dams and canals and in the thoroughness with which colonies prepared for winter; to note cooperation in accomplishing community work, both with and without visible evidence of "management"; to see homeless beavers adopted into colonies and unwanted beavers expelled; to observe beavers releasing water from dams to create a breathing space below the ice and sometimes draining a pond entirely, perhaps for sanitary purposes. He established that the sober water engineers take plenty of time out to play, belying the adage that the beaver is always "busy."

Mills found the most persuasive evidence for beaver "intelligence" in their dam and canal projects, which appeared to require advance planning and the integration of complex parts into a unified whole for results often far in the future. Their skills sometimes exceed, he said, those of the Army Corps of Engineers. Most astonishing was a dam built across *dry ground* and then filled with water — itself a complicated diversion problem — to make a pond across which to float a new food supply. The purpose of this elaborate scheme was to postpone abandonment of the colony by making the new food supply accessible. Yet to forestall using that new food source, the beavers saved closer-in, edible trees by building the dam of nonedible, fire-killed trees.

Mills also found intelligence in the ability of some beavers to fell trees in a desired direction and to avoid cutting trees entangled with others. The claim was already common in beaver literature, though even Seton rejected it, as do virtually all scientists today. Mills offered the observation, however, carefully and not categorically. "Rarely," he said, "does a beaver give any thought to the direction in which the tree will fall." But *"in a few instances . . . I have seen what appeared to be an effort* [italics added] on the part of the beaver to fell a tree in a given direction." And although "the majority will not do so," occasionally a beaver "may be wise enough . . . to look upward to see if the tree about to be felled is entangled at the top." The question, then, was perhaps one of variation in individual aptitude combined with the ability to learn through experience. The case of a beaver (observed by a modern scientist) who learned to spring steel traps by splashing a wave of water over them with a powerful thrust of his tail, is perhaps illustrative.[8]

Mills had precedents to cite in defense of beaver intelligence, notably Morgan's famous work and three books from the 1880s on

Moraine Colony, near Longs Peak Inn, supplied much of the data for Mills's beaver studies. *Courtesy, Enos Mills Cabin Collection.*

animal and human intelligence by George J. Romanes. Both were prominent spokesmen for a nonmechanistic interpretation of animal behavior and are credited with anticipating later developments in the field of ethology. But closer to home and more representative of the prevailing skepticism on the question of intelligence was Edward R. Warren, a Colorado naturalist whose 1910 *The Mammals of Colorado* was considered a definitive sourcebook for species characteristics and type habitats. Warren wrote ungenerously of the beaver:

> While the beaver has always been credited with a sufficient amount of intelligence to fell a tree in any direction it wished, and with a certain amount of engineering skill, some of my observations indicate either a lack of intelligence or very poor judgment, for trees were badly felled when there was no excuse for it, and dams built which were simply labor thrown away from an engineering standpoint.[9]

If Warren failed to deter Mills from publishing his contrary conclusions three years later, Mills may have influenced Warren during the course of their acquaintance. Studying some of the same colonies in the Longs Peak area in the early 1920s and publishing a book-length monograph on beavers for the American Society of Mammalogists in 1927, Warren concluded at last, "My studies of the beaver have led me to the conclusion that it does act intelligently." Though clearly still uncomfortable with the subject ("It is difficult to define my own position in the matter"), he asked forthrightly why, if engineering feats show intelligence "in the case of man, . . . why not also in the case of the beaver?" For some modern ethologists, any discussion of "intelligence" and "reason" is moot because the very terms are anthropomorphic. Others hold as rigidly to mechanistic definitions as Jacques Loeb did seventy-five years ago. But others, called "cognitive ethologists," are finding new and persuasive evidence for bona fide consciousness and intelligent decision-making by animals. The debate, in short, is still open, and Mills's beaver volume remains today a provocative set of observations. Joseph Ewan, in his 1950 biographical compendium, *Rocky Mountain Naturalists,* called it "important to the mammalogist for its original observations and materials." And in 1959 Don J. Neff used it, along with Warren's follow-up studies and Forest Service photographs from the 1930s, to complete a seventy-year chronology of the beaver colony Mills had named Moraine Colony. This exceedingly rare long-term chronology is still referred to in beaver literature.[10]

Because Mills spent large amounts of time outdoors and could go places and endure discomforts few others could, his data on other species often went beyond those recorded by professionals. While Edward Warren notes of the pika, for example, that "little is known of their winter habits [because] these high altitudes in our snowy mountains are not safe places to be investigating [them]," Mills, who spent many winters roaming the snowy mountains, knew their winter habits well. His popular account thus has more to say about the diminutive inhabitant of rock slopes than Warren's handbook account. Warren says that pikas do not seem to hibernate, but he is not sure. Mills says positively that they do not. Warren says that he does not know whether they are a social animal in the strict sense of the word and mentions no instances of contact between any two individuals. While not defining sociability in technical terms, Mills cites instances of snow tracks converging from different dens, of pikas meeting and socializing, of homeless pikas taking refuge in the dens of others, of communication for social or warning purposes, and possible evidence — which he later rejected — of shared labor in harvesting the winter grass supply. Though Warren's accounts were perhaps necessarily brief, we find, for many species, more interesting details in Mills and a fuller sense of each animal's particular essence. Specific topics, such as animals' coping methods for winter survival (profiting from Mills's extraordinary time afield as a snow surveyor) and animal play, important enough to warrant a separate chapter earlier, further enhance our appreciation of Mills as an original field observer.

Right or wrong in specific details, and anthropomorphic or not, Mills thus remains important as a curious and active naturalist at a particular time and place in history. As Mills pondered, and as Barry Lopez notes concerning wolves,[11] we see but a small fraction of an animal's total activity; we must patiently record each new thing we see them do, and may have to wait long for confirmation. According to one professional source, it took fifty years to confirm the observation that a beaver mother sometimes carries her young in her forepaws while walking on her hind legs. Without the luxury of laboratory reproducibility, carefully recorded anecdote remains a necessary tool of behavioral studies. The acute observations of Mills and others of his time warrant review as a source of raw data containing

Mills preached "getting acquainted on the installment plan." *Denver Public Library, Western History Department.*

useful clues to behavior, always open to reinterpretation as knowledge advances. Seton, who worked diligently to compile life histories of mammalian species, stressed the importance of a cumulative data pool gathered by hundreds or thousands of observers, each contributing their small share of ascertained facts. Mills's personal interest in natural history "biographies," was neither odd nor rare. It put him in a tradition going back to Charles George Leroy in the 1700s, John James Audubon in the early and mid 1800s, and Lewis Henry Morgan; and in his own time to Wheeler, Seton, and C. O. Whitman, all of whom called for "a complete biography of every species, which would include the species' individual character, natural appetites, and its particular way of life."[12]

Seton's compilation of data on North American mammals — following a checklist of nearly 500 separate characteristics — culminated in his famous 1925–28 *Lives of Game Animals,* a four-volume popular work so thorough that it remained a standard reference for naturalists at least until the Second World War. Reviewed before publication by top experts for each species, the work guaranteed the authenticity of its facts, said Seton, with a "fullness and force . . . never before equalled in a popular natural history."[13] The *Lives* provide important historical evidence of Mills's standing in natural history circles in the decades following his death. Seton cites him almost six dozen times — nearly twice the combined total for Muir and Burroughs — consulting him on fourteen different species in such categories as mating, denning, and family behavior; diet and hunting habits; territory and range; fighting ability; play behavior; vocalization; life expectancies; and interactions between species. Nearly a dozen times, furthermore, Seton calls attention to the "distinguished" and "ever-delightful" "Longs Peak naturalist," a "keen observer" who combined "rare opportunities with rare gifts," and some of whose accounts were the best on record. Seton unfortunately examined only two of Mills's books — *Adventures of a Nature Guide* (1920) and *Watched by Wild Animals* (1922) — and drew all but seven entries from the latter. *Watched,* the same book that Joseph Ewan called Mills's best work of natural history, was no doubt Seton's most convenient source of data, since it contains many briefer life histories of its own. But many things in Mills's other books — especially his beaver and grizzly volumes — would have been directly relevant to Seton's purposes.

Seton's oversights notwithstanding, he helped to do for Mills what Mills did not do for himself. For Mills's greatest weakness as a naturalist was his failure to document his observations against the existing record of what was known. His writing both gave the illusion of originality where he should have mentioned precedents and failed to secure credit for findings no doubt authentically his. Though Mills clearly made original observations of scientific merit, he published his findings up to twenty years later and as often as not in popular newsstand magazines. He furthermore scattered some important observations randomly in essays on other subjects. In "Winter Mountaineering," for example, he described a lion playing pantomime on the snow above timberline, an observation similar to those of W. H. Hudson in South America; and he recorded an unusual instance of a bird nesting with eggs in February, two months ahead of schedule for that species. Although Seton ensured Mills's reputation a firm standing in prewar literature, later scientists have tended to dismiss his work as "fragmentary and undated" and "primarily intended for popularizing the wilderness and not for scientific study."[14] Those concerned to uphold Mills's historical importance as a naturalist thus need to find in the rest of his popular books the important "flakes of gold" that Seton found in two of them.

A more delicate problem in attributing scientific credit to Mills is the possibility that he supplemented his own observations with an "imaginative extension of facts" according to the rationale discussed in the last chapter. Given his belief in imagination as the highest faculty, reliable through its obedience to the laws of causality, Mills perhaps allowed himself to draw inferences from what he saw and to call some of those inferences observations. We gain a sense in some of his work that he saw too much too often — trees rubbing together and bursting into flame, a squirrel dropping a pine cone just in time for it to stick in a skunk's tail, a tree falling at his feet without waking the sleeping squirrels inside, and many others in the same vein. If Mills created these touches to add spice to his writing, he violated his own belief that the truth is both stranger and better than any fictions about nature we can invent. Rarely referring to or quoting from his actual field notebooks, he was open to the charge of "creative memory" that was said to underlie much of what was called nature faking. He was, in fact, accused of nature faking during his own lifetime. Don J. Neff's study of the seventy-year chronology of Moraine Colony, which on the whole accepts Mills's data, records

Mills often stated that animals "crave human acquaintance." *Denver Public Library, Western History Department.*

Like John Muir, Mills climbed trees both to study them and to ride them in the wind. *Denver Public Library, Western History Department.*

with some annoyance that a fire Mills said he saw devastate the colony was shown by two later investigations to have happened in 1878 — six years before Mills even arrived in Colorado. If Mills reported seeing a fire that he simply knew had occurred, it was a liberty acceptable only by his own rules of discourse. Science, though often rigidly pedantic, submits to caution of necessity, for conclusions drawn about what is unseen, no matter how inspired, can be disastrously wrong. Intuitive guesses are of course in the repertory of most good scientists, but they must always be followed by painstaking verification. Imaginative hypothesizing backed by creative experimentation in the study of animal behavior was brought brilliantly into play by the ethologists Niko Tinbergen and Konrad Lorenz half a generation after Mills.

The possibility of imaginatively derived facts supplementing actual observations also casts a shadow on Mills's famous 1910 essay "The Story of a Thousand Year Pine." Reprinted as a separate book a few years later and translated into several languages, the story describes dissecting a huge western yellow pine in southwestern Colorado that loggers abandoned when it shattered on impact. Mills spent several days analyzing the tree's 1,047–year history from its rings, scars, and embedded objects. Though the essay shows photographs of other large pines, it shows no photograph of the tree he dissected, either standing or fallen, nor photos or diagrams of its ring sequences or other dating evidence.[15] The willing crew from the nearby sawmill, which could have cut him cross sections of this extraordinary specimen, instead burned "every piece and vestige" at Mills's request after he had finished his work. The lack of any hard scientific evidence might be of negligible importance but for the fact that the tree's age would still stand today as the record for its species, older in fact by nearly 200 years than the current record holder, 860 years old, reported by the famous tree analyst Edmund Schulman in 1956. Scientists consulted for this book find the age Mills gave highly improbable, or at best "barely conceivable and at the vanishing end of the distribution curve of longevity for the species." Worse, furthermore, is the absence of detail in large portions of the tree's early centuries ("An even tenor marked his life for nearly three centuries") and Mills's failure to discover any evidence at all of the thirteenth-century drought that drove out the Anasazi culture in precisely that area. Other disturbing aspects of the analysis and missed opportunities to learn more from the tree render Mills's essay useful

Mills was an accomplished photographer, capturing the mood and spirit of nature, especially along the treeline. *Courtesy, Enos Mills Cabin Collection.*

only as sentiment. The record of a tree that might have told scientists a great deal is lost in the mystery of Mills's own personality.[16]

It is significant, finally, that in his experiential approach to discovering nature Mills sometimes slipped into the exaggerated behavior that characterized his heroic adventures. He fell down hillsides with skunks in several variations of the tale told in the last chapter. His hat, left behind when he fell from a tree, became a robin's nest. A lion watching from a branch when he woke up one morning, fell onto *him* when the branch broke. Such events, bringing Mills forcibly into contact with nature, suggest that we should look for metaphor in some of his writings rather than literal truth. Like Mills the adventurer, who acted out or invented a world without limitation, Mills the naturalist perhaps acted out his desire to escape the bondage of the formal and rational world. Searching all day for fossils, he found none; falling, at the end of the day, he landed in a fossil bed. Falling, he discovered bear tracks. Falling, or the illusion of falling, seems to have been one of Mills's direct channels to the inner sanctum of nature.

If we try to judge Mills as a scientist, we discover both great promise, partially realized, and clear evidence that he sought something beyond science. He was to a degree the mystic that Theodore

Cockerell said every true naturalist becomes. If his intuitive reading of nature took him into the realm of invention, he went there with the confidence that he was elaborating truths already present. He measured and counted and behaved in other ways like a scientist, but in the end he sought meanings knowable more from within nature than from an external scientific objectivity. He cultivated and stressed the importance of finely tuned senses, yet he believed that the senses — or at least our human senses — do not receive all the messages nature sends. Imagination is needed to decode the "wireless messages" of scent that make the landscape of the forest a different place for creatures who live by their noses. It is needed to deduce from a few clues what goes on at night and beneath the surfaces of water, soil, and snow. An acute imaginative perception of each animal's mentality is needed to understand the meaning of its sounds, gestures, body language, and codes of behavior. Mills's deepest urge was to know what life is like for each species, and formal science could give him only partial answers.

Nor was Mills willing to allow science to remove nature's magic hold on him. He wanted to absorb nature as well as study it, to appreciate it poetically, to play with and in it. His love of nature gave him patience as well as passion, and a receptivity to plants and animals, however and whenever they presented themselves. Mills acquired all his knowledge under the stimulus of interest, sentiment, and value, and he acquired it casually as well as actively. The revolutionary changes in biology occurring in his lifetime coincided with his own interests and might have offered him the channel for a distinguished scientific career. But he would not submit to the strictures of formal science, even as it entered new territory. He perhaps sensed that science has shifts in its fashions — today's "paradigms" — which do not last; and that he must discover his own truth through his own experience. He remained at heart an artist whose subject was nature; an artist as eager to know his subject as a scientist, but in different ways. He moved between a world of palpable facts, which he sought tenaciously to gather, and a world of hidden facts accessible only to the imagination. He was, as in his adventuring, a romantic idealist who, like even the cautious Burroughs, believed that "it is not so much what we see as what the thing seen suggests."[17] We can view Mills as an intriguing embodiment of the amateur spirit in an age of scientific transition, as interesting for his faults as for his virtues, and a standard of intense involvement by which to measure our own relationship with nature.

CHAPTER 22

Nature's Interpreter: Mills as Writer and Outdoor Educator

Mills's books are simultaneously his written record as a naturalist and the literary record of his effort to reach and inspire a mass audience with what he called "the poetic interpretation of nature." As a nature writer Mills was unfailingly enthusiastic and endowed with an astonishing repertory of subject matter. He showed on every page that he cared deeply about nature, and he believed, like the famous Louis Agassiz, that every man, woman, and child can be made to care, too. What he wrote to Irving Hale as a fledgling public speaker applied equally to his writing: "I want to be effective." Mills succeeded as a nature writer because he created in his persona a figure both appealing and accessible to the popular mind. What he could learn, the masses could learn, and what he could appreciate, so could they. Preaching that once you understand the wilderness it is a wonderland, he created in his writing that same Horatian connection between appreciation and understanding that he and Robert Sterling Yard made the ideal of the national parks. Like vignettes lifted from real parks, Mills's books were a resource for people to enjoy through learning and to learn through enjoying.[1]

Mills's narrative presence as a nature guide has an authenticity not fully realized in his heroic persona. Much of his writing — clearly influenced by his speaking style — has the charm of a trailside conversation. It is loose and associative rather than structured and logical. Guided by spontaneity and curiosity, it creates an experience of constant discovery, showing us all manner of things we had never noticed before or did not have the knowledge to go out and find. At other times Mills's narrator is a journalist reporting on nature "with a nose for news," or a detective reconstructing unseen events from subtle shreds of evidence. He is at times a teacher-ecologist explaining forest, soil, and water conservation, natural insect control, and portions, at least, of what we call today sustainable agriculture. And he is, finally, the biographer par excellence of the living world, adding whatever facts he can to the life histories of species and individuals within species.

The binding element and one of the most admirable qualities of Mills's writing is curiosity. An inquisitive spirit pervades his work and gives him a constant readiness to do whatever is necessary to learn about his subject. The boy who dug into prairie dog colonies to see if they burrow for water later shared the excitement of "procuring tools" with which to dig beneath the sod of meadows for clues to their origins. Finding 100-year-old lodgepole cones embedded in a tree cut open at a sawmill, he brings his readers along as he plants the seeds to see if they will sprout. And wanting to know how long groundhogs hibernate, he describes his rustic experiment: "Near my cabin I marked four ground-hog holes after the fat fellows went in. On September tenth I stuffed a bundle of grass in the entrance of each den. Sometime during the winter one of them had disturbed the grass and thrust out his head. . . . The other groundhogs remained below until between April seventh and twelfth, about seven months."[2]

In many of Mills's essays the desire to know something is announced at the outset. "For years I wondered how big game managed to live through the hard winters," one begins. Mills then takes us on the intriguing odyssey of how he found out. His constant alertness in the field translated easily to the written page and enabled him to articulate the obvious and the subtle, both of which elude less acute observers. Here is the kind of passage, both keenly observant and marked with the stamp of Mills's own personality, that Seton used in his *Lives* to illustrate the lion's patience in hunting:

A friend wished a small blue mule on me. It had been the man's vacation pack animal. The mule loitered around, feeding on the abundant grass near my cabin. The first snow came. Twenty-four hours later the mule was passing a boulder near my cabin when a lion leaped upon him and throttled him. Tracks and scattered hair showed that the struggle had been intense though brief.

Not a track led to the boulder upon which the lion had lain in wait, and as the snow had fallen twenty-four or more hours before the tragedy, he must have been there at least twenty-four hours, and he may have waited twice as long.

Another time I frightened a lion from a cliff where he was waiting for a near-by flock of bighorn sheep to come within leaping distance. Though it was nearly forty-eight hours since snow had ceased falling, not a track led to the lion's watching place or blind.[3]

Sheer fecundity of subject matter was another of Mills's strengths as a writer, and it was, indeed, nature's own abundance that provoked his impressive literary output. He wrote at least one and up to three or four essays on many of the Rocky Mountain mammals, and in addition to his full volumes on the beaver and grizzly, he left material for a posthumous volume on birds.[4] He wrote absorbingly on animal behavior, including his favorite subject, animal play. He wrote numerous articles on trees and covered many other plants more briefly. He wrote thematic essays on what today would be called animal and plant ecology, and on the conservation of forests, wildlife, water, soil, and scenery. He described habitats in deserts, prairies, farmlands, wetlands, hard and softwood forests, high mountains, and alpine tundra. He gave popular accounts of geology and physical geography, including mountain formation and erosion, glaciers and glacial topography, landslides, stream erosion, floods and avalanches, the evolution of alpine lakes, meadows, and parklands, and the influence of fire on landscape formation. A handful of essays on mountain weather showed that he was a first-rate weather observer, especially of severe conditions. His promotional pieces on the Rocky Mountain region were enriched by his observations as a naturalist, as were all of his essays on national parks, park advocacy, the value of the outdoors to individuals and society, and on nature guiding and outdoor interpretation.

Few writers in any era venture such a broad range of subjects, and to the attentive reader no story is devoid of something interesting. Readers prone to coasting quickly through whatever is easy to read will profit from looking at Mills a second time to savor the feast and the resourcefulness of the man who provided it. In the space of one essay, for example, we follow a lynx looking for its next meal; learn that a squirrel near Mills's cabin always eats its cones on a certain branch; see that squirrel scolding a passing coyote; observe

Mills in his writing den. *Denver Public Library, Western History Department.*

a bear, driven out of his den by cold in a snowless winter, carrying mouthfuls of bark and grass back in to improve his bedding; see another bear reopen an old den and flush out a bobcat; watch as Mills hides behind a cornshock in a Missouri field to spy on wild turkeys; observe a rabbit using a high-piled snowdrift to reach a new source of food; conclude from tracks in the snow that a yarding herd of elk successfully resisted a wolf attack; see how a lion ambushed a deer immobilized by soft snow; discover a family of sleeping skunks whose den has been torn open by a snowslide; and first hear and then see the macabre feast of wolves, lions, and grizzlies on the carcasses of over a dozen deer killed by a snowslide. That, by any standard, adds up to a remarkable essay whose facts alone incite wonder.[5]

Mills's willingness as a naturalist to risk personal interpretations of what he saw also made his writing rich in points of view. Calling the coyote, for example, "a clown," "an actor," "something of a philosopher," "wise," "cynical" and "full of wit," was his attempt to define what he called the "peculiar mental makeup" of the species.[6] The interpretation is highly anthropomorphic, but together with Mills's other impressions of the coyote is similar to Native American and other folkloric characterizations. Something in the sensibility of the animal resonates with something in the sensibility of humans to create a common view of the animal's "character" or "soul." Lacking a place in formal science, these impressionistic data find a needed home in nature literature, and Mills's volumes contain them in abundance.

Many readers may nevertheless find some of Mills's portrayals and diction overly anthropomorphic, especially in his early works. While appreciating his always bright and animated spirit, we can grow weary of his brooks, "glad and wild with energy," hickory seeds "bounding down hillsides like merry boys," windborne seeds "flying off on romantic adventures," and winds "delighting in mischievous play." And even as amateurs we sometimes want more explicit biological assurances that the squirrels are really "barking from pure joy," that the ptarmigans are "enjoying the blizzards," that coyotes and beavers are "cavorting like prankish boys," and that migrating birds leisurely stop to "picnic . . . for food and fun." Not infrequently Mills grows maudlin, as in "A Goldfinch Romance," the written version of the talk with which he wooed his future wife. In that late-published tale, the female goldfinch, clad in a "gray-green gown," pauses during her nest building to "call sweetly to her young and handsome husband," who, dressed in a gold vest, sometimes goes to her even "without her calling . . . simply . . . because he [can]not stay away longer." The story continues in that vein.[7]

Quite in contrast, and just as characteristic, however, is Mills's abrupt ending of "Scotch," blown to bits by dynamite, and his stoic lack of commentary on the loggers' abandonment of the thousand-year pine when they found it unfit for milling. Conspicuous in withholding the expected sentiment of the narrator, they have the calculated effect of inviting readers to shed their own tears for Scotch and to gasp with indignation at the callousness of logging. Less premeditated is Mills's biological neutrality in describing the struggle of a beaver colony against a persistent settler who destroys each day what the beavers, each night, have built. His lack of pitying commentary resembles some of Burroughs's accounts of animal mortality from hunting, starvation, and cold.

Mills's natural inclination to see each discovered fact as a "story" and the lives of plants and animals as biographies made his natural history fit conveniently into magazine articles and book chapters. It also enabled him to construct essays around themes such as "nosecraft," "sightseeing by wireless," "the music of the wilds," "the individuality of birds," "animal landowners," and "leisure classes" — essays that, though simple and chatty, depended on extensive knowledge organized in support of a particular point of view. They also make clear Mills's ability to see nature in literary terms, an ability that according to his friend Robert W. Johnson began quite early and made him more a "literary man with artistic and poetic tendencies than a naturalist."[8]

Though Mills's creativity sometimes threatened his objectivity as a naturalist, it served him admirably as a nature writer when he honestly distinguished between speculation and observation. His imaginative visualization of the possible life history of a pine seedling growing miles from any of its kind ("Perhaps the following is its story") is openly speculative but scientifically plausible, accomplishing exactly what nature writing can do. Mills sometimes guessed without claiming proof, suggesting, for example, that hawks and owls rear their young early in order to feed them on the young of other species. When events passed from his sight he sometimes said frankly, "I do not know what happened." He admitted not having seen things he always wanted to see, such as the parting of a grizzly mother from her cubs after two years of constant togetherness. He confessed to observing otters only a few times, to the difficulty of gathering information about grizzly hibernation, and, as already noted, to making mistakes and changing his opinions. He was willing, furthermore, to leave questions unanswered, resisting the temptation to interpret with his imagination what he was not sure of. In this description of a rare partnership between a coyote and a lion, used by Seton in his *Lives,* we see Mills properly in command of scientific caution:

> Just why they were associated in this friendly manner we can only conjecture. It will be readily seen that the coyote, which has all the wisdom of a fox, might follow a game-hog lion about, and thus, with little effort, get a substantial and satisfactory food supply. But why the lion should willingly associate with a coyote is not quite clear. Perhaps this association proved to be of some advantage to the lion in his killing, or it may have been just one of those peculiar, unaccounted-for attachments occasionally seen between animals.[9]

Mills's broad range of subjects, his willingness to express points of view, and his gift for presenting nature in story form enabled him to appeal to his readers' sensibilities over wide latitudes. We gladly follow him in his frequent shifts from fact to mood, from description to evocation. We learn scientifically how a meadow came into existence and a moment later discover its charm as a place to camp. Beauty takes its place as a property of the setting along with technically describable features. Mills's perceptive eye never fails to notice the unusual, pointing for example to a pair of coyotes made to appear headless by a desert mirage. Seeking facts, he discovers poetry: When he climbs up through a storm to measure its vertical depth, he rises out its top and sees the huge cloud mass rotating beneath him: "Like a huge raft becalmed in a quiet harbor, the cloud-sea moved slowly and steadily, almost imperceptibly, a short distance along the mountains; then, as if anchored in the center, it swung in easy rotation a few degrees, hesitated, and slowly drifted back. Occasionally it sank, very slowly, several hundred feet, only to rise easily to its original level."[10]

With his gift for on-the-scene description, Mills has captured the scene as well as today's time-lapse photography. That gift for recording immediate observation, illustrated in earlier chapters by descriptions of a forest fire and wolves at play, was one of Mills's strongest literary assets.

Mills did not, however, penetrate more deeply into his subjects and often suggested ideas without exploring them. His prose abounds in intimations of nature's artistic moods and scenes that remain undeveloped as brief, isolated moments. Mills often sprinkled the epithet "poetic" on scenes and objects without further elaboration. He found certain clumps of trees arranged "artistically" — as did Isabella Bird — but ruminated no further on what he meant. And in such phrases as "[the solitaire's song] puts into utterance the glorious harmonies of the heights,"[11] he leaves his readers to formulate and ponder deeper questions. What, we wonder, *are* the glorious harmonies of the heights? Is bird song a primitive form of expressive art? Has the song of each species developed in response to its specific environment and needs? Is "harmony" thus meaningful in evolutionary terms? As intense as Mills's personal experience of nature was, we do not find in that experience as deep an illumination of the scientific substance as we do, for example, in Muir's intuitive perception of Yosemite's glacial past as he walks barefoot over the sculpted granite, or in Loren Eiseley's meditation on the earth's past as he lies shyly naked in the waters of the Platte River. Nor does Mills's withdrawal from a meadow where he senses that he has disturbed some invisible equilibrium and offended the assembled spirits lead him to anything like the personal and philosophical exploration of Annie Dillard in a remarkably similar situation. Mills both usefully and frustratingly leaves much of the imaginative work to the reader.[12]

Neither nature itself nor Mills's life-and-death adventures were the entry point for him to explore complex states of mind. We saw earlier that he did not investigate the transformative power of nature on his own soul and that even in his most extreme adventures failed to explore the deeper meaning of the experience. He proclaimed but did not show in any detail how nature makes us better men and women. In his first book, which clearly established his literary persona, he occasionally went deeper, to give us as much of a glimpse of his personal self as he ever would:

> One October night I camped in a grass-plot in the depths of a spruce forest. The white moon rose grandly from behind the minareted mountain, hesitated for a moment among the tree-spires, then tranquilly

floated up into space. It was a still night. There was silence in the tree-tops. The river nearby faintly murmured in repose. Everything was at rest. The grass-plot was full of romantic light, and on its eastern margin was an etching of spiry spruce. A dead and broken tree on the edge of the grass-plot looked like a weird prowler just out of the woods, and seemed half-inclined to come out into the light and speak to me. All was still. The moonlit mist clung fantastically to the mossy festoons of the fir trees. I was miles from the nearest human soul, and as I stood in the enchanting scene, amid the beautiful mellow light, I seemed to have been wafted back into the legend-weaving age. The silence was softly invaded by zephyrs whispering in the treetops, and a few moonlit clouds that showed shadow centre-boards came lazily drifting along the bases of the minarets, as though they were looking for some place in particular, although in no hurry to find it. Heavier cloud-flotillas followed, and these floated on the forest sea, touching the treetops with the gentleness of a lover's hand. I lay down by my camp-fire to let my fancy frolic, and fairest dreams came on.[13]

Elsewhere, Mills tells us that if he dies in the wilds — as his friends fear he will — he hopes it will be in summer amid flowers and the sound of the solitaire's song. There, and in the passage just quoted, the real emphasis is on the attributes of nature itself rather than on Mills. His evocation of the moonlit scene is finely drawn, showing him to be alertly and sensitively present. But nothing in his personal history is essential to the mood and no quality beyond a capacity for appreciation is needed to enjoy it. The scene does not turn Mills into a Wordsworth exploring the depths of his own soul, nor into an Ahab confronting unfathomable mysteries of life. The grizzly, his best candidate for a symbolic Moby Dick, had he wanted one, was powerful and full of soul, but a good forest citizen rather than a dark and philosophically charged force. Mills, probably to his credit, neither reduced nor expanded nature to a set of symbols. What might have lurked in his soul in need of expression, he left alone, dismissing the opportunity as "too deep for words." In the scene just described we never learn where his fancy or his dreams took him as he lay by his fire.

The commercial standards of the mass-consumption magazine market were no doubt partly responsible for restricting Mills's deeper exploration of ideas. Defined as a writer by his own mission to bring nature to the masses, Mills thought and saw like a common man, though indeed a common man given energy and alertness by the outdoors. By omitting his deeper identity, Mills excelled in expressing the universal appeal of nature. He experienced more than the ordinary man but provided the assurance that nature's poetry is there for all to discover. He believed as Muir did that if he led people to nature, the trees and rocks and animals would speak for themselves. "My books . . . are only forewords to the great book, and that is Nature herself," he told Philip Ashton Rollins four weeks before he died.[14] Mills's books said what he wanted to say about nature and perhaps all he believed it was possible to say. With his first book he found his style and his voice, and he maintained both throughout his career, with some evolution toward a more strictly graphic portrayal of natural history and the inclusion of his educational ideas.

Virtually all of Mills's critics agree that what his writing lacks in depth and subtlety it gains in enthusiasm, wealth of material, and frank simplicity.[15] And to the extent that problems in his time anticipated problems in all ages, his writing achieved timeless importance. The Enos Mills that was loved by his own generation speaks just as compellingly to ours as we anguish over the fate of the planet:

> How different our history had this wooded and beautiful world been treeless and lonely! Groves stand peaceful and prominent on every hill, in every dale of history that encourages or inspires. If we should lose the hospitality of the trees and the friendship of the forest, our race too would be lost, and the desert's pale, sad sky would come to hover above a rounded, lifeless world. The trees are friends of mankind.[16]

The reissue of seven of Mills's books in recent years has helped to fill a gap on our nature shelves left by several decades of their absence. In them we can re-experience the longing and admiration that Mills's contemporaries — already nostalgic for the vanishing West — felt for the opportunities he had and the ways he used them. We can turn to his books to see what it was like when grizzlies and wolves still roamed the West, yet also learn that they and the forests they roamed faced destruction by a land- and resource-hungry civilization. Mills's greatest single contribution as a nature writer was consciousness raising: consciousness for the exciting place nature is, for the good it does, and for the need to preserve it. That contribution was not accidental. Mills was a proselytizer, aware historically of his role, a writer who used his pen to convey a message to

humanity and who consciously included children in his reading public in order to steer oncoming generations in the direction he
believed was necessary for national survival. Reading his books, we
are inspired by what he experienced, consoled by what he valued in
the outdoors, and determined through his example to put nature
back into our lives. We are interested to see what a man who lived so
abundantly still needed to imagine. And we have no difficulty granting that his importance transcends his faults. Mills's books have a
place in the records of literary history because they help to show the
plenitude of wild nature and the American West as literary
resources; and in the records of social history because they show and
helped shape a stage in our culture. Prominently recognized in Paul
Brooks's 1980 *Speaking for Nature,* Mills was one of the literary
naturalists in the distinguished line from Henry Thoreau forward
who — to repeat an accolade cited earlier — "enlarged our understanding of the natural world and strengthened our sense of kinship
with it." Perhaps Mills's greatest acknowledgment from the literary
world came from the famous English novelist and poet Thomas
Hardy. Probably acquainted with Mills only through his books, the
eighty-two-year-old Hardy wrote when Mills died, "It is as if a
mountain peak had sunk below the horizon."[17]

When Mills told Philip Ashton Rollins that his books were only
forewords to nature's own book, he was probably speaking from
both modesty and genuine conviction. Writers are often the first to
remind us that books are only approximations to life, and John
Muir, Mills no doubt knew, believed that "one day's exposure to
mountains is better than cartloads of books." Even the great and
learned Darwin, for Mills the most influential man of the nineteenth-century, was, he said, "anything but a book-man," and Louis
Agassiz had said tersely, "Study nature, not books." Getting people
outdoors was Mills's consistent and most passionate goal in his writing, lecturing, innkeeping, and park promotion. If he succeeded in
doing that, he told Rollins shortly before he died — perhaps evaluat-
ing his life under a premonition of death — "I won't have lived in
vain." The greatest stimulus to getting people outdoors was nature
guiding, which Mills hoped would become available to people across
the country in national, state, and city parks, and wherever, in fact,
there was a bit of nature to see and experience. The natural extension of Mills's Trail School at Longs Peak Inn, the nature guiding

profession would awaken the outdoor instinct latent in people of all ages, and promote the "right use of leisure time"; that, he said, is how "people are made and nations perpetuated." Though Mills's writing reached his public effectively with all his important messages, he appears to have seen nature guiding as the primary art to which writing was subordinate.

A central inspiration for Mills's ideas on nature guiding was Liberty Hyde Bailey's 1903 *The Nature-Study Idea*. Bailey was a Cornell horticulturalist best remembered today for his book *The Holy Earth*, a pioneering work in environmental ethics. *The Nature-Study Idea* appeared at a strategic time to help Mills give definite shape to the experience he wanted his inn guests to have, including the children in his Trail School. He had already learned, as he gradually added nature lore to his guided peak ascents, to present information in a way that stimulated curiosity and interest. Bailey reinforced his emergent axiom that the guide's job is to help people to look for themselves, to draw their own conclusions from what they see, and to discover relationships rather than isolated facts. The guide must of course have a grasp of relevant technical and popular literature, but does not need to be encyclopedic and should never bookishly propound formal knowledge. For Bailey, "a partial view, if truthful, is worth more than a complete course, if lifeless."[18] Bailey appealed to Mills in prescribing the approach of the artist and poet — experiencing not through "mere knowledge or by analysis," and "in moods, not in details." By the time Mills began using the phrase "the poetic interpretation of nature," he could confidently state that Bailey recommended it too. Stressing the artistic character of guiding, Mills said that it was "more inspirational than informational." And paraphrasing Robert Louis Stevenson, he said that the "essence of nature guiding is to travel gracefully rather than to arrive."

Representing nature biographically, a useful and scientifically acceptable device for his writing, was even more useful for nature guiding. While encouraging people to use their own eyes and ears, the guide could tell the stories of plants and animals, individual stones, a whole canyon, or even a handful of soil — showing that each had a "story stranger than any produced in fairy land." The guide could even speak *auto*biographically for nature, giving first-person renditions of "My life, or How I Came to Be Where I Am and What I Am." In this way, he said, "each plant and animal gave its adventures, its customs, its home territory, its climatic zone, and

Enos Mills, outdoor teacher. *Courtesy, Enos Mills Cabin Collection.*

all the endless and insistent play of the radical and romantic forces of evolution, environment, and ecology." Confirming what is evident in the conversational tone of much of his writing, Mills noted that "what the guide says is essentially nature literature."[19]

It is not surprising that Muir and Burroughs were also among the models for Mills's ideas of nature guiding. Neither conceived of guiding as a formal profession, but both were prototypes of inspirational guides leading people through the outdoors, "frequently . . . stop[ping] to tell the life story of a tree, to describe the manners and customs of a flower." On Sierra Club outings, Mills said, "Muir was closely followed by everyone who could get near."[20] The format of those outings — begun in 1901 — was no doubt an important model for Mills, and as we noted earlier, perhaps helped to define some of the tone he set for Longs Peak Inn generally.

Mills's nature guide was the direct antecedent of today's ranger-naturalist in national parks and the more generic category of outdoor interpreters in other kinds of parks, public and private camps, schools, and in many municipal outdoor recreation departments. Just as he sought to make his Trail School an experiment in alternative education, Mills saw nature guiding as "one of the forces moving for the newer education and for the ideal of internationalism."[21] Because Mills was one of many contributing to the great flood of writing on nature education in the Progressive Era, we cannot attest with certainty to the originality of his ideas. If he was a part of a larger movement rather than an original theorist, he nevertheless deserves historical recognition for having formulated, tested, and published explicit criteria for what nature guiding should be, well before guiding existed in the national parks. He had personally trained nature guides at Longs Peak Inn, spelled out the requisite personal and professional qualifications, and promoted nature guiding as a new profession with important career opportunities for both men and women. Tom Danton, a National Park Service trainer of nature guides — now called "interpreters" — states unequivocally that Mills "founded the profession." James R. Fazio was perhaps the first to give modern recognition to both Mills and Bailey as pioneers of environmental interpretation in a tribute linking them to themes that re-emerged following the 1970 Earth Day. Both men were, he said, "thought leaders" of their own time whose messages and methods richly deserve rediscovery today.[22]

Mills's half dozen principal essays on nature guiding are available to modern readers under one cover in the augmented 1990 reissue of Adventures of a Nature Guide, with a foreword by Danton and further commentary by Enos Mills's grandson Michael Kiley. The first of Mills's essays appeared in the Saturday Evening Post in 1916, the second in Your National Parks in 1917, and the rest in Adventures (1920) and Waiting in the Wilderness (1922). Those in print by 1920 provided a practically tested set of guidelines on nature guiding available to the Park Service by the time it began to implement guided nature tours that same year. Mills was as qualified as anyone to head a pilot program and might easily have been the one chosen to, had his relationship with the Park Service remained cordial. Mather, eager to get nature excursions going in the parks, knew of Mills's expertise and had called him a top authority on the subject at the 1917 National Parks Conference. But with Mills now his bitter antagonist — though not necessarily for that reason — he chose two scientists, Harold Bryant and Loye Miller, to move a program they had begun at Lake Tahoe to Yosemite in 1920. Bryant adopted Mills's term "nature guiding" and acknowledged his debt to Mills in a later pamphlet. He went on to found the famous Yosemite

The modern profession of interpretation continues to pay tribute to methods Mills tested and developed before 1920. *NPS photo.*

School of Field Natural History in 1925 and became the first head of the NPS Education Division in 1930, earning a place in history easily imaginable for Mills had his destiny been only slightly different.[23]

Mills's criteria for a fully professional nature guide give us another glimpse of how he viewed himself and his own professional attainment. The guide, he said, must be a person of "the highest type of culture and refinement," as professionally qualified as an author, lawyer, engineer, doctor, or editor. As a naturalist, he must be a "master of his own locality," and possess a general knowledge "almost as universal as Nature herself." He must be able to "explain miles of geography, talk botany, quote poetry, and . . . give intelligent answers to unintelligible questions." He must be an artist, whose chief ability is to incite interest in others. He must be a "leader rather than a teacher," a "master of the art of suggestion," and a speaker able to address people individually or in groups, in the field or the lecture hall. He must be able to write so that "his ideas will be read by thousands." On the trail the guide requires courage, firmness, good humor, and tact. He must master what we call today "people skills," keeping his party together and focused, dealing with disruptive personalities, and occasionally arbitrating disputes. He must have extraordinary versatility, functioning at times as an "athletic instructor, pack animal, photographer, counselor, physician, and clown." The guide must, in short, "play a big game," managing his party so gracefully that even his occasional use of "iron-hand" discipline is scarcely noticed. We can see in Mills's job description a confident declaration that as a self-made man he had arrived, creating and occupying a profession as prestigious as those traditionally valued in our society. But if Mills defined the profession in his own image, he did not use it for self-advertisement. In his essays on nature guiding we see more than anywhere else in his writing a self-transcending dedication to his cause.

Shep Husted, on whom Edna Ferber lavished high praise, was the finest product of Mills's guide training at Longs Peak Inn. But women, he stressed repeatedly, should have equal entry to the new profession and were "likely to set a new and higher standard for the men to follow." He said that to the Park Service bigwigs at the 1917 conference and throughout his essays on nature guiding. When the Burnell sisters — no doubt his favorite protégées — were licensed as nature guides in RMNP during the summer of 1917, they became, according to Danton, "the first official interpreters in any national park." Pleased with the program's success, Superintendent Way — still on friendly terms with Mills — said it filled a "long-felt want." Woman guides, trained by Enos Mills, can thus be said to have helped lead the way in Park Service interpretation, and within their more limited scope, to have predated Bryant's and Miller's experiments in Yosemite by three years.[24]

If that fact has gotten lost in the intervening seventy-five years, it is partly because nature-related activities took many forms in and around the parks at about the same time. Rangers were sometimes assigned to do educational work along with other tasks. Some produced interpretive handouts or worked on museums and exhibits without necessarily leading outdoor tours. Including education in its 1918 twenty-three-point mandate, the Park Service began to hire local people as seasonal guides without making them staff members — as they did the Burnell sisters. They brought in experts for short-term series of lectures with or without guided excursions, as they did at Yosemite through the University of California extension division. Private hotels and in-park concessions often hired naturalists to lead nature tours, while rangers often gave talks outside the parks in hotels and campgrounds. The same year that Bryant and Miller began the Free Nature Guiding Service in Yosemite, Yellowstone Park created the position of park naturalist and hired the very able Milton D. Skinner away from one of the concessions. Isobel Bassett Wasson, hired at Yellowstone to do interpretive work that same summer, was one of the first female rangers in the Park Service. In RMNP the first official naturalist was J. M. Johnson in 1923 and the first "ranger-naturalist" was Dr. Margaret Fuller Boos in 1928.

By the time Mills's final essays on nature guiding appeared in print he was locked in battle with the Park Service and believed that both park monopolies and "insidious enemy propaganda" were working to keep people away from nature. Nature guiding appears to have been the last refuge of his idealism, his last hope for saving the parks and the people's right to use them. In an undated but evidently very late letter, he wrote his friend Fred Holmes, "I feel that nature guiding is the one thing that will arouse interest in our outdoors and cause the parks to be used . . . and properly managed by the public."[25] Exactly what political process he hoped would mobilize the public, enlightened by nature guiding, to break the stranglehold of the monopolies, he did not — and no doubt could not — say. One of the final ironies in his life was that Superintendent Roger Toll, his last and unyielding adversary in the monopoly battle, was at the same time an enthusiastic supporter of nature programs — as was indeed Mather himself, whom Mills had condemned as a wicked dictator. The 1922 National Parks Conference gave nature interpretation a significant boost and was the topic of greatest interest to the assembled superintendents. We can wonder whether one of Mills's last thoughts was that the Park Service was doing some things right among the many things he believed it was doing wrong.

Nature guiding under its later title "interpretation" has continued to be a successful and central part of the Park Service agenda, with demand often exceeding resources. The NPS Education Division, now also renamed the Interpretation Division, has continued to follow guidelines closely resembling those of Mills and Bailey. One of the most vigorous champions of interpretation in the post–World War II era was Freeman Tilden, for many years a consultant to the Park Service and the author of several books on parks and one on

ENOS MILLS

interpretation. According to Danton, Mills's "general principles of interpretation [were] amazingly similar to the ones Tilden would 'discover' forty years later." Indeed, Tilden's definition of interpretation could have come straight from Mills's pen. It is, Tilden said, "an educational activity which aims to reveal meanings and relationships through the use of original objects, by firsthand experience, and by illustrative media, rather than simply to communicate factual information. [It is] the revelation of a larger truth that lies behind any statement of fact. [Its goal] is not instruction, but provocation."[26]

An Enos Mills centennial, from May to September 1985 (the one hundredth birthday of Mills's homestead cabin) coincided with an "Enos Mills Recognition Year," designated by Estes Park Mayor Bernie Dannels. The series of programs culminated in two "Enos Mills celebration days" on September 21 and 22 (the anniversary of Mills's death) designated by proclamation of Colorado Governor Richard D. Lamm. The theme of the events was the "Enos Mills ethic," a combination of his conservation, park advocacy, and outdoor educational ideas. During the commemorative period, the Estes Park *Trail Gazette* featured a series of "Enos Mills Centennial Notes," in which local writers discussed those ideas and reflected on Mills's life and achievements. Prominently represented in the centennial events were Mills's daughter, Enda Mills Kiley, her husband, Robert Kiley, and their grown children, all ardent Mills aficionados. Since 1965 the Kiley family has operated the Enos Mills homestead cabin as a museum and starting point for guided nature tours, which Enda first learned to conduct as a girl at Longs Peak Inn in the tradition continued by her mother and her aunt Bessie. For nearly twenty years, elementary school children from dozens of Colorado schools as well as many other groups and individuals of all ages have visited the cabin site to explore the meaning of Mills's teachings in his own setting directly from Enda and other family members. The homestead cabin was the site of many of the centennial events, including a repeat presentation of a commemorative award in Mills's name by the national Association of Interpretive Naturalists (AIN). Tim Merriman, AIN president and founder of an Enos Mills Guides Program, believes that Mills "provided leadership and inspiration when no one else would have considered it, . . . [and] that all who provide leadership in our contemporary organizations should remember his early work and its value in creating a future for parks and interpretation and the joy it brings."[27]

We can conclude that time has strengthened Mills's validity as an outdoor theorist. Estes-area educator Mike Donahue sees him "surfacing as the nature educator that he strived to be . . . [and as] a tremendous vehicle through which educators today can stimulate an interest and explore nature as part of the classroom curriculum." Glen Kaye, chief naturalist at RMNP during the Mills centennial, noted that Mills's "understanding of the nature of learning . . . has been confirmed by two generations of psychologists and educators."[28] Mills's legacy as an outdoor educator in fact found expression in his own lifetime when Elizabeth Burnell took it into the Los Angeles schools as Assistant Supervisor of Nature Study, starting in 1918. Though the nature-study movement faltered generally in the 1920s, Mills resurfaced in 1930, when Houghton Mifflin issued a collection of his animal stories with teaching supplements for classroom activities keyed to each story. The supplements, together with a highly appreciative account of Mills's life, were supplied by F. W. Rawcliffe, an Illinois educator. In that same year Esther Burnell Mills donated a set of Enos's books to the RMNP library, in at least a partial thawing of relations with the park following final settlement of the monopoly controversy. Awareness of Mills's life was revived again with the publication of *Enos Mills of the Rockies* by the Houghton Mifflin Junior Literary Guild in 1935, with an endorsement by Eleanor Roosevelt. Books on national parks in the prewar era continued to feature Mills as an inspirational outdoor figure.

The 1985 centennial events revealed a strong desire to reclaim Mills as a regional hero free from the opprobrium of past quarrels. The declaration of one writer, "Colorado needs its own hero," was not unlike the sentiment of Judge Ben Lindsey, who at the time of Mills's death called for men's and women's organizations and school boards across the country to declare an annual Enos Mills day. The "Enos Mills ethic" continues to reach children as a supplement to the curriculum in several Colorado school districts. Seminars in Park Service interpretation given by Danton and others are putting Mills's methods in the repertories of a new generation of interpreters whose assignments are taking them throughout the park system and to invited seminars in the parks of other countries. Assisting them is a new interpreters' guide book (1992) from a university group in Wisconsin that directly acknowledges its debt to Mills and to Freeman

Tilden.[29] National recognition of Mills by the interpretive profession thus appears to be growing as the profession itself grows (the AIN's successor organization, the National Association for Interpretation, now has 3,100 members), bringing Mills increasingly into focus as one of the important pioneers of outdoor education.

CHAPTER 23

Enos Mills in the Stream of Twentieth-Century Conservation

Enos Mills's birthdate, to the very day one century before the first Earth Day on April 22, 1970, is a coincidence enriched by the substance of his own life and work. Mills saw and stated the case not just for preserving the West or the United States, but the earth as a whole. He warned that any civilization that abuses its natural heritage is bound to perish. And his vision of a treeless planet, lifeless under a "pale, sad sky," portrays a scale of tragedy equal to today's worldwide deforestation and its contribution to the risk of irreversible global warming. Convinced that trees are indispensable friends of mankind, Mills belongs as much to the spirit of Earth Day in our time as he did to the spirit of Arbor Day in his own time. He expressed his global conscience symbolically through his hope that sometime all nations will be united under the common flag of a living tree. In the post–Cold War competition for "new world orders," the most essential, according to many, is international cooperation to stop the devastation of the planet's life-support systems. That task, says Lester R. Brown of the Worldwatch Institute, could unite all countries around a common theme for the first time since the birth of the nation state. And Mills's once quaint notion of a universal tree-flag might fittingly symbolize the inseparable destinies of humanity and nature.

If Muir planted the seed of environmental consciousness in his young admirer, germination took time and did not yield a replica of Muir's thought. For a dozen years after Mills met Muir he worked for a mining conglomerate that battered the earth as few in the history of this country have. Like those who work today in environmentally destructive occupations, Mills did not see his own role in that destruction. He was a wage-earning employee beholden to his company for his job and to his union for the amount he earned. Neither taught him to think environmentally, and doing so themselves remains even today a scarcely begun task of both industry and organized labor. Though an activist and reformer by nature, Mills needed more than a decade after he met Muir to prepare for public life — to learn about the outdoors firsthand, to discover what he could and could not learn from books, to immerse himself in remote solitude and the practical affairs of the West, and to form his opinions about right, wrong, justice, equality, and American democracy. In his crucible of self-learning, he mixed the wild and the civilized, seeing in nature both touches of humanity and lessons for humanity's betterment. With that came a lasting duality in his view of the earth's utility: one practical and one that "engenders high ideals." Much of his conservation career would be a quest to make society honor both.

Mills became actively and officially a "conservationist" as the state's snow observer when he systematically reported on Colorado's axed and burned forests. Then, if not earlier, he concluded that the country's reckless waste of its forests needed federal action to be stopped. In Chapter 13 we examined nearly a dozen reasons why Mills followed Pinchot into federal forestry rather than Muir into scenic preservation during the Theodore Roosevelt presidency. He embraced Progressive conservation as the right thing at the right time and the Forest Service as the agency that correctly represented the people and the nation's forests against the larger forces of exploitation. But when he realized that federally managed forestry was itself "plainly and severely a business proposition," he foresaw the dominant direction of forestry through the rest of this century. The renunciation of the Forest Service by one of its loyal spokesmen was an early indicator that something was wrong with the new agency in charge of the nation's forests and is as interesting historically as Muir's more sophisticated refusal to back it in the first place.

Mills's case against the Forest Service was colored by his own volatile temper, by the narrower issue of its opposition to his park plans, and by its apparent reprisals against his own property and business. But his condemnation of the agency as a greed-driven political machine capable of deceit and hypocrisy is little different from the condemnation by today's environmental community. Profound agency misconduct — and outright lawlessness — have been widely documented and helped Congress to pass the 1976 Forest

Management Act to correct decades of prodevelopment bias that had increasingly degraded the nation's forest. If anything, however, abuses worsened during the 1980s, according to sworn testimony in early 1992 by a thirty-three-year veteran of law enforcement. John McCormick, who worked for the Forest Service for fifteen years and for his last two years headed the agency's own whistleblower program, testified before the House Civil Service Subcommittee in January 1992 that the Forest Service has repeatedly violated environmental laws, manipulated scientific evidence to benefit the timber industry, and punished employees who raised objections. "The agency has become comfortable with lying to the public, ignoring long-festering problems, and serving the timber industry as government agents of environmental destruction rather than environmental protection," he said.[1]

With forestry practices worldwide learning from and mirroring those in the United States, "cut-and-run" methods to mine quick, one-time bonanzas of timber are rampant. In the twenty years following Earth Day 1970, the world's forests shrank by an area as large as the whole United States east of the Mississippi River; and deserts, many in the wake of deforestation, grew by an amount equal to all land under cultivation in China. Scientific forestry, born in Mills's generation to rescue forests under siege, has, through mismanagement, corruption, and greed, made forest destruction one of the most severe of all global problems.

Growing public outrage and impulses from within the forestry profession itself — especially the rapidly expanding Association of Forest Service Employees for Environmental Ethics (AFSEEE) — are beginning to demand changes. A new approach to forestry now advocated by the alternative wing of the forestry profession seeks not merely to enforce sustained yield cutting (now violated in most national forests) but to sustain the integrity of whole forest ecosystems. "Sustainable forestry" and "ecosystem management" are forms of holistic resource management with philosophical roots in the ideas of Aldo Leopold who, as a young forester in the 1920s, quickly became disgusted with what was called scientific forestry. He continued to believe that forests must be managed scientifically, but departed from Pinchot's legacy in believing that the guiding science should be ecology rather than economics.[2]

It is reasonable to ask as we review Mills's place in conservation history what he might have contributed to the background for today's emerging new forestry. As a self-taught naturalist and forest expert, he was well qualified to investigate how the nation's forests could provide needed commodities without themselves being seriously degraded. That promise was in fact his assumption when he advertised the forests as "a thing of beauty and profit" while an official spokesman for the Roosevelt administration. There is indeed much in his understanding of the forest that provides inspiration for a biologically based and socially responsible forest ethic. He clearly saw the forest as a community of interrelated species and processes whose health depends on the health of each of its parts. His commentary on forest insects and insect predation by birds, on seed dispersal by small mammals, on the value of dead trees and logs to the health of the forest, on the natural ecology of fire — to the extent he understood it — and much else in his writing can be seen as earlier versions of principles better known today. He saw without today's terminology that biodiversity in the forest is crucial to its long-term health.

Mills also showed convincingly that healthy forests are necessary for healthy societies, providing values up the scale from commodity to amenity to spiritual, in addition to what we call today their crucial "ecological services" of watershed and soil protection, flood control, climate stabilization, and air improvement. His advice to farmers to plant up to 40 percent of their land in trees to shield plowed fields from wind, to stabilize temperature and humidity, to provide bird habitat and hence to help control insects, states principles compatible with today's "sustainable agriculture," a sister science to sustainable forestry. At its best, Mills's conservation message spanned the landscape from forest to farm to inner-city parks. Across that landscape not just trees, but also water, soils, air, other plants, animals, and humans have a right and a need to prosper. The best sense of Mills's forestry suggests what Wendell Berry has articulated for agriculture: that it is more a matter of culture than of mere technique.

As soon as he broke with the Forest Service, Mills denounced its precepts as "radically utilitarian" and no better than "raising hogs for slaughter." We cannot help wondering how carefully he had examined the practices he praised as the agency's official spokesman. Focusing more and more on the agency's opposition to national parks, Mills lost the inclination and the opportunity to explore what practical reforms could make forestry do what he once thought it could. He effectively abandoned the subject of forestry in his later years, convinced that it is an ugly but vaguely necessary business. He thus reached the emotional impasse common to many environmentalists today, not really wanting any trees cut at all. Suffering one of his great philosophical disappointments in discovering the agency's failure to mature into a custodian for the broader values of the forest he had preached as its public voice, Mills turned to the national parks for the "noble profession" he craved and believed the nation needed.

Mills's role as a park promoter locates him most easily in conservation history, and in his own mind must have linked him permanently to John Muir, his "Nestor of National Parks." Parks gave Mills a well-placed axis on which to function between the polarities of "use" and "preservation." Making preservation itself useful to the nation, parks were a "profitable investment" that made the "best economic use of the territory," and "paid large dividends in humanity," with each citizen a "stockholder."[3] Mills's rhetorical fondness for commercial metaphors served him well in selling intangible values to a mass culture conditioned by monetary norms. Mills's park advocacy was exuberant often to the point of hyperbole. Though never less than sincere, he tended to globalize his claims for parks to a virtual panacea for all social ills. To an extent we can say that Mills's park advocacy combined Progressive reformism with the tradition of western boosterism, which since territorial days had promoted settlement, health cures, and See America First vacation packages. But he deepened that genre with genuinely felt emotion and firsthand authority. Mills deserves lasting stature as a spokesman for the young park movement and remains an interesting example of an early environmentalist in a part of the country that still audaciously proclaimed its prodevelopment mentality.

We must say at the same time that although park advocacy was an important and distinctive part of Mills's career, it did not represent a philosophical advance over the forestry movement he abandoned. Parks did not liberate him from the Progressive mindset of utility and efficiency or bring him any closer to a conception of humanity's broader relationship with nature. They in fact represented a narrower spectrum of values than the forests he had interpreted as an integral part of America's functional and psychological landscape. Parks were scenic cameos, places to visit rather than to live. They provided a place for recreation and its deeper incarnation, "re-creation," but were not a promising arena in which Mills could explore basic issues of how human and nonhuman values can be balanced. His own reverence for the rights of nature lacked adequate voice in his park vision to compete with social utility. "The supreme triumph of parks is humanity," he declared; and it was to humanity rather than to nature that he believed John Muir's park advocacy rendered "a vast and heroic service."

Mills's national park vision reflected many of the shortcomings of the early park movement generally. His important and relatively late essay "Why We Need National Parks" focuses almost solely on parks as a social institution. Neither it nor its companion essay "Wildlife in National Parks" explores the conditions the parks must meet to provide truly safe and ecologically durable havens for all park species. Mills was content with the protection parks provided against hunting, and called each park a "wildlife paradise where the animals are safe, free from the fear of being killed by man." Predators such as lions, lynxes, and "problem" bears were, however, not safe from the government's predator control program, which lasted until the 1930s and brought no objection from Mills or other park promoters. And, because only part of their year-round range was protected, animals were easy prey for hunters' rifles in their seasons outside the parks. Though Mills favored enlargement of many existing parks, none of his recommendations were based on biological considerations. Had he turned his attention to that subject, however, it might have been Mills the naturalist rather than a report eleven years after his death that announced the impossibility of protecting animals in areas so small that they live there only a portion of the year.[4]

Park advocates now see the need to reshape and enlarge the parks to manage them as complete biological units but know that doing so after the fact will be virtually impossible. Political compromises vastly reduced proposed park boundaries in the first place, leaving eligible only land not useful for other commercial purposes. That mood still dominates Congress and leaves parks as isolated monuments. The spread of the national park idea to over 1,400 parks in about 125 countries by the 1990s — Mills's fondest dream come true — shows the same pattern: They are often on marginal land not suitable for other commercial development; they were established primarily for scenery and tourist development rather than for ecological preservation; and they are not, therefore, able to protect representative examples of the world's flora and fauna. Increased size, furthermore, would not, according to some critics, necessarily solve the parks' problems. Writing on problems of ecological decline in RMNP, Karl Hess, Jr., cites institutional problems inherent in governmental administration so serious as to suggest removal of the park from the park system to an independent conservation trust. Tourism and nearby urban expansion are less damaging to the park's ecology, Hess states, than damage to vegetation by overpopulated elk herds and the even more pervasive destruction of the plant community and landscape diversity through fire suppression.[5]

Mills was also typical of the early pro-park coalition in his advocacy of mass visitation and of facilities to "get the scenery ready" for a high-volume tourist industry. He — like most others — neglected virtually any reflection on what the impact of the millions he summoned to the parks (a staggering 265 million by 1990) would have on the park experience and on the environments the parks were established to protect. The squalor of today's overcrowded parks and commercial facilities devalues Mills's optimistic promises that "within national parks is room — glorious room — room in which to find ourselves, in which to think and hope, to dream and plan, to rest and resolve." And the impact of mass visitation on the parks' natural systems becomes graver each year, contributing, according to one expert, "to their progressive ecological demise."[6]

Overuse and overdevelopment in national parks are in part the consequences of Mather's original business rationale, which placed a premium on mass visitation to benefit concessioners. Now, critics say, concessions wield power over park management to encourage visitation at the expense of preservation. Wanting continued business growth, they exert constant pressure to attract and hold the disinterested visitor. The result, says Alfred Runte, is that the parks are being not so much "loved to death" as "mismanaged to death." Mills's fear that concessions would acquire enough influence to dictate park policy was to a good degree prophetic, though the consequence he feared was injustice to "the people" and to small entrepreneurs rather than deterioration of parklands. His crusade against concession policy was politically inconclusive but is historically significant as one of the first challenges to a system that has plagued the parks throughout their history. Mills would be sad but not surprised to learn that the Concession Policy Act of 1965 further strengthened the power of concessions; that some now belong to giant conglomerates with powerful political ties; and that details about how concessions operate remain today, as he charged they were in 1919, hidden from the public view. "The biggest secret in the national park system," states a 1991 news report, "is how much profits concessionaires make from selling goods and services to 265 million visitors a year." In 1991, after a thirteen-month legal battle, the government agreed to keep those figures secret from both the public and prospective competitive bidders.[7]

Mills's failure to anticipate problems of overuse can be traced to causes mostly unrelated to business. First was his attempt to promote park use at a time when the fledgling system needed to prove its worth by attracting increasing numbers of visitors. His promotional zeal sacrificed long-term vision to political expediency, but was entirely typical of the young park movement. Second, Mills appeared to take on faith the power of the Park Service's mandate to make parks available to increasing numbers of people while maintaining their quality indefinitely. He did not anticipate the difficulty of applying this wrenchingly paradoxical principle; nor did he foresee which way park managers would lean in the face of strong and immediate pressures. A third factor was Mills's remarkable tolerance for people despite his sometimes crusty temperament in private dealings. As we have seen in several contexts, Mills *was* a man of the masses. He glamorized throngs of tourists as a good thing in their own right — "a world's fair of humanity" cheerfully exchanging ideas and creating new bonds of friendship in a classless and egalitarian setting. This was, furthermore, not necessarily a threat to wildlife, which, "hoping and waiting" for human acquaintance, could exercise its natural inclination to be tame and familiar. Even the grizzly, today's archetypal symbol of the wilderness, would be "happily accessible and friendly again" in national parks.

Mills's idealism about large numbers of people extended to the facilities needed to accommodate them. He believed, as we saw earlier, that tastefully designed lodges and "artistically" laid out roads could actually enhance the scenery, and both increased the parks' popularity. Mills's long-standing attachment to "good roads" as a signature of progress in the West, and his crusade to wrestle park roads away from the demons of monopoly, left him no room to consider discouraging motorized travel in parks altogether. Though he knew that almost none of the things he wanted parks to do for people can take place inside vehicles, he considered road development so essential that he once declared scenery "not usable" without it. Mills was again typical of most early park preservationists who saw that auto accessibility increased middle-class support for the park idea. By the 1930s, as George Horace Lorimer began complaining that autos were spoiling the parks, J. Horace McFarland, who personally disliked them as well, assured him that they were an absolutely necessary compromise. The growth of the park system, simultaneously with the rise of the automobile to its dominant place in American culture, virtually ensured that the parks would cater to a largely motorized public for whom, said Aldo Leopold ruefully, "recreation is mileage." By the midfifties 98 to 99 percent of all park visitors entered in private vehicles, and warnings by a few during Mills's time about the havoc they would wreak had become painfully confirmed. Though Mills's ideas on nature guiding and outdoor education are inseparable from his park vision and can be seen as his most valuable contribution to it, he missed the opportunity to help the Park Service establish them as the dominant feature of the park experience. In RMNP today, only 1 percent of the 2.9 million annual visitors attend ranger walks or campfire programs.

During the 1920s, when park preservationists began seeking with only limited success to give biological protection equal status with public use, the ideas of roadless areas and wilderness protection were gaining fragile footholds in the rival national forests. In the second year of Mills's battle with the Park Service over the transportation concession, Arthur H. Carhart, a Forest Service recreation engineer in nearby Denver, carefully studied and then recommended against agency plans to open Trapper's Lake in western Colorado to an encircling road and waterfront development. Approval of his recommendation in 1920 established the country's first roadless area and helped inspire Leopold, who had joined the Forest Service the year Mills left it, to develop his germinating ideas about wilderness. Mills, still a mortal enemy of the Forest Service, appears not to have known or shared ideas with these two pioneers of the American wilderness movement. Nor, despite his great admiration for Liberty Hyde Bailey, did he publicly state any familiarity with Bailey's 1915 *The Holy Earth,* which influenced Leopold's developing notion of "ecological conscience."

If Mills had lived through the twenties and into the thirties, he would have been astonished but probably still distrustful of the Forest

Service's blossoming emphasis on recreation as a major forest "product" — an emphasis that Horace Albright had condemned as a crude
ploy to eliminate the Park Service. Herbert Wheeler, Mills's old
enemy from the RMNP campaign, had begun closing some national
forest areas to grazing because of their greater recreational value.
Another forest administrator could have taken words from Mills
himself in denying a sawmill permit because the "paltry few dollars"
it would earn did not compare with the "needs for beauty and future
generations." Some forest supervisors waxed downright evangelical
in offering their forests as "scenic empires . . . for the contentment
and health" of the "weary and broken down" — an obvious parrot-
ing of national park rhetoric. Mills's own friend Arthur Chapman
wrote in 1924 that the national forests were now recreational mec-
cas much like national parks.

Even had Mills lived, he might not have noticed the at first
barely perceptible wilderness theme creeping into all of this. Wilderness was not mentioned at a 1924 conference on outdoor recreation
convened by President Coolidge, the same year that Leopold succeeded in getting half a million acres reserved as wilderness in New
Mexico's Gila National Forest. Carhart left the Forest Service in
1923 to pursue a writing career and wrote about gardening and
travel more than about wilderness. His articles in 1923 and 1924
praising scenic mountain roads ("timber-line turnpikes") gave no
hint that the same man had brought about the nation's first roadless
designation. One article in fact praised plans for a road to the edge
of Colorado's largest glacier, where the traveler would be able to
"step out of the machine and in a stride or two stand on age-old
ice."[8] Wilderness was, in short, still only a minor aspect of "recreation," and Leopold's exploratory article on the subject in a 1921
issue of *The Journal of Forestry* stated frankly that most people
wanted mechanized access to their recreation grounds. Would Mills
have agreed with him that some of the rapidly vanishing wilderness
should nevertheless be preserved for those who find their essential
happiness there? By the end of the twenties wilderness was at last
becoming a prominent theme and Leopold its leading voice. Writers
well known to Mills, such as John C. Van Dyke and Emerson
Hough, chimed in their support. In 1933 Bob Marshall (not the
same as Robert B. Marshall, whom Mills knew in the RMNP campaign) added a strong defense of wilderness in the recreation section
of the *National Plan for American Forestry,* and two years later

another Mills acquaintance, Robert Sterling Yard, became the first president of the Wilderness Society. Had Mills lived longer, he would clearly have had a new option to consider in the promotion of his own nature agenda for the country.

Mills's status as an actual precursor of the modern wilderness movement is ambiguous. His books, depicting solitary encounters with wildlife and the raw forces of nature, are books *about* the wilderness, par excellence. They inspire us to love and protect wilderness, and cause Mills frequently to be taken as a wilderness prophet despite the distinctly different character of his public advocacy. Because his notion of wilderness did not automatically exclude people or their works, he could advocate development in national parks, yet claim parks as "wilderness empires . . . snatched from leveling forces of development." And he could advocate mass visitation, yet assure his readers that parks would remain "forever wild, forever mysterious and primeval." Parks were for Mills the best and highest use of the land, and park advocacy the avant-garde of environmental thought.[9]

Socially, parks signified for Mills what wilderness signifies for many of its users today: places to recover our physical and mental health, to discover our deeper selves, to find our roots in nature, and to affirm that we are a nation not wholly consumed by materialism. A great deal of Mills's rhetoric defending national parks serves equally well to defend the "quality of life" values of wilderness and their importance as core national issues. Mills put his distinctive stamp on an important American tradition that began earlier and found both new dimensions and eloquent voice in such later writers as Aldo Leopold and Bob Marshall, the brothers Olaus and Adolph Murie, William O. Douglas, Howard Zahniser, Sigurd Olson, Harvey Broome, Wallace Stegner, David Brower, and others.

If park advocacy fails to address wilderness preservation per se, we must recognize that many of the limitations of national parks also afflict today's wilderness areas. Though wilderness comes packaged in more rhetoric about species and habitat preservation, selection criteria are in fact often more scenic than biological. Like parks, wilderness areas have failed by and large to preserve whole biological units, partly because they, too, are the "rock-and-ice" leftovers from larger proposals in which areas with extractable commodities are first disqualified. Most use of wilderness is strictly recreational and has resulted in similar problems of crowding and overuse. Fears of the wilderness being "loved to death" came swiftly on the heels of the Wilderness Act of 1964 and have precipitated often bitter debate within the environmental community about measures to limit use. Problems of bureaucratic administration also plague wilderness as they plague national parks. Mills's charge that the Forest Service "cannot be trusted with scenery" is by no means obsolete in view of the agency's often inbred antagonism to wilderness, its budgets heavily weighted to commodity extraction, instances of intentional road construction into pristine areas to prevent later wilderness designation, and revelations — more than once — that funds earmarked for wilderness have been secretly diverted to commercial timber sales.

Mills, for better or worse, accepted the passing of the frontier and the American wilderness as historical inevitabilities. He freely confessed that "the days of the wilderness are gone forever" while at the same time rejoicing in the remnants of "wilderness" preserved in national parks. We must not fail to remember that Mills was a part of the developing West and its robust ethic of "progress," yet that he differed from the predominant development mentality in seeing the West's scenery as the most important basis of its economic future. Not destined to be a prophet of wilderness as we now define it, Mills's perceived task at his moment in history was to protect nature in a way that made it universally available and "continuously productive both commercially and spiritually." Arguing for the economic value of high-quality environments both preceded his park advocacy and went beyond it to a general case for scenic preservation. His belief that a shift from consumptive to recreational uses was the West's natural destiny anticipated an environmentalist position popular today and gives him an interesting new relevance.

Echoing both the chronology and conclusions Mills recorded in his 1917 preface to *Your National Parks,* former Arizona governor and now U.S. Interior Secretary Bruce Babbitt noted in 1986 that "we must recognize the new reality that the highest and best, most productive use of western public lands will usually be for public purposes — watershed, wildlife and recreation." Today, recreation and tourism, profiting directly from high-quality environments, are steadily gaining importance in the economies of many western states and may be Colorado's leading industries by the end of the 1990s. A proposed 1984 Colorado Senate resolution acknowledged the link between preservation and recreation, declaring the state's high peaks, wilderness areas, streams, and fish and wildlife to be "natural recreational resources" whose "loss or degradation . . . could result in major economic losses to the state." Today the national forests within the state yield $4 billion in recreational benefits annually. Total tourism and travel expenditures exceed $5.6 billion and generate 54,000 jobs with an annual payroll of $1.4 billion. An earlier study, in 1971, had shown that with a visitor-to-area ratio equal to that of the Swiss Alps, Colorado could accommodate up to 75 million visitors a year.[10]

Mills's thumbnail calculations of the earning power of alpine scenery ("upward of ten thousand dollars to the square mile") versus the few dollars from cattle and sawmills that are "despoiling the Rocky Mountains" also have counterparts today. Economist Thomas M. Power, for example, compared Utah's mining and recreational economies in a study applicable to other resources and to much of the West generally. He found that in counties adjacent to wildlands, recreation, retirement, and "amenity-seeking immigrants offer much greater hope for ongoing economic development than wishful thinking about the recovery of the mineral extraction industries." Mining, subject to fits of boom and bust, is a shrinking part of the Utah economy and guarantees no reliable source of jobs or income. "The future of Utah lies elsewhere," Power concludes, "as Utah continues to develop into a sophisticated 'post-industrial' economy." Other studies have shown that proximity to parks and wilderness may be a major draw for new residents. In the 278 counties in thirty-eight states that contain wilderness, one study reports, average population growth in the 1970s was 31 percent, while growth in rural counties without wilderness averaged just 13 percent.[11]

Environmentalists of course pursue such arguments at no small risk. Quantifying intangible values is philosophically ambiguous and fails to challenge the materialistic bias of our culture. If beauty is secured on the marketplace with economic arguments, its defense can be overturned when new pressures for development reverse the cost-benefit assessment. We saw in Chapter 17 that Hetch Hetchy could not survive the contest of the "greatest good" when San Francisco needed water, even though that water was obtainable elsewhere. None of today's protected lands are entirely safe from the threat of similar invasions, and the guise of "national security" — as Mills's generation knew too — thrives especially in wartime and recessionary economies. It is invoked by today's well-funded "Wise-

Use" movement, which is calling for Congress to allow mining and oil exploration in all national parks, wildlife refuges, and wilderness areas, as well as logging of all old-growth forests, extensive off-road development, and a major weakening of the Endangered Species Act.

The "vast travel industry" that Mills predicted would be spawned by the West's scenery is itself a mixed blessing. "Tourism may not necessarily be the salvation of wildlands being destroyed by logging and other commodity industries," notes one expert.[12] Resorts and "exurbs" developed to create escape zones in scenic areas are in fact urbanizing those areas and making "preservation" the unwitting partner in rapid growth and development projects. In Colorado's mountains the results have often been reduced air and water quality; displacement of wildlife; sacrifice of animal travel routes and wetlands by ski area development; and pressure for increased motorized use of the backcountry. Tourism, furthermore, often fails to create true local economies or to foster any sense of belonging to and caring for the land. Most of the investment capital comes from distant, often multinational, sources whose influence threatens local control and takes profits out of the region. Many of the benefits of resort development are available only to a few at high prices, while many of the jobs are low-paying service jobs staffed by workers who must seek affordable housing elsewhere. Among rural residents reluctant to trade their traditional livelihoods and lifestyles for such a future, economic arguments for scenic preservation are neither popular nor likely to create a unified vision of the West's future. And many environmentalists who once pushed the "recreation-conservation connection," now find its consequences alarming.

Switzerland, where the earning power of scenery is institutionalized as a national asset, was Mills's most influential model for development and one with equally enthusiastic adherents today. Scenery prepared — as Mills said it should be — for access to masses of tourists has contributed vast wealth to the tiny alpine country without interruption from his time to ours. Advocates of Swiss-style development can probably claim Mills as one of their early spokesmen, just as some of the original developers of Aspen, Colorado, as a ski and vacation center claim him as a primary inspiration. Switzerland's efficient cog railroads and aerial lifts take people to spectacular places many could not reach on foot and are the key, some say, to allowing "vast throngs of people to use nature without damage."

And, using the term wilderness much as Mills did, the argument goes that "if Americans were permitted access to Wilderness areas [in this manner] we would create an avid generation of nature lovers."[13]

But even in postcard-perfect Switzerland, the environmental costs are at last becoming clear. By the early 1980s the Alps were experiencing what an alpine protective association called "development madness." Parking lots, aerial lifts, restaurants, and hotels were proliferating, and a construction boom was adding 50,000 new dwellings a year. Blasting and road building had become a growth industry in the neighboring Austrian Alps. And, according to one journalist, "eight glaciers had been offered up to mass tourism." Cog railroads and aerial lifts notwithstanding, hundreds of millions of visitors, supplied by Europe's high-density population, drive to the Alps each year, adding their exhaust gases to the fragile mountain environment. Alpine ground cover and mountain dairy pastures are reported to be under severe stress. Two-thirds of the country's trees, according to one writer, are under stress as well, and half the dairy farms are expected to be gone by the end of the century. In the Canadian Rockies, reports a writer from Alberta, "the development of scenic resources along the lines of the Swiss experience has made once peaceful valleys models of urban expansion into the wilderness. . . . The objective of Swiss-style recreational development is not the aesthetic welfare of people but rather to make a large profit. . . . Is the Swiss way the only way to deal with mountains, glaciers and wilderness?"[14]

The mad rush for recreational development came under criticism from Aldo Leopold nearly half a century ago when he called it a "self-destructive process of seeking but never quite finding, a major frustration of mechanized society." He contrasted the "rudimentary grades of outdoor recreation [that] consume their resource base" with "the only true development in . . . recreation resources . . . the development of the perceptive faculty," which he said can "grow at home as well as abroad" and can be exercised in places as small as a city weedlot. As a naturalist and nature guide, Mills clearly aspired to develop "perception." As a booster of parks and the vacation industry, he was more nearly a product of the "days of the elder Roosevelt," when, said Leopold, "recreation became a problem with a name." However persuasive the economic arguments, recreational development as usually practiced is far from sufficient as a land ethic. And as the West moves further toward a recreational

Mills talked nature wherever he went. At his left is New York Governor and later U.S. Secretary of State and Supreme Court Chief Justice Charles Evans Hughes. *Courtesy, Enos Mills Cabin Collection.*

economy, it will no doubt face value judgments more subtle than it has in deciding between the stark opposites of wilderness and resource extraction. Leopold's timeless dictum that "a thing is right when it tends to preserve the integrity, stability and beauty of the biotic community, . . . [and] wrong when it tends otherwise," will remain crucially relevant.[15]

We can record Mills historically as a transition figure in the maturing of preservation for largely human reasons to preservation for nature's own sake as well. Had he lived another decade or two, Mills could have unquestionably profited from an acquaintance with Leopold's developing ecological philosophy and with the important advances made in the science of ecology during the 1920s. Both could have helped to balance his social goals with a more biologically oriented conservation philosophy and to focus his in many ways already holistic knowledge of nature on the land-ethic question. Given his continued faith in the national park idea, a plausible place for him in the 1920s would have been with Yard and the National Parks Association, which strenuously opposed further commercialization. Were Mills alive today he might see the decline in the health of the national parks as a sign of declining environmental health generally and hence view parks as the best starting place to marshal society's cooperation in reversing the damage. Longtime park observer Michael Frome pursues that theme in his 1992 book *Regreening the National Parks,* noting in socially and politically relevant terms that Mills would applaud, "Considering that we need a revolution of ideas and ideals for all of society, the regreened national parks are marvelous places to begin. Every park is full of lessons to help in the transformation from the Age of Greed and Corruption to the Age of Caring and Integrity." Some of Frome's practical steps to begin that process in the parks consist of items we know Mills favored: reforming the Park Service itself and getting it out of the Department of Interior; reforming concession policy; involving the public in park planning and problem solving; increasing the use of parks for outdoor museums, classrooms, scientific laboratories, and as sources of artistic, literary, and spiritual inspiration. And, given today's conditions in the parks, Frome would probably have no trouble convincing Mills of the need to reduce automobile traffic, limit the number of visitors, and de-emphasize tourism.[16]

Some environmentalists now see the salvation of parks and wilderness not through further isolation to impregnable "fortresses" but as more flexible parts of the total ecological landscape — structured, buffered, and managed by local people directly concerned with their welfare. Biospheric reserves, surrounded by transition zones where people live and work in ways that do not disturb the core area, offer one example of "cooperation over expropriation." Another is the Montana-based Alliance for the Wild Rockies, which seeks to preserve five internationally significant biospheres by enlisting local citizens, Indian tribes, and some developmental interests along with traditional conservationists in a broad program of protective strategies that do not focus solely on wilderness. And long established but awaiting new appreciation is New York State's Adirondack Park (larger than Yellowstone, Yosemite, Grand Canyon and Glacier national parks combined) a de facto wilderness with pockets of settlement, farming, timbering, and tourism. "The Adirondacks are a 'park,'" says writer Bill McKibben, "unlike any other in America: They're a laboratory for figuring out how people might actually live with the world around them, which seems to be the great question we face as a species." The same principle extends, according to ecologist Raymond Dasmann, to the whole vast country "in-between" cities and protected preserves — "the fringe lands, the farmlands, the ranges, the pastures, and managed forests . . . where the real conservation issues of the next two decades will be faced."[17]

Local concern, responsibility, and control are themes permeating much of the environmental movement today, and they find their most concrete expression in the notion of bioregionalism. Stressing "reinhabitation" of the land, learning a "sense of place" (defined by natural features rather than artificial political boundaries), and making that place our "home," bioregionalism promotes living in sustainable equilibrium with the region's own resources to the greatest extent possible. "It is," states the 1990 *Bioregional Reader*, "a proposal to ground human cultures within natural systems . . . in order to fit human communities to the Earth, not distort the Earth to our demands." Much in the life and writing of Enos Mills lends support to the bioregional spirit. His own example as a "true dweller," "at home in the mountains," who knew his territory with a "lover's intimacy" especially struck Thomas J. Lyon in his treatment of Mills in the 1987 *Literary History of the American West*. Mills's personal and professional development, intimately associated with the region around Longs Peak, illustrates the lesson, furthermore, that our self-realization is often best found through our connection to our surroundings. Mills showed the inherent bioregionalism of nature itself through his intimate portraits of the "home lives" of animals and birds — each knowing and making the best use of the resources of its territory, each a reciprocal and inseparable part of its habitat. Mills's growing advocacy of parks and open space at the local level and of nature guiding "in every locale" to acquaint people with the uniqueness of their immediate surroundings matches exactly what today's bioregionalists prescribe to show people that — in the words of Gary Snyder, one of the movement's leaders — "it is not enough to love nature. . . . Our relation to the natural world takes place in a place, and it must be grounded in information and experience."[18]

Bioregionalism is one of the practical expressions of "deep ecology," the rallying concept for much of the American Green movement, which began in the 1980s in the wake of earlier beginnings in Europe. Another of deep ecology's tenets, with inspiration from the Thoreau-Muir-Leopold lineage, is biocentrism, the notion that humanity is part of rather than separate from the biotic community.

Biocentrism rejects human-centered (anthropocentric) standards for judging nature's value, and stresses, in Leopold's words, "man-the-biotic-citizen" in place of "man-the-conqueror." Deep ecology's most strident proponents have appeared to place nature *before* man or to condemn the human race outright as a "blight" on the planet. That in turn has provoked the wrath of the rival social ecologists, who denounce deep ecology as inconsistent, mystical, antihuman, insensitive to humanity's own oppressed classes, and ignorant of the predominantly social causes of environmental degradation. With different motives and different politics, aggressive prodevelopment forces and their minions in "Wise-Use" coalitions, like People for the West, also condemn deep ecology — and environmentalism generally — as deliberate attempts to "destroy industrial civilization." Deep ecology nevertheless continues to mature as a genuine branch of applied philosophy, with its most careful thinkers mindful of criticism from social ecologists, third world ecologists (who insist that human deprivation must be treated as part and parcel of the environmental crisis), and ecofeminists (who stress the destructive role of "patriarchial structures" in environmental degradation and the guiding role of "the feminine" in preserving life-giving resources). Just as Thoreau, Muir, and Leopold, examined more deeply, all survive the charge of being "antisocial," so deep ecology cannot help being committed in the long run to just and sustainable societies. And bioregionalism may be only one of many explorations of the kinds of social reconstruction and ethical principles needed to improve the human condition and its relationship with nature.

Mills should be of historical interest to deep ecologists not only for his nascent sense of bioregionalism, but for the primal energy and direct experiential connection with nature expressed in his writings. His passion for awakening in people a sense of being in nature and having an active relationship with it, free of fear or arrogance and enriched by adventure, emotion, intuition, inspiration, imagination, play, and sensory experience is precisely what deep ecologists prescribe to reverse industrial civilization's alienation from nature. Mills also expressed something of what deep ecologists call "biospheric egalitarianism," the belief that all members of the biotic community share with humans intrinsic moral value. Reading Mills convinces us that "wild folk" are our valued friends, often our teachers, and never our inferiors. His assumption that they possess intelligence and reasoning ability — an assumption readmitted in some biological circles — strengthens the case implied throughout his writing that they deserve moral and ethical standing. And the belief that "ethical standing does not begin and end with human beings," says Roderick Nash in his 1989 history of environmental ethics, *The Rights of Nature,* "is one of the most remarkable ideas of our time."[19] Current debate over ethical and even legal standing for nonhumans is complex far beyond what is relevant here. We should note instead that Mills's egalitarian sense was colored and somewhat diminished by his overriding humanism, which biased his partnership with the animal world by making humans the defining species — the species whose acquaintance animals "crave" and whose qualities when found in animals make those animals all the more lovable. Lacking Leopold's degree of ecological objectivity, Mills could not develop his sense of citizenship in nature to the depth of Leopold's "man-the-biotic-citizen." Mills welcomed animals into an anthropocentric world rather than seeking a way for humanity to reintegrate itself into a biocentric world.

As a practical conservationist, Mills was not, in key respects, an early deep ecologist. The national parks, his most advanced concept in wildland preservation, have shown their inability to promote a "biospheric egalitarianism" and have in fact demanded heavy sacrifices from the biotic community. Mills was not a close enough disciple of Muir to sense the deeper biocentric strain in his thinking, and he characteristically praised Muir's achievement in humanistic terms. He wrote in 1917, for example, that Muir's "practical labors and books are likely to prove the most influential force in this century for the profitable use of leisure hours." But though Mills subordinated his allegiance to nature to his hopes for an improved society, we sense throughout his writing deeper instincts which, had he lived longer and absorbed new currents of thinking, might have shaped his trajectory more explicitly toward that of Muir and Leopold. At the most basic level, Mills wanted humans to achieve a mutually supportive alliance with nature and a conservation ethic which would impel us to respect and care for nature by merging our interests with those of nature. At the very least Mills would have probably achieved — or did in large measure achieve — what Rene Dubos called an "enlightened anthropocentrism," which acknowledges that over the long run "the world's good always coincides with man's own most meaningful good."[20]

Mills's desire to make nature a guiding force for society was, for its part, limited by the lack of a broader sense of what he wanted society to be. Without a consistent body of social theory to guide him, Mills did not know how far nature could or should go to remaking society. He remained as a result largely bound by the reformism that characterized his age and left its deeper problems untouched. As we saw earlier, most of the wares in Mills's medicine chest for social ailments helped people cope with their stressed lives but did not challenge them to seek fundamental changes in the society that sapped their energies and spirit. By returning vacationing Americans to their jobs with renewed efficiency and "happy hands," nature remained only a palliative in the service of the status quo. Neither Mills's socialist sentiment, however long it lasted, nor his conspicuous championing of women were lenses for him to examine structural injustices in society or to at least glimpse the parallels between the oppression of social classes and the exploitation of nature which concerns today's social ecologists. The influence of Mills's socialist friend Eugene Debs remains obscure, as does any practical right-left orientation in his politics after about 1905. His increasing revulsion for bureaucracy would have perhaps caused him to reject a socialist bureaucratic state, yet the bureaucratic injustices he alleged and fought against were those of his own federal government. He appeared to champion small business against the tyranny of corporate-government hegemony, but never, apparently, evaluated the relative merits of capitalism and socialism as systems best able to harmonize man's relation with nature. That question persists today in the Green debates of many countries: Does a society, fully egalitarian in social terms, necessarily imply a society that is ecologically benign? And if not, is a competitive, market-driven society ecologically preferable? Will the "powerful market forces" widely praised by those who profit from them bring blessings on today's stricken environment and the world's starving millions, or is the market economy, as one critic insists, the most efficient mechanism imaginable "to bring the planet to the edge of ruin"?[21]

Many bioregionalists and social ecologists, despite other differences, share a desire for autonomous local politics and economy unconstrained by higher authority and combining individual freedom and diversity, social equity, participatory democracy, and community responsibility. "Radical municipalism" or "communitarian anarchism" — two of several names now being used — could resemble a natural ecosystem in which diversity of the parts contributes to the identity and functioning of the whole. "Anarchy does not mean out of control," writes one bioregionalist, aware of the negative connotations of the word. "It means out of *their* control." Even Thomas Jefferson, according to historian Richard K. Matthews, can be seen as leaning toward a communitarian anarchism based on the belief that humans can live in community without the need for formal government. That, Matthews adds, "raises serious challenges to the Madison-Hamilton view of market man as universal man; and it offers a kind of metaphoric ideal of the type of communal life — without regressing backward historically in terms of science, technology and enlightenment — toward which modern humans ought to aspire."[22]

An important source of inspiration for an ecologically based and self-governing society in Mills's own time (and an important inspiration to many of today's social ecologists) was the work of Peter Kropotkin, a Russian naturalist and anarchist who saw mutual aid as a stronger force in nature than competition and advocated a balanced community of all living things in place of centralized governmental structures. "Kropotkin might well," notes John Henry Wadland, "displace Aldo Leopold as the father of the 'ecological conscience.'" Mills owned Kropotkin's *Mutual Aid,* and Ernest Thompson Seton applied Kropotkin's social principles in a youth movement that drew additional inspiration from the North American Indian.[23] It is tempting to wonder whether Mills, finding big government increasingly pernicious and being regionally attuned, attracted to the idea of mutual aid in nature, and respectful of American Indians as "people of culture and refinement," might at some point have brought Kropotkin's ideas or Seton's practical application of them into his own Trail School. Suggestive — but insufficient — evidence of Mills's attraction to a communitarian society based on mutual respect and mutual aid was the remarkable, self-governing road crew of convicts in whose midst he spent a week — an uplifting and socially significant experience for Mills.

The inspiration that Mills drew from the convict crew reminds us of deeper, more radical currents trying to stretch the boundaries of his reformist impulse. He may in his last years have believed that government dishonesty had become a permanent condition, with propaganda and disinformation its weapons against the people. His conviction by 1919 that the public "is given only such selected nature lore as it can be trusted with and still remain loyal to public institutions" was one of his most pungent political statements, which, had he explored it farther, might help us to see in any age how information and attitudes about nature can be used to manipulate society. If, Mills seemed to believe, the government can deprive people of the clear-headedness and innate common sense they acquire through direct contact with nature, it can deprive them of their last defense against control. Against that background we can understand the desperation of his effort to "save" the national parks — not simply as parks but as refuges of American democracy where people learn to see, think, and feel without distortion. His conviction that a national park does more for international peace than a battleship is trenchantly relevant in our own time, when the annual budget for the entire national park system is less than the cost of one strategic bomber. And his plea for rehabilitating convicted wrongdoers through outdoor living and self-determination rather than in spirit-crushing prisons seems urgently relevant today, when imprisonment, increasingly the solution for our social problems, has given us the world's highest incarceration rate. Mills's example challenges us to oppose national priorities gone amok and to make nature our most trusted teacher in becoming an alert, concerned, and emotionally healthy citizenry.

The life of Enos Mills illustrates a response to personal conscience and a respect for both nature and humanity as moral forces in arousing himself to public action. He was an almost archetypal example of a man acting on his beliefs, a man with a Faustian drive to pursue noble ideals in the face of any obstacle. Some modern activists will see in Mills the prototypical "ecowarrior" — defending his flowers against marauding cattle, waving his fist at the Forest Service, provoking his arrest by the Park Service. We have tried to enter the complex terrain of Mills's public and private psyches, his heroic self-image, the persona that expressed it, and the borderland he sometimes inhabited between fact and imagination. In his crusading persona Mills expressed a kind of holy and sacrosanct anger that was both his greatest liability and his most powerful weapon. Enos Mills, wilderness man turned fierce wilderness defender, still stands for many as the primary image of the Rocky Mountain conservationist. Let us grant substantial truth in that while at the same time qualifying it on several fronts.

As an "environmental activist" Mills was a personality type recognizable by anyone who has participated in public campaigns: intelligent, idealistic, energetic, inflammatory, distrustful, and uncompromising both toward his adversaries and members of his own coalition. Like Thoreau 150 years ago and Edward Abbey in our own time, he was regarded as a "problem" by many on his own side of the issues. Mills easily mistook structural problems for the machinations of individual scoundrels, tended to demonize his adversaries, and at times resorted to name calling. He committed the grave political mistake of allowing his opponents to fault his own character and motives. It is significant that some of the opposition to the RMNP campaign was raised solely from dislike for Mills himself. And it is equally significant that Mills's own force of personality prevailed over that opposition where the most crucial support was needed.

Action campaigns must inevitably deal with difficult personalities and internal conflicts. "Conservationists," wrote Aldo Leopold over four decades ago, "are notorious for their dissensions." Yet diversity of types can in fact strengthen a movement, and in the RMNP campaign the sometimes obstreperous Mills and the diplomatic but sometimes wavering James Grafton Rogers can be seen as two parts of a successful movement, more powerful than either alone. Both were citizens with a common goal and, to borrow Michael Frome's words, "human frailty notwithstanding, citizen concern more than any other force has made and saved the national parks." Though Mills needed buffering by his colleagues, they on the other hand needed his uncompromising example not to yield, not to make deals that lead to co-optation by the opposition. Mills's example helps us to focus our own attention on such questions as How much do we work within the system and how much oppose it outright? Do we join the Sierra Club or Earth First!? Do we have to be radical to get something moderate or moderate to get anything at all? How far can we push public officials before they begin to ignore us, leaving us marginalized and without further influence?[24]

We leave the subject of Enos Mills with the memory of a man of puzzling and perhaps impenetrable complexity, of a man who involved his whole being in all he did and sought unstintingly to leave the earth a better place than he found it. He stands as one of those intriguing figures who cause us to ask, Do we judge the man or his achievement? And to realize that neither choice yields simple answers. Mills's example will not let us forget that however the environmental movement evolves — and evolve it surely will — "conservation" and human character cannot be separated. What we humans decide to do about the earth will depend increasingly on what human character, itself a product of nature, is made of. Can we dare to hope for the best?

Notes

The notes that follow are abstracted from a much larger set, which contains additional information and citations, as well as a further discussion of certain subjects. The larger set is available from the author, care of the University Press of Colorado.

Works assigned abbreviations are cited without author. Works not assigned abbreviations are cited in full the first time only; in subsequent citations, square brackets immediately following the title indicate the chapter in the Notes section where the full reference appears.

ABBREVIATIONS

BOOKS (ALL BY ENOS A. MILLS, EXCEPT EMOR)

ANG   *Adventures of a Nature Guide and Essays in Interpretation,* ed. Enda Mills Kiley (1920; Friendship, WI: New Past Press, 1990).

BGB   *Being Good to Bears and Other True Animal Stories,* ed. F. W. Rawcliffe (1919; Boston: Houghton Mifflin, 1930). BGB is a reprint of earlier Mills stories and contains no new material.

BMR   *Bird Memories of the Rockies* (Boston: Houghton Mifflin, 1931).

EEP   *The Story of Early Estes Park, Rocky Mountain National Park, and Grand Lake,* 5th ed., eds. Robert H. and Enda M. Kiley (1905; Longs Peak, Estes Park: Enos Mills Cabin: 1980); other editions of the booklet are occasionally cited and are identified by the year of publication.

EMOR   *Enos Mills of the Rockies,* biography by Hildegarde Hawthorne and Esther Burnell Mills (New York: Juvenile Guild [Houghton Mifflin], 1935).

GGWA   *The Grizzly, Our Greatest Wild Animal* (1919; Sausalito, CA: Comstock Editions, 1973).

IBW   *In Beaver World,* ed. James H. Pickering (1913; Lincoln and London: University of Nebraska Press, 1990).

RG   *Romance of Geology* (1926; Boston and New York: Houghton Mifflin, 1932).

RMNP   *The Rocky Mountain National Park, Memorial Edition* (Garden City, NY: Doubleday, Page, 1924).

RMW   *The Rocky Mountain Wonderland,* ed. James H. Pickering (1915; Lincoln and London: University of Nebraska Press, 1991).

SR   *The Spell of the Rockies,* ed. James H. Pickering (1911; Lincoln and London: University of Nebraska Press, 1989).

SS   *The Story of Scotch* (Boston: Houghton Mifflin, 1916).

STYP   *The Story of a Thousand Year Pine* (Boston: Houghton Mifflin, 1914); separate edition of a story in WLR.

WAH   *Wild Animal Homesteads* (Garden City, NY: Doubleday, Page, 1923).

WLR   *Wild Life on the Rockies,* ed. James H. Pickering (1909; Lincoln and London: University of Nebraska Press, 1988).

WW   *Waiting in the Wilderness* (Garden City, NY: Doubleday, Page, 1921).

WWA   *Watched by Wild Animals* (Garden City, NY: Doubleday, Page, 1922).

YNP   *Your National Parks* (Boston: Houghton Mifflin, 1917).

COLLECTIONS

CHS   Colorado Historical Society, Denver, CO

CPF   Colorado Pamphlet File, in EPPL

EMCC   Enos Mills Cabin Collection (papers in possession of Mills Family)

EPAHM   Estes Park Area Historical Museum

EPOHP   Estes Park Oral History Project, transcripts in EPPL

EPPL   Estes Park [CO] Public Library

HWP   Herbert Wheeler Papers, in WHD

IHP   Irving Hale Papers, in WHD

JGRP   James Grafton Rogers Papers, in CHS

JHMP   J. Horace McFarland Papers, in Pennsylvania State Archives, Harrisburg; copies of many are also in RMNPL

LCHS   Lynn County [KS] Historical Society

MMC   Mills-Muir correspondence; letters from Mills to Muir are in the Hanna-Muir Trust, Holt Atherton Center for Western Studies, University of the Pacific, Stockton, CA; letters from Muir to Mills are in the Huntington Library, San Marino, CA, and are cited with their call numbers.

MP   Mills Papers, in WHD

RMNPL   Rocky Mountain National Park Library

WHD   Western History Department, Denver Public Library

PROLOGUE

1. Accounts of the meeting are given in the following works: "The Friend of the Rocky Mountains," *Literary Digest* 55 (July 14, 1917), p. 44; Arthur Chapman, *Enos A Mills: Author, Speaker, Nature Guide* (Longs Peak, CO: Trail Book Store, 1921), p. 11; Mills, "Enos Mills — Himself, by Himself," *Saturday Evening Post* (Sep. 1, 1917), p. 25; and Mills to Fred L. Holmes, July 21, 1921,

MP. Mills thanked Muir personally in letters of Jan. 24, 1903; May 1, 1906; Jan. 31, 1913; and Nov. 24, 1914, all in MMC.

2. Stephen Fox, *John Muir and His Legacy: The American Conservation Movement* (Boston and Toronto: Little, Brown, 1981), pp. 27–28.

3. Michael P. Cohen, *The Pathless Way: John Muir and American Wilderness* (Madison: University of Wisconsin Press, 1984).

4. Robert Shankland, *Steve Mather of the National Parks*, 3rd ed. (New York: Alfred A. Knopf, 1970), p. 79.

5. Carl Abbott, "The Active Force: Enos A. Mills and the National Park Movement," *Colorado Magazine* 56 (1979), pp. 59, 67.

6. *EEP*, p. xviii.

7. *EMOR*'s primary author, Hildegarde Hawthorne, had already published works of poetry, fiction, opinion, travel, and biography.

8. Hans Huth, *Nature and the American: Three Centuries of Changing Attitudes* (1957; reprint ed., Lincoln and London: University of Nebraska Press, 1972), p. 182; Roderick Nash, *Wilderness and the American Mind,* revised ed. (New Haven: Yale University Press, 1973), 189. Other works of interest include Frederick Turner, *Rediscovering America: John Muir in His Time and Ours* (1985; reprint ed., San Francisco: Sierra Club Books, n.d.); G. Michael McCarthy, *Hour of Trial: The Conservation Conflict in Colorado and the West, 1891–1907* (Norman: University of Oklahoma Press, 1977); Gifford Pinchot, *Breaking New Ground* (1946; reprint ed., Washington, D.C.: Island Press, 1987); Harold K. Steen, *The U.S. Forest Service: A History* (Seattle: University of Washington Press, 1976), p. 119; Carl Abbott, "The Literary Career of Enos Mills," *Montana: The Magazine of Western History* (April 1981); John Ise, *Our National Park Policy: A Critical History* (Baltimore: Johns Hopkins Press, 1961); Horace M. Albright, *The Birth of the National Park Service: The Founding Years, 1913–1933* (Salt Lake City: Howe Brothers, 1985); Donald C. Swain, *Wilderness Defender: Horace M. Albright and Conservation* (Chicago: University of Chicago Press, 1970); C. W. Buchholtz, *Rocky Mountain National Park: A History* (Boulder: Colorado Associated University Press, 1983); Patricia M. Fazio, *Cragged Crusade: The Fight for Rocky Mountain National Park, 1909–1915,* M.S. thesis, University of Wyoming, 1982. State histories of interest are Carl Abbott, Stephen J. Leonard, and David McComb, *Colorado: A History of the Centennial State* (Boulder: Colorado Associated University Press, 1982); Carl Ubbelohde, Maxine Benson, and Duane A. Smith, *A Colorado History,* revised ed. (Boulder, CO: Pruett Publishing, 1976); Marshall Sprague, *Colorado: A Bicentennial History* (New York: W. W. Norton, 1976). Other relevant works on the Forest Service, Park Service, and state or regional history are cited elsewhere.

9. Peter Wild, *Pioneer Conservationists of Western America* (Missoula, MT: Mountain Press Publishing, 1979), p. 73; Wild, *Enos Mills* (Boise, ID: Boise State University Western Writers Series, 1979), pp. 8–9; James H. Pickering, introduction to *WLR,* p. xii; Paul Brooks, *Speaking for Nature* (Boston: Houghton Mifflin, 1980), p. 212.

10. Abbott, "Literary Career," p. 4.

11. Emerson E. Lynn, "The Preacher's Son," in *The Scottage* (1959), p. 28, in CPF.

CHAPTER 1

1. Mills, "Himself, by Himself" [Prologue]: p. 25; Joe Mills to Esther Mills, Feb. 7, 1934, EMCC; *Proceedings of the National Parks Conference: Held in the Auditorium of the New National Museum, Washington, D.C. January 2–6, 1917* (Washington: Government Printing Office, 1917), pp. 43, 172, 270.

2. *BMR,* p. 39; *YNP,* p. 313.

3. *YNP,* p. 363.

4. Rev. E. J. Lamb, *Memories of the Past and Thoughts of the Future* (United Brethren Publishing House, 1906), p. 49.

5. Joe Mills, *A Mountain Boyhood* (1926; reprint ed., Lincoln and London: University of Nebraska Press, 1988), p. 5.

6. Lamb, *Memories,* pp. 44–48; Enos Mills, Sr., in an autobiographical memoir of Dec. 26, 1909, repr. in *Pleasanton* [KS] *Observer* (Feb. 25, 1910), copy in LCHS, stated that the families came "for the avowed purpose of helping to make Kansas a free state." Joe Mills, *Boyhood,* p. 3.

7. Lamb, *Memories,* p. 15.

8. Enos Mills, Sr., to Mills, Sep. 16, 1895, EMCC; as a Mason, Enos, Sr. was supposed to believe in the existence of a Supreme Being and in the immortality of the soul. Ann Lamb Mills also drifted away from the Quaker faith and at the time of her death was a member of the local Baptist parish. Emerson E. Lynn, who knew Enos Mills during his last five years, from 1917 to 1922, said that his "disbelief in religion was intense" ("Preacher's Son" [Prologue], p. 28); Robert W. Johnson (foreword to *RMNP,* pp. xviii–xix) briefly discusses Mills's agnosticism, and the inspirations he took from Tolstoy and the freethinker Robert Ingersoll. Enos Mills's grandson, Michael M. Kiley (personal communication, April 18, 1994) believes that Mills *was* a religious man, with inspiration from Tom Paine and other deists, Freemason esotericism, and paranormal experiences in the wilds.

9. Though Enos Mills never mentioned his father in his writings, Joe Mills portrayed him as positively as he did his mother. He noted (*Boyhood,* p. 2) that he could "laugh heartily," and that both parents, rather than his mother alone, gave him his adventurous spirit. The obituary for Enos Mills, Sr., (copy in LCHS) described him as being "held in high esteem by a wide circle of friends." As both a Freemason and an Odd Fellow, he appears to have been a man of sociable temperament. His 1895 letter to Enos (the only letter so far discovered) is comradely, offering Mills (at age twenty-five) winter quarters at home and the enticement of hunting and fishing together.

10. Mills, undated fragment, MP; in *YNP,* p. 9, Mills quotes Kant's idea that "geography lies at the basis of history"; William Allen White quoted in *Encyclopedia Americana* (Danbury, CT: Grolier, 1978), vol. 16, p. 295.

11. Stephen E. Whicher, ed., *Selections from Ralph Waldo Emerson* (Boston: Houghton Mifflin, 1957), p. 362.

12. Turner, *Rediscovering America* [Prologue], p. 183.

13. Isabella L. Bird, *A Lady's Life in the Rockies* (1879; reprint ed., Sausalito, CA: Comstock Editions, 1980), p. 62.

14. *WWA,* pp. 34–35.

15. Though Mills later referred explicitly to Burroughs as a "dear friend" (*New York Times,* Mar. 30, 1921), concrete evidence of a significant personal relationship is lacking, and no correspondence has been located in the records of either man.

CHAPTER 2

1. F. J. Bancroft to Board of Immigration to Colorado Territory, Nov. 15, 1873, in Carl Ubbelohde, ed., *A Colorado Reader,* revised ed. (Boulder, CO: Pruett Publishing, 1964), p. 173. The large portion of Colorado settlers classifiable as health seekers in the decade of the 1880s is "an index to a facet of Colorado's development that has never been fully considered or described," note Ubbelohde, Benson, and Smith in *A Colorado History* [Prologue], p. 156.
2. F. C. Nims, *Health, Wealth and Pleasure in Colorado and New Mexico* (1881; reprint ed., Santa Fe: Museum of New Mexico Press, 1980), p. 15.
3. Sandra Dallas, *No More than Five in a Bed* (Norman: University of Oklahoma Press, 1967), p. 182; Bird, *Lady's Life* [Ch. 1], pp. 37–38.
4. George A. Crofutt, *Crofutt's Grip-Sack Guide of Colorado: A Complete Encyclopedia of the State,* vol. 2 (1885; reprint ed., Boulder, CO: Johnson Books, 1981), p. 24.
5. Ibid., pp. 27–28.
6. Bird, *Lady's Life,* p. 30.
7. Ibid., pp. 67, 51.
8. See Abner Sprague, "William E. James," *Estes Park Trail* 3 (Apr. 27, 1923), p. 3; and Dr. Homer James, transcript of interview, Nov. 14, 1940, EPOHP.
9. Eleanor E. Hondius, *Memoirs of Eleanor E. Hondius of Elkhorn Lodge* (Boulder CO: Pruett Press, 1964), p. 7.
10. John Muir, *Journal,* Jan. 6, 1873, quoted in Fox, *Muir and His Legacy* [Prologue], p. 15; "longest is the life" is from *EMOR,* p. 250, quoted without source.
11. *YNP,* pp. ix–x.

CHAPTER 3

1. *EEP,* p. 69; Mills said that he climbed Longs Peak a total of 305 times (*ANG,* p. 95) and that "after one climb to the summit, I decided to be a Longs Peak guide" (*RMNP,* p. 149).
2. Mark Twain, *The Adventures of Tom Sawyer* (Garden City, NY: Nelson Doubleday, n.d.), p. 14; quoted in Paul W. Nesbitt, *Longs Peak: Its Story and a Climbing Guide,* 8th ed. (Boulder, CO: Johnson Publishing, 1972), p. 57.
3. Quoted by Johnson, foreword to *RMNP,* p. xii.
4. *RMW,* p. 56; *WLR,* pp. 253–54.
5. Peter Matthiessen describing his own son in *The Snow Leopard* (New York:

Viking Press, 1978), p. 41; in an obituary notice following Mills's death, one
writer speculated that in his first years at Longs Peak he had still been "a faun
unconscious of his dominion" (H. J. Haskell, as quoted by Philip Ashton Rollins in *RMNP*, p. 216; "bite the twigs" quoted in Farida A. Wiley, ed., *Ernest
Thompson Seton's America: Selections from the Writings of the Artist-Natural-
ist* (New York: Devin-Adair, 1954), p. 394.

CHAPTER 4

1. Mills, quoted in *EMOR*, p. 54.
2. Michael Malone, *The Battle for Butte: Mining and Politics on the Northern
    Frontier, 1864–1906* (Seattle and London: University of Washington Press,
    1981), p. 40.
3. Robert W. Johnson, foreword to *RMNP*, p. x.
4. Mills, quoted in ibid., p. xviii; Robert Louis Stevenson, "An Apology for
    Idlers," in George Scott-Moncrieff, ed., *Robert Louis Stevenson: Selected
    Essays* (Chicago: Henry Regnery, 1959), p. 4.
5. Ibid., pp. 6–7.
6. Mills, quoted in *EMOR*, p. 50.
7. Fox, *Muir and His Legacy* [Prologue], pp. 72, 86.
8. Ibid., p. 15.
9. *EMOR*, p. 78 (an invented quotation, not necessarily reliable); in one of Mills's
    rare references to time actually spent with Muir, he wrote (*WW*, p. 240) that
    Muir "kindly showed me the Redwoods."

CHAPTER 5

1. This and all subsequent quotations about the Uncompahgre adventure are
    from *SR*, pp. 223–44.
2. Frank Munsey, quoted in Earle Labor, Robert C. Leitz, III, and I. Milo Shep-
    ard, eds., *The Letters of Jack London, Vol. One, 1896–1905* (Stanford, CA:
    Stanford University Press, 1988), p. xiv. George Horace Lorimer, who became
    Mills's most influential editor, tightly controlled the tone and content of the
    Saturday Evening Post (personally reading every word that went into print)
    and several times praised Mills's stories as "just right."
3. *Denver Daily News* (June 7, 1903) wrote, for example, that Mills possessed
    "the enviable reputation of being the most daring and successful mountain
    climber in the West."
4. *WW*, p. 94.
5. Ibid., p. 90; *WLR*, p. 90.
6. *WW*, pp. 93, 96.
7. *ANG*, p. 100.
8. *SR*, p. 240; Mills's sole reference to his "theory of nonresistance" is ibid., p.
    242.

9. John Muir, *My First Summer in the Sierra* (1916; reprint ed., Boston: Hough-ton Mifflin, 1979), p. 80; C. Hart Merriam, quoted in Edwin Way Teale, ed., *The Wilderness World of John Muir* (Boston: Houghton Mifflin, 1954), p. xii.

10. *YNP,* p. 361.

11. If Muir ate sparingly and indifferently, he could not, it appears, fast for long, says Muir biographer Frederick Turner (*Rediscovering America* [Prologue], p. 189); after two days without bread, Muir grew weak and dreamed of food — which he considered a danger signal.

12. *SR,* p. 119.

13. *New Orleans Daily States* (Feb. 11, 1908).

14. *YNP,* pp. 337–38; *BMR,* p. 172.

15. *SR,* pp. 149–50 and *GGWA,* pp. 44–45.

16. *ANG,* p. 19; Mills lost his goggles in mid morning and was snowblind by noon, though normally about eight hours are required. See James A. Wilker-son, MD, ed., *Medicine for Mountaineering and Other Wilderness Activities,* 4th ed. (Seattle: The Mountaineers, 1992), p. 324. Mills's snowblind adventure is discussed further in Ch. 20.

17. Stefansson, quoted in Roland Huntford, *Scott and Amundsen* (New York: Ath-eneum, 1984), p. 177.

18. Bill McKibben, "Hero of the Wilderness," *New York Review of Books* 36/17 (Nov. 9, 1989), p. 20–25.

19. Quotations, in order, are from: *WLR,* p. 14; *SR,* pp. 226, 235, 242; *ANG,* p. 20; Mills partially retracted his bravado later: For example, "How I ever man-aged to go through that black, storm-filled night without breaking my neck amid the innumerable opportunities for accident is a thing I cannot explain," he confessed of the Uncompahgre adventure (*SR,* p. 226).

20. *SR,* pp. 109–19; ibid., pp. 10–11; William M. Bueler, in *Roof of the Rockies: A History of Mountaineering in Colorado* (Boulder, CO: Pruett Publishing, 1974), p. 120, expresses doubt that Mills could have climbed the peak's entire northeast ridge — difficult even by modern standards. He suggests that Mills "must have climbed one of the lesser summits of the Sierra Blanca massif rather than Blanca Peak. Even that, however, was no mean achievement."

21. Quotations, in order, are from: *SR,* pp. 277–78; *RMW,* pp. 53–54, and *ANG,* pp. 57, 64. Mills told an interviewer in 1917 that climbing Longs Peak in gale winds had demonstrated "just plain lack of sense."

22. *GGWA,* p. 112.

CHAPTER 6

1. *SR,* 139.

2. This and other quotations from the bluebird experience are from *BMR,* pp. 3–32.

3. John Muir, quoted in Lisa Mighetto, ed., *Muir Among the Animals: The Wild-life Writings of John Muir* (San Francisco: Sierra Club Books, 1986), p. xviii; see also Cohen, *Pathless Way* [Prologue], pp. 346–50.

4. *WW,* p. 226.
5. John Burroughs, quoted in Farida A. Wiley, ed., *John Burroughs' America: Selections from the Writings of the Hudson River Naturalist* (New York: Devin-Adair, 1967), pp. 3–5; see also John Burroughs, "The Gospel of Nature," in *The Works of John Burroughs* (Boston and New York: Houghton Mifflin, 1912), vol. 14, pp. 243–73: *ANG,* p. 30; Muir quoted in Turner, *Rediscovering America* [Prologue], p. 128.
6. Philip Ashton Rollins, "Champion of Wildlife," in *RMNP,* p. 214.
7. Burroughs, *Works,* vol. 14, pp. 249–50.
8. Muir, quoted in Fox, *Muir and His Legacy* [Prologue], p. 23.
9. Teale, *Wilderness World of Muir* [Ch. 5], pp. 320–21 (see Chs. 20 and 21 for a discussion of Mills's notion and use of imagination).
10. *SR,* p. 217.
11. *WWA,* pp. 184, 187.
12. *ANG,* pp. 77–78.

CHAPTER 7

1. This and subsequent quotations are from "American Liberty," typed manuscript, July 4, 1898, MP; his oration a year earlier was entitled "The Growth and Prospects of Liberty."
2. Undated fragment, MP.
3. Mills, "Right Vs. Wrong," typed manuscript, May 17, 1899, MP.
4. Quotations about Kansas from untitled, typed manuscript, n.d., MP.
5. Joel Estes, quoted in Milton Estes, "The Memoirs of Estes Park," *Colorado Magazine* 16/4 (July 1939), p. 124.
6. *EEP,* p. 19.
7. Mills, "Government Ownership of Roads," letter to *Loveland* [CO] *Reporter* (Feb. 1903).
8. Ibid., Feb. 18, 1903.
9. Edward Bellamy, *Looking Backward* (1887; Modern Library ed., New York: Random House, 1951), pp. 41–42.
10. The connection with Clark, stated in *EMOR,* pp. 82–84, cannot be verified.
11. Malone, *Battle for Butte* [Ch. 4], p. 210.
12. Hondius, *Memoirs* [Ch. 2], p. 15.
13. Debs described the meeting in a letter to his brother Theo, Oct. 30, 1913, concluding, "From now on we're friends in the closest bonds and I'll tell you he's a friend worth having." J. Robert Constantine, ed., *Letters of Eugene V. Debs, Vol. 2, 1913–1919* (Urbana and Chicago: University of Illinois Press, 1990), pp. 78–79; EMCC contains four letters from Debs to Mills and two to his widow following Mills's death; all express high regard for Mills.
14. Muir, quoted in Roderick Nash, *Wilderness and the American Mind* [Prologue], p. 158.

15. For White's "conversion," see E. Jay Jernigan, William Allen White (Boston: Twayne Publishers, 1983), pp. 1–26, and *The Autobiography of William Allen White* (New York: Macmillan, 1964), pp. 297–99.
16. *ANG*, p. 147.

CHAPTER 8

1. *RMW*, p. 348; John Muir, *The Yosemite* (1912; reprint ed., Garden City, NY: Doubleday, 1962), p. 20.
2. Eunice H. Kauffman to Mills, Nov. 21, 1909, MP.
3. *ANG*, p. 156.
4. This and other Harding quotations from Earl Harding, "Climbing Longs Peak," *Outing* 44 (July 1904), pp. 461–68.
5. This and subsequent Longs Peak anecdotes from *RMW*, pp. 3–19.
6. Mills discusses climbing and romance in ibid., pp. 11–12, and *EEP*, 1905 ed., p. 99.
7. Mills wrote two accounts of the climb with Harriet: *WLR*, pp. 99–112, and *ANG*, pp. 149–54; EMCC contains a charming letter from Harriet herself, recalling the climb.

CHAPTER 9

1. *ANG*, p. 138; most ethologists agree that life forms below vertebrates do not play, but some naturalists before and during Mills's time believed that insects enjoy "motion play." Mills wrote (ibid., p. 101): "Play appears to be a common and enlivening and beneficial habit of the entire world of wild life."
2. *ANG*, pp. 139, 133; *BMR*, p. 21; Mills cites Darwin and Wallace in *GGWA*, p. 91.
3. Karl Groos, *The Play of Animals*, English ed. (1898; New York and London: D. Appleton, 1911), p. 82.
4. *WWA*, pp. 240, 101.
5. *ANG*, p. 139.
6. Ibid., p. 134.
7. *GGWA*, p. 85.
8. Ibid., pp. 105, 112; Sally Carrighar, *Wild Heritage* (New York: Ballantine Books, 1971), pp. 193–94.
9. *GGWA*, pp. 110, 107.
10. Ibid., p. 141.
11. *WWA*, p. 102.
12. Ibid., p. 221.
13. Ibid., p. 225.
14. Quotations, in order, are from *GGWA*, pp. 33, 112, 111, 13.

CHAPTER 10

1. This and subsequent quotations from the European tour are from Lamb, *Memories* [Ch. 1], pp. 201–38.

2. *EEP,* 1905 ed., p. 107.

3. Undated letter, Frank S. Harrison to Mills, MP.

4. Mills, quoted in *EMOR,* p. 106 (Mills also posted cloth signs at various places on the inn grounds saying RESERVED FOR WILD FLOWERS).

5. Charles Hewes, *Song of the Rockies* (Estes Park, CO: The Egerton-Palmer Press, 1922), p. 14.

6. News clipping, ca. 1913, MP.

7. Irving Hale to Mills, Dec. 20, 1905, IHP.

8. Robert P. Gookins (former Longs Peak Inn employee) to Atkins Ferrel, Aug. 19, 1975, CPF. Mills's charm as a fireside talker is described in Philip Ashton Rollins, "Champion of Wildlife," *RMNP,* pp. 222–23.

9. The anecdotes are in *RMW,* pp. 14–15, and *RMNP,* pp. 52–53. Although Longs Peak Inn did not allow tipping, it was one of the priciest inns of the area (see *YNP,* p. 492).

10. *EMOR,* pp. 107, 217; Frank S. Harrison to Esther Burnell Mills, July 11, 1934, MP.

11. See, for example, Edna Ferber, *A Peculiar Treasure* (Garden City, NY: Doubleday, 1938, 1960), p. 242.

12. *SS,* pp. 24–25.

13. Ibid.

14. Mills to Irving Hale, June 11 and 15, 1906, IHP.

15. John T. Jacobs, introduction to *BMR,* p. xvii; the inn is described in M. Kennedy Bailey, "A Forest House," *Craftsman* 20 (May 1911), pp. 205–7.

16. Mills, "A Home of Forest Fire Logs," *Sunset Magazine* (May 1921), pp. 11–12; Frank Lloyd Wright, *An Autobiography* (1932; reprint ed., New York: Horizon Press, 1977), p. 192.

17. Mills, "A Home of Forest Fire Logs," p. 5.

18. "Beautiful New Hotel for Horseshoe Park," *The Estes Park Mountaineer* (June 4, 1908).

CHAPTER 11

1. Alva Adams, quoted in *Official Proceedings of the Eighteenth National Irrigation Congress,* Pueblo, CO, 1910.

2. "Master of Irrigation," typed manuscript, n.d., MP; biographical sketches of Carpenter can be found in Ansel Watrous, *History of Larimer County, Colorado* (Ft. Collins, CO: Courier Printing and Publishing, 1911), pp. 342–44, and Joseph Ewan, *Rocky Mountain Naturalists* (Denver: University of Denver Press, 1950), p. 178.

3. Mills to Carpenter, Feb. 20, 1904, MP.

4. *Rocky Mountain News* (Feb. 19, 1904).

5. Quotations compiled from letters from Mills to Carpenter, Nov. 5 and Dec. 8, 1903, and Jan. 18, Feb. 20, Mar. 1, Sep. 26, and Dec. 20, 1904, all in MP.

6. L. G. Carpenter, in a talk to the Denver Chamber of Commerce, reproduced in Enos A. Mills and W.G.M. Stone, *Forests and Trees: An Arbor Day Souvenir* (Denver: Denver Chamber of Commerce and Board of Trade, 1905), p. 16.

7. Mills, quoted in *Riverside* [CA] *Daily Press* (Apr. 17, 1909); *SR*, p. 128; *BMR*, p. 181.

8. Mills to Carpenter, Sep. 26, 1904, MP; Mills wrote about the value of beavers as water conservationists in *WLR*, pp. 53–67; *SR*, pp. 17–48; and *IBW*, pp. 211–21.

9. *Denver Times* (Jan. 5, 1903).

10. *WLR*, pp. 123–24.

11. *Denver Post* (Sep. 12, 1935).

12. Mills, "Snowfalls of Colorado: Distribution and Snowslides," *Denver Times Friday Magazine* (Feb. 24, 1905).

13. Mills, "The Rockies' Heart and Summit," *Denver Times* (Jan. 16, 1904).

14. Ibid.; Mills, "Some of Colorado's Mountaineers," *Friday Evening Times Illustrated Weekly Magazine* (Dec. 30, 1904).

CHAPTER 12

1. *WLR*, p. 6.

2. Ibid.

3. Mills, "Some of Colorado's Mountaineers," *Friday Evening Times Illustrated Weekly Magazine* (Dec. 30, 1904); Mills, "A Home on the Snowy Range," *Denver Times* (Jan. 2, 1904), p. 5.

4. Mills, "One of the Earliest Pioneers," *Denver Times* (Jan. 23, 1904), p. 7.

5. Mills, "A Home on the Snowy Range."

6. *Denver Times* (Jan. 16, 1904).

7. Mills, "The Rockies' Heart and Summit" [Ch. 11].

8. Mills, "Some of Colorado's Mountaineers."

9. Writing virtually nothing about his Butte years, Mills does not mention these examples, but he probably knew of them, since they were a well known part of Butte lore; see Malone, *Battle for Butte* [Ch. 4], pp. 72–73.

10. *WLR*, pp. 119, 127.

11. *The Autobiography of Will Rogers* (1921; reprint ed., New York: Avon Books, 1975), pp. 9–10.

12. *WLR*, p. 217.

CHAPTER 13

1. The text of Mills's talk is reproduced in Mills and Stone, *Forests and Trees* [Ch. 11]; Mills had expressed similar views a year earlier in "The Forests of Colorado," *Outdoor Life* (July 1904), pp. 432–37.
2. Gifford Pinchot, quoted in McCarthy, *Hour of Trial* [Prologue], p. 71.
3. Quoted in Fox, *Muir and His Legacy* [Prologue], p. 115.
4. Quoted in McCarthy, *Hour of Trial*, p. 78. "Better help a poor man make a living for his family than help a rich man get richer still," said Pinchot himself (ibid., p. 79). For renunciations of Pinchot, see ibid., pp. 85–91.
5. Mills and Stone [Ch. 11].
6. Mills, "The Forests of Colorado," p. 434.
7. Mills and Stone [Ch. 11].
8. John Muir, quoted in Cohen, *Pathless Way* [Prologue], p. 250; McCarthy, *Hour of Trial*, p. 26. Many authors have linked Muir's conservation philosophy to a negative view of civilization. But, as Thomas J. Lyon notes in his monograph *John Muir* (Boise, ID: Boise State College Western Writers Series, 1972, p. 9), "[Muir's] philosophy is not renegade misanthropy; it attempts a view which is beyond either misanthropy or conventional humanism. . . . Like Thoreau he was most deeply concerned not to escape man and his besmirching of the beautiful world, but to know the place of man in the great scheme of things, which is to say, the wild scheme." For discussion of Muir's own sense of public conscience, see Turner, *Rediscovering America* [Prologue], pp. 340–41.
9. John Muir, quoted in Nash, *Wilderness and the American Mind* [Prologue], pp. 134–35.
10. Theodore Roosevelt, quoted in Cohen, *Pathless Way*, pp. 327, 298; Mills, quoted in the *Denver Times* (Jan. 31, 1907).
11. Fox, *Muir and His Legacy*, p. 130; McCarthy, *Hour of Trial*, p. 130; Mills, quoted in the *Denver Times* (Jan. 31, 1907).
12. Gifford Pinchot, quoted in Alfred Runte, *National Parks: The American Experience* (Lincoln and London: University of Nebraska Press, 1979), p. 70. Cohen's central theme in *The Pathless Way* is to trace Muir's "spiritual journey" and the development of his ethics (see Cohen's overview, pp. xii-xv).
13. For further discussion, see ibid., pp. 282, 315–17, 322–23, 332–33; and Cohen's *History of the Sierra Club, 1892–1970* (San Francisco: Sierra Club Books, 1988), p. 17: "The ideas of a younger and more radical Muir were not rediscovered until the Club was half a century old." On Muir's probably conscious suppression of his true beliefs, see Roderick Frazier Nash, *The Rights of Nature: A History of Environmental Ethics* (Madison: University of Wisconsin Press, 1989), p. 78.
14. Muir, *Our National Parks*, pp. 33–34.
15. Wendell Berry, *The Unsettling of America: Culture and Agriculture* (San Francisco: Sierra Club Books, 1977, 1986), p. 30; Berry notes (p. 72) that "neither the agricultural specialist nor the conservation specialist has any idea where people belong in the order of things."
16. Mills, "The Forests of Colorado," p. 435.

17. W.G.M. Stone to Mills, Jan. 8, 1906, MP.
18. Mills, *The Forestry Situation in Colorado, Report to the Colorado State Forestry Association,* Jan. 1907, copy in MP.
19. McCarthy, *Hour of Trial,* pp. 234–35; Stone had nevertheless written to Mills on May 8, 1907, that with renewed opposition to the reserves "the situation was about as bad as it could be."
20. Mills, *The Forestry Situation in Colorado.*

CHAPTER 14

1. Irving Hale to Theodore Roosevelt, Jan 7, 1907, IHP; all other cited correspondence to and from Hale is from the same source.
2. Mills to Hale, Jan. 10, 1907.
3. "Mills Honored by Uncle Sam," *Denver Times* (Jan. 31, 1907), copy in MP. Unless otherwise noted, all other cited news stories are from clipping files in MP. Official letter of appointment: G. G. Anderson to Mills, Jan. 23, 1907, copy in MP; his salary was $1,800 per year plus $500 for travel costs; his appointment was renewed in Sept. 1907, and his salary increased to $2,400 per year in Nov. 1907.
4. *Denver Daily News* (Dec. 10, 1905).
5. Mills to Hale, June 5, 1906; Hale to fifty of his friends during 1907.
6. Mills to Hale, Dec. 20, 1905, Nov. 17, 1906.
7. Undated news clipping, MP.
8. Mills to Herbert A. Smith (USFS), Apr. 10, 1907, copy in EMCC.
9. William C. Reynolds (president of Georgia Military College) to Bristow Adams (USFS), n.d., MP.
10. Mills to Pinchot, May 28, 1907, copy in EMCC; all other cited letters between Mills and Pinchot are from EMCC. Mills told Pinchot his experience had convinced him that schools and women's clubs "are the best places for forestry addresses."
11. *Proceedings of the 18th National Irrigation Congress* [Ch. 13], p. 277.
12. Mills quoted in the *Denver Times* (Jan. 31, 1907).
13. Mills, "Our Faithful Servant and Constant Friend, the Forest," transcript of talk to GFWC, St. Paul, MN, June 1906, copy in MP.
14. Ibid.
15. Ibid.
16. Mills to Pinchot, May 23, 1907.
17. Irving Dilliard, "Historian in Cowboy Boots: Jay Monaghan, 1893–1980," *Journal of the Illinois State Historical Society* 74/4 (Winter 1981), p. 269.
18. *Bulletin of Evanston Academy of Northwestern University,* May 1909, MP.
19. Mills to Pinchot, May 23, 1907.
20. Pinchot, quoted in Roderick Nash, *The American Environment: Readings in the History of Conservatlon* (Reading, MA: Addison-Wesley Publishing, 1976),

p. 59; Mills quoted in *Beaumont* [TX] *Enterprise* (n.d.) and the *Denver Daily News* (Dec. 19, 1905).

21. *Charlotte* [NC] *News* (Apr. 3, 1908).
22. Quotations are from files in MP. Identifiable sources are *Omaha World Herald* (Apr. 24, 1907), *Charleston Evening Post* (Apr. 1, 1908), and *Charlotte News* (Apr. 3, 1908).
23. Dean Babcock, "Enos A. Mills," *The* [Canton, IL] *Pennant"* (Mar. 9, 1907).
24. Sprague, *Bicentennial History* [Prologue], p. 145; Pinchot biographer Harold T. Pinkett (*Gifford Pinchot: Private and Public Forester* [Urbana, Chicago, and London: University of Illinois Press, 1970], p. 85) illustrates Mills's effectiveness with testimony from one conservation organization: "If the Service had not sent Mills . . . to Delaware . . . a forestry bill would not have passed the state legislature two years later." Numerous news clippings also testify to Mills's direct influence on local and state conservation measures and give evidence that he was offered positions of state forester or equivalent in Massachusetts, Texas, and Maine.
25. Quotations from the *Atlanta Constitution* (Jan. 24, 1908).
26. Mills quoted in ibid.
27. Theodore Roosevelt, "Opening Address by the President," *Proceedings of Conference of Governors in the White House, May 13 to 15, 1908,* ed. Newton C. Blanchard et al. (Washington: Government Printing Office, 1909), p. 3; Muir's exclusion and the bitterness it caused in the preservationist camp are discussed in Nash, *Wilderness and the American Mind* [Prologue], p. 139; Cohen, *Pathless Way* [Prologue], p. 316; and Fox, *Muir and His Legacy* [Prologue], p. 130.
28. Pinchot, *Breaking New Ground* [Prologue], p.352.
29. *Proceedings of the Governors' Conference,* p. 1; the invocation was by U.S. Senate Chaplain Edward Everett Hale, who Mills said had helped him with his forestry lectures.
30. Pinchot, *Breaking New Ground,* pp. 352–53; Robert Underwood Johnson, quoted in Nash, *American Environment,* pp. 68–69; McFarland, quoted in Nash, *Wilderness and the American Mind,* p. 165.
31. *RMW,* p. 330; John Muir to Robert Underwood Johnson, June 2, 1908, quoted in Fox, *Muir and His Legacy,* p. 130.
32. W. Hays (acting secretary of agriculture) to Mills, May 15, 1909; Pinchot to Mills, Apr. 13, 1909. Pinkett (*Gifford Pinchot,* pp. 85–86) notes that while Mills was said to have been "remarkably successful" and that "the demand for his instruction in forest principles reportedly came from every part of the United States," an internal memorandum on the lecture work of the Forest Service, dated Mar. 9, 1909, had recommended the program's discontinuation because it was the "least effective and most costly" method to "bring home to the people its work and aims and to disseminate information." The timing of the memorandum suggests that Mills's termination two months later was a routine action. An amendment to the Agricultural Appropriation Act in 1909 had already eliminated travel reimbursement for lecturing activities.

CHAPTER 15

1. Muir wrote: "I'm glad to congratulate [you] on the success of your fine wild book & sincerely thank you for the dedication. I read the copy you sent me through at a sitting & never dreamed I had failed to acknowledge it. Go ahead and write another." Muir to Mills, Feb. 21, 1910 (HM31335), MMC.

2. *SR,* p. 168.

3. Ibid., p. 148.

4. Dyer to Mills, Dec. 10, 1910; Lorimer to Mills, Jan 29, 1912; Page to Mills, July 22, 1908, all in MP; Lorimer published eleven of Mills's stories between 1910 and 1913 and over three dozen more during the rest of Mills's life.

5. Quotations from *EEP,* pp. 93–107.

6. Ibid.

7. Edna Ferber, *A Kind of Magic* (New York: Lancer Books, 1963), p. 130.

8. *YNP,* p. 322.

9. Quotations from Mills, "National Forests vs. National Parks," typescript, n.d. (probably 1910 or 1911), MP. Mills expressed similar sentiments in *RMW,* pp. 327–29 and *YNP,* pp. 272–77.

10. J. Horace McFarland, quoted in Cohen, *Pathless Way* [Prologue], p. 283.

11. For an excellent review of Joe's life, see Pickering, introduction to Joe Mills, *Mountain Boyhood* [Ch. 1], pp. ix–li.

12. The interpretation is by Patricia Yeager Washburn (granddaughter of Joe Mills), "Remembering the Thirties in Estes Park," transcript of a talk, Aug. 12, 1979, EPOHP.

13. Mills, quoted in undated news clipping; Mills to Lydia Phillips Williams, Mar. 6, 1906; Mills quoted in *Omaha World Herald* (Jan. 4, 1914), all in MP.

14. Norman G. Neuhoff, interview with author, July 9, 1984; Roy and Hazel Baldwin, transcript of a museum talk, July 6, 1974, EPOHP, p. 3.

15. Pickering, introduction to Joe Mills, *Mountain Boyhood,* p. xxv; Emerson E. Lynn, "Preacher's Son" [prologue], p. 29.

16. Joe Mills, *Mountain Boyhood,* pp. 283–84. Even allowing for disagreement about how much credit Enos deserved for founding RMNP, no account of the subject is thinkable without mentioning him; it must, therefore, at some level have strained Joe's own sense of integrity to omit Enos from the account altogether.

17. Robert W. Johnson, foreword to Mills, *RMNP,* pp. xx–xxi; Mills's neighbor Charles Edwin Hewes, his most vocal critic, excoriated him many times in his 1,116-page journal, maintained from 1913 to 1944. His Jan. 1, 1914, entry attributes Mills's behavior to a "confirmed egotism" and complained that "he refuses to conform to any opinion save his own, and it is quite impossible to persuade, suggest, or present anything different." Quoted in Pickering, introduction to Mills, *WLR,* p. xxxix.

18. *ANG,* p. 93; J. A. Maguire in the *Denver Post,* n.d. (probably 1919), copy in MP; John Tebbel, *George Horace Lorimer and the Saturday Evening Post* (Garden City, NY: Doubleday, 1948), p. 146.

19. Eugene V. Debs to Theodore Debs, Oct. 30, 1913, in Constantine, ed., *Letters,* vol. 2 [Ch. 7], pp. 78–79. Other opinions: (1) Neuhoff (interview) believes that

Mills's main failing was "taking on more than he could carry"; (2) Charles Merton Tresner, who accepted a job at Longs Peak Inn in 1914 despite warnings that Mills was difficult to work for, found him "very nice to get along with" (transcript of interview with Flossie Maud Jones Tresner, oral history file, Ft. Collins, CO, Public Library, pp. 22–24); (3) Henry Dannels, an employee at Joe Mills's hotel, the Crags, said that he knew and liked Enos Mills, finding him "kind and gentle, a kook of sorts," (*Estes Park Trail Gazette* [June 5, 1981], p. 8); (4) Roy and Hazel Baldwin (transcript, p. 3) hearing that Mills was "a shorttempered crab," found him on closer acquaintance, "warm, talkative, and willing to express his views"; (5) for McClellan Dings (transcript of interview, Sep. 14, 1981, EPOHP, p. 9) Mills's relationships with his neighbors were "just perpetual squabble"; but Mills had carried Dings piggyback to see the beaver ponds during Dings's first summer in the Tahosa Valley when he was unable to walk that distance. The testimony of many, in short, was that Mills could be as likable as he was difficult.

CHAPTER 16

1. [Mrs.] C. E. Jones, letter to *Rocky Mountain Motorist* 57/6 (June 1982), p. 4; many press accounts at the time of the 1915 dedication credited Mills with a "one-man campaign" and at once established his reputation as the park's "father." Mills himself wrote (*RMNP*, pp. 90–91): "Nearly all the fighting, the debating, speaking and writing, was my lot. Occasionally I was left alone. The opposition tried for a time to discredit the proposition by circulating the story that 'Mills was the only one who wanted the park.' . . . But it was not dead and buried, for I never stopped fighting. . . . For six years there was not a day that I failed to plan or work for it." Of his support, he wrote, "Organizations and hundreds of people helped; many worked for a year or longer and then either from necessity or discouragement, dropped out."

2. *EEP*, p. 104; Herbert Wheeler, autobiographical memoir (pp. 80–81), HWP.

3. Ibid., pp. 55–56.

4. Statement by Mills to a hearing on the RMNP bill, S. 6309, by House Committee on Public Lands, 63rd Congress, 3rd Session, U.S. House of Representatives, Report No. 1275, p. 18.

5. Undated letter (probably early 1910), entitled "The Proposed Estes National Park and Game Preserve," quoted in Fazio, *Cragged Crusade* [Prologue], p. 90.

6. A. F. Potter to Mills, May 28, 1910, quoted in *RMNP*, pp. 88–89; for an interpretation of the Forest Service's evolving position on recreational uses in the national forests and the question of national parks, see Steen, *Forest Service History* [Prologue], pp. 113–22.

7. McFarland to Mills, Feb. 1, 6, 13, and 25, 1911, and from Mills to McFarland, Feb. 1, 7, and 20, 1911, all in JHMP; further correspondence to and from McFarland is from the same source. In a long letter to James Grafton Rogers (Oct. 15, 1912, in JGRP), Graves lamented that the Forest Service was misunderstood on the question of national parks and that, having studied parks in Europe, he favored a separate bureau of parks with a far-reaching planning process.

8. Mills to Henry S. Graves, June 6, 1911, copy in JHMP.

9. Wheeler, memoir, p. 81.

10. McFarland to Mills, June 12, 1911.

11. McFarland to Thorndike DeLand, Denver Chamber of Commerce, Dec. 19, 1910.

12. *RMNP*, p. 89; Fazio, *Cragged Crusade*, p. 119; "Enos Mills Fined Limit for Assault on Neighbor," *Boulder Daily Camera* (Sep. 21, 1910).

13. *Denver Republican* (June 28, 1910).

14. Front Range Settlers' League, *The Proposed Estes National Park, A Matter Affecting Colorado Homes, Colorado People, Colorado State, Colorado Visitors* (Summer 1911), copy in RMNPL; Mills was right that the Forest Service helped and plotted with the FRSL. Burns Will, a Forest Service ranger and nearby lodge owner, was part of the FRSL, and Charles Hewes (*Journal*, Jan. 5, 1912, copy in EPAHM), confided that the "forest people are secretly supporting our organization . . . against the pro-park people."

15. *RMNP*, pp. 89–90.

16. Rev. E. J. Lamb, *Miscellaneous Meditations* (Publisher's Press Room and Bindery, Dec. 1913), p. 119.

17. Hewes, *Journal*, Mar. 4, 1913.

18. Marshall, letter to Walter Fisher, secretary of the interior, Jan. 9, 1913, quoted in Fazio, *Cragged Crusade*, p. 205.

19. Marshall, quoted in ibid., pp. 142, 145.

20. Mills to Muir, Jan. 31, 1913; Muir to Mills, Feb. 16, 1913, both in MCC.

21. Correspondence between Mills and Rogers clearly establishes Mills's influence in conceiving the idea for a mountain club. Relevant letters are Mills to Rogers, July 24, 1911, and Apr. 24, 1912; and Rogers to Mills, July 27, 1911, and Apr. 22 and 27, 1912, all in JGRP. Correspondence during summer 1912 and into 1913 also shows that Mills provided valuable advice (and specific names) for building the club's membership. Possibly because of later antagonisms, Rogers forgot Mills's influential role, noting (*Trail and Timberline* 280 [Apr. 1942], p. 38) that "the seed of the CMC was really planted by Miss Mary Sabin [a former high school teacher of Rogers]." The club's seventy-five-year history egregiously omits Mills's role in the club's founding. See Hugh E. Kingery (assisted by Eleanor Eppich Kingery), *The Colorado Mountain Club: The First Seventy-Five Years of a Highly Individual Corporation, 1912–1987* (Evergreen, CO: Cordillera Press, 1981), p. 25.

22. This interesting and somewhat involved subject, which included positive participation by Mills and Mills's rancorous opposition to naming the Tahosa Valley after Elkanah Lamb, is described in Louisa Ward Arps and Elinor Eppich Kingery, *High Country Names* (Estes Park, CO: Rocky Mountain Nature Association, 1977), pp. 1–15 and 185–86; see also letters from Mills to Rogers, Sep. 24, 1914, and May 18, 1915, copies in JGRP; and Oliver W. Toll, *Arapahoe Names and Trails* (n.d., reprinted 1962). Mills advocated Indian place names in *YNP*, pp. 120, 153.

23. Henry S. Graves to Rogers, Mar. 8, 1913, JGRP; B. F. Galloway to Scott Ferris, chairman of House Committee on Public Lands, Aug. 1913, quoted in Fazio, *Cragged Crusade*, p. 157. In a long letter to Ferris, however, Rogers carefully refuted Galloway's criticism, showing that many of the provisions he stipulated did, in fact, have precedents in existing national parks (Rogers to Ferris, Sep. 18, 1913, JGRP).

24. *RMNP,* p. 88; Rogers to Robert B. Marshall, Feb. 28, 1913, JGRP; disagreement with Mills over strategy is especially evident in letters from Rogers to Mills, Sep. 20, 1913, and Mills to Rogers, Sep. 29, 1913.

25. Rogers to Graves, Sep. 26, 1912.

26. Graves to Rogers, Oct. 21, 1913.

27. Resolution adopted by CMC board of directors, Apr. 16, 1914; *Colliers* (Apr. 16, 1910); see Alfred Runte's chapter on this theme, "Worthless Lands," in his *National Parks: The American Experience* (Lincoln and London: University of Nebraska Press, 1979), pp. 48–64, and its application to Glacier and RMNP, pp. 75–77.

28. Mills to Rogers, May 3, 1914.

29. Rogers to Frederick R. Ross, May 12, 1914.

30. Fazio, *Cragged Crusade,* p. 133.

31. Granville Liles, May 14, 1965, quoted in ibid., p. 115; James Grafton Rogers, "The Creation of Rocky Mountain Park," *Trail and Timberline* 558 (June 1965), p. 99; Kingery, *The Colorado Mountain Club,* pp. 48, 71.

32. *Denver Republican* (Jan. 7, 1910).

33. Muir to Mills, Feb. 21, 1910, Aug. 14, 1912, and Feb. 16, 1913 (HM 31335, HM 31336, and HM 31337); and Mills to Muir, Nov. 24, 1914, all in MMC; McFarland to Mills, Apr. 20, 1912.

34. Robert B. Marshall, testimony for House Hearing on S. 6309.

35. Mills, "The Rocky Mountain National Park," *Estes Park Trail* 3/9 (Aug. 15, 1914), p. 182; McFarland to Mills, Dec. 28, 1914.

36. Senator Edward T. Taylor to House Hearing on S. 6309.

37. McFarland to Mills, Jan. 23, 1915.

38. *RMNP,* p. 95.

39. For relevant discussion, see Albright, *Birth of the National Park Service* [Prologue], pp. 32–43. Mills had supported earlier attempts to found a national park agency, writing, for example, "Why House Bill 8668 for the Creation of a National Park Service Should be Passed" (Jan. 30, 1911, MP). He had strategized with McFarland on the possibility of creating a parks division within the Department of Interior rather than a separate parks bureau (Mills to McFarland, Sep. 16, 1912).

40. Mills to McFarland, Feb. 17, 1915; he also told McFarland (Apr. 9, 1915) that the campaign "made me almost a physical and financial wreck."

41. *Denver Post* (Sept. 4, 1915, Jan. 20, 1915).

42. Mills to a Judge Jacobs, Jan. 1, 1914, MP; "Mills, Himself by Himself" [Prologue]; Eugene V. Debs to Mills, Jan. 2, 1915, EMCC.

CHAPTER 17

1. For relevant discussion, see Runte, *National Parks* [Ch. 16], p. 82.

2. *Proceedings of the 1917 National Parks Conference* [Ch. 1], p. 36.

3. *RMW,* pp. 315, 317; *YNP,* pp. 271, 384.

4. Robert Sterling Yard, *The Book of the National Parks* (New York: Charles Scribner's Son, 1919), pp. 18–19; *YNP*, pp. 199, 122; *RMW*, pp. 314, 296.

5. Runte, *National Parks,* p. 118; Yard, quoted in Fox, *Muir and His Legacy* [Prologue], p. 204.

6. Cohen, *Pathless Way* [Prologue], pp. 282–83.

7. *YNP*, pp. 378–87.

8. Ibid., pp. 296–315; *RMNP*, p. 93.

9. *YNP*, p. 322.

10. *RMW*, pp. 10–11; *EEP*, 1917 ed., p. 99.

11. Mills described the Pikes Peak study in *RMW*, pp. 302–4; a modern account is in Charles S. Houston, M.D., *Going High: The Story of Man and Altitude* (Burlington, VT: Charles S. Houston and the American Alpine Club, 1980), pp. 99–100.

12. Theodore Roosevelt, quoted in *WWA,* p. 200; *WW,* p. 130.

13. *YNP*, pp. 313–14.

14. For a fuller account, see Buchholtz, *RMNP History* [Prologue], pp. 139–40, 169–70 (no evidence has surfaced to show whether Mills was part of the plot or was himself taken in by it).

15. *YNP*, pp. x-xi; see also Runte, *National Parks*, pp. 109–11.

16. Yard, *Book of the National Parks,* p. 5.

17. Ibid., pp. 6, 8.

18. *YNP*, p. 366. In referring to Mills at the 1917 Parks Conference, Yard said his "whole life is the life of a teacher" (*Proceedings*, p. 111).

19. *YNP*, p. 269; Mills served a term as National Parks chairman for the American Civic Association and in 1917 was lending his support to numerous proposals for new parks.

20. Ronald A. Foresta, *America's National Parks and Their Keepers* (Washington, D.C., Resources for the Future, 1984), p. 20.

21. Robert B. Marshall, quoted in Runte, *National Parks,* p. 96 (see ibid., pp. 82–105 for a fuller discussion of evolving justifications and defenses for the park system).

22. *YNP*, p. 264; Mills's idea for a Board of Commissioners probably came from a similar idea suggested by Olmsted to the small group (which included Mills) formulating ideas for the creation of the Park Service. According to Albright (*Birth of the National Park Service* [Prologue], p. 36) the idea was dropped in the interest of simplicity.

23. Ibid., pp. 62, 73.

24. Ibid., p. 77.

25. Woodrow Wilson, *The New Freedom* (New York and Garden City, NY: Doubleday Page, 1913), p. 130; Swain, *Albright and Conservation* [Prologue], pp. 86, 94–96.

26. Shankland, *Steve Mather* [Prologue], pp. 186–87.

CHAPTER 18

1. Front Range Settlers' League, *The Proposed Estes National Park* [Ch. 16]; Mills, "Exploiting Our National Parks," *New Republic* 24 (Nov. 10, 1920), p. 272.

2. Don Hummel, *Stealing the National Parks: The Destruction of Concessions and Park Access* (Bellevue, WA: Free Enterprise Press, 1987), p. 56.

3. William C. Everhart, *The National Park Service* (Boulder, CO: Westview Press, 1983), p. 111; Hummel, *Stealing the National Parks,* p. 60.

4. Mills, "Warden of the Nation's Mountain Scenery," *Review of Reviews* 51 (Apr. 1915), p. 428; Mills to Edward Marshall, Nov. 29, 1915, MP.

5. Mills, "The Kingdom of National Parks," *Estes Park Trail Talk* (Aug. 27, 1920), p. 6.

6. J. Horace McFarland, "Economic Destiny of the National Parks," in *Proc. 1917 National Parks Conference* [Ch. 1], p. 110.

7. Stephen Tyng Mather, "The National Parks on a Business Basis," *Review of Reviews* 51 (Apr. 1915), p. 430.

8. McFarland, "Economic Destiny," p. 110.

9. See Way to Mills, Aug. 18, 1919, in Way vs. Mills correspondence file, RMNPL; and Way, "Letter to the Director of the National Park Service, Aug. 20, 1910, published in *Estes Park Trail* 1/10 (Sep. 3, 1920).

10. Paul W. Lee, "Litigation Concerning the Rocky Mountain National Park," in *RMNP,* p. 232.

11. Mills, "Kingdom of National Parks," p. 6; Mills, "Exploiting Our National Parks."

12. Section 3 of the act (S. 6309) establishing Rocky Mountain National Park; *RMW,* p. 325, citing the decision of Judge Robert E. Lewis; Howard Zinn, *A People's History of the United States* (New York: Harper and Row, 1980), p. 255, quoting Supreme Court justice David J. Brewer in 1893.

13. Mills, "National Parks Monopolies," *New York Times* (Jan. 30, 1921).

14. Freelan O. Stanley, *Denver Post* (Dec. 4, 1921), copy in EMCC.

15. *EMOR,* p. 232; *EEP,* pp. xi–xii.

16. McFarland to Mills, Sep. 25, 1920; Mills to McFarland, Oct. 6, 1920, both in JHMP.

17. McFarland to Mills, Oct. 11, 1920, JHMP; *Estes Park Trail* (Sep. 30 and Oct. 5, 1921).

18. Albright, *Birth of the National Park Service* [Prologue], p. 125.

19. L. Claude Way, "Letter to the Director," Aug. 1920 (Way mentioned specifically "the Hewes boys" and two lodges near Longs Peak Inn as being "well satisfied" with "no complaints to make or suggestions to offer"); Mills, "Kingdom of National Parks," p. 6.

20. Report adopted by the board of directors, Denver Civic and Commercial Association, Nov. 3, 1921, p. 5, copy in JHMP.

21. *EMOR,* p. 231; Shankland, *Steve Mather* [Prologue], p. 187; Ise, *National Park Policy* [Prologue], p. 317. Musselman's analysis of the controversy is found in Lloyd K. Musselman, *Rocky Mountain National Park: Administrative History, 1915–1965* (Washington, D.C.: Department of Interior, 1971).

22. Testimony of Enos A. Mills to House Hearing on S. 6309.

23. Secretary Payne, quoted in *Rocky Mountain News* (Jan. 23, 1921), copy in EMCC.

24. *Houston Chronicle* (Mar. 1920), copy in EMCC; *St. Louis Post Dispatch* (Feb. 1921), copy in EMCC.

25. John Muir, quoted in Shankland, *Steve Mather,* pp. 48–49.

26. Mills, "National Park Roads," *New York Times* (July 10, 1921); *EMOR,* p. 249.

27. *Sterling* [CO] *Advocate* (Feb. 5, 1927).

28. *Boulder* [CO] *Daily Camera* (Feb. 5, 1927); for a discussion of the legal aspects of the cede-jurisdication controversy, see William Sherman Bell, "The Legal Phases of Cession of Rocky Mountain National Park," *Rocky Mountain Law Review* 1 (1928), pp. 35–46.

29. "Park Vendors' Profits Called Excessive; Monopoly Pacts Enrich Concessioners," *Denver Post* (May 25, 1990).

CHAPTER 19

1. Katherine G. Garetson, *Homesteading Big Owl* (Allenspark, CO: *Allenspark Wind,* 1989), pp. 40–41, 44.

2. Mills wrote of Esther Burnell in *ANG,* pp. 163–71; a native Kansan, she was the daughter of the Reverend and Mrs. Arthur Burnell and had lived in Cleveland and Des Moines before settling in Colorado.

3. *EMOR,* p. 206.

4. Garetson, *Homesteading,* p. 41.

5. *ANG,* p. 164.

6. Garetson, *Homesteading,* p. 49.

7. Esther portrayed the courtship in *EMOR,* pp. 205–19; "A Goldfinch Romance" was anthologized in Mills's posthumous *BMR* (1924).

8. *ANG,* p. 110.

9. Ibid., p. 112.

10. Ibid., p. 120.

11. Ibid., p. 122.

12. The essays appeared in the *Saturday Evening Post* (Mar. 1, 1919) and *Nature Study* 17 (Mar. 1921), pp. 95–98.

13. Charles W. Eliot, quoted in *ANG,* p. 121.

14. Ibid., p. 142.

15. Ibid., p. 145.

16. Mills, "The Mayor of Five Points," undated typescript, MP.

17. Ibid.; the remarkable record of Thomas Tynan, the enlightened warden who Mills said "had a real and consistently kindly interest in every convict," is described in Elinor McGinn, "Trying to Profit: Inmate Labor at Canyon City," *Colorado Heritage* (1987, issue 2), pp. 21–24.

18. *EEP*, p. vii.

19. Rollins, "Champion of Wildlife," in *RMNP*, p. 226.

20. Ferber, *Peculiar Treasure* [Ch. 10], p. 241; Ferber mentions specifically her sto-
    ries "The Afternoon of a Faun" and "Nobody's in Town" as having profited
    from her stay at the inn.

21. Rollins, "Champion of Wildlife," p. 223; Lynn, "Preacher's Son" [Prologue], p.
    28; Ferber, *Peculiar Treasure*, p. 240.

22. Frank G. Craighead, Jr., *Track of the Grizzly* (San Francisco: Sierra Club
    Books, 1979), p. 7; *GGWA*, pp. vii–viii, 1, 174.

23. Russell Doubleday, quoted in *Colorado Prospector* 16/4 (May 1985), p. 10.

24. Roger W. Toll to Emerson E. Lynn, Aug. 9, 1922, superintendent's file,
    RMNPL.

25. The cause of death entered on the death certificate was myocardial infarction,
    but blood poisoning from the abscessed tooth was probably responsible,
    according to Anne Matlack of Longmont, CO, daughter of Mills's dentist, who
    treated him for ulcerated teeth on the day he died (*Estes Park Trail Gazette*
    [June 25, 1982]); deaths from tooth infection were not rare in the days before
    antibiotics.

26. *BMR*, p. 167; Lindsey's remarks can be found in *Estes Park Trail* (Sep. 1922);
    in his typescript entitled "Appreciation" (copy in EMCC); and in a commemo-
    rative article, "The Passing of Enos Mills," *Sunset Magazine* (Jan. 1923), p. 44.

27. *ANG*, p. 69.

CHAPTER 20

1. Quotations, in order, are from *WLR*, pp. 11, 17, 188, 171–72, 154, 139.

2. John T. Jacobs, introduction to *BMR*, p. xvi.

3. See Lynn, "Preacher's Son" [Prologue], pp. 28–29.

4. *ANG*, pp. 121–23; on the uses of the imagination by nineteenth-century
   romantic writers, see C. M. Bowra, *The Romantic Imagination* (New York:
   Oxford University Press, 1961), pp. 1–24, 271–92.

5. *ANG*, p. 25; the original version is in *Country Life* 33 (Feb. 1918), pp. 41–44.

6. Opinions cited are, in order, Norman Neuhoff, interview with author, July 9,
   1984; Charles Eagle Plume, transcript of museum talk, Feb. 19, 1981, EPOHP,
   p. 15; Jack Moomaw, transcript of interview, Jan. 22, 1972, EPOHP, pp. 18–
   19; William B. Bueler, "Who was Enos Mills?" *Trail and Timberline* 689 (May
   1976), p. 109; Robert W. Johnson, foreword to *RMNP*, pp. xx–xxi; Earl Harding, "Climbing Longs Peak," *Outing* 44 (July 1904). Modern appraisals of
   Mills's snowblind adventure were supplied, in private communications to the
   author, by expert mountaineers Dale Johnson, Stu Krebs, Stanley Boucher, and
   Janet Robertson.

7. See Nash, *Wilderness and the American Mind* [Prologue], pp. 141–42; his
   chapter "The Wilderness Cult" (pp. 141–60) describes the great popularity of
   outdoor heroes, including fictional ones such as Tarzan of the Apes, created by
   Edgar Rice Burroughs in 1914.

8. Julius Stone, quoted in *YNP*, p. 208.

9. *ANG*, p. 64.

10. *EEP*, pp. 87–88; Henry C. King, "Snow-Blind," *Outdoor Life* (Apr. 1904), pp. 231–32.

11. Bill McKibben, "Hero of the Wilderness," *New York Review of Books* 36/17 (Nov. 9, 1989), p. 25. Shortly after Mills's death the publisher Russell Double-day, inspired by walks with Mills that summer, wrote that "his books will live, for they contain the spirit of living truth" (Dec. 2, 1922, quoted in *Colorado Prospector* [May 1985], p. 10).

CHAPTER 21

1. *Peoria* [IL] *Star* (Sep. 24, 1922); "An Historian of Birds and Flowers and Animals," *World's Work* 45 (Jan. 1923), p. 252; Henry Fairfield Osborn, *Impressions of the Great Naturalists* (New York: Charles Scribner's Sons, 1924), pp. 190–91; Osborne notes that Burroughs's "powers of original observation of nature were not great powers as would entitle him to be called a great naturalist." Burroughs was in fact always slightly embarrassed when his admirers called him that.

2. Rollins, "Champion of Nature," in *RMNP*, p. 214.

3. Thoreau, quoted in Brooks, *Speaking for Nature* [Prologue], pp. xiv, 8.

4. Mills, quoted in *New York Times* (Mar. 30, 1921).

5. See Ralph H. Lutts, *The Nature Fakers: Wildlife, Science & Sentiment* (Golden, CO: Fulcrum Publishing, 1990); and John Henry Wadland, *Ernest Thompson Seton: Man in Nature in the Progressive Era, 1880–1915* (New York: Arno Press, 1978), pp. 288–89, 296.

6. Mills discusses animal reasoning ability in *WLR*, p. 59; *IBW*, p. 57; *YNP*, p. 314; *GGWA*, entire opening chapter; and *WWA*, p. 148; he nowhere mentions Burroughs's articles denying animal reason.

7. Unsigned review, *Chicago Inter-Ocean* (June 29, 1913).

8. *IBW*, pp. 31–32; Mills had earlier noted (*WLR*, p. 55–56) that "the majority of beaver do not plan how the trees are to fall;" Morrell Allred, *Beaver Behavior: Architect of Fame and Bane!* (Happy Camp, CA: Naturegraph Publishers, 1986), pp. 8–9.

9. Edward Royal Warren, S.B., *Mammals of Colorado* (New York and London: G.P. Putnam's Sons, 1910), p. 144.

10. Warren, *The Beaver: Its Work and Its Ways* (Baltimore: Williams & Wilkins, 1927), pp. 24, 27 (his discussion is less a confession of full belief in beaver intelligence than of uncertainty and perplexity about the vagueness of definitions); Ewan, *Rocky Mountain Naturalists* [Ch. 11], p. 268; Don J. Neff, "A Seventy-Year History of a Colorado Beaver Colony," *Journal of Mammalogy* 40/3 (1959), pp. 381–87.

11. Barry Holston Lopez, in *Of Wolves and Men* (New York: Charles Scribner's Sons, 1978), p. 3, calculates that "observed behavior amounts to about three one-thousandths of 1 percent of wolf behavior."

12. Charles George Leroy, quoted in Wadland, *Ernest Thompson Seton*, p. 193.

13. Ernest Thompson Seton, *Lives of Game Animals,* 4 vols. (1925–1928; reprint ed., Boston: Charles T. Branford, 1953), vol. 4, p. x.

14. Neff, "Seventy-Year History," p. 382; though not reporting research results, Mills approached more technical publication with his *Forest and Exotic Trees of Colorado* (pamphlet coauthored with W.G.M. Stone, Denver, n.d.) and his "Wars of the Winds at Timberline," *Natural History* 19 (1919), pp. 427–35.

15. Though Mills was an accomplished photographer of mountain landscapes, he rarely used his camera for scientific documentation and was neither a botanical nor a wildlife photographer; for a description of advances already made by Mills's time, see A. G. Wallihan, "Photographing Wild Life in Early Colorado," *Colorado Magazine* 21/5 (Sep. 1944), pp. 171–77.

16. Edmund Schulman, *Dendroclimatic Changes in Semiarid America* (Tucson: University of Arizona Press, 1956), p. 32. Mills's count may have been inflated by the presence of false rings, fequently present in ponderosa pine and requiring cross comparison in groups of trees in the same area (see ibid., p. 19); F. P. Keen, in "Longevity of Ponderosa Pine," *Journal of Forestry* 38 (1940), pp. 597–98, surveyed the published literature on the exact ages of old ponderosa pines and reported that the oldest of nearly 6,000 dated stumps was 726 years; scientists at the Colorado State University Department of Forestry, the University of Arizona Tree Ring Laboratory, and the Laboratory of Mesa Verde National Park (close to the site of Mills's 1,047-year-old pine) all expressed doubt about the correctness of Mills's dating.

17. Wiley, ed., *Burroughs' America* [Ch.6], p. 8.

CHAPTER 22

1. The following will illustrate Mills's high status as a writer while he lived and in the first years following his death: "To say that the book . . . was written by the late Enos Mills is introduction enough." *Sierra Club Bulletin* 12 (1924), p. 107. "[Mills] may be called a combination of naturalist and prose-poet [whose work] has reached a high plane of literary merit." Wilbur Fisk Stone, *History of Colorado* (Chicago: S. J. Clarke Publishing, 1918), vol. 1, p. 880. "[In the years following his death, Mills remained] perhaps the most widely known of all recent Colorado authors." Irene Pettit McKeehan, in *Colorado: Short Studies of Its Past and Present* (Boulder; University of Colorado, 1927), p. 180. Letters to Mills in EMCC contain high praise for him as a writer from other writers, including Gene Stratton Porter, Helen Keller, Philip Ashton Rollins, and John Niehart.

2. *WWA,* p. 164.

3. Ibid., pp. 195–96.

4. Mills was elected an Associate of the American Ornithological Union in 1916 and the Union's journal (*Auk* 40 [1923], p. 721) said that he was "not an ornithologist in the strict sense of the term" but was a keen observer familiar with most Rocky Mountain species.

5. The example chosen is "Winter Ways of Animals," *WWA,* pp. 158–74.

6. The examples are from *WWA,* pp. 84–97.

7. *BMR,* pp. 59–64.

8. Robert W. Johnson, foreword to *RMNP*, p. xxi.

9. *WWA*, p. 204.

10. *YNP*, pp. 318–19.

11. *BMR*, p. 120; commenting on the same problem, Thomas J. Lyon in *Literary History of the American West* (Ft. Worth: Texas Christian University Press, 1987), p. 242, notes that Mills "was reticent about deeper interpretations, seeming to pass them off in almost formulaic sentences."

12. Compare Mills, *RMW*, p. 244, with Annie Dillard, "A Field of Silence," in *Teaching a Stone to Talk: Expeditions and Encounters* (New York: Harper and Row, 1982), pp. 132–38; other opinions: (1) Mills "wrote about what he saw instead of what he thought, and he let the reader draw his own conclusions." Enda Mills Kiley, quoted in *Estes Park Trail Gazette* (June 25, 1982); (2) "[The American wilds] offered something new to observe, to describe, to philosophize and poetize over. Enos Mills confined himself largely to the first two activities." *World's Work* 45 (Jan. 1923), p. 252.

13. *WLR*, pp. 255–56.

14. Mills, quoted in Rollins, "Champion of Wildlife," *RMNP*, p. 220.

15. Though modern literary appraisals of Mills as a nature writer are relatively scarce, examinations of his writing by Carl Abbott, Peter Wild, James H. Pickering, Thomas J. Lyon, and Paul Brooks (all cited elsewhere in these notes) show many similar themes and give us the following composite portrait: Mills was important as a distinctive Rocky Mountain writer, indeed one of the best portrayers of that region at a time when California and Southwest-desert writers dominated the western nature essay. He excelled in depicting a strong, immediate awareness of place — even the small spaces where he sat for hours — and the wealth of detail in each place. His extensive, direct, fearless involvement with nature and its creatures rivaled Muir's, gave his writing impressive vitality, and made a unique contribution to western literature. His portrayal of the wilds as a place to be at home, to love, to play, to grow, and to find oneself transcended geographic boundaries and created a larger feeling of bondedness with the natural world, which inspired others and made his books a strengthening companion to the young conservation movement. As a first-person narrator, Mills was original, strongly individual, sometimes eccentric; homey, fun-loving, easily accessible, and more typically western and more human than many of greater literary stature. Yet his deeper character was also masked by a persona of cheerful optimism, heroic posturing, and sometimes trite attitudes. He left much of the real experience of the wilds unexplored and lacked in general the ability to explore ideas and human emotions. He was nevertheless a skilled storyteller with superb descriptive abilities and a capacity for close observation. His prose is uncomplicated, entertaining, at times wryly humorous, at times repetitious and poorly organized, at times preachy and sentimental. Passages imitating Muir fall short of Muir in both substance and evocative power. Mills the writer is important historically for portraying changes in his own era as the West became more settled, its wilderness exploited and reduced, yet recognized by a few as a national resource for human regeneration. He was unusual among his contemporary writers for his growing shift in sensibility, gradually abandoning overdramatized, anthropomorphized and sometimes improbable scenarios in favor of a more documentary and purely biological depiction of nature. That shift influenced and reflected what was becoming and what continues in our own time to be a shift in American sensibility from see-

ing and experiencing nature in idealized, romantic terms to accepting nature on its own terms. Society, like Mills, has moved toward a more ecological understanding of nature — an understanding that increases our allegiance to the natural world and our place in it. Within these parameters Mills's nature writing has literary, scientific, historical, and ecological significance.

16. *YNP,* p. 283.
17. Thomas Hardy, quoted in *EMOR,* p. 257; the orignal source cannot be located. Hardy had access to Mills's books in England, where, according to Chapman (*Enos A. Mills* [Prologue], p. 25) they had a "large sale, . . . showing that the Colorado naturalist's appeal is international."
18. Liberty Hyde Bailey, *The Nature Study Idea* (New York: Doubleday, Page, 1903); see especially his chapter "The Poetic Interpretation of Nature" (pp. 116–23); Mills discusses Bailey in *ANG,* pp. 129, 162; "essence of nature guiding" is *ANG,* p. 125.
19. *ANG,* pp. 126–27.
20. *RMNP,* p. 157.
21. *ANG,* p. 129.
22. Danton credits Mills's orginality in his foreword to ibid., pp. 6–7; James Fazio in "Liberty Hyde Bailey and Enos A. Mills, Pioneers in Environmental Interpretation," *Nature Study* (Summer 1975), pp. 1–3, credits Mills and Bailey equally, and traces historical antecedents of their approach.
23. See Albright, *Birth of the National Park Service* [Prologue], pp. 121–22, and Ise, *National Park Policy* [Prologue], pp. 199–02; Alfred Runte in *Yosemite: The Embattled Wilderness* (Lincoln and London: University of Nebraska Press, 1990), pp. 114–16, notes the role of Joseph Grinnell, director of the University of California Museum of Vertebrate Zoology, in encouraging the Park Service to implement Bryant's kind of instruction. Correspondence in the museum's records shows that Grinnell also praised and encouraged Mills's outdoor educational activities.
24. *RMNP,* pp. 144–45; Danton, foreword to *ANG,* p. 11.
25. Mills to Fred L. Holmes, undated letter, MP.
26. Danton, in *Sharing, Newsletter of the Office of Interpretation,* NPS Midwest Region (Dec. 30, 1985); Tilden, quoted in Ise, *National Park Policy,* p. 201; Tilden's principal work on the subject is his 1957 *Interpreting Our Heritage.*
27. Merriman to the author, Apr. 30, 1993.
28. Mike Donahue, "The Enos Mills Legacy," undated transcript, CPF; Glen Kaye, "RMNP's Master of the Trail," *Estes Park Trail Gazette* (Apr. 5, 1985).
29. Kathleen Regnier, Michael Gross, and Ron Zimmerman, *The Interpreter's Guidebook: Techniques for Programs and Presentations* (Stevens Point: University of Wisconsin-Stevens Point Foundation Press, 1992).

CHAPTER 23

1. "FS Whistle-Blowers Head for the Hills," *AFSEEE Activist* 2 (Feb. 1992), p. 1.
2. In 1990 the Forest Service itself announced a public commitment to ecosystem management; for evaluation after two years, see Richard Manning, "Forest

Service is Trying to Turn Over a New Leaf, But Critics Have Doubts," *High Country News* 24/24 (Dec. 28, 1992), p. 18.

3. *RMW*, pp. 311–331.

4. Details of attempts to increase biological protection in the early decades of the park system are given in Runte, *National Parks* [Ch. 16], pp. 106–54.

5. Hess's views are presented in *Rocky Times in Rocky Mountain National Park: An Unnatural History* (Boulder: University Press of Colorado, 1993).

6. *YNP*, p. 379; Todd Wilkinson quoting William Bryan in "Experts Say Tourism Threatens Yellowstone," *Denver Post* (June 2, 1991).

7. Jim Carrier, quoting Alfred Runte in "Crowd Crunch, Budget Bind Tarnish Nation's Crown Jewels," ibid., Aug. 25, 1991; see also "Profits Concessionaires' Domain," ibid., Aug. 27, 1991. For an overview of the concession controversy, see William C. Everhart, *The National Park Service* [Ch. 18], pp. 107–21.

8. Arthur Carhart, "Our Most Accessible Glaciers," *Outlook* (May 23, 1923), pp. 23–25; in 1961, Carhart wrote a handbook on wilderness-area planning for land-use professionals.

9. *YNP*, pp. xi–xii; Mills also wrote (ibid., p. 10) that as undeveloped wilderness "the Yellowstone environing factor arrested, deflected and retarded the movement and the development of society. To-day [as a national park] it attracts, arouses, energizes and ennobles a multitude."

10. Bruce Babbitt, quoted in Charles F. Wilkinson, "The End of Multiple Use," *High Country News* (Mar. 20, 1987); following his governorship, Babbitt served as president of the League of Conservation Voters before being appointed Secretary of Interior in the Clinton Administration; Senate Joint Resolution 12, State of Colorado, 54th General Assembly, LDO No. *84 0095/1 (agricultural and water interests killed the resolution in committee); Phyllis T. Thompson, *The Use of Mountain Recreational Resources: A Comparison of Recreation and Tourism in the Colorado Rockies and the Swiss Alps* (Boulder: University of Colorado Business Research Division, 1971), p. 7.

11. *RMW*, p. 315; Thomas M. Power, "Wildland Preservation and the Economy of Utah," insert to *Newsletter of the Southern Utah Wilderness Alliance* (Summer 1992), p. 11; Gundars Rudzitis and Harley E. Johansen, "Migration into Western Wilderness Counties: Causes and Consequences," *Western Wildlands* (Spring 1989), pp. 19–23.

12. Todd Wilkinson, quoting William Bryant in "Experts Say Tourism Threatens Yellowstone" *Denver Post* (June 2, 1991).

13. Elizabeth Nitze Paepcke, influenced by Enos Mills while a guest at Longs Peak Inn in 1917, and her husband, Walter Paepcke, helped to develop Aspen to a modern cultural center and established the Aspen Center for Environmental Studies; Eric Julber, quoted in Nash, *Wilderness and the American Mind* [Prologue], p. 265.

14. Georg Karp, "Saving the Alps," *World Press Review* (Nov. 1981), p. 57; Dennis R. Jaques, letter, *Alaska* (Jan. 1980), p. 28.

15. Aldo Leopold, *A Sand County Almanac and Sketches Here and There* (New York: Oxford University Press, 1949, repr. 1976), pp. 165–66, 174, 224–25; for comment on the limitations of scenic and wilderness conservation generally, see Wendell Berry, The *Unsettling of America* [Ch. 13], pp. 25–26.

16. Michael Frome, *Regreening the National Parks* (Tucson: University of Arizona Press, 1992), pp. 229–32.

17. David Western and Mary C. Pearl, eds., *Conservation for the Twenty-First Century* (New York: Oxford University Press, 1989); Bill McKibben, "Adirondack Reprieve," *Outside* (Nov. 1991), p. 126; Raymond F. Dasmann, "The Country In-Between," Sierra Club Calendar essay, 1982.

18. Van Andruss, et al., eds. *Home: A Bioregional Reader* (Philadelphia: New Society Publisher, 1990), p. 2; Thomas J. Lyon, *Literary History* [Ch. 22], pp. 241–42; Gary Snyder, in *Bioregional Reader,* p. 18. Mills's regional perspective was acknowledged in his own time: "Mr. Mills has scored an excellent point. . . . Companionship with nature shall begin at home. When once the friendship has been established, it will be carried to the far corners of the earth." *Denver Republican* (Jan. 1912).

19. Nash, *Rights of Nature* [Ch. 13], p. xi.

20. *YNP,* p. 364; Rene Dubos, quoted in Nash, *Rights of Nature,* p. 78.

21. Jeremy Seabrook, quoted in Kirkpatrick Sale, "The Trouble with Earth Day," *The Nation* (Apr. 30, 1990), p. 597.

22. Jim Dodge in *Bioregional Reader,* pp. 1–9; Richard K. Matthews, *The Radical Politics of Thomas Jefferson: A Revisionist View* (Lawrence: University Press of Kansas, 1984; paperback ed., 1986), pp. 124–25.

23. Wadland, *Ernest Thompson Seton,* [Ch. 21]; see further discussion of Kropotkin in ibid., pp. vii, 14; and of Seton's youth program, pp. 298–445.

24. Leopold, *Sand County Almanac,* p. 221; Frome, *Regreening,* p. 210. Mills was an honorary vice president of the Sierra Club from 1915 to 1920 and Colorado chapters of both the Sierra Club and the Colorado Mountain Club are named for him.

Index